THE URANTIA BOOK WORKBOOKS

URANTIA_®

URANTIA FOUNDATION
533 WEST DIVERSEY PARKWAY
CHICAGO, ILLINOIS 60614
U.S.A.

URANTIA_®

®: Registered Mark of URANTIA Foundation

THE URANTIA BOOK WORKBOOKS

VOLUME II

Science

This series of workbooks originally was published in the 1950s and 1960s to assist those early students who wanted to pursue an in-depth study of *The Urantia Book*. The workbook creators recognized that the materials were imperfect and were far from being definitive works on these subjects. Current students may be able to make more exhaustive analyses due to advances in knowledge and computerization of the text that are available today. Nevertheless, we recognize the enormous effort that went into this attempt to enhance understanding of *The Urantia Book* by some of its earliest students. We think these materials will be of interest to many and are therefore republishing them for their historic and educational value.

FIRST PRINTING 2003

THE URANTIA BOOK WORKBOOKS
VOLUME II
SCIENCE

The Urantia Book Workbooks

Volume I: Transcripts of Lecture and Discussion of the Foreword and An Analytic Study of Part One of *The Urantia Book*
Volume II: Science in *The Urantia Book*
Volume III: Topical Studies in *The Urantia Book* and A Short Course in Doctrine
Volume IV: The Teachings of Jesus in *The Urantia Book*, The Life of Jesus Compared to the four Gospels

"URANTIA", "URANTIAN", "THE URANTIA BOOK", and ⓘ are the trademarks, service marks, and collective membership marks of URANTIA Foundation.

© 1959, 1961, 2003 URANTIA Foundation

All rights reserved, including translation, under the Berne Convention, Universal Copyright Convention, and other international copyright conventions.

To request permission to translate or to reproduce material contained in *The Urantia Book Workbooks* or the *The Urantia Book* by any means (including electronic, mechanical, or other—such as photocopying, recording, or any information storage and retrieval system), please contact Urantia Foundation. Copies of Urantia Foundation's current Copyright and Trademark Policies are available upon request.

ISBN:
0-942430-98-0

PUBLISHED BY URANTIA FOUNDATION
Original Publisher since 1955
533 Diversey Parkway
Chicago, Illinois 60614 U.S.A.
Telephone: +1 (773) 525-3319
Fax: +1 (773) 525-7739
Website: http://www.urantia.org
E-mail: urantia@urantia.org

Information

URANTIA Foundation has Representatives in Argentina, Belgium, Brazil, Bulgaria, Colombia, Ecuador, Estonia, Greece, Indonesia, Korea, Lithuania, México, Norway, Perú, Senegal, Spain, Uruguay, and Venezuela. If you require information on study groups, where you can obtain *The URANTIA Book*, or a Representative's telephone number, please contact the office nearest you or the head office in Chicago, Illinois.

International Offices:

Head Office
533 West Diversey Parkway
Chicago, Illinois 60614 U.S.A.
Tel.: +(773) 525-3319
Fax: +(773) 525-7739
Website: www.urantia.org
E-mail: urantia@urantia.org

Canada—English
PO Box 92006
West Vancouver, BC Canada V7V 4X4
Tel: +(604) 926-5836
Fax: +(604) 926-5899
E-mail: urantia@telus.net

Finland / Estonia / Sweden
PL 18,
15101 Lahti Finland
Tel./Fax: +(358) 3 777 8191
E-mail: urantia-saatio@urantia.fi

Great Britain / Ireland
Tel./Fax: +(44) 1491 641-922
E-Mail: urantia@easynet.co.uk

Australia / New Zealand / Asia
Tel./Fax: +(61) 2 9970-6200
E-mail: urantia@urantia.org.au

Canada—French
C. P. 233
Cap-Santé (Québec) Canada G0A 1L0
Tel.: +(418) 285-3333
Fax: +(418) 285-0226
E-mail: fondation@urantia-quebec.org

St. Petersburg, Russia
Tel./Fax: +(7) 812-580-3018
E-mail: vitgen@peterlink.ru

Other books available from URANTIA Foundation:

The URANTIA Book	hard cover		ISBN 0-911560-02-5
The URANTIA Book	leather collector	($7^5/_8$" x $5^3/_4$")	ISBN 0-911560-75-0
The URANTIA Book	small hard cover	($8^7/_{16}$" x $5^1/_2$")	ISBN 0-911560-07-6
The URANTIA Book	paperback	($8^7/_{16}$" x $5^1/_2$")	ISBN 0-911560-51-3
The URANTIA Book	gift-box leather	($8^7/_{16}$" x $5^1/_2$")	ISBN 0-911560-08-4
The URANTIA Book	softcover*	($8^7/_{16}$" x $5^1/_2$")	ISBN 0-911560-50-5
Le Livre d'URANTIA	hard cover	French	ISBN 0-911560-05-X
Le Livre d'URANTIA	soft cover	French	ISBN 0-911560-53-X
El libro de URANTIA	paperback	Spanish ($8^7/_{16}$" x $5^1/_2$")	ISBN 1-883395-02-X
El libro de URANTIA	hard cover	Spanish ($8^7/_{16}$" x $5^1/_2$")	ISBN 1-883395-03-8
URANTIA-kirja	hard cover	Finnish	ISBN 0-911560-03-3
URANTIA-kirja	soft cover	Finnish	ISBN 0-911560-52-1
Книга Урантии	hard cover	Russian* ($8^7/_{16}$" x $5^1/_2$")	ISBN 0-911560-80-7
Het URANTIA Boek	hard cover	Dutch	ISBN 0-911560-54-6
유란시아서	hard cover	Korean	ISBN 0-911560-40-8
The URANTIA Book Concordance		English Index	ISBN 0-911560-00-9
URANTIA-kirja Hakemisto		Finnish Index	ISBN 0-911560-04-1
The URANTIA Book	Audio	English*	ISBN 0-911560-30-0
The URANTIA Book	CD ROM	English, Finnish, French	ISBN 0-911560-63-7

The URANTIA Book Workbooks

Title	Format	Language	ISBN
Forward and Part I	Paperback	English	ISBN 0-942430-99-9
Science	Paperback	English	ISBN 0-942430-98-0
Topical and Doctrinal Study	Paperback	English	ISBN 0-942430-97-2
Jesus	Paperback	English	ISBN 0-942430-96-4

INTRODUCTION

Much has already been written regarding the study groups called "The Forum" and "The Seventy". Therefore I will try to confine my remarks more closely to the compiling and printing of several workbooks by Dr. William Sadler to be used in conjunction with *The Urantia Book*.

"The Forum" was the larger of the two groups and met on Sunday afternoons. The Wednesday night group was much smaller, studied in more depth, and was called "The Seventy" as that was the number of its members. Both met at the home of Dr. Sadler at 533 Diversey Parkway in Chicago. Doctor and some others in the group felt that something concrete was needed to train teachers for the future. Workbooks would help the teachers to form classes in the state or country in which they lived and use them to understand and present the concepts and new ideas from the Book in a uniform manner.

For several years members of the Wednesday night group were asked to prepare topical papers and teach the contents to the others in the group thus giving them experience in teaching. Dr. Sadler and his son, Bill, also taught the members of the group the information contained in the Papers of *The Urantia Book*. From the information Dr. Sadler taught at these classes the workbooks were developed for use by the group and for future teachers of the revelation.

The titles of the workbooks were:
Urantia Doctrine;
The Theology of *The Urantia Book*, Part I, Part II, and Part III;
Worship and Wisdom;
The Short Course in Doctrine,
Summary Of The Theology Of *The Urantia Book*;
Science in *The Urantia Book* Volume I (with the collaboration of Alvin Kulieke); and
The Teachings Of Jesus.

Dr. Sadler possessed a great intellect, which may be one of the reasons he was selected by the Contact Commission to be the recipient of the *Urantia Papers*. He was able to understand and present, in a form that is understandable for others, many of the more difficult concepts and information in *The Urantia Book*. This is a great advantage for students who may be teaching these concepts in the future. The reprinting of these study aids will help many students of *The Urantia Book* gain a more comfortable understanding of the more difficult teachings in the book and an insight into Dr. Sadler's plan for instructing the future teachers of the revelation.

What a legacy has been left to us!

Katharine

Katharine Lea Jones Harries

SCIENCE IN *THE URANTIA BOOK*

PAGE

PART I. ASTRONOMY 12

Sec. 1. Over-all Picture of the Master Universe 12
Sec. 2. Orvonton—the Seventh Superuniverse 31
Sec. 3. Local Universes 38
Sec. 4. Satania and Monmatia 45
Sec. 5. Nebulae 52
Sec. 6. The Origin of Space Bodies 56
Sec. 7. The Spheres of Space 59

PART II. GEOLOGY 71

Sec. 1. Early Ages of Urantia 71
Sec. 2. The Geologic Scheme (Primordial Life) 74
Sec. 3. Early Geologic History of Urantia 76
Sec. 4. The Life-dawn Era - the Proterozoic 80
Sec. 5. The Marine-life Era - the Paleozoic 84
Sec. 6. The Early Land-life Era - the Mesozoic 96
Sec. 7. The Mammalian Era - the Cenozoic 104

PART III. PHYSICS AND CHEMISTRY 116

Sec. 1. Origins and Cosmic Control of Forces and Energies 116
Sec. 2. Force, Energy, Power, Matter 128
Sec. 3. Physical-energy Controllers and Regulators 149
Sec. 4. Chemical Phenomena 163
Sec. 5. Physical Aspects of the Grand Universe 175

PART IV. BIOLOGY 185

Introduction - The Source of Life 185
Sec. 1. The Local Universe - The Creative Domain of a Creator son 186
Sec. 2. Urantia Biology 199
Conclusion 235

PART V. ANTHROPOLOGY 238

Sec. 1. Components and Attributes of Urantia Mortals 238
Sec. 2. Prehuman Mammals 246
Sec. 3. Human Beings 255
Sec. 4. The Evolutionary Races 267
Sec. 5. Second and Third Planetary Mortal Epochs 296
Sec. 6. The Races of Urantia after the Second Garden 325
Sec. 7. The Development of Civilization 257
Sec. 8. The Culmination of Human Evolution 393
Conclusion 402

SCIENCE IN
THE URANTIA BOOK

PART I — ASTRONOMY

Section One
OVER-ALL PICTURE OF THE MASTER UNIVERSE

I. **Space**

   A. **Description of total space.**

   1. **Space is a bestowal of Paradise.**
      "Space is neither a subabsolute condition within, nor the presence of, the Unqualified Absolute, neither is it a function of the Ultimate. It is a bestowal of Paradise, and the space of the grand universe and that of all outer regions is believed to be actually pervaded by the ancestral space potency of the Unqualified Absolute. From near approach to peripheral Paradise, this pervaded space extends horizontally outward through the fourth space level and beyond the periphery of the master universe, but how far beyond we do not know." P. 124.

   2. **Paradise is the nucleus of quiescent zones separating pervaded and unpervaded space.**
      "Paradise is the actually motionless nucleus of the relatively quiescent zones existing between pervaded and unpervaded space. Geographically these zones appear to be a relative extension of Paradise, but there probably is some motion in them. We know very little about them, but we observe that these zones of lessened space motion separate pervaded and unpervaded space. Similar zones once existed between the levels of pervaded space, but these are now less quiescent." P. 124.

      "Space does not exist on any of the surfaces of Paradise. If one 'looked' directly up from the upper surface of Paradise, one would 'see' nothing but unpervaded space going out or coming in, just now coming in. Space does not touch Paradise; only the quiescent *midspace zones* come in contact with the central Isle." P. 124.

   3. **Cross section of total space—pervaded and unpervaded.**
      "The vertical cross section of total space would slightly resemble a maltese cross, with the horizontal arms representing pervaded (universe) space and the vertical arms representing unpervaded (reservoir) space. The areas between the four arms would separate them somewhat as the midspace zones separate pervaded and unpervaded space. These quiescent midspace zones grow larger and larger at greater and greater

PART I — *Astronomy*

distances from Paradise and eventually encompass the borders of all space and completely incapsulate both the space reservoirs and the entire horizontal extension of pervaded space." P. 124.

4. **Outline of pervaded space.**

   "If you imagine a finite, but inconceivably large, V-shaped plane situated at right angles to both the upper and lower surfaces of Paradise, with its point nearly tangent to peripheral Paradise, and then visualize this plane in elliptical revolution about Paradise, its revolution would roughly outline the volume of pervaded space." P. 124.

B. **Space respiration.**

1. **Vertical extensions of unpervaded space contract as unpervaded space is transmitted into pervaded space and the horizontal extensions of pervaded space expand, and the converse.**

   "We do not know the actual mechanism of space respiration; we merely observe that all space alternately contracts and expands. This respiration affects both the horizontal extension of pervaded space and the vertical extensions of unpervaded space which exist in the vast space reservoirs above and below Paradise. In attempting to imagine the volume outlines of these space reservoirs, you might think of an hourglass." P. 123.

   "As the universes of the horizontal extension of pervaded space expand, the reservoirs of the vertical extension of unpervaded space contract and vice versa. There is a confluence of pervaded and unpervaded space just underneath nether Paradise. Both types of space there flow through the transmuting regulation channels, where changes are wrought making pervadable space nonpervadable and vice versa in the contraction and expansion cycles of the cosmos." P. 123.

2. **Description of unpervaded space—unpervaded by those forces, energies, powers, and presences known to exist in pervaded space.**

   "'Unpervaded' space means: unpervaded by those forces, energies, powers, and presences known to exist in pervaded space. We do not know whether vertical (reservoir) space is destined always to function as the equipoise of horizontal (universe) space; we do not know whether there is a creative intent concerning unpervaded space; we really know very little about the space reservoirs, merely that they exist, and that they seem to counterbalance the space-expansion-contraction cycles of the universe of universes." P. 123.

3. **Cycles of space respiration—approximately 2 billion years.**
"The cycles of space respiration extend in each phase for a little more than one billion Urantia years. During one phase the universes expand; during the next they contract. Pervaded space is now approaching the mid-point of the expanding phase, while unpervaded space nears the mid-point of the contracting phase, and we are informed that the outermost limits of both space extensions are, theoretically, now approximately equidistant from Paradise. The unpervaded-space reservoirs now extend vertically above upper Paradise and below nether Paradise just as far as the pervaded space of the universe extends horizontally outward from peripheral Paradise to and even beyond the fourth outer space level." P. 123.

"For a billion years of Urantia time the space reservoirs contract while the master universe and the force activities of all horizontal space expand. It thus requires a little over two billion Urantia years to complete the entire expansion-contraction cycle." P. 124.

4 **Errors and distortions of observations and calculations are due to space respiration.**
"The present relationship of your sun and its associated planets, while disclosing many relative and absolute motions in space, tends to convey the impression to astronomic observers that you are comparatively stationary in space, and that the surrounding starry clusters and streams are engaged in outward flight at everincreasing velocities as your calculations proceed outward in space. But such is not the case. You fail to recognize the present outward and uniform expansion of the physical creations of all pervaded space. Your own local creation (Nebadon) participates in this movement of universal outward expansion. The entire seven superuniverses participate in the two-billion-year cycles of space respiration along with the outer regions of the master universe." P. 134.

Errors are also due to angles of observation and other time-space distortions.

"Although your spectroscopic estimations of astronomic velocities are fairly reliable when applied to the starry realms belonging to your superuniverse and its associate

PART I — *Astronomy*

superuniverses, such reckonings with reference to the realms of outer space are wholly unreliable. Spectral lines are displaced from the normal towards the violet by an approaching star; likewise these lines are displaced towards the red by a receding star. Many influences interpose to make it appear that the recessional velocity of the external universes increases at the rate of more than one hundred miles a second for every million light-years increase in distance. By this method of reckoning, subsequent to the perfection of more powerful telescopes, it will appear that these far-distant systems are in flight from this part of the universe at the unbelievable rate of more than thirty thousand miles a second. But this apparent speed of recession is not real; it results from numerous factors of error embracing angles of observation and other time-space distortions." P. 134. Greatest distortions are due to opposite direction of revolution of the seven superuniverses and the first outer space level.

"But the greatest of all such distortions arises because the vast universes of outer space in the realms next to the domains of the seven superuniverses, seem to be revolving in a direction opposite to that of the grand universe. That is, these myriads of nebulae and their accompanying suns and spheres are at the present time revolving clockwise about the central creation. The seven superuniverses revolve about Paradise in a counterclockwise direction. It appears that the second outer universe of galaxies, like the seven superuniverses, revolves counterclockwise about Paradise. And the astronomic observers of Uversa think they detect evidence of revolutionary movements in a third outer belt of far-distant space which are beginning to exhibit directional tendencies of a clockwise nature." P. 134.

5. **Work done in space respiration is space work, not power-energy work.**

"When the universes expand and contract, the material masses in pervaded space alternately move against and with the pull of Paradise gravity. The work that is done in moving the material energy mass of creation is *space* work but not *power-energy* work." P. 134.

II. Paradise-Havona System

A. Paradise.

1. **General description. (P. 118)**

- 15 -

- a. Paradise, at the center of the universe of universes, is the most gigantic body in the master universe, a worthy capital of the universe of universes.
- b. Paradise is the:
    - (1) Eternal center of the universe of universes.
    - (2) Abiding place of the Universal Father, Eternal Son, Infinite Spirit, and their divine co-ordinates and associates.
    - (3) Most gigantic organized body of cosmic reality in all the master universe.
- c. The glory and spiritual splendor of the divine abode are impossible of mortal comprehension.
- d. Paradise is from eternity; there are neither records nor traditions respecting the origin of this nuclear Isle of Light and Life.

2. **Its shape and dimensions—elliptical, flat.**
"In form Paradise differs from the inhabited space bodies: it is not spherical. It is definitely ellipsoid, being one sixth longer in the north-south diameter than in the east-west diameter. The central Isle is essentially flat, and the distance from the upper surface to the nether surface is one tenth that of the east-west diameter." P. 119.

3. **Its composition—stationary, unique; composed of absolutum.**
"The eternal Isle is composed of a single form of materialization—stationary systems of reality. This literal substance of Paradise is a homogeneous organization of space potency not to be found elsewhere in all the wide universe of universes. It has received many names in different universes, and the Melchizedeks of Nebadon long since named it *absolutum*. This Paradise source material is neither dead nor alive; it is the original nonspiritual expression of the First Source and Center; it is *Paradise*, and Paradise is without duplicate." P. 120.

4. **Its relation to space, time, motion, and distance.**
"It appears to us that the First Source and Center has concentrated all absolute potential for cosmic reality in Paradise as a part of his technique of self-liberation from infinity limitations, as a means of making possible subinfinite, even time-space, creation. But it does not follow that Paradise is time-space limited just because the universe of universes discloses these qualities. Paradise exists without time and has no location in space." P. 120.

Part I — *Astronomy*

"Roughly: space seemingly originates just below nether Paradise; time just above upper Paradise. Time, as you understand it, is not a feature of Paradise existence, though the citizens of the central Isle are fully conscious of nontime sequence of events. Motion is not inherent on Paradise; it is volitional. But the concept of distance, even absolute distance, has very much meaning as it may be applied to relative locations on Paradise. Paradise is nonspatial; hence its areas are absolute and therefore serviceable in many ways beyond the concept of mortal mind." P. 120.

5. **Its geographical divisions.**
   a. *Upper Paradise. (P. 120)*
      (1) Central area—Deity presence.
      (2) Most Holy Sphere—immediately surrounding Deity presence— for worship, trinitization, high spiritual attainment.
      (3) Outer region—Holy Area—seven concentric zones—residential region
   b. *Peripheral Paradise. (P. 121)*
      (1) Landing and dispatching fields.
      (2) Force-focal headquarters of Seven Master Spirits.
      (3) Historic and prophetic exhibits of Creator Sons.
   c. *Nether Paradise. (P. 122)*
      (1) Central unknown and unrevealed Zone of Infinity.
      (2) Unnamed area—immediately surrounding Zone of Infinity.
      (3) Outer margin consisting of three concentric elliptical zones—concerned with space potency and force-energy.
         (a) Inner zone—functions as a gigantic heart whose pulsations direct and modify force-energies.
         (b) Mid-zone—pulsating control mechanism of midspace or quiet zones.
            —related to nonpervaded-space mechanism of the master universe.
         (c) Outer zone—central focalization of the space presence of the Unqualified Absolute.
            —central circuit point of emanations of pace-force pulsating in 2-billion-year cycles

in synchrony with space respiration.
—source and destiny of all force-energy.

6. **Space conditions and motions surrounding Paradise.**
"From the periphery of Paradise to the inner borders of the seven superuniverses there are the following seven space conditions and motions:

"1. The quiescent midspace zones impinging on Paradise.
"2. The clockwise processional of the three Paradise and the seven Havona circuits.
"3. The semiquiet space zone separating the Havona circuits from the dark gravity bodies of the central universe.
"4. The inner, counterclockwise-moving belt of the dark gravity bodies.
"5. The second unique space zone dividing the two space paths of the dark gravity bodies.
"6. The outer belt of dark gravity bodies, revolving clockwise around Paradise.
"7. A third space zone—a semiquiet zone—separating the outer belt of dark gravity bodies from the innermost circuits of the seven superuniverses." P. 152

B. **The sacred worlds of Paradise.**

1. **Description of the three seven-world circuits of the Father, Son, and Spirit.**
"Between the central Isle of Paradise and the innermost of the Havona planetary circuits there are situated in space three lesser circuits of special spheres. The innermost circuit consists of the seven secret spheres of the Universal Father; the second group is composed of the seven luminous worlds of the Eternal Son; in the outermost are the seven immense spheres of the Infinite Spirit, the executive-headquarters worlds of the Seven Master Spirits.

"These three seven-world circuits of the Father, the Son, and the Spirit are spheres of unexcelled grandeur and unimagined glory. Even their material or physical construction is of an order unrevealed to you. Each circuit is diverse in material, and each world of each circuit is different excepting the seven worlds of the Son, which are alike in physical constitution. All twenty-one are enormous spheres, and each group of seven is differently eternalized. As far as we know they have always been; like Paradise they are eternal. There exists neither record nor tradition of their origin." P. 143.

PART I — *Astronomy*

C. **Havona.**

1. **Havona—eternal central universe, consisting of one billion worlds.**

   "*Havona*, the central universe, is not a time creation; it is an eternal existence. This never-beginning, never-ending universe consists of one billion spheres of sublime perfection and is surrounded by the enormous dark gravity bodies. At the center of Havona is the stationary and absolutely stabilized Isle of Paradise, surrounded by its twenty-one satellites. Owing to the enormous encircling masses of the dark gravity bodies about the fringe of the central universe, the mass content of this central creation is far in excess of the total known mass of all seven sectors of the grand universe." P. 129.

2. **Arrangement—seven concentric circuits not superimposed.**

   "The billion worlds of Havona are arranged in seven concentric circuits immediately surrounding the three circuits of Paradise satellites. There are upwards of thirty-five million worlds in the innermost Havona circuit and over two hundred and forty-five million in the outermost, with proportionate numbers intervening. Each circuit differs, but all are perfectly balanced and exquisitely organized, and each is pervaded by a specialized representation of the Infinite Spirit, one of the Seven Spirits of the Circuits. In addition to other functions this impersonal Spirit co-ordinates the conduct of celestial affairs throughout each circuit.

   "The Havona planetary circuits are not superimposed; their worlds follow each other in an orderly linear procession. The central universe whirls around the stationary Isle of Paradise in one vast plane, consisting of ten concentric stabilized units—the three circuits of Paradise spheres and the seven circuits of Havona worlds. Physically regarded, the Havona and the Paradise circuits are all one and the same system; their separation is in recognition of functional and administrative segregation." P. 152-3.

3. **Time on Havona—the Paradise-Havona standard day: one day equals one thousand years of Urantia time.**

   "Time is not reckoned on Paradise; the sequence of successive events is inherent in the concept of those who are indigenous to the central Isle. But time is germane to the Havona circuits and to numerous beings of both celestial and terrestrial origin sojourning thereon. Each Havona world has its own local time, determined by its circuit. All worlds in a given circuit have the same length of year since they uniformly swing around Paradise, and the length of these planetary years decreases from the outermost to the innermost circuit." P. 153.

"Besides Havona-circuit time, there is the Paradise-Havona standard day and other time designations which are determined on, and are sent out from, the seven Paradise satellites of the Infinite Spirit. The Paradise-Havona standard day is based on the length of time required for the planetary abodes of the first or inner Havona circuit to complete one revolution around the Isle of Paradise; and though their velocity is enormous, owing to their situation between the dark gravity bodies and gigantic Paradise, it requires almost one thousand years for these spheres to complete their circuit. You have unwittingly read the truth when your eyes rested on the statement 'A day is as a thousand years with God, as but a watch in the night.' One Paradise-Havona day is just seven minutes, three and one-eighth seconds less than one thousand years of the present Urantia leap-year calendar.

"This Paradise-Havona day is the standard time measurement for the seven superuniverses, although each maintains its own internal time standards." P. 153.

D. **Dark gravity bodies.**
   1. **Nature and form—unlike other space bodies.**

   "On the outskirts of this vast central universe, far out beyond the seventh belt of Havona worlds, there swirl an unbelievable number of enormous dark gravity bodies. These multitudinous dark masses are quite unlike other space bodies in many particulars; even in form they are very different. These dark gravity bodies neither reflect nor absorb light; they are nonreactive to physical-energy light, and they so completely encircle and enshroud Havona as to hide it from the view of even near-by inhabited universes of time and space.

   "The great belt of dark gravity bodies is divided into two equal elliptical circuits by a unique space intrusion. The inner belt revolves counterclockwise; the outer revolves clockwise. These alternate directions of motion, coupled with the extraordinary mass of the dark bodies, so effectively equalize the lines of Havona gravity as to render the central universe a physically balanced and perfectly stabilized creation.

   "The inner procession of dark gravity bodies is tubular in

arrangement, consisting of three circular groupings. A cross section of this circuit would exhibit three concentric circles of about equal density. The outer circuit of dark gravity bodies is arranged perpendicularly, being ten thousand times higher than the inner circuit. The up-and-down diameter of the outer circuit is fifty thousand times that of the transverse diameter.

"The intervening space which exists between these two circuits of gravity bodies is *unique* in that nothing like it is to be found elsewhere in all the wide universe. This zone is characterized by enormous wave movements of an up-and-down nature and is permeated by tremendous energy activities of an unknown order.

"In our opinion, nothing like the dark gravity bodies of the central universe will characterize the future evolution of the outer space levels; we regard these alternate processions of stupendous gravity-balancing bodies as unique in the master universe." P. 153-4.

III. THE SEVEN SUPERUNIVERSES

The grand universe embraces the central creation and the seven superuniverses, having a potential of seven trillion inhabited worlds.

"*The Grand Universe* is the present organized and inhabited creation. It consists of the seven superuniverses, with an aggregate evolutionary potential of around seven trillion inhabited planets, not to mention the eternal spheres of the central creation. But this tentative estimate takes no account of architectural administrative spheres, neither does it include the outlying groups of unorganized universes. The present ragged edge of the grand universe, its uneven and unfinished periphery, together with the tremendously unsettled condition of the whole astronomical plot, suggests to our star students that even the seven superuniverses are, as yet, uncompleted. As we move from within, from the divine center outward in any one direction, we do, eventually, come to the outer limits of the organized and inhabited creation; we come to the outer limits of the grand universe. And it is near this outer border, in a far-off corner of such a magnificent creation, that your local universe has its eventful existence." P. 129.

A. Composition of the seven superuniverses.

"*The Seven Superuniverses* are not primary physical organizations; nowhere do their boundaries divide a nebular family, neither do they cross a local universe, a prime creative unit. Each superuniverse is simply a geographic space clustering of approximately one seventh of the organized and partially inhabited post-Havona creation, and each is about equal in the number of local universes embraced and in the space encompassed. *Nebadon*, your local universe, is one of the newer creations in *Orvonton*, the seventh superuniverse." P. 129.

B. **Total superuniverse motion.**
   1. **Counterclockwise elliptical course around the central universe.**
      "Within the limited range of the records, observations, and memories of the generations of a million or a billion of your short years, to all practical intents and purposes, Urantia and the universe to which it belongs are experiencing the adventure of one long and uncharted plunge into new space; but according to the records of Uversa, in accordance with older observations, in harmony with the more extensive experience and calculations of our order, and as a result of conclusions based on these and other findings, we know that the universes are engaged in an orderly, well-understood, and perfectly controlled processional, swinging in majestic grandeur around the First Great Source and Center and his residential universe." P. 164.
      "We have long since discovered that the seven superuniverses traverse a great ellipse, a gigantic and elongated circle. Your solar system and other worlds of time are not plunging headlong, without chart and compass, into unmapped space. The local universe to which your system belongs is pursuing a definite and well-understood counterclockwise course around the vast swing that encircles the central universe. This cosmic path is well charted and is just as thoroughly known to the superuniverse star observers as the orbits of the planets constituting your solar system are known to Urantia astronomers." P. 165.
   2. **The order of the superuniverse processional around Paradise.**
      "In this age and as direction is regarded on Urantia, superuniverse number one swings almost due north, approximately opposite, in an easterly direction, to the Paradise residence of the Great Sources and Centers and the central universe of Havona. This position, with the corresponding one to the west, represents the nearest physical approach of the

PART I — *Astronomy*

spheres of time to the eternal Isle. Superuniverse number two is in the north, preparing for the westward swing, while number three now holds the northernmost segment of the great space path, having already turned into the bend leading to the southerly plunge. Number four is on the comparatively straightaway southerly flight, the advance regions now approaching opposition to the Great Centers. Number five has about left its position opposite the Center of Centers while continuing on the direct southerly course just preceding the eastward swing; number six occupies most of the southern curve, the segment from which your superuniverse has nearly passed." P. 165.

3. **Position of Urantia and location of our solar system in the superuniverse swing around Paradise.**

"Your local universe of Nebadon belongs to Orvonton, the seventh superuniverse, which swings on between superuniverses one and six, having not long since (as we reckon time) turned the southeastern bend of the superuniverse space level. Today, the solar system to which Urantia belongs is a few billion years past the swing around the southern curvature so that you are just now advancing beyond the southeastern bend and are moving swiftly through the long and comparatively straightaway northern path. For untold ages Orvonton will pursue this almost direct northerly course.

"Urantia belongs to a system which is well out towards the border-land of your local universe; and your local universe is at present traversing the periphery of Orvonton. Beyond you there are still others, but you are far removed in space from those physical systems which swing around the great circle in comparative proximity to the Great Source and Center." P. 165

C. **Description of headquarters worlds.**

1. **Location and lighting.**

"While each superuniverse government presides near the center of the evolutionary universes of its space segment, it occupies a world made to order and is peopled by accredited personalities. These headquarters worlds are architectural spheres, space bodies specifically constructed for their special purpose. While sharing the light of near-by suns, these spheres are independently lighted and heated. Each has a sun which gives forth light without heat, like the satellites of Paradise, while each is supplied with heat by the circulation of certain energy currents near the surface of the sphere. These headquarters worlds belong to one of the greater systems situated near the astronomical center of their respective superuniverses." P. 174.

   2. **Their grandeur.**
   "The headquarters worlds of the seven superuniverses partake of the nature and grandeur of Paradise, their central pattern of perfection. In reality, all headquarters worlds are paradisiacal. They are indeed heavenly abodes, and they increase in material size, morontia beauty, and spirit glory from Jerusem to the central Isle. And all the satellites of these headquarters worlds are also architectural spheres.

   "The various headquarters worlds are provided with every phase of material and spiritual creation. All kinds of material, morontial, and spiritual beings are at home on these rendezvous worlds of the universes. As mortal creatures ascend the universe, passing from the material to the spiritual realms, they never lose their appreciation for, and enjoyment of, their former levels of existence." P. 174.

D. **Approximate organization of the superuniverses. (Paper 15, Sec. 2)**

   1. Each superuniverse contains ten major sectors.
   2. Each major sector contains one hundred minor sectors.
   3. Each minor sector contains one hundred local universes.
   4. Each local universe contains one hundred constellations.
   5. Each constellation contains one hundred systems.
   6. Each system contains one thousand inhabited or inhabitable worlds.

IV. THE MASTER UNIVERSE—OUTER SPACE

A. **General description of space levels.**

   1. **A zone of quiet, four hundred thousand light-years in width, separates the seven superuniverses from a gigantic outer belt of unbelievable energy action.**
   "The relatively quiet zone between the space levels, such as the one separating the seven superuniverses from the first outer space level, are enormous elliptical regions of quiescent space activities. These zones separate the vast galaxies which race around Paradise in orderly procession. You may visualize the first outer space level, where untold universes are now in process of formation, as a vast procession of galaxies swinging around Paradise, bounded above and below by the midspace

PART I — *Astronomy*

zones of quiescence and bounded on the inner and outer margins by relatively quiet space zones.

"A space level thus functions as an elliptical region of motion surrounded on all sides by relative motionlessness. Such relationships of motion and quiescence constitute a curved space path of lessened resistance to motion which is universally followed by cosmic force and emergent energy as they circle forever around the Isle of Paradise.

"This alternate zoning of the master universe, in association with the alternate clockwise and counterclockwise flow of the galaxies, is a factor in the stabilization of physical gravity designed to prevent the accentuation of gravity pressure to the point of disruptive and dispersive activities. Such an arrangement exerts antigravity influence and acts as a brake upon otherwise dangerous velocities." P. 125.

2. **The mighty transactions of this vast realm of outer space constitute the domains of the Unqualified Absolute.**
"When Urantia astronomers peer through their increasingly powerful telescopes into the mysterious stretches of outer space and there behold the amazing evolution of almost countless physical universes, they should realize that they are gazing upon the mighty outworking of the unsearchable plans of the Architects of the Master Universe. True, we do possess evidences which are suggestive of the presence of certain Paradise personality influences here and there throughout the vast energy manifestations now characteristic of these outer regions, but from the larger viewpoint the space regions extending beyond the outer borders of the seven superuniverses are generally recognized as constituting the domains of the Unqualified Absolute." P. 130.

3. **Millions of universes are revealed by our telescopes.**
"Although the unaided human eye can see only two or three nebulae outside the borders of the superuniverse of Orvonton, your telescopes literally reveal millions upon millions of these physical universes in process of formation. Most of the starry realms visually exposed to the search of your present-day telescopes are in Orvonton, but with photographic technique the larger telescopes penetrate far beyond the borders of the grand universe into the domains of outer space, where untold universes are in process of organization. And there are yet other millions of universes beyond the range of your present instruments." P. 130.

"In the not-distant future, new telescopes will reveal to the wondering gaze of Urantian astronomers no less than 375 million new galaxies in the remote stretches of outer space. At the same time these more powerful telescopes will disclose that many island universes formerly believed to be in outer space are really a part of the galactic system of Orvonton. The seven superuniverses are still growing; the periphery of each is gradually expanding; new nebulae are constantly being stabilized and organized; and some of the nebulae which Urantian astronomers regard as extragalactic are actually on the fringe of Orvonton and are traveling along with us." P. 130.

B. First outer space level.

"The Outer Space Levels. Far out in space, at an enormous distance from the seven inhabited superuniverses, there are assembling vast and unbelievably stupendous circuits of force and materializing energies. Between the energy circuits of the seven superuniverses and this gigantic outer belt of force activity, there is a space zone of comparative quiet, which varies in width but averages about four hundred thousand light-years. These space zones are free from star dust—cosmic fog. Our students of these phenomena are in doubt as to the exact status of the space-forces existing in this zone of relative quiet which encircles the seven superuniverses. But about one-half million light-years beyond the periphery of the present grand universe we observe the beginnings of a zone of an unbelievable energy action which increases in volume and intensity for over twenty-five million light-years. These tremendous wheels of energizing forces are situated in the first outer space level, a continuous belt of cosmic activity encircling the whole of the known, organized, and inhabited creation." P. 129.

C. Second outer space level.

1. **Far beyond the first outer space level is a zone of still greater activity.**
   "Still greater activities are taking place beyond these regions, for the Uversa physicists have detected early evidence of force manifestations more than fifty million light-years beyond the outermost ranges of the phenomena in the first outer space level. These activities undoubtedly presage the organization of the material creations of the second outer space level of the master universe." P. 130.

PART I — *Astronomy*

D. **Direction of revolution of space levels.**

"But the greatest of all such distortions arises because the vast universes of outer space in the realms next to the domains of the seven superuniverses, seem to be revolving in a direction opposite to that of the grand universe. That is, these myriads of nebulae and their accompanying suns and spheres are at the present time revolving clockwise about the central creation. The seven superuniverses revolve about Paradise in a counterclockwise direction. It appears that the second outer universe of galaxies, like the seven superuniverses, revolves counterclockwise about Paradise. And the astronomic observers of Uversa think they detect evidence of revolutionary movements in a third outer belt of far-distant space which are beginning to exhibit directional tendencies of a clockwise nature." P. 134.

E. **Relative quantity of material in the grand universe and in the outer space zones.**

1. **Gravity researchers have found that about five per cent of the active functioning of the Paradise absolute-gravity grasp is used by the central and superuniverses. Ninety-five per cent is engaged in controlling material systems beyond the borders of the present organized universes. (P. 132)**
2. **Uversa physicists calculate that the energy and matter of outer space regions already equals many times the total of all seven superuniverses.**

"The Uversa star students observe that the grand universe is surrounded by the ancestors of a series of starry and planetary clusters which completely encircle the present inhabited creation as concentric rings of outer universes upon universes. The physicists of Uversa calculate that the energy and matter of these outer and uncharted regions already equal many times the total material mass and energy charge embraced in all seven superuniverses. We are informed that the metamorphosis of cosmic force in these outer space levels is a function of the Paradise force organizers. We also know that these forces are ancestral to those physical energies which at present activate the grand universe. The Orvonton power directors, however, have nothing to do with these far-distant realms, neither are the energy movements therein discernibly connected with the power circuits of the organized and inhabited creations." P. 131.

F. **Sources of information concerning outer space levels.**
1. **Outer space domain is beyond the jurisdiction of the superuniverse governments.**
   "We know very little of the significance of these tremendous phenomena of outer space. A greater creation of the future is in process of formation. We can observe its immensity, we can discern its extent and sense its majestic dimensions, but otherwise we know little more about these realms than do the astronomers of Urantia. As far as we know, no material beings on the order of humans, no angels or other spirit creatures, exist in this outer ring of nebulae, suns, and planets. This distant domain is beyond the jurisdiction and administration of the superuniverse governments." P. 131.
2. **At the present time practically the entire spirit gravity of the Eternal Son is observable as functioning in the grand universe. (P. 132)**
3. **Eighty-five per cent of the mind-gravity response to the intellectual drawing of the Conjoint Actor takes origin in the existing grand universe, indicating that intelligent force organizers are at present directing universe evolution in the space levels beyond the present outer limits of the grand universe. (P. 132)**
4. **Solitary Messengers.**
   a. *Solitary Messengers volunteer as explorers of the cosmos.*
      "When the reserve corps of the Solitary Messengers is over-recruited, there issues from one of the Seven Supreme Power Directors a call for exploration volunteers; and there is never a lack of volunteers, for they delight to be dispatched as free and untrammeled explorers, to experience the thrill of finding the organizing nucleuses of new worlds and universes." P. 259.
   b. *Solitary Messengers are experts in discovering materializing energy centers and planets adapted for habitation.*
      "They go forth to investigate the clues furnished by the space contemplators of the realms. Undoubtedly the Paradise Deities know of the existence of these undiscovered energy systems of space, but they never divulge such information. If the Solitary Messengers did not explore and chart these newly organizing energy centers, such phenomena would long remain unnoticed even by the intelligences of adjacent realms. Solitary Messengers, as a class, are highly sensitive to gravity; accordingly they can

sometimes detect the probable presence of very small dark planets, the very worlds which are best adapted to life experiments." P. 259.

 c. *They patrol the master universe and much of our knowledge of outer space comes from their explorations.*
"These messenger-explorers of undirected assignment patrol the master universe. They are constantly out on exploring expeditions to the uncharted regions of all outer space. Very much of the information which we possess of transactions in the realms of outer space, we owe to the explorations of the Solitary Messengers as they often work and study with the celestial astronomers." P. 260.

 d. *Solitary Messengers function as emergency lines of communication.*
"The Solitary Messengers are able to function as emergency lines of communication throughout remote space regions, realms not embraced within the established circuits of the grand universe. It develops that one messenger, when so functioning, can transmit a message or send an impulse through space to a fellow messenger about one hundred light-years away as Urantia astronomers estimate stellar distances." P. 261.

G. **Architects of the Master Universe. (P. 351, Sec. 9)**

The Master Architects are in essence the living blueprints of the seven levels of the master universe. The numbers of Architects concerned with each level may be an indication of the ultimate physical size of each level.

1. One functions on the Paradise level.
2. Three are concerned with the Havona level.
3. Seven function on the superuniverse level.
4. Seventy deal with plans for the first outer space level.
5. 490 are concerned with the second outer space level.
6. 3,430 are occupied with plans for the tertiary space level.
7. 24,010 are related to the fourth outer space level.

H. **The summation of all our knowledge points to the existence of a well-nigh limitless, but, nonetheless, finite universe.**

"And all this confirms our belief in a circular, somewhat limited, but orderly and far-flung universe of universes. If this were not true, then evidence of energy depletion at some point would sooner or later appear. All laws, organizations, administration, and the testimony of universe explorers—everything points to the existence of an infinite God but, as yet, a finite universe, a circularity of endless existence, well-nigh limitless but, nevertheless, finite in contrast with infinity." P. 468.

PART I — *Astronomy*

SECTION TWO
ORVONTON - THE SEVENTH SUPERUNIVERSE

I. GENERAL ASPECTS OF SUPERUNIVERSES

A. Relation of the superuniverses to the Paradise Deities.

"As far as the Universal Father is concerned—as a Father—the universes are virtually nonexistent; he deals with personalities; he is the Father of personalities. As far as the Eternal Son and the Infinite Spirit are concerned—as creator partners—the universes are localized and individual under the joint rule of the Creator Sons and the Creative Spirits. As far as the Paradise Trinity is concerned, outside Havona there are just seven inhabited universes, the seven superuniverses which hold jurisdiction over the circle of the first post-Havona space level. The Seven Master Spirits radiate their influence out from the central Isle, thus constituting the vast creation one gigantic wheel, the hub being the eternal Isle of Paradise, the seven spokes the radiations of the Seven Master Spirits, the rim the outer regions of the grand universe." P. 164.

B. Superuniverse organization and government.

"Early in the materialization of the universal creation the sevenfold scheme of the superuniverse organization and government was formulated. The first post-Havona creation was divided into seven stupendous segments, and the headquarters worlds of these superuniverse governments were designed and constructed. The present scheme of administration has existed from near eternity, and the rulers of these seven superuniverses are rightly called Ancients of Days." P. 164.

II. ORGANIZATION OF ORVONTON

A. "*The Superuniverse.* Ten major sectors (about 1,000,000,000,000 inhabitable planets) constitute a superuniverse. Each superuniverse is provided with an enormous and glorious headquarters world and is ruled by three Ancients of Days." P. 166.

"The Satania system of inhabited worlds is far removed from Uversa and that great sun cluster which functions as the physical or astronomic center of the seventh superuniverse. From Jerusem, the headquarters of Satania, it is over two hundred thousand light-years to the physical center of the superuniverse of Orvonton, far, far away in the dense diameter of the Milky Way. Satania is on the periphery of the local universe, and Nebadon is now well out towards the edge of Orvonton. From the outermost system of inhabited worlds to the center of the superuniverse is a trifle less than two hundred and fifty thousand light-years." P. 359-60.

B. **The Milky Way - the central nucleus.**
  1. **Most of the starry realms visible to the naked eye—the Milky Way—belong to the superuniverse of Orvonton.**
    "Practically all of the starry realms visible to the naked eye on Urantia belong to the seventh section of the grand universe, the superuniverse of Orvonton. The vast Milky Way starry system represents the central nucleus of Orvonton, being largely beyond the borders of your local universe. This great aggregation of suns, dark islands of space, double stars, globular clusters, star clouds, spiral and other nebulae, together with myriads of individual planets, forms a watchlike, elongated-circular grouping of about one seventh of the inhabited evolutionary universes.
    "From the astronomical position of Urantia, as you look through the cross section of near-by systems to the great Milky Way, you observe that the spheres of Orvonton are traveling in a vast elongated plane, the breadth being far greater than the thickness and the length far greater than the breadth." P. 167.
  2. **When the angle of observation is right, the central universe is in the line of the main body of the Milky Way.**
    "Observation of the so-called Milky Way discloses the comparative increase in Orvonton stellar density when the heavens are viewed in one direction, while on either side the density diminishes; the number of stars and other spheres decreases away from the chief plane of our material superuniverse. When the angle of observation is propitious, gazing through the main body of this realm of maximum density, you are looking toward the residential universe and the center of all things." P. 167.
C. **Uversa - the headquarters of Orvonton.**
  1. "The personal abodes of each trio of the Ancients of Days are located at the point of spiritual polarity on their headquarters sphere. Such a sphere is divided into seventy administrative sectors and has seventy divisional capitals in which the Ancients of Days reside from time to time." P. 209.
  2. **Uversa is surrounded by seven clusters of seven worlds, universities of advanced special training. When completed, the seven superuniverses will contain slightly less than five hundred billion architectural worlds.**
    "*Uversa*, the headquarters of Orvonton, your superuniverse, is immediately surrounded by the seven higher universities of

advanced spiritual training for ascending will creatures. Each of these seven clusters of wonder spheres consists of seventy specialized worlds containing thousands upon thousands of replete institutions and organizations devoted to universe training and spirit culture wherein the pilgrims of time are re-educated and re-examined preparatory to their long flight to Havona. The arriving pilgrims of time are always received on these associated worlds, but the departing graduates are always dispatched for Havona direct from the shores of Uversa.

"Uversa is the spiritual and administrative headquarters for approximately one trillion inhabited or inhabitable worlds. The glory, grandeur, and perfection of the Orvonton capital surpass any of the wonders of the time-space creations.

"If all the projected local universes and their component parts were established, there would be slightly less than five hundred billion architectural worlds in the seven superuniverses." P. 175.

D. Standard superuniverse time.

    1. The standard day is equal to almost 30 days of Urantia time; the year equals one hundred standard days.

"Time is standardized on the headquarters of the superuniverses. The standard day of the superuniverse of Orvonton is equal to almost thirty days of Urantia time, and the Orvonton year equals one hundred standard days. This Uversa year is standard in the seventh superuniverse, and it is twenty-two minutes short of three thousand days of Urantia time, about eight and one fifth of your years." P. 174.

E. The major sectors.

    1. "*The Major Sector*. One hundred minor sectors (about 100,000,000,000 inhabitable worlds) make one major sector. Each major sector is provided with a superb headquarters and is presided over by three Perfections of Days, Supreme Trinity Personalities." P. 166.

    2. Eight of the major sectors of Orvonton have been astronomically identified.

"Of the ten major divisions of Orvonton, eight have been roughly identified by Urantian astronomers. The other two are difficult of separate recognition because you are obliged to view these phenomena from the inside. If you could look upon the superuniverse of Orvonton from a position far-distant in space, you would immediately recognize the ten major sectors of the seventh galaxy." P. 167.

"...Better methods of space measurement and improved telescopic technique will sometime more fully disclose the ten grand divisions of the superuniverse of Orvonton; you will at least recognize eight of these immense sectors as enormous and fairly symmetrical star clusters." P. 459.

3. "*Umajor the fifth*, the headquarters of your major sector, Splandon, is surrounded by the seventy spheres of the advancing intellectual training of the superuniverse." P. 174.

"A *major sector* comprises about one tenth of a superuniverse and consists of one hundred minor sectors, ten thousand local universes, about one hundred billion inhabitable worlds. These major sectors are administered by three Perfections of Days, Supreme Trinity Personalities." P. 181.

F. **The minor sectors.**

1. "*The Minor Sector*. One hundred local universes (about 1,000,000,000 inhabitable planets) constitute a minor sector of the superuniverse government; it has a wonderful headquarters world, wherefrom its rulers, the Recents of Days, administer the affairs of the minor sector. There are three Recents of Days, Supreme Trinity Personalities, on each minor sector headquarters." P. 166.

2. "*Uminor the third*, the headquarters of your minor sector, Ensa, is surrounded by the seven spheres of the higher physical studies of the ascendant life." P. 174.

3. **The rotational center of Ensa is the star cloud of Sagittarius.**

   "The rotational center of your minor sector is situated far away in the enormous and dense star cloud of Sagittarius, around which your local universe and its associated creations all move, and from opposite sides of the vast Sagittarius subgalactic system you may observe two great streams of star clouds emerging in stupendous stellar coils." P. 168.

4. **Minor sector government.**

   "The *minor sector* governments are presided over by three Recents of Days. Their administration is concerned mainly with the physical control, unification, stabilization, and routine coordination of the administration of the component local universes. Each minor sector embraces as many as one hundred local universes, ten thousand constellations, one million systems, or about one billion inhabitable worlds.

PART I — *Astronomy*

"Minor sector headquarters worlds are the grand rendezvous of the Master Physical Controllers. These headquarters worlds are surrounded by the seven instruction spheres which constitute the entrance schools of the superuniverse and are the centers of training for physical and administrative knowledge concerning the universe of universes." P. 181.

G. **The local universes.**
   1. "*The Local Universe*. One hundred constellations (about 10,000,000 inhabitable planets) constitute a local universe. Each local universe has a magnificent architectural headquarters world and is ruled by one of the co-ordinate Creator Sons of God of the order of Michael. Each universe is blessed by the presence of a Union of Days, a representative of the Paradise Trinity." P. 166.
   2. "*Salvington*, the capital of Nebadon, your local universe, is surrounded by ten university clusters of forty-nine spheres each. Hereon is man spiritualized following his constellation socialization." P. 174.

H. **The constellations.**
   1. "*The Constellation*. One hundred systems (about 100,000 inhabitable planets) make up a constellation. Each constellation has an architectural headquarters sphere and is presided over by three Vorondadek Sons, the Most Highs. Each constellation also has a Faithful of Days in observation, an ambassador of the Paradise Trinity." P. 166.
   2. "*Edentia*, the headquarters of your constellation of Norlatiadek, has its seventy satellites of socializing culture and training, on which ascenders sojourn upon the completion of the Jerusem regime of personality mobilization, unification, and realization." P. 174.

I. **The systems.**
   1. "*The System*. The basic unit of the supergovernment consists of about one thousand inhabited or inhabitable worlds. Blazing suns, cold worlds, planets too near the hot suns, and other spheres not suitable for creature habitation are not included in this group. These one thousand worlds adapted to support life are called a system, but in the younger systems only a comparatively small number of these worlds may be inhabited. Each inhabited planet is presided over by a Planetary Prince, and each local system has an architectural sphere as its head

quarters and is ruled by a System Sovereign." P. 166.

2. "Satania has a headquarters world called Jerusem, and it is system number twenty-four in the constellation of Norlatiadek. Your constellation, Norlatiadek, consists of one hundred local systems and has a headquarters world called Edentia. Norlatiadek is number seventy in the universe of Nebadon. The local universe of Nebadon consists of one hundred constellations and has a capital known as Salvington. The universe of Nebadon is number eighty-four in the minor sector of Ensa." P. 182.

3. "*Jerusem*, the headquarters of your local system of Satania, has its seven worlds of transition culture, each of which is encircled by seven satellites, among which are the seven mansion worlds of morontia detention, man's first post-mortal residence. As the term heaven has been used on Urantia, it has sometimes meant these seven mansion worlds, the first mansion world being denominated the first heaven, and so on to the seventh." P. 174.

J. Description of the seven different astronomic revolutions which confuse astronomers.

"The Sagittarius sector and all other sectors and divisions of Orvonton are in rotation around Uversa, and some of the confusion of Urantian star observers arises out of the illusions and relative distortions produced by the following multiple revolutionary movements:

"1. The revolution of Urantia around its sun.

"2. The circuit of your solar system about the nucleus of the former Andronover nebula.

"3. The rotation of the Andronover stellar family and the associated clusters about the composite rotation-gravity center of the star cloud of Nebadon.

"4. The swing of the local star cloud of Nebadon and its associated creations around the Sagittarius center of their minor sector.

"5. The rotation of the one hundred minor sectors, including Sagittarius, about their major sector.

"6. The whirl of the ten major sectors, the so-called star drifts, about the Uversa headquarters of Orvonton.

"7. The movement of Orvonton and six associated superuniverses around Paradise and Havona, the counterclockwise processional of the superuniverse space level.

PART I — *Astronomy*

"These multiple motions are of several orders: The space paths of your planet and your solar system are genetic, inherent in origin. The absolute counterclockwise motion of Orvonton is also genetic, inherent in the architectural plans of the master universe. But the intervening motions are of composite origin, being derived in part from the constitutive segmentation of matter-energy into the superuniverses and in part produced by the intelligent and purposeful action of the Paradise force organizers." P. 168.

Section Three
LOCAL UNIVERSES

I. Creator Sons - Makers and Rulers of Local Universes

A. Local universes are the creations of the unique Paradise Creator Sons.

"The Creator Sons are the makers and rulers of the local universes of time and space. These universe creators and sovereigns are of dual origin, embodying the characteristics of God the Father and God the Son. But each Creator Son is different from every other; each is unique in nature as well as in personality; each is the 'only-begotten Son' of the perfect deity ideal of his origin." P. 234.

B. Creator Sons undergo long courses of training before undertaking the work of universe organization.

"The Paradise Sons of the primary order are the designers, creators, builders, and administrators of their respective domains, the local universes of time and space, the basic creative units of the seven evolutionary superuniverses. A Creator Son is permitted to choose the space site of his future cosmic activity, but before he may begin even the physical organization of his universe, he must spend a long period of observation devoted to the study of the efforts of his older brothers in various creations located in the superuniverse of his projected action. And prior to all this, the Michael Son will have completed his long and unique experience of Paradise observation and Havona training." P. 235.

C. In time, the Creator Son, in union with the Creative Daughter of the Infinite Spirit, begins the creation of numerous universe children.

"When such a perfect and divine Son has taken possession of the space site of his chosen universe; when the initial problems of universe materialization and of gross equilibrium have been resolved; when he has formed an effective and co-operative working union with the complemental Daughter of the Infinite Spirit—then do this Universe Son and this Universe Spirit initiate that liaison which is designed to give origin to the innumerable hosts of their local universe children. In connection with this event the Creative Spirit focalization of the Paradise Infinite Spirit becomes changed in nature, taking on the personal qualities of the Mother Spirit of a local universe." P. 236.

II. Evolution of Local Universes

A. Physical emergence of universes.

PART I — *Astronomy*

1. "A local universe is the handiwork of a Creator Son of the Paradise order of Michael. It comprises one hundred constellations, each embracing one hundred systems of inhabited worlds. Each system will eventually contain approximately one thousand inhabited spheres." P. 357.
   "The preuniverse manipulations of space-force and the primordial energies are the work of the Paradise Master Force Organizers; but in the superuniverse domains, when emergent energy becomes responsive to local or linear gravity, they retire in favor of the power directors of the superuniverse concerned.
   "These power directors function alone in the prematerial and post-force phases of a local universe creation. There is no opportunity for a Creator Son to begin universe organization until the power directors have effected the mobilization of the space-energies sufficiently to provide a material foundation—literal suns and material spheres—for the emerging universe.
   "The local universes are all approximately of the same energy potential, though they differ greatly in physical dimensions and may vary in visible-matter content from time to time. The power charge and potential-matter endowment of a local universe are determined by the manipulations of the power directors and their predecessors as well as by the Creator Son's activities and by the endowment of the inherent physical control possessed by his creative associate." P. 357-58.
2. Creator Sons materialize visible matter from pre-existent energy. The first act of physical creation to be completed is the organization of the headquarters world and its 490 satellites. This is immediately followed by the creation of the constellation headquarters worlds. In Nebadon this required almost a million years. (Paper 32.)

III. Evolution of Nebadon

A. A local universe is not composed of a single astronomical system but of diverse nebular ancestry that has enough commonness of motion to be adjusted into a contiguous unit.

"The characteristic space phenomenon which sets off each local creation from all others is the presence of the Creative Spirit. All Nebadon is certainly pervaded by the space presence of the Divine Minister of Salvington, and such presence just as certainly terminates at the outer borders of our local universe. That which is pervaded by our local universe Mother Spirit *is* Nebadon; that which extends beyond her space presence is outside Nebadon, being the extra-Nebadon space regions of the superuniverse of Orvonton—other local universes." P. 455.

"One or more—even many—such nebulae may be encompassed within the domain of a single local universe even as Nebadon was physically assembled out of the stellar and planetary progeny of Andronover and other nebulae. The spheres of Nebadon are of diverse nebular ancestry, but they all had a certain minimum commonness of space motion which was so adjusted by the intelligent efforts of the power directors as to produce our present aggregation of space bodies, which travel along together as a contiguous unit over the orbits of the superuniverse.

"Such is the constitution of the local star cloud of Nebadon, which today swings in an increasingly settled orbit about the Sagittarius center of that minor sector of Orvonton to which our local creation belongs." P. 455.

B. "Salvington, the headquarters of Nebadon, is situated at the exact energy-mass center of the local universe. But your local universe is not a single astronomic system, though a large system does exist at its physical center." P. 359.

C. Development of Nebadon.

1. **The beginnings of the Andronover nebula.**
"987,000,000,000 years ago associate force organizer and then acting inspector number 811,307 of the Orvonton series, traveling out from Uversa, reported to the Ancients of Days that space conditions were favorable for the initiation of materialization phenomena in a certain sector of the, then, easterly segment of Orvonton.
"900,000,000,000 years ago the Uversa archives testify, there was recorded a permit issued by the Uversa Council of Equilibrium to the superuniverse government authorizing the dispatch of a force organizer and staff to the region previously designated by inspector number 811,307. The Orvonton authorities commissioned the original discoverer of this potential universe to execute the mandate of the Ancients of Days calling for the organization of a new material creation." P. 651.

2. **The force organizers initiate the Andronover nebula.**
"875,000,000,000 years ago the enormous Andronover

nebula number 876,926 was duly initiated. Only the presence of the force organizer and the liaison staff was required to inaugurate the energy whirl which eventually grew into this vast cyclone of space. Subsequent to the initiation of such nebular revolutions, the living force organizers simply withdraw at right angles to the plane of the revolutionary disk, and from that time forward, the inherent qualities of energy insure the progressive and orderly evolution of such a new physical system." P. 652.

3. **Andronover was well established 800,000,000,000 years ago.**
"800,000,000,000 years ago the Andronover creation was well established as one of the magnificent primary nebulae of Orvonton. As the astronomers of near-by universes looked out upon this phenomenon of space, they saw very little to attract their attention. Gravity estimates made in adjacent creations indicated that space materializations were taking place in the Andronover regions, but that was all." P. 652.

4. **600,000,000,000 years ago Andronover attained its height of energy mobilization and mass.**
"600,000,000,000 years ago the height of the Andronover energy-mobilization period was attained; the nebula had acquired its maximum of mass. At this time it was a gigantic circular gas cloud in shape somewhat like a flattened spheroid. This was the early period of differential mass formation and varying revolutionary velocity. Gravity and other influences were about to begin their work of converting space gases into organized matter." P. 652.

5. **The nebula becomes spiral and vast systems of solid matter appear in the gaseous cloud.**
"About the time of the attainment of the maximum of mass, the gravity control of the gaseous content commenced to weaken, and there ensued the stage of gas escapement, the gas streaming forth as two gigantic and distinct arms, which took origin on opposite sides of the mother mass. The rapid revolutions of this enormous central core soon imparted a spiral appearance to these two projecting gas streams. The cooling and subsequent condensation of portions of these protruding arms eventually produced their knotted appearance. These denser portions were vast systems and subsystems of physical matter whirling through space in the midst of the gaseous cloud of the nebula while being held securely within the gravity grasp of the mother wheel." P. 653.

6. **Next, comes the era of increased gas escapement and the critical centrifugal stage preceding sun formation.**

   "But the nebula had begun to contract, and the increase in the rate of revolution further lessened gravity control; and erelong, the outer gaseous regions began actually to escape from the immediate embrace of the nebular nucleus, passing out into space on circuits of irregular outline, returning to the nuclear regions to complete their circuits, and so on. But this was only a temporary stage of nebular progression. The ever-increasing rate of whirling was soon to throw enormous suns off into space on independent circuits.

   "And this is what happened in Andronover ages upon ages ago. The energy wheel grew and grew until it attained its maximum of expansion, and then, when contraction set in, it whirled on faster and faster until, eventually, the critical centrifugal stage was reached and the great breakup began." P. 653.

7. **The first Andronover sun was born 500,000,000,000 years ago and started out on its adventure in the cosmos.**

   "500,000,000,000 years ago the first Andronover sun was born. This blazing streak broke away from the mother gravity grasp and tore out into space on an independent adventure in the cosmos of creation. Its orbit was determined by its path of escape. Such young suns quickly become spherical and start out on their long and eventful careers as the stars of space. Excepting terminal nebular nucleuses, the vast majority of Orvonton suns have had an analogous birth. These escaping suns pass through varied periods of evolution and subsequent universe service." P. 653.

8. **Andronover next entered the recaptive period of its history.**

   "400,000,000,000 years ago began the recaptive period of the Andronover nebula. Many of the near-by and smaller suns were recaptured as a result of the gradual enlargement and further condensation of the mother nucleus. Very soon there was inaugurated the terminal phase of nebular condensation, the period which always precedes the final segregation of these immense space aggregations of energy and matter." P. 653.

9. **Soon after this era Michael began the creation of the universe of Nebadon. The architectural worlds were finished about five billion years ago.**

"It was scarcely a million years subsequent to this epoch that Michael of Nebadon, a Creator Son of Paradise, selected this disintegrating nebula as the site of his adventure in universe building. Almost immediately the architectural worlds of Salvington and the one hundred constellation headquarters groups of planets were begun. It required almost one million years to complete these clusters of specially created worlds. The local system headquarters planets were constructed over a period extending from that time to about five billion years ago." P. 654.

10. **300,000,000,000 years ago Andronover was temporarily stabilized and Michael's staff arrived on Salvington.**
"300,000,000,000 years ago the Andronover solar circuits were well established, and the nebular system was passing through a transient period of relative physical stability. About this time the staff of Michael arrived on Salvington, and the Uversa government of Orvonton extended physical recognition to the local universe of Nebadon." P. 654.

11. **100,000,000,000 years ago the height of tension was reached—heat was winning over gravity—and the stage was set for final sun dispersion.**
"100,000,000,000 years ago the nebular apex of condensation tension was reached; the point of maximum heat tension was attained. This critical stage of gravity-heat contention sometimes lasts for ages, but sooner or later, heat wins the struggle with gravity, and the spectacular period of sun dispersion begins. And this marks the end of the secondary career of a space nebula." P. 654.

12. **Completion of the first period of sun losses—the tertiary cycle of the nebula.**
"75,000,000,000 years ago this nebula had attained the height of its sun-family stage. This was the apex of the first period of sun losses. The majority of these suns have since possessed themselves of extensive systems of planets, satellites, dark islands, comets, meteors, and cosmic dust clouds.
"50,000,000,000 years ago this period of sun dispersion was completed; the nebula was fast finishing its tertiary cycle of existence, during which it gave origin to 876,926 sun systems." P. 654.

13. **Completion of the tertiary cycle 25,000,000,000 years ago brought relative stabilization.**
"25,000,000,000 years ago witnessed the completion of the

tertiary cycle of nebular life and brought about the organization and relative stabilization of the far-flung starry systems derived from this parent nebula. But the process of physical contraction and increased heat production continued in the central mass of the nebular remnant." P. 654.

14. **8,000,000,000 years ago the terminal eruption began—the end of the nebula.**

    "8,000,000,000 years ago the terrific terminal eruption began. Only the outer systems are safe at the time of such a cosmic upheaval. And this was the beginning of the end of the nebula. This final sun disgorgement extended over a period of almost two billion years.

    "7,000,000,000 years ago witnessed the height of the Andronover terminal breakup. This was the period of the birth of the larger terminal suns and the apex of the local physical disturbances." P. 655.

15. **6,000,000,000 years ago marked the birth of our sun—fifty-sixth from the last of Andronover's second solar family.**

    "6,000,000,000 years ago marks the end of the terminal breakup and the birth of your sun, the fifty-sixth from the last of the Andronover second solar family. This final eruption of the nebular nucleus gave birth to 136,702 suns, most of them solitary orbs. The total number of suns and sun systems having origin in the Andronover nebula was 1,013,628. The number of the solar system sun is 1,013,572." P. 655.

16. "And now the great Andronover nebula is no more, but it lives on in the many suns and their planetary families which originated in this mother cloud of space. The final nuclear remnant of this magnificent nebula still burns with a reddish glow and continues to give forth moderate light and heat to its remnant planetary family of one hundred and sixty-five worlds, which now revolve about this venerable mother of two mighty generations of the monarchs of light." P. 655.

17. "The organization of planetary abodes is still progressing in Nebadon, for this universe is, indeed, a young cluster in the starry and planetary realms of Orvonton. At the last registry there were 3,840,101 inhabited planets in Nebadon, and Satania, the local system of your world, is fairly typical of other systems." P. 359.

Part I — *Astronomy*

Section Four
SATANIA AND MONMATIA

I. General Description of Satania

A. Satania is composed of many astronomical systems.

"Satania itself is composed of over seven thousand astronomical groups, or physical systems, few of which had an origin similar to that of your solar system. The astronomic center of Satania is an enormous dark island of space which, with its attendant spheres, is situated not far from the headquarters of the system government." P. 457.

B. Satania contains 619 inhabited worlds located in over 500 physical systems.

"Satania is not a uniform physical system, a single astronomic unit or organization. Its 619 inhabited worlds are located in over five hundred different physical systems. Only five have more than two inhabited worlds, and of these only one has four peopled planets, while there are forty-six having two inhabited worlds." P. 359

C. More than 2000 suns serve Satania. Power Directors control the energy circuits.

"There are upward of two thousand brilliant suns pouring forth light and energy in Satania, and your own sun is an average blazing orb. Of the thirty suns nearest yours, only three are brighter. The Universe Power Directors initiate the specialized currents of energy which play between the individual stars and their respective systems. These solar furnaces, together with the dark giants of space, serve the power centers and physical controllers as way stations for the effective concentrating and directionizing of the energy circuits of the material creations." P. 458.

II. Evolution of Our Solar System

A. The origin of Monmatia.

1. **The story of our pulsating sun and its disruptive response to the gravity pull of Angona.**
"5,000,000,000 years ago your sun was a comparatively isolated blazing orb, having gathered to itself most of the near-by circulating matter of space, remnants of the recent upheaval which attended its own birth.

"Today, your sun has achieved relative stability, but its eleven and one-half year sunspot cycles betray that it was a variable star in its youth. In the early days of your sun the continued contraction and consequent gradual increase of temperature initiated tremendous convulsions on its surface. These titanic heaves required three and one-half days to complete a cycle of varying brightness. This variable state, this periodic pulsation, rendered your sun highly responsive to certain outside influences which were to be shortly encountered.

"Thus was the stage of local space set for the unique origin of *Monmatia*, that being the name of your sun's planetary family, the solar system to which your world belongs. Less than one per cent of the planetary systems of Orvonton have had a similar origin.

"4,500,000,000 years ago the enormous Angona system began its approach to the neighborhood of this solitary sun. The center of this great system was a dark giant of space, solid, highly charged, and possessing tremendous gravity pull." P. 655.

2. **First stages of the planets of our solar system.**

"As Angona more closely approached the sun, at moments of maximum expansion during solar pulsations, streams of gaseous material were shot out into space as gigantic solar tongues. At first these flaming gas tongues would invariably fall back into the sun, but as Angona drew nearer and nearer, the gravity pull of the gigantic visitor became so great that these tongues of gas would break off at certain points, the roots falling back into the sun while the outer sections would become detached to form independent bodies of matter, solar meteorites, which immediately started to revolve about the sun in elliptical orbits of their own." P. 656.

3. **Completion of the birth of the solar system.**

"As the Angona system drew nearer, the solar extrusions grew larger and larger; more and more matter was drawn from the sun to become independent circulating bodies in surrounding space. This situation developed for about five hundred thousand years until Angona made its closest approach to the sun; whereupon the sun, in conjunction with one of its periodic internal convulsions, experienced a partial disruption; from opposite sides and simultaneously, enormous volumes of matter were disgorged. From the Angona side there was drawn out a vast column of solar gases, rather pointed at both ends and markedly bulging at the center, which became permanently detached from the immediate gravity control of the sun.

Part I — *Astronomy*

"This great column of solar gases which was thus separated from the sun subsequently evolved into the twelve planets of the solar system. The repercussional ejection of gas from the opposite side of the sun in tidal sympathy with the extrusion of this gigantic solar system ancestor, has since condensed into the meteors and space dust of the solar system, although much, very much, of this matter was subsequently recaptured by solar gravity as the Angona system receded into remote space." P. 656.

4. **While drawing off the solar system, Angona did not secure any of the sun's substance for itself.**
"Although Angona succeeded in drawing away the ancestral material of the solar system planets and the enormous volume of matter now circulating about the sun as asteroids and meteors, it did not secure for itself any of this solar matter. The visiting system did not come quite close enough to actually steal any of the sun's substance, but it did swing sufficiently close to draw off into the intervening space all of the material comprising the present-day solar system." P. 656.

5. **Formation of the twelve planets of the solar system.**
"The five inner and five outer planets soon formed in miniature from the cooling and condensing nucleuses in the less massive and tapering ends of the gigantic gravity bulge which Angona had succeeded in detaching from the sun, while Saturn and Jupiter were formed from the more massive and bulging central portions. The powerful gravity pull of Jupiter and Saturn early captured most of the material stolen from Angona as the retrograde motion of certain of their satellites bears witness." P. 656.

6. **Origin and evolution of Jupiter and Saturn.**
"Jupiter and Saturn, being derived from the very center of the enormous column of superheated solar gases, contained so much highly heated sun material that they shone with a brilliant light and emitted enormous volumes of heat; they were in reality secondary suns for a short period after their formation as separate space bodies. These two largest of the solar system planets have remained largely gaseous to this day, not even yet having cooled off to the point of complete condensation or solidification." P. 656.

7. **Solidification and evolution of the ten minor planets.**
"The gas-contraction nucleuses of the other ten planets soon

reached the stage of solidification and so began to draw to themselves increasing quantities of the meteoric matter circulating in near-by space. The worlds of the solar system thus had a double origin: nucleuses of gas condensation later on augmented by the capture of enormous quantities of meteors. Indeed they still continue to capture meteors, but in greatly lessened numbers." P. 656.

8. **The planets swing around the sun in the plane of the Angona extrusion.**

"The planets do not swing around the sun in the equatorial plane of their solar mother, which they would do if they had been thrown off by solar revolution. Rather, they travel in the plane of the Angona solar extrusion, which existed at a considerable angle to the plane of the sun's equator." P. 657.

9. **The new solar system steals three of Angona's outer tributaries.**

"While Angona was unable to capture any of the solar mass, your sun did add to its metamorphosing planetary family some of the circulating space material of the visiting system. Due to the intense gravity field of Angona, its tributary planetary family pursued orbits of considerable distance from the dark giant; and shortly after the extrusion of the solar system ancestral mass and while Angona was yet in the vicinity of the sun, three of the major planets of the Angona system swung so near to the massive solar system ancestor that its gravitational pull, augmented by that of the sun, was sufficient to overbalance the gravity grasp of Angona and to permanently detach these three tributaries of the celestial wanderer." P. 657.

10. **Retrograde motions in the solar system are derived from matter stolen from Angona.**

"All of the solar system material derived from the sun was originally endowed with a homogeneous direction of orbital swing, and had it not been for the intrusion of these three foreign space bodies, all solar system material would still maintain the same direction of orbital movement. As it was, the impact of the three Angona tributaries injected new and foreign directional forces into the emerging solar system with the resultant appearance of *retrograde motion*. Retrograde motion in any astronomic system is always accidental and always appears as a result of the collisional impact of foreign space bodies. Such collisions may not always produce retrograde motion, but no retrograde ever appears except in a system containing masses which have diverse origins." P. 657.

11. **The later evolution of the solar system.**
"Subsequent to the birth of the solar system a period of diminishing solar disgorgement ensued. Decreasingly, for another five hundred thousand years, the sun continued to pour forth diminishing volumes of matter into surrounding space. But during these early times of erratic orbits, when the surrounding bodies made their nearest approach to the sun, the solar parent was able to recapture a large portion of this meteoric material." P. 657.

12. **The influence of gravitation and tidal friction on planetary axial revolution.**
"The planets nearest the sun were the first to have their revolutions slowed down by tidal friction. Such gravitational influences also contribute to the stabilization of planetary orbits while acting as a brake on the rate of planetary-axial revolution, causing a planet to revolve ever slower until axial revolution ceases, leaving one hemisphere of the planet always turned toward the sun or larger body, as is illustrated by the planet Mercury and by the moon, which always turns the same face toward Urantia." P. 657.

13. **Tidal friction as concerns the earth and the moon and the possible future disruption of the moon.**
"When the tidal frictions of the moon and the earth become equalized, the earth will always turn the same hemisphere toward the moon, and the day and month will be analogous—in length about forty-seven days. When such stability of orbits is attained, tidal frictions will go into reverse action, no longer driving the moon farther away from the earth but gradually drawing the satellite toward the planet. And then, in that far-distant future when the moon approaches to within about eleven thousand miles of the earth, the gravity action of the latter will cause the moon to disrupt, and this tidal-gravity explosion will shatter the moon into small particles, which may assemble about the world as rings of matter resembling those of Saturn or may be gradually drawn into the earth as meteors." P. 657-58.

14. **Laws governing the disruption or collision of space bodies.**
"If space bodies are similar in size and density, collisions may occur. But if two space bodies of similar density are relatively

unequal in size, then, if the smaller progressively approaches the larger, the disruption of the smaller body will occur when the radius of its orbit becomes less then two and one-half times the radius of the larger body. Collisions among the giants of space are rare indeed, but these gravity-tidal explosions of lesser bodies are quite common." P. 658.

15. **The completed organization of the Jupiter and Saturn systems.**

"4,000,000,000 years ago witnessed the organization of the Jupiter and Saturn systems much as observed today except for their moons, which continued to increase in size for several billions of years. In fact, all of the planets and satellites of the solar system are still growing as the result of continued meteoric captures." P. 658.

16. **Story of the further evolution and organization of the solar system.**

"3,500,000,000 years ago the condensation nucleuses of the other ten planets were well formed, and the cores of most of the moons were intact, though some of the smaller satellites later united to make the present-day larger moons. This age may be regarded as the era of planetary assembly.

"3,000,000,000 years ago the solar system was functioning much as it does today. Its members continued to grow in size as space meteors continued to pour in upon the planets and their satellites at a prodigious rate.

"About this time your solar system was placed on the physical registry of Nebadon and given its name, Monmatia.

"2,500,000,000 years ago the planets had grown immensely in size. Urantia was a well-developed sphere about one tenth its present mass and was still growing rapidly by meteoric accretion." P. 658.

17. **Description of the astronomic location of Urantia in the distorted Andronover nebula.**

"The nucleus of the physical system to which your sun and its associated planets belong is the center of the onetime Andronover nebula. This former spiral nebula was slightly distorted by the gravity disruptions associated with the events which were attendant upon the birth of your solar system, and which were occasioned by the near approach of a large neighboring nebula. This near collision changed Andronover into a somewhat globular aggregation but did not wholly destroy the two-way procession of the suns and their associated physical groups. Your solar system now occupies a fairly central position in one of the arms of this distorted spiral, situated about halfway from the center out towards the edge of the star stream." P. 168.

18. **The majority of solar systems had an origin different from ours.**

"The majority of solar systems, however, had an origin entirely different from yours, and this is true even of those which were produced by gravity-tidal technique. But no matter what technique of world building obtains, gravity always produces the solar system type of creation; that is, a central sun or dark island with planets, satellites, subsatellites, and meteors." P. 466.

Section Five
NEBULAE

I. Function of Force Organizers

A. Transmutation of space potency into physical reality.

1. **The force-charge of space and the ultimaton are not fully understood.**

   "While creation and universe organization remain forever under the control of the infinite Creators and their associates, the whole phenomenon proceeds in accordance with an ordained technique and in conformity to the gravity laws of force, energy, and matter. But there is something of mystery associated with the universal force-charge of space; we quite understand the organization of the material creations from the ultimatonic stage forward, but we do not fully comprehend the cosmic ancestry of the ultimatons. We are confident that these ancestral forces have a Paradise origin because they forever swing through pervaded space in the exact gigantic outlines of Paradise. Though nonresponsive to Paradise gravity, this force-charge of space, the ancestor of all materialization, does always respond to the presence of nether Paradise, being apparently circuited in and out of the nether Paradise center." P. 169.

2. **Function of force organizers and power directors in the transmutation of space potency into physical reality.**

   "The Paradise force organizers transmute space potency into primordial force and evolve this prematerial potential into the primary and secondary energy manifestations of physical reality. When this energy attains gravity-responding levels, the power directors and their associates of the superuniverse regime appear upon the scene and begin their never-ending manipulations designed to establish the manifold power circuits and energy channels of the universes of time and space. Thus does physical matter appear in space, and so is the stage set for the inauguration of universe organization." P. 169.

3. **The segmentation of energy has never been solved by Nebadon physicists due to the inaccessibility of the Paradise force organizers.**

   "This segmentation of energy is a phenomenon which has never been solved by the physicists of Nebadon. Their chief difficulty lies in the relative inaccessibility of the Paradise force organizers, for the living power directors, though they are competent to deal with space-energy, do not have the least

PART I — *Astronomy*

conception of the origin of the energies they so skillfully and intelligently manipulate." P. 169.

4. **Paradise force organizers are the originators of the ten varieties of nebulae to be observed throughout the master universe.**

   "Paradise force organizers are nebulae originators; they are able to initiate about their space presence the tremendous cyclones of force which, when once started, can never be stopped or limited until the all-pervading forces are mobilized for the eventual appearance of the ultimatonic units of universe matter. Thus are brought into being the spiral and other nebulae, the mother wheels of the direct-origin suns and their varied systems. In outer space there may be seen ten different forms of nebulae, phases of primary universe evolution, and these vast energy wheels had the same origin as did those in the seven superuniverses." P. 169.

II. Additional Facts about Nebulae (P. 169-70)

A. **Nebulae vary in size, some of the larger ones giving origin to one hundred million suns.**

   "Nebulae vary greatly in size and in the resulting number and aggregate mass of their stellar and planetary offspring. A sun-forming nebula just north of the borders of Orvonton, but within the superuniverse space level, has already given origin to approximately forty thousand suns, and the mother wheel is still throwing off suns, the majority of which are many times the size of yours. Some of the larger nebulae of outer space are giving origin to as many as one hundred million suns." P. 169.

B. **Nebulae are not directly related to the administrative units of the superuniverses.**

   "Nebulae are not directly related to any of the administrative units, such as minor sectors or local universes, although some local universes have been organized from the products of a single nebula. Each local universe embraces exactly one one-hundred-thousandth part of the total energy charge of a superuniverse irrespective of nebular relationship, for energy is not organized by nebulae—it is universally distributed." P. 169.

C. **Not all spiral nebulae are engaged in sun making.**

   "Not all spiral nebulae are engaged in sun making. Some have retained control of many of their segregated stellar offspring, and their spiral appearance is occasioned by the fact that their suns pass

- 53 -

out of the nebular arm in close formation but return by diverse routes, thus making it easy to observe them at one point but more difficult to see them when widely scattered on their different returning routes farther out and away from the arm of the nebula. There are not many sun-forming nebulae active in Orvonton at the present time, though Andromeda, which is outside the inhabited superuniverse, is very active. This far-distant nebula is visible to the naked eye, and when you view it, pause to consider that the light you behold left those distant suns almost one million years ago." P. 170.

D. **The Milky Way is composed of vast numbers of nebulae; some through rearrangement appear as clouds, like the Magellanic Cloud.**

"The Milky Way galaxy is composed of vast numbers of former spiral and other nebulae, and many still retain their original configuration. But as the result of internal catastrophes and external attraction, many have suffered such distortion and rearrangement as to cause these enormous aggregations to appear as gigantic luminous masses of blazing suns, like the Magellanic Cloud. The globular type of star clusters predominates near the outer margins of Orvonton." P. 170.

E. **Many Orvonton star clouds are comparable to nebulae. Some, however, consist of gaseous materials only.**

"The vast star clouds of Orvonton should be regarded as individual aggregations of matter comparable to the separate nebulae observable in the space regions external to the Milky Way galaxy. Many of the so-called star clouds of space, however, consist of gaseous material only. The energy potential of these stellar gas clouds is unbelievably enormous, and some of it is taken up by near-by suns and redispatched in space as solar emanations." P. 170.

III. Hydrogen Clouds in Space Regions— Later Sources of Energy

"During the earlier times of universe materialization the space regions are interspersed with vast hydrogen clouds, just such astronomic dust clusters as now characterize many regions throughout remote space. Much of the organized matter which the blazing suns break down and disperse as radiant energy was originally built up in these early appearing hydrogen clouds of space. Under certain unusual conditions atom disruption also occurs at the nucleus of the larger hydrogen masses. And all of these phenomena of atom building and atom dissolution, as in the highly heated nebulae, are attended by the emergence of flood tides of short space rays of radiant energy. Accompanying these diverse radiations is a form of space-energy unknown on Urantia." P. 666.

Section Six
THE ORIGIN OF SPACE BODIES

"The bulk of the mass contained in the suns and planets of a superuniverse originates in the nebular wheels; very little of superuniverse mass is organized by the direct action of the power directors (as in the construction of architectural spheres), although a constantly varying quantity of matter originates in open space.

"As to origin, the majority of the suns, planets, and other spheres can be classified in one of the following ten groups:

"1. *Concentric Contraction Rings*. Not all nebulae are spiral. Many an immense nebula, instead of splitting into a double star system or evolving as a spiral, undergoes condensation by multiple-ring formation. For long periods such a nebula appears as an enormous central sun surrounded by numerous gigantic clouds of encircling, ring-appearing formations of matter.

"2. *The Whirled Stars* embrace those suns which are thrown off the great mother wheels of highly heated gases. They are not thrown off as rings but in right- and left-handed processions. Whirled stars are also of origin in other-than-spiral nebulae.

"3. *Gravity-explosion Planets*. When a sun is born of a spiral or of a barred nebula, not infrequently it is thrown out a considerable distance. Such a sun is highly gaseous, and subsequently, after it has somewhat cooled and condensed, it may chance to swing near some enormous mass of matter, a gigantic sun or a dark island of space. Such an approach may not be near enough to result in collision but still near enough to allow the gravity pull of the greater body to start tidal convulsions in the lesser, thus initiating a series of tidal upheavals which occur simultaneously on opposite sides of the convulsed sun. At their height these explosive eruptions produce a series of varying-sized aggregations of matter which may be projected beyond the gravity-reclamation zone of the erupting sun, thus becoming stabilized in orbits of their own around one of the two bodies concerned in this episode. Later on the larger collections of matter unite and gradually draw the smaller bodies to themselves. In this way many of the solid planets of the lesser systems are brought into existence. Your own solar system had just such an origin.

"4. *Centrifugal Planetary Daughters*. Enormous suns, when in certain stages of development, and if their revolutionary rate greatly accelerates, begin to throw off large quantities of matter which may subsequently be assembled to form small worlds that continue to encircle the parent sun.

"5. *Gravity-deficiency Spheres.* There is a critical limit to the size of individual stars. When a sun reaches this limit, unless it slows down in revolutionary rate, it is doomed to split; sun fission occurs, and a new double star of this variety is born. Numerous small planets may be subsequently formed as a by-product of this gigantic disruption.

"6. *Contractural Stars.* In the smaller systems the largest outer planet sometimes draws to itself its neighboring worlds, while those planets near the sun begin their terminal plunge. With your solar system, such an end would mean that the four inner planets would be claimed by the sun, while the major planet, Jupiter, would be greatly enlarged by capturing the remaining worlds. Such an end of a solar system would result in the production of two adjacent but unequal suns, one type of double star formation. Such catastrophes are infrequent except out on the fringe of the superuniverse starry aggregations.

"7. *Cumulative Spheres.* From the vast quantity of matter circulating in space, small planets may slowly accumulate. They grow by meteoric accretion and by minor collisions. In certain sectors of space, conditions favor such forms of planetary birth. Many an inhabited world has had such an origin.

"Some of the dense dark islands are the direct result of the accretions of transmuting energy in space. Another group of these dark islands have come into being by the accumulation of enormous quantities of cold matter, mere fragments and meteors, circulating through space. Such aggregations of matter have never been hot and, except for density, are in composition very similar to Urantia.

"8. *Burned-out Suns.* Some of the dark islands of space are burned-out isolated suns, all available space-energy having been emitted. The organized units of matter approximate full condensation, virtual complete consolidation; and it requires ages upon ages for such enormous masses of highly condensed matter to be recharged in the circuits of space and thus to be prepared for new cycles of universe function following a collision or some equally revivifying cosmic happening.

"9. *Collisional Spheres.* In those regions of thicker clustering, collisions are not uncommon. Such an astronomic readjustment is accompanied by tremendous energy changes and matter transmutations. Collisions involving dead suns are peculiarly influential in creating widespread energy fluctuations. Collisional debris often constitutes the material nucleuses for the subsequent formation of planetary bodies adapted to mortal habitation.

"10. *Architectural Worlds.* These are the worlds which are built according to plans and specifications for some special purpose, such as Salvington, the headquarters of your local universe, and Uversa, the seat of government of our superuniverse.

"There are numerous other techniques for evolving suns and segregating planets, but the foregoing procedures suggest the methods whereby the vast majority of stellar systems and planetary families are brought into existence. To undertake to describe all the various techniques involved in stellar metamorphosis and planetary evolution would require the narration of almost one hundred different modes of sun formation and planetary origin. As your star students scan the heavens, they will observe phenomena indicative of all these modes of stellar evolution, but they will seldom detect evidence of the formation of those small, nonluminous collections of matter which serve as inhabited planets, the most important of the vast material creations." P. 170-2.

Part I — *Astronomy*

Section Seven
THE SPHERES OF SPACE

"Irrespective of origin, the various spheres of space are classifiable into the following major divisions:

"1.   The suns—the stars of space.

"2.   The dark islands of space.

"3.   Minor space bodies—comets, meteors, and planetesimals.

"4.   The planets, including the inhabited worlds.

"5.   Architectural spheres—worlds made to order." P. 172.

"With the exception of the architectural spheres, all space bodies have had an evolutionary origin, evolutionary in the sense that they have not been brought into being by fiat of Deity, evolutionary in the sense that the creative acts of God have unfolded by a time-space technique through the operation of many of the created and eventuated intelligences of Deity." P. 172.

I.   Suns

A.   Types of suns.

"*The Suns.* These are the stars of space in all their various stages of existence. Some are solitary evolving space systems; others are double stars, contracting or disappearing planetary systems. The stars of space exist in no less than a thousand different states and stages. You are familiar with suns that emit light accompanied by heat; but there are also suns which shine without heat." P. 172.

B.   Number of suns.

1. **Orvonton is illuminated and warmed by more than ten trillion suns.**

   "The superuniverse of Orvonton is illuminated and warmed by more than ten trillion blazing suns. These suns are the stars of your observable astronomic system. More than two trillion are too distant and too small ever to be seen from Urantia. But in the master universe there are as many suns as there are glasses of water in the oceans of your world." P. 172.

2. **There are over two thousand suns in Satania.**

   "There are upward of two thousand brilliant suns pouring forth light and energy in Satania, and your own sun is an average blazing orb. Of the thirty suns nearest yours, only three are brighter. The Universe Power Directors initiate the specialized currents of energy which play between the individual stars and their respective systems. These solar furnaces, together with the dark giants of space, serve the power centers and physical controllers as way stations for the effective concentrating and directionizing of the energy circuits of the material creations." P. 458.

C. Critical size.

"When suns that are too large are thrown off a nebular mother wheel, they soon break up or form double stars. All suns are originally truly gaseous, though they may later transiently exist in a semiliquid state. When your sun attained this quasi-liquid state of supergas pressure, it was not sufficiently large to split equatorially, this being one type of double star formation." P. 458.

"When less than one tenth the size of your sun, these fiery spheres rapidly contract, condense, and cool. When upwards of thirty times its size—rather thirty times the gross content of actual material—suns readily split into two separate bodies, either becoming the centers of new systems or else remaining in each other's gravity grasp and revolving about a common center as one type of double star." P. 458.

"The most recent of the major cosmic eruptions in Orvonton was the extraordinary double star explosion, the light of which reached Urantia in A.D. 1572. This conflagration was so intense that the explosion was clearly visible in broad daylight." P. 458.

D. Composition of suns.

1. **The composition of all suns, dark islands, planets, satellites, and meteors is quite identical.**
   "The suns of Nebadon are not unlike those of other universes. The material composition of all suns, dark islands, planets, and satellites, even meteors, is quite identical. These suns have an average diameter of about one million miles, that of your own solar orb being slightly less. The largest star in the universe, the stellar cloud Antares, is four hundred and fifty times the diameter of your sun and is sixty million times its volume. But there is abundant space to accommodate all of these enormous suns. They have just as much comparative elbow room in space as one dozen oranges would have if they were circulating about throughout the interior of Urantia, and were the planet a hollow globe." P. 458.

2. **Suns vary in state, mass, and density.**
   "Not all stars are solid, but many of the older ones are. Some of

the reddish, faintly glimmering stars have acquired a density at the center of their enormous masses which would be expressed by saying that one cubic inch of such a star, if on Urantia, would weigh six thousand pounds. The enormous pressure, accompanied by loss of heat and circulating energy, has resulted in bringing the orbits of the basic material units closer and closer together until they now closely approach the status of electronic condensation. This process of cooling and contraction may continue to the limiting and critical explosion point of ultimatonic condensation." P. 458.

E. Relation of a sun's age to light.

"Most of the giant suns are relatively young; most of the dwarf stars are old, but not all. The collisional dwarfs may be very young and may glow with an intense white light, never having known an initial red stage of youthful shining. Both very young and very old suns usually shine with a reddish glow. The yellow tinge indicates moderate youth or approaching old age, but the brilliant white light signifies robust and extended adult life." P. 459.

F. Variable stars.

   1. Pulsating suns.

"While all adolescent suns do not pass through a pulsating stage, at least not visibly, when looking out into space you may observe many of these younger stars whose gigantic respiratory heaves require from two to seven days to complete a cycle. Your own sun still carries a diminishing legacy of the mighty upswellings of its younger days, but the period has lengthened from the former three and one-half day pulsations to the present eleven and one-half year sunspot cycles." P. 459.

   2. Pulsating suns may give rise to solar systems.

"Some of the variable stars, in or near the state of maximum pulsation, are in process of giving origin to subsidiary systems, many of which will eventually be much like your own sun and its revolving planets. Your sun was in just such a state of mighty pulsation when the massive Angona system swung into near approach, and the outer surface of the sun began to erupt veritable streams—continuous sheets—of matter. This kept up with ever-increasing violence until nearest apposition, when the limits of solar cohesion were reached and a vast pinnacle of matter, the ancestor of the solar system, was disgorged. In similar circumstances the closest approach of the attracting body sometimes draws off whole planets, even a quarter or third of a sun. These major extrusions form certain peculiar cloud-bound types of worlds, spheres much like Jupiter and Saturn." P. 465.

3. **Other causes of variable stars.**

"Stellar variables have numerous origins. In some double stars the tides caused by rapidly changing distances as the two bodies swing around their orbits also occasion periodic fluctuations of light. These gravity variations produce regular and recurrent flares, just as the capture of meteors by the accretion of energy-material at the surface would result in a comparatively sudden flash of light which would speedily recede to normal brightness for that sun. Sometimes a sun will capture a stream of meteors in a line of lessened gravity opposition, and occasionally collisions cause stellar flare-ups, but the majority of such phenomena are wholly due to internal fluctuations.

"In one group of variable stars the period of light fluctuation is directly dependent on luminosity, and knowledge of this fact enables astronomers to utilize such suns as universe lighthouses or accurate measuring points for the further exploration of distant star clusters. By this technique it is possible to measure stellar distances most precisely up to more than one million light-years." P. 459.

G. **Density of suns.**

1. **Though gaseous, the specific gravity of our sun is one and one-half.**

"The mass of your sun is slightly greater than the estimate of your physicists, who have reckoned it as about two octillion (2×10^{27}) tons. It now exists about halfway between the most dense and the most diffuse stars, having about one and one-half times the density of water. But your sun is neither a liquid nor a solid—it is gaseous—and this is true notwithstanding the difficulty of explaining how gaseous matter can attain this and even much greater densities." P. 459.

2. **Physical state and density—supergases.**

"Gaseous, liquid, and solid states are matters of atomic-molecular relationships, but density is a relationship of space and mass. Density varies directly with the quantity of mass in space and inversely with the amount of space in mass, the space between the central cores of matter and the particles which whirl around these centers as well as the space within such material particles." P. 459.

"Cooling stars can be physically gaseous and tremendously dense at the same time. You are not familiar with the solar *supergases*, but these and other unusual forms of matter explain how even nonsolid suns can attain a density equal to iron—about the same as Urantia—and yet be in a highly heated gaseous state and continue to function as suns. The atoms in these dense supergases are exceptionally small; they contain few electrons. Such suns have also largely lost their free ultimatonic stores of energy." P. 459.

3. **Comparative density of suns.**

"One of your near-by suns, which started life with about the same mass as yours, has now contracted almost to the size of Urantia, having become sixty thousand times as dense as your sun. The weight of this hot-cold gaseous-solid is about one ton per cubic inch. And still this sun shines with a faint reddish glow, the senile glimmer of a dying monarch of light." P. 460.

"The massive sun of Veluntia, one of the largest in Orvonton, has a density only one one-thousandth that of Urantia's atmosphere. Were it in composition similar to your atmosphere and not superheated, it would be such a vacuum that human beings would speedily suffocate if they were in or on it." P. 460.

"Another of the Orvonton giants now has a surface temperature a trifle under three thousand degrees. Its diameter is over three hundred million miles—ample room to accommodate your sun and the present orbit of the earth. And yet, for all this enormous size, over forty million times that of your sun, its mass is only about thirty times greater. These enormous suns have an extending fringe that reaches almost from one to the other." P. 460.

H. **Solar energy.**

1. **Energy function of suns.**

    a. *There are numerous techniques of sun formation and planetary origin.*

    "There are numerous other techniques for evolving suns and segregating planets, but the foregoing procedures suggest the methods whereby the vast majority of stellar systems and planetary families are brought into existence. To undertake to describe all the various techniques involved in stellar metamorphosis and planetary evolution would require the narration of almost one hundred different modes of sun formation and planetary origin. As your star students scan the heavens, they will observe phenomena indicative of all these modes of stellar evolution, but they will seldom detect evidence of the formation of those small, nonluminous collections of matter which serve as inhabited planets, the most important of the vast material creations." P. 172.

b. *Some suns shine on forever—others are destined to burn out.*
"Only those suns which function in the direct channels of the main streams of universe energy can shine on forever. Such solar furnaces blaze on indefinitely, being able to replenish their material losses by the intake of space-force and analogous circulating energy. But stars far removed from these chief channels of recharging are destined to undergo energy depletion—gradually cool off and eventually burn out." P. 464.

c. *Sun rejuvenation.*
"Such dead or dying suns can be rejuvenated by collisional impact or can be recharged by certain nonluminous energy islands of space or through gravity-robbery of near-by smaller suns or systems. The majority of dead suns will experience revivification by these or other evolutionary techniques. Those which are not thus eventually recharged are destined to undergo disruption by mass explosion when the gravity condensation attains the critical level of ultimatonic condensation of energy pressure. Such disappearing suns thus become energy of the rarest form, admirably adapted to energize other more favorably situated suns." P. 464.

2. **Sun temperatures.**

"The internal temperature of many of the suns, even your own, is much higher than is commonly believed. In the interior of a sun practically no whole atoms exist; they are all more or less shattered by the intensive X-ray bombardment which is indigenous to such high temperatures. Regardless of what material elements may appear in the outer layers of a sun, those in the interior are rendered very similar by the dissociative action of the disruptive X rays. X ray is the great leveler of atomic existence.

PART I — *Astronomy*

"The surface temperature of your sun is almost 6,000 degrees, but it rapidly increases as the interior is penetrated until it attains the unbelievable height of about 35,000,000 degrees in the central regions. (All of these temperatures refer to your Fahrenheit scale.)" P. 463.

"There exists a regulating blanket of hot gases (sometimes millions of degrees in temperature) which envelops the suns, and which acts to stabilize heat loss and otherwise prevent hazardous fluctuations of heat dissipation. During the active life of a sun the internal temperature of 35,000,000 degrees remains about the same quite regardless of the progressive fall of the external temperature." P. 463.

3. **Sources of solar energy.**

"All of these phenomena are indicative of enormous energy expenditure, and the sources of solar energy, named in the order of their importance, are:

"1. Annihilation of atoms and, eventually, of electrons.
"2. Transmutation of elements, including the radioactive group of energies thus liberated.
"3. The accumulation and transmission of certain universal space-energies.
"4. Space matter and meteors which are incessantly diving into the blazing suns.
"5. Solar contraction; the cooling and consequent contraction of a sun yields energy and heat sometimes greater than that supplied by space matter.
"6. Gravity action at high temperatures transforms certain circuitized power into radiative energies.
"7. Recaptive light and other matter which are drawn back into the sun after having left it, together with other energies having extrasolar origin." P. 463.

4. **35 million degrees—the electronic boiling point**

"You might try to visualize 35,000,000 degrees of heat, in association with certain gravity pressures, as the electronic boiling point. Under such pressure and at such temperature all atoms are degraded and broken up into their electronic and other ancestral components; even the electrons and other associations of ultimatons may be broken up, but the suns are not able to degrade the ultimatons.

"These solar temperatures operate to enormously speed up the ultimatons and the electrons, at least such of the latter as continue to maintain their existence under these conditions. You will realize what high temperature means by way of the acceleration of ultimatonic and electronic activities when you pause to consider that one drop of ordinary water contains over one billion trillions of atoms. This is the energy of more than one hundred horsepower exerted continuously for two years. The total heat now given out by the solar system sun each second is sufficient to boil all the water in all the oceans on Urantia in just one second of time." P. 463.

I. Sun stability.

1. Equilibrium between the pressures of gravity and heat determines the stability of a sun.

"Sun stability is wholly dependent on the equilibrium between gravity-heat contention—tremendous pressures counterbalanced by unimagined temperatures. The interior gas elasticity of the suns upholds the overlying layers of varied materials, and when gravity and heat are in equilibrium, the weight of the outer materials exactly equals the temperature pressure of the underlying and interior gases. In many of the younger stars continued gravity condensation produces ever-heightening internal temperatures, and as internal heat increases, the interior X-ray pressure of supergas winds becomes so great that, in connection with the centrifugal motion, a sun begins to throw its exterior layers off into space, thus redressing the imbalance between gravity and heat." P. 465.

2. Present and future state of our sun.

"Your own sun has long since attained relative equilibrium between its expansion and contraction cycles, those disturbances which produce the gigantic pulsations of many of the younger stars. Your sun is now passing out of its six billionth year. At the present time it is functioning through the period of greatest economy. It will shine on as of present efficiency for more than twenty-five billion years. It will probably experience a partially efficient period of decline as long as the combined periods of its youth and stabilized function." P. 465.

3. Sun depletion—the result of light escape and ultimatonic leakage.

"The larger suns maintain such a gravity control over their electrons that light escapes only with the aid of the powerful X rays. These helper rays penetrate all space and are concerned in the maintenance of the basic ultimatonic associations of energy. The great energy losses in the early days of a sun, subsequent to its attainment of maximum temperature—upwards of 35,000,000 degrees—are not so much due to light escape as to ultimatonic leakage. These ultimaton energies escape out into space, to engage in the adventure of electronic association and energy materialization, as a veritable energy blast during adolescent solar times." P. 465.

J. **Sun collapse.**

"In large suns—small circular nebulae—when hydrogen is exhausted and gravity contraction ensues, if such a body is not sufficiently opaque to retain the internal pressure of support for the outer gas regions, then a sudden collapse occurs. The gravity-electric changes give origin to vast quantities of tiny particles devoid of electric potential, and such particles readily escape from the solar interior, thus bringing about the collapse of a gigantic sun within a few days. It was such an emigration of these 'runaway particles' that occasioned the collapse of the giant nova of the Andromeda nebula about fifty years ago. This vast stellar body collapsed in forty minutes of Urantia time." P. 464.

II. THE DARK ISLANDS OF SPACE

A. **The dark islands of space—control functions.**

"*The Dark Islands of Space.* These are the dead suns and other large aggregations of matter devoid of light and heat. The dark islands are sometimes enormous in mass and exert a powerful influence in universe equilibrium and energy manipulation. The density of some of these large masses is well-nigh unbelievable. And this great concentration of mass enables these dark islands to function as powerful balance wheels, holding large neighboring systems in effective leash. They hold the gravity balance of power in many constellations; many physical systems which would otherwise speedily dive to destruction in near-by suns are held securely in the gravity grasp of these guardian dark islands. It is because of this function that we can locate them accurately. We have measured the gravity pull of the luminous bodies, and we can therefore calculate the exact size and location of the dark islands of space which so effectively function to hold a given system steady in its course." P. 173.

III. Minor Space Bodies

A. Comets, meteors, and other bodies.

"*Minor Space Bodies.* The meteors and other small particles of matter circulating and evolving in space constitute an enormous aggregate of energy and material substance.

> "Many comets are unestablished wild offspring of the solar mother wheels, which are being gradually brought under control of the central governing sun. Comets also have numerous other origins. A comet's tail points away from the attracting body or sun because of the electrical reaction of its highly expanded gases and because of the actual pressure of light and other energies emanating from the sun. This phenomenon constitutes one of the positive proofs of the reality of light and its associated energies; it demonstrates that light has weight. Light is a real substance, not simply waves of hypothetical ether." P. 173.

IV. The Planets

"*The Planets.* These are the larger aggregations of matter which follow an orbit around a sun or some other space body; they range in size from planetesimals to enormous gaseous, liquid, or solid spheres. The cold worlds which have been built up by the assemblage of floating space material, when they happen to be in proper relation to a near-by sun, are the more ideal planets to harbor intelligent inhabitants. The dead suns are not, as a rule, suited to life; they are usually too far away from a living, blazing sun, and further, they are altogether too massive; gravity is tremendous at the surface.

"In your superuniverse not one cool planet in forty is habitable by beings of your order. And, of course, the superheated suns and the frigid outlying worlds are unfit to harbor higher life. In your solar system only three planets are at present suited to harbor life. Urantia, in size, density, and location, is in many respects ideal for human habitation." P. 173.

A. Basic universe life patterns are varied by local physical conditions.

"The laws of physical-energy behavior are basically universal, but local influences have much to do with the physical conditions which prevail on individual planets and in local systems. An almost endless variety of creature life and other living manifestations characterizes the countless worlds of space. There are, however, certain points of similarity in a group of worlds associated in a given system, while there also is a universe pattern of intelligent life. There are physical relationships among those planetary systems which belong to the same physical circuit, and which closely follow each other in the endless swing around the circle of universes." P. 173.

B. **Planets were made to be inhabited.**

"The myriads of planetary systems were all made to be eventually inhabited by many different types of intelligent creatures, beings who could know God, receive the divine affection, and love him in return. The universe of universes is the work of God and the dwelling place of his diverse creatures. 'God created the heavens and formed the earth; he established the universe and created this world not in vain; he formed it to be inhabited.'" P. 21.

C. **Urantia—its number and location.**

"The grand universe number of your world, Urantia, is 5,342,482,337,666. That is the registry number on Uversa and on Paradise, your number in the catalogue of the inhabited worlds. I know the physical-sphere registry number, but it is of such an extraordinary size that it is of little practical significance to the mortal mind." P. 182.

"Urantia is comparatively isolated on the outskirts of Satania, your solar system, with one exception, being the farthest removed from Jerusem, while Satania itself is next to the outermost system of Norlatiadek, and this constellation is now traversing the outer fringe of Nebadon. You were truly among the least of all creation until Michael's bestowal elevated your planet to a position of honor and great universe interest. Sometimes the last is first, while truly the least becomes greatest." P. 466.

V. ARCHITECTURAL SPHERES

A. **Headquarters worlds of superuniverses and other administrative units are architectural spheres.**

"While each superuniverse government presides near the center of the evolutionary universes of its space segment, it occupies a world made to order and is peopled by accredited personalities. These headquarters worlds are architectural spheres, space bodies specifically constructed for their special purpose. While sharing the light of nearby suns, these spheres are independently lighted and heated. Each has a sun which gives forth light without heat, like the satellites of Paradise, while each is supplied with heat by the circulation of certain energy currents near the surface of the sphere. These headquarters worlds belong to one of the greater systems situated near the astronomical center of their respective superuniverses." P. 174.

"The headquarters world of the seven superuniverses partake of the nature and grandeur of Paradise, their central pattern of perfection. In reality, all headquarters worlds are paradisiacal. They are indeed heavenly abodes, and they increase in material size, morontia beauty, and spirit glory from Jerusem to the central Isle. And all the satellites of these headquarters worlds are also architectural spheres." P. 174.

B. **Summary of architectural worlds.**

1. Superuniverse—491—capital surrounded by 7 clusters of 70 worlds each.
2. Major sector—71—capital surrounded by 70 spheres.
3. Minor sector—8—capital surrounded by 7 spheres.
4. Local universe—491—capital surrounded by 70 primary spheres in 10 groups, each surrounded by 6 tributary spheres.
5. Constellation—771—capital surrounded by 70 major spheres each with 10 satellites.
6. System—57—capital surrounded by 7 transition worlds each surrounded by 7 sub-satellites.

CONCLUSION

"The creation of energy and the bestowal of life are the prerogatives of the Universal Father and his associate Creator personalities. The river of energy and life is a continuous outpouring from the Deities, the universal and united stream of Paradise force going forth to all space. This divine energy pervades all creation. The force organizers initiate those changes and institute those modifications of space-force which eventuate in energy; the power directors transmute energy into matter; thus the material worlds are born. The Life Carriers initiate those processes in dead matter which we call life, material life. The Morontia Power Supervisors likewise perform throughout the transition realms between the material and the spiritual worlds. The higher spirit Creators inaugurate similar processes in divine forms of energy, and there ensue the higher spirit forms of intelligent life." P. 468.

PART II — GEOLOGY

Introduction
THE LOCAL UNIVERSE CREATION

I. THE ORIGIN AND EARLY EXPERIENCE OF THE CREATIVE SPIRIT CONSORT OF A MICHAEL CREATOR SON.

"At the time the creatorship charge is administered to a Michael Son by the Eternal Son, the Master Spirit who directs the superuniverse to which this new Creator Son is destined gives expression to the 'prayer of identification' in the presence of the Infinite Spirit; and for the first time, the entity of the subsequent Creative Spirit appears as differentiated from the person of the Infinite Spirit. And proceeding directly to the person of the petitioning Master Spirit, this entity is immediately lost to our recognition, becoming apparently a part of the person of this Master Spirit. The newly identified Creative Spirit remains with the Master Spirit until the moment of the departure of the Creator Son for the adventure of space; whereupon the Master Spirit commits the new Spirit consort to the keeping of the Creator Son, at the same time administering to the Spirit consort the charge of eternal fidelity and unending loyalty. And then occurs one of the most profoundly touching episodes which ever take place on Paradise. The Universal Father speaks in acknowledgment of the eternal union of the Creator Son and the Creative Spirit and in confirmation of the bestowal of certain joint powers of administration by the Master Spirit of superuniverse jurisdiction." P. 204.

II. THE ASSOCIATION OF THE FATHER-UNITED CREATOR SON AND THE CREATIVE SPIRIT.

"The Father-united Creator Son and Creative Spirit then go forth on their adventure of universe creation. And they work together in this form of association throughout the long and arduous period of the material organization of their universe." P. 204.

Section One
EARLY AGES OF URANTIA

I. THE EARLY GEOLOGIC EXPERIENCE OF DIFFERENT TYPES OF PLANETS

"The physical aspects of the individual worlds are largely determined by mode of origin, astronomical situation, and physical environment. Age, size, rate of revolution, and velocity through space are also determining factors. Both the gas-contraction and the solid-accretion worlds are characterized by mountains and, during their earlier life, when not too small, by water and air. The molten-split and collisional worlds are sometimes without extensive mountain ranges.

"During the earlier ages of all these new worlds, earthquakes are frequent, and they are all characterized by great physical disturbances; especially is this true of the gas-contraction spheres, the worlds born of the immense nebular rings which are left behind in the wake of the early condensation and contraction of certain individual suns. Planets having a dual origin like Urantia pass through a less violent and stormy youthful career. Even so, your world experienced an early phase of mighty upheavals, characterized by volcanoes, earthquakes, floods, and terrific storms." P. 466.

II. Geologic Prehistory of Urantia

A. 2,500,000,000 years ago.

1. **Urantia at about the time of the registry of the solar system.**

   "2,500,000,000 years ago the planets had grown immensely in size. Urantia was a well-developed sphere about one tenth its present mass and was still growing rapidly by meteoric accretion.

   "All of this tremendous activity is a normal part of the making of an evolutionary world on the order of Urantia and constitutes the astronomic preliminaries to the setting of the stage for the beginning of the physical evolution of such worlds of space in preparation for the life adventures of time." P. 658.

B. 2,000,000,000 years ago.

1. **The size and condition of Urantia.**

   "2,000,000,000 years ago the earth began decidedly to gain on the moon. Always had the planet been larger than its satellite, but there was not so much difference in size until about this time, when enormous space bodies were captured by the earth. Urantia was then about one fifth its present size and had become large enough to hold the primitive atmosphere which had begun to appear as a result of the internal elemental contest between the heated interior and the cooling crust." P. 659.

2. **The radium clock.**

   "Definite volcanic action dates from these times. The internal heat of the earth continued to be augmented by the deeper and deeper burial of the radioactive or heavier elements brought in from space by the meteors. The study of these radioactive elements will reveal that Urantia is more than one billion years old on its surface. The radium clock is your most reliable timepiece for making scientific estimates of the age of the

PART II — *Geology*

planet, but all such estimates are too short because the radioactive materials open to your scrutiny are all derived from the earth's surface and hence represent Urantia's comparatively recent acquirements of these elements." P. 659.

C. 1,500,000,000 years ago.

1. Size of the earth and moon.

"*1,500,000,000* years ago the earth was two thirds its present size, while the moon was nearing its present mass. Earth's rapid gain over the moon in size enabled it to begin the slow robbery of the little atmosphere which its satellite originally had." P. 659.

2. The volcanic age on Urantia.

"Volcanic action is now at its height. The whole earth is a veritable fiery inferno, the surface resembling its earlier molten state before the heavier metals gravitated toward the center. *This is the volcanic age*. Nevertheless, a crust, consisting chiefly of the comparatively lighter granite, is gradually forming. The stage is being set for a planet which can someday support life." P. 659.

3. Primitive atmosphere. (P. 659-60)

The atmosphere now contains water vapor, carbon monoxide, and hydrogen chloride, but little free oxygen or nitrogen. Meteoric combustion keeps exhausting the oxygen supply. Presently the atmosphere becomes sufficiently cool to cause condensation of the water vapor and precipitation of rain upon the hot rocks. For many years the sun did not penetrate the hot blanket of steam that enveloped the planet. Oxygen did not appear in significant quantities until it was later generated by vegetation. The oxygen-deficient atmosphere was little protection against the impact of meteors.

Section Two
THE GEOLOGIC SCHEME (PRIMORDIAL LIFE)

I. The Prelife Era - the Archeozoic
(Formerly Called Azoic—Lifeless)

450,000,000 years' duration, from 1,000,000,000 to 550,000,000 years ago.

II. The Life-dawn Era - the Proterozoic
(Beginning of Life)

150,000,000 years' duration, from 550,000,000 to 400,000,000 years ago.

III. The Marine-life Era - the Paleozoic
(Ancient Life)

250,000,000 years' duration, from 400,000,000 to 150,000,000 years ago.

    A. The Trilobite Age - the Cambrian Period.

    50,000,000 years' duration, from 400,000,000 to 350,000,000 years ago.

    B. The Invertebrate-animal Age - the Ordovician Period.

    50,000,000 years' duration, from 350,000,000 to 300,000,000 years ago.

    C. The Brachiopod Age - the Silurian Period.

    25,000,000 years' duration, from 300,000,000 to 275,000,000 years ago.

    D. The Age of Fishes - the Devonian Period.

    50,000,000 years' duration, from 275,000,000 to 225,000,000 years ago.

    E. The Age of Frogs - the Carboniferous Period.

    50,000,000 years' duration, from 225,000,000 to 175,000,000 years ago.

    F. The Age of Biologic Tribulation - the Permian Period.

    25,000,000 years' duration, from 175,000,000 to 150,000,000 years ago.

IV. The Early Land-life Era - the Mesozoic
(Middle Life)

100,000,000 years' duration, from 150,000,000 to 50,000,000 years ago.

    A. The Early Reptilian Age - the Triassic Period.

    25,000,000 years' duration, from 150,000,000 to 125,000,000 years ago.

B. **The Later Reptilian Age - the Jurassic Period.**

25,000,000 years' duration, from 125,000,000 to 100,000,000 years ago.

C. **The Final Age of Reptiles, the Age of Birds, the Flowering-plant Period - the Cretaceous Age.**

50,000,000 years' duration, from 100,000,000 to 50,000,000 years ago.

V. **THE MAMMALIAN ERA - THE CENOZOIC AGE**
(Recent Life)

50,000,000 years' duration, from 50,000,000 years ago to about the present.

   A. **The New Continental Land Stage, the Age of Early Mammals - the Eocene Period.**

15,000,000 years' duration, from 50,000,000 to 35,000,000 years ago.

   B. **The Recent Flood Stage, the Age of Advanced Mammals - the Oligocene Period.**

10,000,000 years' duration, from 35,000,000 to 25,000,000 years ago.

   C. **The Modern Mountain Stage, the Age of the Elephant and the Horse - the Miocene Period.**

15,000,000 years' duration, from 25,000,000 to 10,000,000 years ago.

   D. **The Recent Continental-elevation Stage, the Last Great Mammalian Migration - the Pliocene Period.**

About 8,000,000 years' duration, from 10,000,000 to about 2,000,000 years ago.

   E. **The Ice Age - the Pleistocene Period.**

About 2,000,000 years' duration, from about 2,000,000 to 35,000 years ago.

SCIENCE IN *THE URANTIA BOOK*

SECTION THREE
EARLY GEOLOGIC HISTORY OF URANTIA
THE PRELIFE ERA - THE ARCHEOZOIC PERIOD

I. CRUSTAL STABILIZATION

   A. 1,000,000,000 years ago.

      1. **Conditions at the time of the Nebadon registry of Urantia.**
"*1,000,000,000* years ago is the date of the actual beginning of Urantia history. The planet had attained approximately its present size. And about this time it was placed upon the physical registries of Nebadon and given its name, *Urantia*.
"The atmosphere, together with incessant moisture precipitation, facilitated the cooling of the earth's crust. Volcanic action early equalized internal-heat pressure and crustal contraction; and as volcanoes rapidly decreased, earthquakes made their appearance as this epoch of crustal cooling and adjustment progressed." P. 660.

      2. **The hydrosphere. (P. 660)**
The geologic history of Urantia begins when the crust becomes sufficiently cool to permit the formation of the first ocean. The earth was covered with salt-free water to an average depth of one mile. Later lava flows depressed the Pacific Ocean and forced up the first continental land mass.

   B. 950,000,000 to 900,000,000 years ago.

      1. **Conditions at the time Urantia was assigned to Satania.**
"*950,000,000* years ago Urantia presents the picture of one great continent of land and one large body of water, the Pacific Ocean. Volcanoes are still widespread and earthquakes are both frequent and severe. Meteors continue to bombard the earth, but they are diminishing in both frequency and size. The atmosphere is clearing up, but the amount of carbon dioxide continues large. The earth's crust is gradually stabilizing." P. 660.

      2. **Selection of Urantia as the sixtieth Satania experimental planet. (P. 661)**
After a painstaking survey a commission of twenty-four recommended Urantia as a life experiment planet. It was soon registered in the minor and major sectors and on Uversa.

      3. **The age of violent storms.**
"This entire age was characterized by frequent and violent storms. The early crust of the earth was in a state of continual flux. Surface cooling alternated with immense lava flows.

- 76 -

Nowhere can there be found on the surface of the world anything of this original planetary crust. It has all been mixed up too many times with extruding lavas of deep origins and admixed with subsequent deposits of the early world-wide ocean." P. 661.

4. **Remnants of preocean age around Hudson Bay.**
"Nowhere on the surface of the world will there be found more of the modified remnants of these ancient preocean rocks than in northeastern Canada around Hudson Bay. This extensive granite elevation is composed of stone belonging to the preoceanic ages. These rock layers have been heated, bent, twisted, up-crumpled, and again and again have they passed through these distorting metamorphic experiences." P. 661.

5. **Deposition of fossil-free stone.**
"Throughout the oceanic ages, enormous layers of fossil-free stratified stone were deposited on this ancient ocean bottom. (Limestone can form as a result of chemical precipitation; not all of the older limestone was produced by marine-life deposition.) In none of these ancient rock formations will there be found evidences of life; they contain no fossils unless, by some chance, later deposits of the water ages have become mixed with these older prelife layers." P. 661.

C. **850,000,000 to 800,000,000 years ago.**

1. **Crustal stabilization.**
"*850,000,000* years ago the first real epoch of the stabilization of the earth's crust began. Most of the heavier metals had settled down toward the center of the globe; the cooling crust had ceased to cave in on such an extensive scale as in former ages. There was established a better balance between the land extrusion and the heavier ocean bed. The flow of the subcrustal lava bed became well-nigh world-wide, and this compensated and stabilized the fluctuations due to cooling, contracting, and superficial shifting." P. 662.

2. **The first great land epoch.**
"*800,000,000* years ago witnessed the inauguration of the first great land epoch, the age of increased continental emergence.
"Since the condensation of the earth's hydrosphere, first into the world ocean and subsequently into the Pacific Ocean, this latter body of water should be visualized as then covering nine tenths of the earth's surface. Meteors falling into the sea accumulated on the ocean bottom, and meteors are, generally

speaking, composed of heavy materials. Those falling on the land were largely oxidized, subsequently worn down by erosion, and washed into the ocean basins.

"Thus the ocean bottom grew increasingly heavy, and added to this was the weight of a body of water at some places ten miles deep." P. 662.

3. **The first climatic difference. (P. 662)**

The upthrust of land continued until almost one third of the earth's surface consisted of land, all in one continental body, reaching a height of almost nine miles. The ice age was delayed because of the lack of sufficient moisture at these heights.

D. **750,000,000 to 650,000,000 years ago.**

1. **The first great land-mass crackings.**

"750,000,000 years ago the first breaks in the continental land mass began as the great north-and-south cracking, which later admitted the ocean waters and prepared the way for the westward drift of the continents of North and South America, including Greenland. The long east-and-west cleavage separated Africa from Europe and severed the land masses of Australia, the Pacific Islands, and Antarctica from the Asiatic continent." P. 663.

2. **Continental land drift.**

"700,000,000 years ago Urantia was approaching the ripening of conditions suitable for the support of life. The continental land drift continued; increasingly the ocean penetrated the land as long fingerlike seas providing those shallow waters and sheltered bays which are so suitable as a habitat for marine life." P. 663.

3. **Increase of saltiness of the seas.**

"650,000,000 years ago witnessed the further separation of the land masses and, in consequence, a further extension of the continental seas. And these waters were rapidly attaining that degree of saltiness which was essential to Urantia life.

"It was these seas and their successors that laid down the life records of Urantia, as subsequently discovered in well-preserved stone pages, volume upon volume, as era succeeded era and age grew upon age. These inland seas of olden times were truly the cradle of evolution." P. 663.

PART II — *Geology*

II. THE CONTINENTAL DRIFT

A. 600,000,000 to 550,000,000 years ago. (P.664-5)
   1. Period of evolution toward conditions suitable to marine life. Since a sodium chloride pattern of life had been projected for Urantia, life could not be planted until the ocean waters had become sufficiently briny. During this period the further breakup of land masses, providing more sheltered bays, and an increase in the saltiness of the ocean, brought about conditions favorable for the support of life. The carbon dioxide content of the atmosphere was suitable to plant growth, but would not permit animal life.

Section Four
THE LIFE-DAWN ERA - THE PROTEROZOIC

I. Life Implantation and Development (P. 667-8)

Three life implantations, the central or Eurasian, the eastern or Australasian, and the western, the Americas, were made as these areas continued to drift apart.

II. Description of the Earth's Composition

A. The continental drift.

1. **The earth's internal heat and pressure increased and the continental drift continued.**
   "The continental land drift continued. The earth's core had become as dense and rigid as steel, being subjected to a pressure of almost 25,000 tons to the square inch, and owing to the enormous gravity pressure, it was and still is very hot in the deep interior. The temperature increases from the surface downward until at the center it is slightly above the surface temperature of the sun." P. 668.

2. **Outer one thousand miles of the earth is chiefly rock— the heavy metals are mostly deep in the interior.**
   "The outer one thousand miles of the earth's mass consists principally of different kinds of rock. Underneath are the denser and heavier metallic elements. Throughout the early and preatmospheric ages the world was so nearly fluid in its molten and highly heated state that the heavier metals sank deep into the interior. Those found near the surface today represent the exudate of ancient volcanoes, later and extensive lava flows, and the more recent meteoric deposits." P. 668.

3. **Underneath the forty-mile-thick outer crust of the earth there existed a molten mobile basalt layer.**
   "The outer crust was about forty miles thick. This outer shell was supported by and rested directly upon, a molten sea of basalt of varying thickness, a mobile layer of molten lava held under high pressure but always tending to flow hither and yon in equalization of shifting planetary pressures, thereby tending to stabilize the earth's crust." P. 668.

4. **Even today the continents are still floating on this molten basalt.**
   "Even today the continents continue to float upon this noncrystallized cushiony sea of molten basalt. Were it not for this protective condition, the more severe earthquakes would

literally shake the world to pieces. Earthquakes are caused by sliding and shifting of the solid outer crust and not by volcanoes." P. 668.

5. **Relative density of granite and basalt as concerns continental stability.**

    "The lava layers of the earth's crust, when cooled, form granite. The average density of Urantia is a little more than five and one half times that of water; the density of granite is less than three times that of water. The earth's core is twelve times as dense as water.

    "The sea bottoms are more dense than the land masses, and this is what keeps the continents above water. When the sea bottoms are extruded above the sea level, they are found to consist largely of basalt, a form of lava considerably heavier than the granite of the land masses. Again, if the continents were not lighter than the ocean beds, gravity would draw the edges of the oceans up onto the land, but such phenomena are not observable." P. 668.

6. **Factors causing the continents to flow towards the ocean beds.**

    "The weight of the oceans is also a factor in the increase of pressure on the sea beds. The lower but comparatively heavier ocean beds, plus the weight of the overlying water, approximate the weight of the higher but much lighter continents. But all continents tend to creep into the oceans. The continental pressure at ocean-bottom levels is about 20,000 pounds to the square inch. That is, this would be the pressure of a continental mass standing 15,000 feet above the ocean floor. The ocean-floor water pressure is only about 5,000 pounds to the square inch. These differential pressures tend to cause the continents to slide toward the ocean beds." P. 668.

7. **Factors concerned in the differential behavior of the eastern and western land masses.**

    "Depression of the ocean bottom during the prelife ages had upthrust a solitary continental land mass to such a height that its lateral pressure tended to cause the eastern, western, and southern fringes to slide downhill, over the underlying semiviscous lava beds into the waters of the surrounding Pacific Ocean. This so fully compensated the continental pressure that a wide break did not occur on the eastern shore of this ancient Asiatic continent, but ever since has that eastern coast line hovered over the precipice of its adjoining oceanic depths, threatening to slide into a watery grave." P. 669.

B. **The transition period.**

The metamorphosis from vegetable to animal life came about in tropical shallow waters *gradually*, about 450,000,000 years ago.

C. **The geologic history book.**

1. **Little of the Proterozoic era rock is now found on the surface of the earth.**

    "The vast group of rock systems which constituted the outer crust of the world during the life-dawn or Proterozoic era does not now appear at many points on the earth's surface. And when it does emerge from below all the accumulations of subsequent ages, there will be found only the fossil remains of vegetable and early primitive animal life. Some of these older water-deposited rocks are commingled with subsequent layers, and sometimes they yield fossil remains of some of the earlier forms of vegetable life, while on the topmost layers occasionally may be found some of the more primitive forms of the early marine-animal organisms. In many places these oldest stratified rock layers, bearing the fossils of the early marine life, both animal and vegetable, may be found directly on top of the older undifferentiated stone." P. 670.

2. **This era yields fossils of algae, corallike, Protozoa, and spongelike organisms.**

    "Fossils of this era yield algae, corallike plants, primitive Protozoa, and spongelike transition organisms. But the absence of such fossils in the early rock layers does not necessarily prove that living things were not elsewhere in existence at the time of their deposition. Life was sparse throughout these early times and only slowly made its way over the face of the earth." P. 670.

3. **Thickness and extent of transition rocks at or near the earth's surface.**

    "The rocks of this olden age are now at the earth's surface, or very near the surface, over about one eighth of the present land area. The average thickness of this transition stone, the oldest stratified rock layers, is about one and one-half miles. At some points these ancient rock systems are as much as four miles thick, but many of the layers which have been ascribed to this era belong to later periods." P. 670.

Part II — *Geology*

4. **The Proterozoic stone layer. (P. 670-1)**
   The Proterozoic stone layer comes to the surface in various regions on the North American continent, but can best be interpreted in the Lake Superior region and in the Grand Canyon. This stone layer has been greatly folded and twisted, and has many lava flows interspersed between the strata.

5. **The mineral deposits of this period.**
   "Some of the upper layers of these transition rock deposits contain small amounts of shale or slate of dark colors, indicating the presence of organic carbon and testifying to the existence of the ancestors of those forms of plant life which overran the earth during the succeeding Carboniferous or coal age. Much of the copper in these rock layers results from water deposition. Some is found in the cracks of the older rocks and is the concentrate of the sluggish swamp water of some ancient sheltered shore line. The iron mines of North America and Europe are located in deposits and extrusions lying partly in the older unstratified rocks and partly in these later stratified rocks of the transition periods of life formation." P. 671.

6. **"The dust we tread upon was once alive."**
   "All of this story is graphically told within the fossil pages of the vast 'stone book' of world record. And the pages of this gigantic biogeologic record unfailingly tell the truth if you but acquire skill in their interpretation. Many of these ancient sea beds are now elevated high upon land, and their deposits of age upon age tell the story of the life struggles of those early days. It is literally true, as your poet has said, 'The dust we tread upon was once alive.'" P. 671.

Science In *The Urantia Book*

Section Five
THE MARINE-LIFE ERA - THE PALEOZOIC
I. The Cambrian Period - the Trilobite Age

By the dawn of this period of relative quiet on the earth's surface, life is confined to the seas. Single cell animals are well established. (P. 673)

A. 400,000,000 years ago. (P. 673)

Vegetable and animal life is distributed over the world. Vegetation crawls out upon the land, and suddenly multicellular animals appear. The trilobites have evolved. The land remains elevated.

B. 380,000,000 years ago.

1. **When Arctic, Atlantic, and Gulf waters were connected. The Alp-like Appalachians.**
"*380,000,000* years ago Asia was subsiding, and all other continents were experiencing a short-lived emergence. But as this epoch progressed, the newly appearing Atlantic Ocean made extensive inroads on all adjacent coast lines. The northern Atlantic or Arctic seas were then connected with the southern Gulf waters. When this southern sea entered the Appalachian trough, its waves broke upon the east against mountains as high as the Alps, but in general the continents were uninteresting lowlands, utterly devoid of scenic beauty." P. 673.

2. **The Cambrian sedimentary deposits.**
"The sedimentary deposits of these ages are of four sorts:
"1. Conglomerates—matter deposited near the shore lines.
"2. Sandstones—deposits made in shallow water but where the waves were sufficient to prevent mud settling.
"3. Shales—deposits made in the deeper and more quiet water.
"4. Limestone—including the deposits of trilobite shells in deep water." P. 673.

3. **Trilobite fossils and the three different life groups.**
"The trilobite fossils of these times present certain basic uniformities coupled with certain well-marked variations. The early animals developing from the three original life implantations were characteristic; those appearing in the Western Hemisphere were slightly different from those of the Eurasian group and from the Australasian or Australian-Antarctic type." P. 673.

PART II — *Geology*

C. **370,000,000 years ago.**

1. **North and South America together with Africa and Australia are submerged.**
   "*370,000,000* years ago the great and almost total submergence of North and South America occurred, followed by the sinking of Africa and Australia. Only certain parts of North America remained above these shallow Cambrian seas. Five million years later the seas were retreating before the rising land. And all of these phenomena of land sinking and land rising were undramatic, taking place slowly over millions of years." P. 674.

2. **Manifold geologic changes during this epoch.**
   "The trilobite fossil-bearing strata of this epoch outcrop here and there throughout all the continents except in central Asia. In many regions these rocks are horizontal, but in the mountains they are tilted and distorted because of pressure and folding. And such pressure has, in many places, changed the original character of these deposits. Sandstone has been turned into quartz, shale has been changed to slate, while limestone has been converted into marble." P. 674.

D. **360,000,000 years ago.**

1. **The continents emerge and Greenland is a tropic Paradise.**
   "360,000,000 years ago the land was still rising. North and South America were well up. Western Europe and the British Isles were emerging, except parts of Wales, which were deeply submerged. There were no great ice sheets during these ages. The supposed glacial deposits appearing in connection with these strata in Europe, Africa, China, and Australia are due to isolated mountain glaciers or to the displacement of glacial debris of later origin. The world climate was oceanic, not continental. The southern seas were warmer then than now, and they extended northward over North America up to the polar regions. The Gulf Stream coursed over the central portion of North America, being deflected eastward to bathe and warm the shores of Greenland, making that now ice-mantled continent a veritable tropic Paradise." P. 674.

2. **This is the geologic picture of the long fifty-million-year Cambrian period.**
   "This was the biogeologic picture of Urantia at the end of that long period of the world's history, embracing fifty million years, designated by your geologists as the *Cambrian*." P. 674.

- 85 -

II. The Ordovician Period - The First Continental Flood Stage - The Invertebrate-animal Age

"The periodic phenomena of land elevation and land sinking characteristic of these times were all gradual and nonspectacular, being accompanied by little or no volcanic action. Throughout all of these successive land elevations and depressions the Asiatic mother continent did not fully share the history of the other land bodies. It experienced many inundations, dipping first in one direction and then another, more particularly in its earlier history, but it does not present the uniform rock deposits which may be discovered on the other continents. In recent ages Asia has been the most stable of all the land masses." P. 674.

A. **350,000,000 years ago - the first great flood period.**
   1. **Three great land submergences characterized this period.**
      "*350,000,000* years ago saw the beginning of the great flood period of all the continents except central Asia. The land masses were repeatedly covered with water; only the coastal highlands remained above these shallow but widespread oscillatory inland seas. Three major inundations characterized this period, but before it ended, the continents again arose, the total land emergence being fifteen per cent greater than now exists. The Caribbean region was highly elevated. This period is not well marked off in Europe because the land fluctuations were less, while the volcanic action was more persistent." P. 675.

B. **340,000,000 years and 330,000,000 years ago - the second land sinking and rising.**
   1. **The great limestone age.**
      "*340,000,000* years ago there occurred another extensive land sinking except in Asia and Australia. The waters of the world's oceans were generally commingled. This was a great limestone age, much of its stone being laid down by lime-secreting algae.
      "A few million years later large portions of the American continents and Europe began to emerge from the water. In the Western Hemisphere only an arm of the Pacific Ocean remained over Mexico and the present Rocky Mountain regions; but near the close of this epoch the Atlantic and Pacific coasts again began to sink." P. 675.
   2. **A long period of comparative quiet except for the Kentucky volcano.**

Part II — *Geology*

"*330,000,000* years ago marks the beginning of a time sector of comparative quiet all over the world, with much land again above water. The only exception to this reign of terrestrial quiet was the eruption of the great North American volcano of eastern Kentucky, one of the greatest single volcanic activities the world has ever known. The ashes of this volcano covered five hundred square miles to a depth of from fifteen to twenty feet." P. 675.

C. **320,000,000 and 310,000,000 years ago - the third cycle of land submergence and rising.**

1. **The third great flood of this period occurs.**
   "*320,000,000* years ago the third major flood of this period occurred. The waters of this inundation covered all the land submerged by the preceding deluge, while extending farther in many directions all over the Americas and Europe. Eastern North America and western Europe were from 10,000 to 15,000 feet under water." P. 675.

2. **The land masses emerge and world is quiet and peaceful.**
   "*310,000,000* years ago the land masses of the world were again well up excepting the southern parts of North America. Mexico emerged, thus creating the Gulf Sea, which has ever since maintained its identity.
   "The life of this period continues to evolve. The world is once again quiet and relatively peaceful; the climate remains mild and equable; the land plants are migrating farther and farther from the seashores. The life patterns are well developed, although few plant fossils of these times are to be found." P. 675.

III. THE SILURIAN PERIOD - THE SECOND GREAT FLOOD STAGE - THE CORAL PERIOD - THE BRACHIOPOD AGE

A. **300,000,000 and 290,000,000 years ago - the first Silurian land submergence and emergence.**

1. **The first great Silurian inundation.**
   "*300,000,000* years ago another great period of land submergence began. The southward and northward encroachment of the ancient Silurian seas made ready to engulf most of Europe and North America. The land was not elevated far above the sea so that not much deposition occurred about the shore lines. The seas teemed with lime-shelled life, and the falling of these shells to the sea bottom gradually built up very thick layers of

limestone. This is the first widespread limestone deposit, and it covers practically all of Europe and North America but only appears at the earth's surface in a few places. The thickness of this ancient rock layer averages about one thousand feet, but many of these deposits have since been greatly deformed by tilting, upheavals, and faulting, and many have been changed to quartz, shale, and marble.

"No fire rocks or lava are found in the stone layers of this period except those of the great volcanoes of southern Europe and eastern Maine and the lava flows of Quebec. Volcanic action was largely past. This was the height of great water deposition; there was little or no mountain building." P. 676.

2. **Birth of the Caledonian Mountains.**
"290,000,000 years ago the sea had largely withdrawn from the continents, and the bottoms of the surrounding oceans were sinking. The land masses were little changed until they were again submerged. The early mountain movements of all the continents were beginning, and the greatest of these crustal upheavals were the Himalayas of Asia and the great Caledonian Mountains, extending from Ireland through Scotland and on to Spitzbergen." P. 676.

3. **Deposits of this period.**
"It is in the deposits of this age that much of the gas, oil, zinc, and lead are found, the gas and oil being derived from the enormous collections of vegetable and animal matter carried down at the time of the previous land submergence, while the mineral deposits represent the sedimentation of sluggish bodies of water. Many of the rock salt deposits belong to this period." P. 677.

4. **Other characteristics of the period. (P. 677)**
Trilobites declined, yielding to larger mollusks or cephalopods. Great volcanic action took place in Europe. The climate remained mild and uniform.

B. **280,000,000 years ago - conditions following the second flood and emergence.**

1. **Emergence from the second Silurian flood.**
"280,000,000 years ago the continents had largely emerged from the second Silurian inundation. The rock deposits of this submergence are known in North America as Niagara limestone because this is the stratum of rock over which Niagara Falls now flows. This layer of rock extends from the eastern

PART II — *Geology*

mountains to the Mississippi valley region but not farther west except to the south. Several layers extend over Canada, portions of South America, Australia, and most of Europe, the average thickness of this Niagara series being about six hundred feet. Immediately overlying the Niagara deposit, in many regions may be found a collection of conglomerate, shale, and rock salt. This is the accumulation of secondary subsidences. This salt settled in great lagoons which were alternately opened up to the sea and then cut off so that evaporation occurred with deposition of salt along with other matter held in solution. In some regions these rock salt beds are seventy feet thick." P. 677.

2. **Climate and animal developments. (P. 677-8)**
The climate remains even and mild. The sea becomes excessively salt so that marine life declines. Mollusks continue as monarchs of the seas, but suddenly scorpions—air breathers—appear.

IV. THE DEVONIAN PERIOD - THE GREAT LAND-EMERGENCE STAGE VEGETATIVE LAND-LIFE PERIOD - THE AGE OF FISHES

"In the agelong struggle between land and water, for long periods the sea has been comparatively victorious, but times of land victory are just ahead. And the continental drifts have not proceeded so far but that, at times, practically all of the land of the world is connected by slender isthmuses and narrow land bridges.

"As the land emerges from the last Silurian inundation, an important period in world development and life evolution comes to an end. It is the dawn of a new age on earth. The naked and unattractive landscape of former times is becoming clothed with luxuriant verdure, and the first magnificent forests will soon appear." P. 678.

A. **270,000,000 and 260,000,000 years ago - the great Devonian land-emergence and land-depression epoch.**

1. **The greatest of all land eras—more land above water.**
"270,000,000 years ago the continents were all above water. In millions upon millions of years not so much land had been above water at one time; it was one of the greatest land-emergence epochs in all world history.
"Five million years later the land areas of North and South America, Europe, Africa, northern Asia, and Australia were briefly inundated, in North America the submergence at one

time or another being almost complete; and the resulting limestone layers run from 500 to 5,000 feet in thickness. These various Devonian seas extended first in one direction and then in another so that the immense arctic North American inland sea found an outlet to the Pacific Ocean through northern California." P. 678.

2. **The first Devonian flood—coral deposits near Louisville, Kentucky.**

"260,000,000 years ago, toward the end of this land-depression epoch, North America was partially overspread by seas having simultaneous connection with the Pacific, Atlantic, Arctic, and Gulf waters. The deposits of these later stages of the first Devonian flood average about one thousand feet in thickness. The coral reefs characterizing these times indicate that the inland seas were clear and shallow. Such coral deposits are exposed in the banks of the Ohio River near Louisville, Kentucky, and are about one hundred feet thick, embracing more than two hundred varieties. These coral formations extend through Canada and northern Europe to the arctic regions." P. 678.

"Following these submergences, many of the shore lines were considerably elevated so that the earlier deposits were covered by mud or shale. There is also a red sandstone stratum which characterizes one of the Devonian sedimentations, and this red layer extends over much of the earth's surface, being found in North and South America, Europe, Russia, China, Africa, and Australia. Such red deposits are suggestive of arid or semiarid conditions, but the climate of this epoch was still mild and even.

"Throughout all of this period the land southeast of the Cincinnati Island remained well above water. But very much of western Europe, including the British Isles, was submerged. In Wales, Germany, and other places in Europe the Devonian rocks are 20,000 feet thick." P. 678-9.

B. **250,000,000 to 230,000,000 years ago - fishes, ferns, mountains.**

1. "250,000,000 years ago witnessed the appearance of the fish family, the vertebrates, one of the most important steps in all prehuman evolution." P. 679.

"Veritable bone beds of fish teeth and skeletons may be found in the deposits laid down toward the close of this period, and rich fossil beds are situated along the coast of California since many sheltered bays of the Pacific Ocean extended into the land of that region." P. 679.

2. Suddenly the fern family appeared and quickly spread over the face of the rising land. These ferns had only rudimentary foliage. North America was connected with Europe by land bridges. (P. 679)

3. **The last of the Devonian floods—one of its monuments, the Catskill Mountains.**

"240,000,000 years ago the land over parts of both Europe and North and South America began to sink. This subsidence marked the appearance of the last and least extensive of the Devonian floods. The arctic seas again moved southward over much of North America, the Atlantic inundated a large part of Europe and western Asia, while the southern Pacific covered most of India. This inundation was slow in appearing and equally slow in retreating. The Catskill Mountains along the west bank of the Hudson River are one of the largest geologic monuments of this epoch to be found on the surface of North America." P. 679.

4. **The land emerges. The Susquehanna River reveals the strata of this period.**

"230,000,000 years ago the seas were continuing their retreat. Much of North America was above water, and great volcanic activity occurred in the St. Lawrence region. Mount Royal, at Montreal, is the eroded neck of one of these volcanoes. The deposits of this entire epoch are well shown in the Appalachian Mountains of North America where the Susquehanna River has cut a valley exposing these successive layers, which attained a thickness of over 13,000 feet." P. 679.

V. THE CARBONIFEROUS PERIOD - CRUSTAL SHIFTING STAGE - THE AGE OF FROGS

"The appearance of fish during the preceding period marks the apex of marine-life evolution. From this point onward the evolution of land life becomes increasingly important. And this period opens with the stage almost ideally set for the appearance of the first land animals." P. 680.

A. 220,000,000 and 210,000,000 years ago - ferns and frogs.

1. **The age of ferns—the land is up and overrun with vegetation.**

"220,000,000 years ago many of the continental land areas, including most of North America, were above water. The land was overrun by luxurious vegetation; this was indeed the *age of ferns*. Carbon dioxide was still present in the atmosphere but in lessening degree." P. 680.

2. **Atlantic and Pacific waters unite across North America.**
   "Shortly thereafter the central portion of North America was inundated, creating two great inland seas. Both the Atlantic and Pacific coastal highlands were situated just beyond the present shore lines. These two seas presently united, commingling their different forms of life, and the union of these marine fauna marked the beginning of the rapid and world-wide decline in marine life and the opening of the subsequent land-life period." P. 680.

3. **Now comes the sudden development of land animals.**
   "210,000,000 years ago the warm-water arctic seas covered most of North America and Europe. The south polar waters inundated South America and Australia, while both Africa and Asia were highly elevated.

   "When the seas were at their height, a new evolutionary development *suddenly* occurred. Abruptly, the first of the land animals appeared. There were numerous species of these animals that were able to live on land or in water. These air-breathing amphibians developed from the arthropods, whose swim bladders had evolved into lungs." P. 680.

B. **200,000,000 to 180,000,000 years ago -**
   The coal-deposition period.

1. **The active stages of the Carboniferous period—twenty-five million years of coal-making.**
   "200,000,000 years ago the really active stages of the Carboniferous period began. For twenty million years prior to this time the earlier coal deposits were being laid down, but now the more extensive coal-formation activities were in process. The length of the actual coal-deposition epoch was a little over twenty-five million years.

   "The land was periodically going up and down due to the shifting sea level occasioned by activities on the ocean bottoms. This crustal uneasiness—the settling and rising of the land—in connection with the prolific vegetation of the coastal swamps, contributed to the production of extensive coal deposits, which have caused this period to be known as the *Carboniferous*. And the climate was still mild the world over.

   "The coal layers alternate with shale, stone, and conglomerate. These coal beds over central and eastern United States vary in thickness from forty to fifty feet. But many of these deposits

were washed away during subsequent land elevations. In some parts of North America and Europe the coal-bearing strata are 18,000 feet in thickness." P. 681.

2. **The carbonizing process.**
"The presence of roots of trees as they grew in the clay underlying the present coal beds demonstrates that coal was formed exactly where it is now found. Coal is the water-preserved and pressure-modified remains of the rank vegetation growing in the bogs and on the swamp shores of this faraway age. Coal layers often hold both gas and oil. Peat beds, the remains of past vegetable growth, would be converted into a type of coal if subjected to proper pressure and heat. Anthracite has been subjected to more pressure and heat than other coal." P. 681.

3. **The coal layers vary from ten to seventy-five.**
"In North America the layers of coal in the various beds, which indicate the number of times the land fell and rose, vary from ten in Illinois, twenty in Pennsylvania, thirty-five in Alabama, to seventy-five in Canada. Both fresh- and salt-water fossils are found in the coal beds." P. 681.

4. **Continued coal deposition.**
"190,000,000 years ago witnessed a westward extension of the North American Carboniferous sea over the present Rocky Mountain region, with an outlet to the Pacific Ocean through northern California. Coal continued to be laid down throughout the Americas and Europe, layer upon layer, as the coastlands rose and fell during these ages of seashore oscillations." P. 682.

5. **The close of the Carboniferous period.**
"180,000,000 years ago brought the close of the Carboniferous period, during which coal had been formed all over the world—in Europe, India, China, North Africa, and the Americas. At the close of the coal-formation period North America east of the Mississippi valley rose, and most of this section has ever since remained above the sea. This land-elevation period marks the beginning of the modern mountains of North America, both in the Appalachian regions and in the west. Volcanoes were active in Alaska and California and in the mountain-forming regions of Europe and Asia. Eastern America and western Europe were connected by the continent of Greenland." P. 682.

6. **The development of variable climate.**
   "Land elevation began to modify the marine climate of the preceding ages and to substitute therefor the beginnings of the less mild and more variable continental climate." P. 682.

VI. THE PERMIAN PERIOD - THE CLIMATIC TRANSITION STAGE SEED-PLANT PERIOD - THE AGE OF BIOLOGIC TRIBULATION

The increasing elevation of land masses caused a harsher climate and the consequent disappearance of over ninety-nine percent of the living species. (P. 682)

A. **170,000,000 years ago—climatic changes.**
   1. **Land is rising, mountains develop, glaciation and aridity appear.**
      "170,000,000 years ago great evolutionary changes and adjustments were taking place over the entire face of the earth. Land was rising all over the world as the ocean beds were sinking. Isolated mountain ridges appeared. The eastern part of North America was high above the sea; the west was slowly rising. The continents were covered by great and small salt lakes and numerous inland seas which were connected with the oceans by narrow straits. The strata of this transition period vary in thickness from 1,000 to 7,000 feet.
      "The earth's crust folded extensively during these land elevations. This was a time of continental emergence except for the disappearance of certain land bridges, including the continents which had so long connected South America with Africa and North America with Europe.
      "Gradually the inland lakes and seas were drying up all over the world. Isolated mountain and regional glaciers began to appear, especially over the Southern Hemisphere, and in many regions the glacial deposit of these local ice formations may be found even among some of the upper and later coal deposits. Two new climatic factors appeared—glaciation and aridity. Many of the earth's higher regions had become arid and barren." P. 683.
   2. **Variations in plants and animals.**
      Seed plants appeared. A resting stage for insects evolved. New animal species with better survival qualities developed. (P. 683)

B. **160,000,000 years ago - conclusion of the Permian period of the Paleozoic era.**
   1. "The vast oceanic nursery of life on Urantia has served its

purpose. During the long ages when the land was unsuited to support life, before the atmosphere contained sufficient oxygen to sustain the higher land animals, the sea mothered and nurtured the early life of the realm. Now the biologic importance of the sea progressively diminishes as the second stage of evolution begins to unfold on the land." P. 684.

2. "The era of exclusive marine life has ended. Land elevation, cooling crust and cooling oceans, sea restriction and consequent deepening, together with a great increase of land in northern latitudes, all conspired greatly to change the world's climate in all regions far removed from the equatorial zone. "The closing epochs of the preceding era were indeed the age of frogs, but these ancestors of the land vertebrates were no longer dominant, having survived in greatly reduced numbers. Very few types outlived the rigorous trials of the preceding period of biologic tribulation. Even the spore-bearing plants were nearly extinct." P. 685.

Section Six
THE EARLY LAND-LIFE ERA - THE MESOZOIC

I. The Triassic Period. The Early Reptilian Age.

A. The deposits of the Triassic Period.

1. **Much of the latter part of this period was arid—indicated by red layer deposits.**

   "The erosion deposits of this period were mostly conglomerates, shale, and sandstone. The gypsum and red layers throughout these sedimentations over both America and Europe indicate that the climate of these continents was arid. These arid districts were subjected to great erosion from the violent and periodic cloudbursts on the surrounding highlands." P. 685.

2. **Few fossils are to be found in the extensive deposits of this period.**

   "Few fossils are to be found in these layers, but numerous sandstone footprints of the land reptiles may be observed. In many regions the one thousand feet of red sandstone deposit of this period contains no fossils. The life of land animals was continuous only in certain parts of Africa." P. 685.

3. **The Palisades of the Hudson River, New Red Sandstone in England, dolomite formations in the Alps, and Carrara marble were produced in this period.**

   "These deposits vary in thickness from 3,000 to 10,000 feet, even being 18,000 on the Pacific coast. Lava was later forced in between many of these layers. The Palisades of the Hudson River were formed by the extrusion of basalt lava between these Triassic strata. Volcanic action was extensive in different parts of the world.

   "Over Europe, especially Germany and Russia, may be found deposits of this period. In England the New Red Sandstone belongs to this epoch. Limestone was laid down in the southern Alps as the result of a sea invasion and may now be seen as the peculiar dolomite limestone walls, peaks, and pillars of those regions. This layer is to be found all over Africa and Australia. The Carrara marble comes from such modified limestone. Nothing of this period will be found in the southern regions of South America as that part of the continent remained down and hence presents only a water or marine deposit continuous with the preceding and succeeding epochs." P. 685.

B. 150,000,000 years ago.

1. **The land is above water. North American troughs formed and were later filled with deposits.**

PART II — *Geology*

"As this era opens, the eastern and central parts of North America, the northern half of South America, most of Europe, and all of Asia are well above water. North America for the first time is geographically isolated, but not for long as the Bering Strait land bridge soon again emerges, connecting the continent with Asia.

"Great troughs developed in North America, paralleling the Atlantic and Pacific coasts. The great eastern-Connecticut fault appeared, one side eventually sinking two miles. Many of these North American troughs were later filled with erosion deposits, as also were many of the basins of the fresh- and salt-water lakes of the mountain regions. Later on, these filled land depressions were greatly elevated by lava flows which occurred underground. The petrified forests of many regions belong to this epoch." P. 686.

2. **The Pacific coast went down and deposits rich in marine fossils were formed.**

"The Pacific coast, usually above water during the continental submergences, went down excepting the southern part of California and a large island which then existed in what is now the Pacific Ocean. This ancient California sea was rich in marine life and extended eastward to connect with the old sea basin of the mid-western region." P. 686.

C. **140,000,000 years ago.**

Reptiles appeared and rapidly evolved into the dinosaurs. Marine life was meager, but improved rapidly, and fossil beds are to be found in Europe and Asia. (P. 686)

D. **130,000,000 years ago.**

This was a period of rich and changing marine life. North America and Asia were connected by a land bridge.

"130,000,000 years ago the seas had changed very little. Siberia and North America were connected by the Bering Strait land bridge. A rich and unique marine life appeared on the Californian Pacific coast, where over one thousand species of ammonites developed from the higher types of cephalopods. The life changes of this period were indeed revolutionary notwithstanding that they were transitional and gradual.

"This period extended over twenty-five million years and is known as the *Triassic*." P. 686.

II. The Jurassic Period. The Later Reptilian Age.

A. 120,000,000 years ago.

Dinosaurs evolved and declined, ultimately becoming extinct. North America was invaded by the Atlantic and Pacific Oceans and the northern sea up to the Dakota Black Hills. There were also many fresh-water lakes and consequent fresh-water fossils. All of South America but the Andes Mountains was covered, as well as China, Russia, and especially Europe. The lithographic stone of southern Germany, which contained unusual fossils, was deposited. The climate became even and mild. (P. 687)

B. 110,000,000 years ago.

1. Dinosaurs continued to decline, and evolution from this time forth followed the growth of brains rather than physical bulk. (P. 688)
2. "This period, embracing the height and the beginning decline of the reptiles, extended nearly twenty-five million years and is known as the *Jurassic*." P. 688.

III. The Cretaceous Stage. The Flowering-plant Period. The Age of Birds.

"The great Cretaceous period derives its name from the predominance of the prolific chalk-making foraminifers in the seas. This period brings Urantia to near the end of the long reptilian dominance and witnesses the appearance of flowering plants and bird life on land. These are also the times of the termination of the westward and southward drift of the continents, accompanied by tremendous crustal deformations and concomitant widespread lava flows and great volcanic activities.

"Near the close of the preceding geologic period much of the continental land was up above water, although as yet there were no mountain peaks. But as the continental land drift continued, it met with the first great obstruction on the deep floor of the Pacific. This contention of geologic forces gave impetus to the formation of the whole vast north and south mountain range extending from Alaska down through Mexico to Cape Horn.

"This period thus becomes the *modern mountain-building stage* of geologic history. Prior to this time there were few mountain peaks, merely elevated land ridges of great width. Now the Pacific coast range was beginning to elevate, but it was located seven hundred miles west of the present shore line. The Sierras were beginning to form, their gold-bearing quartz

Part II — *Geology*

strata being the product of lava flows of this epoch. In the eastern part of North America, Atlantic sea pressure was also working to cause land elevation." P. 688-9.

A. 100,000,000 years ago.

1. **Land elevation and mountain development.**

    "100,000,000 years ago the North American continent and a part of Europe were well above water. The warping of the American continents continued, resulting in the metamorphosing of the South American Andes and in the gradual elevation of the western plains of North America. Most of Mexico sank beneath the sea, and the southern Atlantic encroached on the eastern coast of South America, eventually reaching the present shore line. The Atlantic and Indian Oceans were then about as they are today." P. 689.

B. 95,000,000 years ago.

1. **Land submergence and volcanic action.**

    "95,000,000 years ago the American and European land masses again began to sink. The southern seas commenced the invasion of North America and gradually extended northward to connect with the Arctic Ocean, constituting the second greatest submergence of the continent. When this sea finally withdrew, it left the continent about as it now is. Before this great submergence began, the eastern Appalachian highlands had been almost completely worn down to the water's level. The many colored layers of pure clay now used for the manufacture of earthenware were laid down over the Atlantic coast regions during this age, their average thickness being about 2,000 feet." P. 689.

    "Great volcanic actions occurred south of the Alps and along the line of the present California coast-range mountains. The greatest crustal deformations in millions upon millions of years took place in Mexico. Great changes also occurred in Europe, Russia, Japan, and southern South America. The climate became increasingly diversified." P. 689.

C. 85,000,000 years ago.

1. **Bering Strait closed. Chalk was deposited.**

    "85,000,000 years ago Bearing Strait closed, shutting off the cooling waters of the northern seas. Theretofore the marine life of the Atlantic-Gulf waters and that of the Pacific Ocean had differed greatly, owing to the temperature variations of

these two bodies of water, which now became uniform.
"The deposits of chalk and greensand marl give name to this period. The sedimentations of these times are variegated, consisting of chalk, shale, sandstone, and small amounts of limestone, together with inferior coal or lignite, and in many regions they contain oil. These layers vary in thickness from 200 feet in some places to 10,000 feet in western North America and numerous European localities. Along the eastern borders of the Rocky Mountains these deposits may be observed in the uptilted foothills.

"All over the world these strata are permeated with chalk, and these layers of porous semirock pick up water at upturned outcrops and convey it downward to furnish the water supply of much of the earth's present arid regions." P. 689-90.

D. 80,000,000 and 75,000,000 years ago.

1. As the continental drift came to a standstill, the enormous energy of the momentum caused great upheavals and the crumpling of the Pacific shore line of the Americas with repercussional changes along the Pacific shores of Asia. (P. 690)

2. **The Pacific Coast mountain ranges were completed— from Alaska to Cape Horn.**
   "75,000,000 years ago marks the end of the continental drift. From Alaska to Cape Horn the long Pacific coast mountain ranges were completed, but there were as yet few peaks.
   "The backthrust of the halted continental drift continued the elevation of the western plains of North America, while in the east the worn-down Appalachian Mountains of the Atlantic coast region were projected straight up, with little or no tilting." P. 690.

E. 70,000,000 to 55,000,000 years ago.

1. **The Rocky Mountains attain their maximum elevation.**
   "70,000,000 years ago the crustal distortions connected with the maximum elevation of the Rocky Mountain region took place. A large segment of rock was overthrust fifteen miles at the surface in British Columbia; here the Cambrian rocks are obliquely thrust out over the Cretaceous layers. On the eastern slope of the Rocky Mountains, near the Canadian border, there was another spectacular overthrust; here may be found the prelife stone layers shoved out over the then recent Cretaceous deposits." P. 690.

PART II — *Geology*

2. **Volcanic activity over all the world.**
   "This was an age of volcanic activity all over the world, giving rise to numerous small isolated volcanic cones. Submarine volcanoes broke out in the submerged Himalayan region. Much of the rest of Asia, including Siberia, was also still under water." P. 690.
3. **The great lava flows.**
   "65,000,000 years ago there occurred one of the greatest lava flows of all time. The deposition layers of these and preceding lava flows are to be found all over the Americas, North and South Africa, Australia, and parts of Europe." P. 690.
4. **Biologic developments.**
   The climate remained warm and uniform. Land animals were little changed. Great plant-life evolution took place, many present-day trees first appearing. Suddenly the flowering plants mutated and suddenly true birds appeared. (P. 690-91)

F. **Summation.**
   1. **The sea invasions.**
      "The great Cretaceous period was drawing to a close, and its termination marks the end of the great sea invasions of the continents. Particularly is this true of North America, where there had been just twenty-four great inundations. And though there were subsequent minor submergences, none of these can be compared with the extensive and lengthy marine invasions of this and previous ages. These alternate periods of land and sea dominance have occurred in million-year cycles. There has been an agelong rhythm associated with this rise and fall of ocean floor and continental land levels. And these same rhythmical crustal movements will continue from this time on throughout the earth's history but with diminishing frequency and extent." P. 691.
   2. **The causes of mountain building.**
      "This period also witnesses the end of the continental drift and the building of the modern mountains of Urantia. But the pressure of the continental masses and the thwarted momentum of their age-long drift are not the exclusive influences in mountain building. The chief and underlying factor in determining the location of a mountain range is the pre-existent lowland, or trough, which has become filled up with the comparatively lighter deposits of the land erosion and marine

drifts of the preceding ages. These lighter areas of land are sometimes 15,000 to 20,000 feet thick; therefore, when the crust is subjected to pressure from any cause, these lighter areas are the first to crumple up, fold, and rise upward to afford compensatory adjustment for the contending and conflicting forces and pressures at work in the earth's crust or underneath the crust. Sometimes these upthrusts of land occur without folding. But in connection with the rise of the Rocky Mountains, great folding and tilting occurred, coupled with enormous overthrusts of the various layers, both underground and at the surface." P. 691-2.

3. **The age of mountains.**

"The oldest mountains of the world are located in Asia, Greenland, and northern Europe among those of the older east-west systems. The mid-age mountains are in the circumpacific group and in the second European east-west system, which was born at about the same time. This gigantic uprising is almost ten thousand miles long, extending from Europe over into the West Indies land elevations. The youngest mountains are in the Rocky Mountain system, where, for ages, land elevations had occurred only to be successively covered by the sea, though some of the higher lands remained as islands. Subsequent to the formation of the mid-age mountains, a real mountain highland was elevated which was destined, subsequently, to be carved into the present Rocky Mountains by the combined artistry of nature's elements.

"The present North American Rocky Mountain region is not the original elevation of land; that elevation had been long since leveled by erosion and then re-elevated. The present front range of mountains is what is left of the remains of the original range which was re-elevated. Pikes Peak and Longs Peak are outstanding examples of this mountain activity, extending over two or more generations of mountain lives. These two peaks held their heads above water during several of the preceding inundations." P. 692.

4. **Conclusion.**

"And thus ends a long era of world evolution, extending from the early appearance of land life down to the more recent times of the immediate ancestors of the human species and its collateral branches. This, the *Cretaceous age*, covers fifty million years and brings to a close the premammalian era of land life, which extends over a period of one hundred million years and is known as the *Mesozoic*." P. 692.

Science In *The Urantia Book*

Section Seven
THE MAMMALIAN ERA - THE CENOZOIC

"During this Cenozoic age the world's landscape presented an attractive appearance—rolling hills, broad valleys, wide rivers, and great forests. Twice during this sector of time the Panama Isthmus went up and down; three times Bering Strait land bridge did the same. The animal types were both many and varied. The trees swarmed with birds, and the whole world was an animal paradise, notwithstanding the incessant struggle of the evolving animal species for supremacy." P. 693.

I. **The Eocene Period. The New Continental Land Stage. The Age of Early Mammals.**

   A. 50,000,000 years ago.

      Land areas were generally above water. *Suddenly* placental *mammals* with their immense survival advantages *appeared*. (P. 693-4)

   B. 40,000,000 years ago.

      1. Land began to elevate. The Isthmus of Panama, the Bering Strait land bridge, and the bridge across Greenland and Ireland were up. Only Europe was submerged, the Arctic Ocean being connected with the Mediterranean. Considerable limestone was deposited in Europe and Asia. (P. 694)

      2. "Throughout this so-called *Eocene* period the evolution of mammalian and other related forms of life continued with little or no interruption. North America was then connected by land with every continent except Australia, and the world was gradually overrun by primitive mammalian fauna of various types." P. 694.

II. **The Oligocene Period. The Recent Flood Stage. The Age of Advanced Mammals.**

   A. 35,000,000 years ago.

      1. The world climate remained mild because of the enormous size of the tropic seas and because the land was not elevated sufficiently to produce glaciers. Many present day marine species and insects developed, as well as rodents and dogs, some hoofed grazing species, and most modern birds. (P. 695-6)

      2. "By the close of this *Oligocene* period, covering ten million years, the plant life, together with the marine life and the land animals, had very largely evolved and was present on earth much as today. Considerable specialization has subsequently

appeared, but the ancestral forms of most living things were then alive." P. 696.

III. The Miocene Period. The Modern Mountain Stages. Age of The Elephant and The Horse.

"Land elevation and sea segregation were slowly changing the world's weather, gradually cooling it, but the climate was still mild. Sequoias and magnolias grew in Greenland, but the subtropical plants were beginning to migrate southward. By the end of this period these warm-climate plants and trees had largely disappeared from the northern latitudes, their places being taken by more hardy plants and the deciduous trees." P. 696.

A. 25,000,000 to 15,000,000 years ago.
1. **Western North American land elevation and lowering.**
"25,000,000 years ago there was a slight land submergence following the long epoch of land elevation. The Rocky Mountain region remained highly elevated so that the deposition of erosion material continued throughout the lowlands to the east. The Sierras were well re-elevated; in fact, they have been rising ever since. The great four-mile vertical fault in the California region dates from this time." P. 696.
2. **The golden age of mammals.**
"20,000,000 years ago was indeed the golden age of mammals. Bering Strait land bridge was up, and many groups of animals migrated to North America from Asia, including the four-tusked mastodons, short-legged rhinoceroses, and many varieties of the cat family." P. 696.
3. **Eurasian mountains rise, the Straits of Gibraltar close, the Iceland land bridge is submerged. Ocean currents functioned, affecting the climate as they do today.**
"15,000,000 years ago the mountain regions of Eurasia were rising, and there was some volcanic activity throughout these regions, but nothing comparable to the lava flows of the Western Hemisphere. These unsettled conditions prevailed all over the world." P. 697.
"The Strait of Gibraltar closed, and Spain was connected with Africa by the old land bridge, but the Mediterranean flowed into the Atlantic through a narrow channel which extended across France, the mountain peaks and highlands appearing as islands above this ancient sea. Later on, these European seas began to withdraw. Still later, the Mediterranean was connected

with the Indian Ocean, while at the close of this period the Suez region was elevated so that the Mediterranean became, for a time, an inland salt sea." P. 697.

"The Iceland land bridge submerged, and the arctic waters commingled with those of the Atlantic Ocean. The Atlantic coast of North America rapidly cooled, but the Pacific coast remained warmer than at present. The great ocean currents were in function and affected climate much as they do today." P. 697.

B. Biologic developments.

1. The elephant survived because its brain was sufficiently large and of superior quality. Enormous herds of horses joined the camels. The dog and cat families continued to increase, being represented by wolves and foxes, panthers and saber-toothed tigers. (P. 697)
2. "The biologic developments of this period contributed much toward the setting of the stage for the subsequent appearance of man. In central Asia the true types of both the primitive monkey and the gorilla evolved, having a common ancestor, now extinct. But neither of these species is concerned in the line of living beings which were, later on, to become the ancestors of the human race." P. 697.

C. Conclusion.

"Thus drew to a close a very eventful and interesting period of the world's history. This age of the *elephant* and the *horse* is known as the *Miocene*." P. 698.

IV. THE PLIOCENE. THE RECENT CONTINENTAL-DEVELOPMENT STAGE. THE LAST GREAT MAMMALIAN MIGRATION.

"This is the period of preglacial land elevation in North America, Europe, and Asia. The land was greatly altered in topography. Mountain ranges were born, streams changed their courses, and isolated volcanoes broke out all over the world." P. 698.

A. 10,000,000 years ago.

1. **The geologic situation just before the ice age.**
   "10,000,000 years ago began an age of widespread local land deposits on the lowlands of the continents, but most of these sedimentations were later removed. Much of Europe, at this time, was still under water, including parts of England, Belgium, and France, and the Mediterranean Sea covered much

PART II — *Geology*

of northern Africa. In North America extensive depositions were made at the mountain bases, in lakes, and in the great land basins. These deposits average only about two hundred feet, are more or less colored, and fossils are rare. Two great fresh-water lakes existed in western North America. The Sierras were elevating; Shasta, Hood, and Rainier were beginning their mountain careers. But it was not until the subsequent ice age that North America began its creep toward the Atlantic depression." P. 698.

2. **Once again, all land is connected except Australia. There was a great interchange of animal life.**

"For a short time all the land of the world was again joined excepting Australia, and the last great world-wide animal migration took place. North America was connected with both South America and Asia, and there was a free exchange of animal life. Asiatic sloths, armadillos, antelopes, and bears entered North America, while North American camels went to China. Rhinoceroses migrated over the whole world except Australia and South America, but they were extinct in the Western Hemisphere by the close of this period." P. 698.

B. **5,000,000 years ago.**

1. The climate was getting cooler. Plants and animals moved southward. The major land bridges were finally submerged. (P. 698)

C. **Conclusion.**

"And thus does this period of almost ten million years' duration draw to a close, and not yet has the ancestor of man appeared. This is the time usually designated as the *Pliocene*." P. 699.

V. THE PLEISTOCENE. THE EARLY ICE AGE.

A. **Development of the glaciers.**

1. **The northern lands of America and Europe were highly elevated.**

"By the close of the preceding period the lands of the northeastern part of North America and of northern Europe were highly elevated on an extensive scale, in North America vast areas rising up to 30,000 feet and more. Mild climates had formerly prevailed over these northern regions, and the arctic waters were all open to evaporation, and they continued to be ice-free until almost the close of the glacial period." P. 699.

2. **Snow falls to a depth of twenty thousand feet on the cold northern highlands.**

   "Simultaneously with these land elevations the ocean currents shifted, and the seasonal winds changed their direction. These conditions eventually produced an almost constant precipitation of moisture from the movement of the heavily saturated atmosphere over the northern highlands. Snow began to fall on these elevated and therefore cool regions, and it continued to fall until it had attained a depth of 20,000 feet. The areas of the greatest depth of snow, together with altitude, determined the central points of subsequent glacial pressure flows. And the ice age persisted just as long as this excessive precipitation continued to cover these northern highlands with this enormous mantle of snow, which soon metamorphosed into solid but creeping ice." P. 699.

3. **Extent of the ice sheets.**

   "The great ice sheets of this period were all located on elevated highlands, not in mountainous regions where they are found today. One half of the glacial ice was in North America, one fourth in Eurasia, and one fourth elsewhere, chiefly in Antarctica. Africa was little affected by the ice, but Australia was almost covered with the antarctic ice blanket." P. 699.

4. **The six ice invasions.**

   "The northern regions of this world have experienced six separate and distinct ice invasions, although there were scores of advances and recessions associated with the activity of each individual ice sheet. The ice in North America collected in two and, later, three centers. Greenland was covered, and Iceland was completely buried beneath the ice flow. In Europe the ice at various times covered the British Isles excepting the coast of southern England, and it overspread western Europe down to France." P. 699.

B. **2,000,000 years ago.**

1. **The first North American glacier.**

   "2,000,000 years ago the first North American glacier started its southern advance. The ice age was now in the making, and this glacier consumed nearly one million years in its advance from, and retreat back toward, the northern pressure centers. The central ice sheet extended south as far as Kansas; the eastern and western ice centers were not then so extensive." P. 699.

PART II — *Geology*

C. **1,500,000 years ago.**
  1. **The second ice invasion.**
    "1,500,000 years ago the first great glacier was retreating northward. In the meantime, enormous quantities of snow had been falling on Greenland and on the northeastern part of North America, and ere long this eastern ice mass began to flow southward. This was the second invasion of the ice." P. 699.
  2. **Limits of the effect of the first two ice sheets.**
    The first two ice invasions were not extensive in Eurasia. Away from the ice the land and water were little changed and between invasions the climate was mild as at present. Glaciers, even though greatly spread out, are local phenomena. (P. 699-700)

D. **1,000,000 years ago.**
  1. "The great event of this glacial period was the evolution of primitive man." "1,000,000 years ago Urantia was registered as an inhabited planet." "This event occurred at about the time of the beginning of the third glacial advance." P. 700.
  2. "Throughout the glacial period other activities were in progress, but the action of the ice overshadows all other phenomena in the northern latitudes. No other terrestrial activity leaves such characteristic evidence on the topography. The distinctive boulders and surface cleavages, such as potholes, lakes, displaced stone, and rock flour, are to be found in connection with no other phenomenon in nature. The ice is also responsible for those gentle swells, or surface undulations, known as drumlins. And a glacier, as it advances, displaces rivers and changes the whole face of the earth. Glaciers alone leave behind them those telltale drifts—the ground, lateral, and terminal moraines. These drifts, particularly the ground moraines, extend from the eastern seaboard north and westward in North America and are found in Europe and Siberia." P. 700-1.

E. **750,000 and 700,000 years ago.**
  1. **The fourth glacier was a union of the central and eastern ice fields.**
    "750,000 years ago the fourth ice sheet, a union of the North American central and eastern ice fields, was well on its way south; at its height it reached to southern Illinois, displacing the Mississippi River fifty miles to the west, and in the east it extended as far south as the Ohio River and central Pennsylvania.

"In Asia the Siberian ice sheet made its southernmost invasion, while in Europe the advancing ice stopped just short of the mountain barrier of the Alps." P. 701.

2. **The fourth glacier drove the Neanderthalers and other peoples southward.**

    "750,000 years ago the fourth ice sheet was well on its way south. With their improved implements the Neanderthalers made holes in the ice covering the northern rivers and thus were able to spear the fish which came up to these vents. Ever these tribes retreated before the advancing ice, which at this time made its most extensive invasion of Europe.

    "In these times the Siberian glacier was making its southernmost march, compelling early man to move southward, back toward the lands of his origin. But the human species had so differentiated that the danger of further mingling with its nonprogressive simian relatives was greatly lessened." P. 721.

3. **As the fourth glacier retreats, mammalian animal life has been but little changed.**

    "700,000 years ago the fourth glacier, the greatest of all in Europe, was in recession; men and animals were returning north. The climate was cool and moist, and primitive man again thrived in Europe and western Asia. Gradually the forests spread north over land which had been so recently covered by the glacier.

    "Mammalian life had been little changed by the great glacier. These animals persisted in that narrow belt of land lying between the ice and the Alps and, upon the retreat of the glacier, again rapidly spread out over all Europe. There arrived from Africa, over the Sicilian land bridge, straight-tusked elephants, broad-nosed rhinoceroses, hyenas, and African lions, and these new animals virtually exterminated the saber-toothed tigers and the hippopotamuses." P. 721.

F. **650,000 and 600,000 years ago.**

1. **As the glacier retreated the climate was mild.**

    "650,000 years ago witnessed the continuation of the mild climate. By the middle of the interglacial period it had become so warm that the Alps were almost denuded of ice and snow." P. 721.

2. **The interglacial period.**
   "600,000 years ago the ice had reached its then northern most point of retreat and, after a pause of a few thousand years, started south again on its fifth excursion. But there was little modification of climate for fifty thousand years. Man and the animals of Europe were little changed. The slight aridity of the former period lessened, and the alpine glaciers descended far down the river valleys." P. 721.

G. **550,000 and 500,000 years ago.**
   1. **During the fourth and fifth glaciers there was little improvement in human culture.**
      "550,000 years ago the advancing glacier again pushed man and the animals south. But this time man had plenty of room in the wide belt of land stretching northeast into Asia and lying between the ice sheet and the then greatly expanded Black Sea extension of the Mediterranean.
      "These times of the fourth and fifth glaciers witnessed the further spread of the crude culture of the Neanderthal races. But there was so little progress that it truly appeared as though the attempt to produce a new and modified type of intelligent life on Urantia was about to fail. For almost a quarter of a million years these primitive peoples drifted on, hunting and fighting, by spells improving in certain directions, but, on the whole, steadily retrogressing as compared with their superior Andonic ancestors." P. 721.
   2. **During the fifth glacier the Sangik colored races appeared and the Planetary Prince arrived.**
      "500,000 years ago, during the fifth advance of the ice, a new development accelerated the course of human evolution. *Suddenly* and in one generation the six colored races mutated from the aboriginal human stock. This is a doubly important date since it also marks the arrival of the Planetary Prince." P. 701.
      "In North America the advancing fifth glacier consisted of a combined invasion by all three ice centers. The eastern lobe, however, extended only a short distance below the St. Lawrence valley, and the western ice sheet made little southern advance. But the central lobe reached south to cover most of the State of Iowa. In Europe this invasion of the ice was not so extensive as the preceding one." P. 701.

H. **250,000 to 150,000 years ago.**
   1. **The sixth and last glacier. Three great ice sheets coalesced into one. This was the largest ice invasion in North America.**
      "250,000 years ago the sixth and last glaciation began. And despite the fact that the northern highlands had begun to sink slightly, this was the period of greatest snow deposition on the northern ice fields.
      "In this invasion the three great ice sheets coalesced into one vast ice mass, and all of the western mountains participated in this glacial activity. This was the largest of all ice invasions in North America; the ice moved south over fifteen hundred miles from its pressure centers, and North America experienced its lowest temperatures." P. 701.
   2. **The Lucifer rebellion.**
      "200,000 years ago, during the advance of the last glacier, there occurred an episode which had much to do with the march of events on Urantia—the Lucifer rebellion." P. 701.
   3. **Extent of the sixth glacier.**
      "150,000 years ago the sixth and last glacier reached its farthest points of southern extension, the western ice sheet crossing just over the Canadian border; the central coming down into Kansas, Missouri, and Illinois; the eastern sheet advancing south and covering the greater portion of Pennsylvania and Ohio.
      "This is the glacier that sent forth the many tongues, or ice lobes, which carved out the present-day lakes, great and small. During its retreat the North American system of Great Lakes was produced. And Urantian geologists have very accurately deduced the various stages of this development and have correctly surmised that these bodies of water did, at different times, empty first into the Mississippi valley, then eastward into the Hudson valley, and finally by a northern route into the St. Lawrence. It is thirty-seven thousand years since the connected Great Lakes system began to empty out over the present Niagara route." P. 701.

I. **100,000 years ago.**
   1. **Retreat of the last glacier and the formation of the polar ice sheets.**
      "100,000 years ago, during the retreat of the last glacier, the vast polar ice sheets began to form, and the center of ice accumulation moved considerably northward. And as long as the polar regions continue to be covered with ice, it is hardly

PART II — *Geology*

possible for another glacial age to occur, regardless of future land elevations or modification of ocean currents.

"This last glacier was one hundred thousand years advancing, and it required a like span of time to complete its northern retreat. The temperate regions have been free from the ice for a little over fifty thousand years." P. 702.

2. **Effect of glaciers upon biologic species.**

"The rigorous glacial period destroyed many species and radically changed numerous others. Many were sorely sifted by the to-and-fro migration which was made necessary by the advancing and retreating ice. Those animals which followed the glaciers back and forth over the land were the bear, bison, reindeer, musk ox, mammoth, and mastodon." P. 702.

"The enforced migration of life before the advancing ice led to an extraordinary commingling of plants and of animals, and with the retreat of the final ice invasion, many arctic species of both plants and animals were left stranded high upon certain mountain peaks, whither they had journeyed to escape destruction by the glacier. And so, today, these dislocated plants and animals may be found high up on the Alps of Europe and even on the Appalachian Mountains of North America." P. 702.

3. **End of the ice age.**

"The ice age is the last completed geologic period, the so-called *Pleistocene*, over two million years in length." P. 702.

VI. **Recent times.**

A. **End of the Cenozoic.**

1. "This narrative, extending from the rise of mammalian life to the retreat of the ice and on down to historic times, covers a span of almost fifty million years. This is the last—the current—geologic period and is known to your researchers as the *Cenozoic* or recent-times era." P. 702.

B. **The post-glacial or Holocene Period.**

1. **The Ice Age terminated about the time Adam and Eve arrived on Urantia.**

"35,000 years ago marks the termination of the great ice age excepting in the polar regions of the planet. This date is also significant in that it approximates the arrival of a Material Son and Daughter and the beginning of the Adamic dispensation, roughly corresponding to the beginning of the Holocene or post-glacial period." P. 702.

2. **The retreat of the glacier turned the Sahara into a desert.**

   "The early expansion of the violet race into Europe was cut short by certain rather sudden climatic and geologic changes. With the retreat of the northern ice fields the water-laden winds from the west shifted to the north, gradually turning the great open pasture regions of Sahara into a barren desert. This drought dispersed the smaller-statured brunets, dark-eyed but long-headed dwellers of the great Sahara plateau." P. 890.

3. **England separates from the continent, Denmark arises from the sea, the Mediterranean connects with the Atlantic Ocean.**

   "About the time of these climatic changes in Africa, England separated from the continent, and Denmark arose from the sea, while the isthmus of Gibraltar, protecting the western basin of the Mediterranean, gave way as the result of an earthquake, quickly raising this inland lake to the level of the Atlantic Ocean. Presently the Sicilian land bridge submerged, creating one sea of the Mediterranean and connecting it with the Atlantic Ocean. This cataclysm of nature flooded scores of human settlements and occasioned the greatest loss of life by flood in all the world's history." P. 890.

CONCLUSION

All of this story is graphically told within the fossil pages of the vast "stone book" of world record. And the pages of this gigantic biogeologic record unfailingly tell the truth if you but acquire skill in their interpretation.

PART III — PHYSICS AND CHEMISTRY

Section One
ORIGINS AND COSMIC CONTROL OF FORCES AND ENERGIES

I. Philosophical Basis for Time-space Creation

A. Universe mechanisms.

1. **Time and space are a conjoined mechanism whereby finite creatures exist in a universe controlled by the Infinite.**
   "Time and space are a conjoined mechanism of the master universe. They are the devices whereby finite creatures are enabled to co-exist in the cosmos with the Infinite. Finite creatures are effectively insulated from the absolute levels by time and space. But these insulating media, without which no mortal could exist, operate directly to limit the range of finite action. Without them no creature could act, but by them the acts of every creature are definitely limited." P. 1303.

2. **The mechanisms of higher minds somewhat limit the action of subordinate intelligences. There are limitations on man's free will.**
   "Mechanisms produced by higher minds function to liberate their creative sources but to some degree unvaryingly limit the action of all subordinate intelligences. To the creatures of the universes this limitation becomes apparent as the mechanism of the universes. Man does not have unfettered free will; there are limits to his range of choice, but within the radius of this choice his will is relatively sovereign." P. 1303.

3. **Man does not perfectly control the mortal body as he will the self-created mechanism after fusion.**
   "The life mechanism of the mortal personality, the human body, is the product of supermortal creative design; therefore it can never be perfectly controlled by man himself. Only when ascending man, in liaison with the fused Adjuster, self-creates the mechanism for personality expression, will he achieve perfected control thereof." P. 1303.

4. **The grand universe is mechanism as well as organism—activated by Supreme Mind and co-ordinated by Supreme Spirit.**
   "The grand universe is mechanism as well as organism, mechanical and living—a living mechanism activated by a Supreme Mind, co-ordinating with a Supreme Spirit, and

finding expression on maximum levels of power and personality unification as the Supreme Being. But to deny the mechanism of the finite creation is to deny fact and to disregard reality." P. 1303.

5. **Mechanisms are the product of Creator thought—their purpose is discovered in their origin—not in their function.**
"Mechanisms are the products of mind, creative mind acting on and in cosmic potentials. Mechanisms are the fixed crystallizations of Creator thought, and they ever function true to the volitional concept that gave them origin. But the purposiveness of any mechanism is in its origin, not in its function." P. 1303.

6. **Universe mechanisms are the patterns of the expression of Deity. They exist in response to the will of the First Source and Center.**
"These mechanisms should not be thought of as limiting the action of Deity; rather is it true that in these very mechanics Deity has achieved one phase of eternal expression. The basic universe mechanisms have come into existence in response to the absolute will of the First Source and Center, and they will therefore eternally function in perfect harmony with the plan of the Infinite; they are, indeed, the nonvolitional patterns of that very plan." P. 1303.

7. **On all universe levels, there exists some relationship between person and pattern. With the Supreme and the Ultimate this is a new relationship.**
"We understand something of how the mechanism of Paradise is correlated with the personality of the Eternal Son; this is the function of the Conjoint Actor. And we have theories regarding the operations of the Universal Absolute with respect to the theoretical mechanisms of the Unqualified and the potential person of the Deity Absolute. But in the evolving Deities of Supreme and Ultimate we observe that certain impersonal phases are being actually united with their volitional counterparts, and thus there is evolving a new relationship between pattern and person." P. 1303.

II. SOURCE AND CONTROL OF UNIVERSE ENERGIES AND FORCES

A. The First Source and Center.

1. "God, as the First Source and Center, is primal in relation to total reality—unqualifiedly." P. 5.

"*The First Source and Center* is related to the universes as:

"1. The gravity forces of the material universes are convergent in the gravity center of nether Paradise." P. 5.

2. "As a physical controller in the material universe of universes, the First Source and Center functions in the patterns of the eternal Isle of Paradise, and through this absolute gravity center the eternal God exercises cosmic over control of the physical level equally in the central universe and throughout the universe of universes." P. 24.

3. "Viewed as an unspiritual phenomenon, God is energy. This declaration of physical fact is predicated on the incomprehensible truth that the First Source and Center is the primal cause of the universal physical phenomena of all space. Prom this divine activity all physical energy and other material manifestations are derived." P. 47.

4. "God controls all power; he has made 'a way for the lightning'; he has ordained the circuits of all energy. He has decreed the time and manner of the manifestation of all forms of energy-matter. And all these things are held forever in his everlasting grasp—in the gravitational control centering on nether Paradise. The light and energy of the eternal God thus swing on forever around his majestic circuit, the endless but orderly procession of the starry hosts composing the universe of universes. All creation circles eternally around the Paradise-Personality center of all things and beings." P. 47.

B. **Nether Paradise.**

1. **Personalities do not sojourn on nether Paradise. All physical-energy and cosmic-force circuits take origin there. It consists of three concentric zones.**

    "Concerning nether Paradise, we know only that which is revealed; personalities do not sojourn there. It has nothing whatever to do with the affairs of spirit intelligences, nor does the Deity Absolute there function. We are informed that all physical-energy and cosmic-force circuits have their origin on nether Paradise, and that it is constituted as follows:

    "1. Directly underneath the location of the Trinity, in the central portion of nether Paradise, is the unknown and unrevealed Zone of Infinity.

    "2. This Zone is immediately surrounded by an unnamed area.

    "3. Occupying the outer margins of the under surface is a region having mainly to do with space potency and force-energy. The activities of this vast elliptical force center are

PART III — *Physics and Chemistry*

not identifiable with the known functions of any triunity, but the primordial force-charge of space appears to be focalized in this area. This center consists of three concentric elliptical zones: The innermost is the focal point of the force-energy activities of Paradise itself; the outermost may possibly be identified with the functions of the Unqualified Absolute, but we are not certain concerning the space functions of the mid-zone." P. 122.

2. **Force-energy enters at the south of the inner pulsating zone and flows out at the north.**
"*The inner zone* of this force center seems to act as a gigantic heart whose pulsations direct currents to the outermost borders of physical space. It directs and modifies force-energies but hardly drives them. The reality pressure-presence of this primal force is definitely greater at the north end of the Paradise center than in the southern regions; this is a uniformly registered difference. The mother force of space seems to flow in at the south and out at the north through the operation of some unknown circulatory system which is concerned with the diffusion of this basic form of force-energy. From time to time there are also noted differences in the east-west pressures. The forces emanating from this zone are not responsive to observable physical gravity but are always obedient to Paradise gravity." P. 122.

3. **The function of the three-way pulsating mid-zone is unknown. Many believe that it is the control mechanism of the midspace or quiet zones of the master universe, since it is somehow related to the functioning of unpervaded space.**
"*The mid-zone* of the force center immediately surrounds this area. This mid-zone appears to be static except that it expands and contracts through three cycles of activity. The least of these pulsations is in an east-west direction, the next in a north-south direction, while the greatest fluctuation is in every direction, a generalized expansion and contraction. The function of this mid-area has never been really identified, but it must have something to do with reciprocal adjustment between the inner and the outer zones of the force center. It is believed by many that the midzone is the control mechanism of the midspace or quiet zones which separate the successive space levels of the master universe, but no evidence or revelation confirms this. This inference is derived from the knowledge that this mid-

4. **The enormous outer zone is the center of emanations to the domains of all outer space. It is in some way responsive to the Trinity and is the central focalization of the space presence of the Unqualified Absolute.**

   "*The outer zone* is the largest and most active of the three concentric and elliptical belts of unidentified space potential. This area is the site of unimagined activities, the central circuit point of emanations which proceed spaceward in every direction to the outermost borders of the seven superuniverses and on beyond to overspread the enormous and incomprehensible domains of all outer space. This space presence is entirely impersonal notwithstanding that in some undisclosed manner it seems to be indirectly responsive to the will and mandates of the infinite Deities when acting as the Trinity. This is believed to be the central focalization, the Paradise center, of the space presence of the Unqualified Absolute." P. 122.

5. **The outer zone pulsates in cycles of one billion Urantia years—it is synchronized with the respiration of all pervaded space.**

   "All forms of force and all phases of energy seem to be encircuited; they circulate throughout the universes and return by definite routes. But with the emanations of the activated zone of the Unqualified Absolute there appears to be either an outgoing or an incoming—never both simultaneously. This outer zone pulsates in agelong cycles of gigantic proportions. For a little more than one billion Urantia years the space-force of this center is outgoing; then for a similar length of time it will be incoming. And the space-force manifestations of this center are universal; they extend throughout all pervadable space." P. 123.

6. **Originally, all force came from nether Paradise, but many forms of energy and matter take origin in the womb of space.**

   "All physical force, energy, and matter are one. All force-energy originally proceeded from nether Paradise and will eventually return thereto following the completion of its space circuit. But the energies and material organizations of the universe of universes did not all come from nether Paradise in their present phenomenal states; space is the womb of several forms of matter and prematter." P. 123.

PART III — *Physics and Chemistry*

7. **Space does not originate on nether Paradise. Neither do the pulsations of the outer zone give origin to space respiration.**
   "Though the outer zone of the Paradise force center is the source of space-energies, space does not originate there. Space is not force, energy, or power. Nor do the pulsations of this zone account for the respiration of space, but the incoming and outgoing phases of this zone are synchronized with the two-billion-year expansion-contraction cycles of space." P. 123.

C. Space.

1. **Space is a bestowal of Paradise. It is pervaded by the ancestral space potency of the Unqualified Absolute.**
   "Space is neither a subabsolute condition within, nor the presence of, the Unqualified Absolute, neither is it a function of the Ultimate. It is a bestowal of Paradise, and the space of the grand universe and that of all outer regions is believed to be actually pervaded by the ancestral space potency of the Unqualified Absolute. From near approach to peripheral Paradise, this pervaded space extends horizontally outward through the fourth space level and beyond the periphery of the master universe, but how far beyond we do not know." P. 124.

2. **The space levels are curved paths of lessened resistance to motion.**
   "A space level thus functions as an elliptical region of motion surrounded on all sides by relative motionlessness. Such relationships of motion and quiescence constitute a curved space path of lessened resistance to motion which is universally followed by cosmic force and emergent energy as they circle forever around the Isle of Paradise." P. 125.

3. **Everything in space is in motion; only Paradise is stationary.**
   "All units of cosmic energy are in primary revolution, are engaged in the execution of their mission, while swinging around the universal orbit. The universes of space and their component systems and worlds are all revolving spheres, moving along the endless circuits of the master universe space levels. Absolutely nothing is stationary in all the master universe except the very center of Havona, the eternal Isle of Paradise, the center of gravity." P. 133.

4. **While the Unqualified Absolute is functionally limited to space, his relation to motion is not clear.**
   "The Unqualified Absolute is functionally limited to space, but we are not so sure about the relation of this Absolute to

motion. Is motion inherent therein? We do not know. We know that motion is not inherent in space; even the motions *of* space are not innate. But we are not so sure about the relation of the Unqualified to motion. Who, or what, is really responsible for the gigantic activities of force-energy transmutations now in progress out beyond the borders of the present seven superuniverses?" P. 133.

5. **Three theories concerning the origin of motion in space.**
    "Concerning the origin of motion we have the following opinions:
    "1. We think the Conjoint Actor initiates motion *in* space.
    "2. If the Conjoint Actor produces the motions *of* space, we cannot prove it.
    "3. The Universal Absolute does not originate initial motion but does equalize and control all of the tensions originated by motion." P. 133.

6. **Relation of force organizers to the origin of nebulae.**
    "In outer space the force organizers are apparently responsible for the production of the gigantic universe wheels which are now in process of stellar evolution, but their ability so to function must have been made possible by some modification of the space presence of the Unqualified Absolute." P. 133.

7. **Space is real and there are four classes of space motion.**
    "Space is, from the human viewpoint, nothing—negative; it exists only as related to something positive and nonspatial. Space is, however, real. It contains and conditions motion. It even moves. Space motions may be roughly classified as follows:
    "1. Primary motion—space respiration, the motion of space itself.
    "2. Secondary motion—the alternate directional swings of the successive space levels.
    "3. Relative motions—relative in the sense that they are not evaluated with Paradise as a base point. Primary and secondary motions are absolute, motion in relation to unmoving Paradise.
    "4. Compensatory or correlating movement designed to co-ordinate all other motions." P. 133.

8. **Space is neither infinite nor absolute.**
    "Space is not infinite, even though it takes origin from Paradise; not absolute, for it is pervaded by the Unqualified Absolute.

PART III — *Physics and Chemistry*

We do not know the absolute limits of space, but we do know that the absolute of time is eternity." P. 135.

9. **Space is absolutely ultimate. While material bodies exist in space, space also exists in material bodies.**

    "Space comes the nearest of all nonabsolute things to being absolute. Space is apparently absolutely ultimate. The real difficulty we have in understanding space on the material level is due to the fact that, while material bodies exist in space, space also exists in these same material bodies. While there is much about space that is absolute, that does not mean that space is absolute.

    "It may help to an understanding of space relationships if you would conjecture that, relatively speaking, space is after all a property of all material bodies. Hence, when a body moves through space, it also takes all its properties with it, even the space which is in and of such a moving body." P. 1297.

D. **Gravity.**

"The Universal Controller is potentially present in the gravity circuits of the Isle of Paradise in all parts of the universe at all times and in the same degree, in accordance with the mass, in response to the physical demands for this presence, and because of the inherent nature of all creation which causes all things to adhere and consist in him." P. 45.

"*The Isle of Paradise*—Paradise not otherwise qualified—is the Absolute of the material-gravity control of the First Source and Center." P. 7.

1. **Gravity is the all-powerful grasp of the physical presence of Paradise.**

    "The inescapable pull of gravity effectively grips all the worlds of all the universes of all space. Gravity is the all-powerful grasp of the physical presence of Paradise. Gravity is the omnipotent strand on which are strung the gleaming stars, blazing suns, and whirling spheres which constitute the universal physical adornment of the eternal God, who is all things, fills all things, and in whom all things consist." P. 125.

2. **All energy and matter is unerringly responsive to the gravity pull of Paradise.**

    "The center and focal point of absolute material gravity is the Isle of Paradise, complemented by the dark gravity bodies encircling Havona and equilibrated by the upper and nether space reservoirs. All known emanations of nether Paradise invariably and unerringly respond to the central gravity pull operating upon the endless circuits of the elliptical space levels of the master universe. Every known form of cosmic reality has the bend of the ages, the trend of the circle, the swing of the great ellipse." P. 125.

3. **The relation of space to gravity.**

   "Space is nonresponsive to gravity, but it acts as an equilibrant on gravity. Without the space cushion, explosive action would jerk surrounding space bodies. Pervaded space also exerts an antigravity influence upon physical or linear gravity; space can actually neutralize such gravity action even though it cannot delay it. Absolute gravity is Paradise gravity. Local or linear gravity pertains to the electrical stage of energy or matter; it operates within the central, super-, and outer universes, wherever suitable materialization has taken place." P. 125.

4. **Energy and matter disclose three forms of response to Paradise gravity.**

   "The numerous forms of cosmic force, physical energy, universe power, and various materializations disclose three general, though not perfectly clear-cut, stages of response to Paradise gravity:

   "1. *Pregravity Stages (Force).* This is the first step in the individuation of space potency into the pre-energy forms of cosmic force. This state is analogous to the concept of the primordial force-charge of space, sometimes called *pure energy* or *segregata.*

   "2. *Gravity Stages (Energy).* This modification of the force-charge of space is produced by the action of the Paradise force organizers. It signalizes the appearance of energy systems responsive to the pull of Paradise gravity. This emergent energy is originally neutral but consequent upon further metamorphosis will exhibit the so-called negative and positive qualities. We designate these stages *ultimata.*

   "3. *Postgravity Stages (Universe Power).* In this stage, energy-matter discloses response to the control of linear gravity. In the central universe these physical systems are threefold organizations known as *triata.* They are the superpower mother systems of the creations of time and space. The physical systems of the superuniverses are mobilized by the Universe Power Directors and their associates.

PART III — *Physics and Chemistry*

These material organizations are dual in constitution and are known as *gravita*. The dark gravity bodies encircling Havona are neither triata nor gravita, and their drawing power discloses both forms of physical gravity, linear and absolute." P. 125-6.

5. **Space potency is not subject to gravity. It emanates from Paradise and constitutes the space presence of the Unqualified Absolute.**

   "Space potency is not subject to the interactions of any form of gravitation. This primal endowment of Paradise is not an actual level of reality, but it is ancestral to all relative functional nonspirit realities—all manifestations of force-energy and the organization of power and matter. Space potency is a term difficult to define. It does not mean that which is ancestral to space; its meaning should convey the idea of the potencies and potentials existent within space. It may be roughly conceived to include all those absolute influences and potentials which emanate from Paradise and constitute the space presence of the Unqualified Absolute." P. 126.

6. **Relation of the Unqualified Absolute to Paradise. Why gravity acts in the plane perpendicular to the mass.**

   "Paradise is the absolute source and the eternal focal point of all energy-matter in the universe of universes. The Unqualified Absolute is the revealer, regulator, and repository of that which has Paradise as its source and origin. The universal presence of the Unqualified Absolute seems to be equivalent to the concept of a potential infinity of gravity extension, an elastic tension of Paradise presence. This concept aids us in grasping the fact that everything is drawn inward towards Paradise. The illustration is crude but nonetheless helpful. It also explains why gravity always acts preferentially in the plane perpendicular to the mass, a phenomenon indicative of the differential dimensions of Paradise and the surrounding creations." P. 126.

7. **The Universal Father can make use of all four absolute gravity circuits.**

   "All forms of force-energy—material, mindal, or spiritual—are alike subject to those grasps, those universal presences, which we call gravity. Personality also is responsive to gravity—to the Father's exclusive circuit; but though this circuit is exclusive to the Father, he is not excluded from the other circuits; the Universal Father is infinite and acts over *all* four

absolute-gravity circuits in the master universe:
"1. The Personality Gravity of the Universal Father.
"2. The Spirit Gravity of the Eternal Son.
"3. The Mind Gravity of the Conjoint Actor.
"4. The Cosmic Gravity of the Isle of Paradise.
"These four circuits are not related to the nether Paradise force center; they are neither force, energy, nor power circuits. They are absolute *presence* circuits and like God are independent of time and space." P. 131.

8. **The present grand universe engages only five per cent of the total Paradise gravity action.**
"Having formulated an estimate of the summation of the entire physical-gravity capacity of the grand universe, they have laboriously effected a comparison of this finding with the estimated total of absolute gravity presence now operative. These calculations indicate that the total gravity action on the grand universe is a very small part of the estimated gravity pull of Paradise, computed on the basis of the gravity response of basic physical units of universe matter. These investigators reach the amazing conclusion that the central universe and the surrounding seven superuniverses are at the present time making use of only about five per cent of the active functioning of the Paradise absolute-gravity grasp. In other words: At the present moment about ninety-five per cent of the active cosmic-gravity action of the Isle of Paradise, computed on this totality theory, is engaged in controlling material systems beyond the borders of the present organized universes. These calculations all refer to absolute gravity; linear gravity is an interactive phenomenon which can be computed only by knowing the actual Paradise gravity." P. 132.

9. **Nature and function of Gravity Messengers.**
"Gravity Messengers hail from Divinington, and they are modified and personalized Adjusters, but no one of our Uversa group will undertake to explain the nature of one of these messengers. We know they are highly personal beings, divine, intelligent, and touchingly understanding, but we do not comprehend their timeless technique of traversing space. They seem to be competent to utilize any and all energies, circuits, and even gravity. Finaliters of the mortal corps cannot defy time and space, but they have associated with them and subject to their command all but infinite spirit personalities who can.

We presume to call Gravity Messengers personalities, but in reality they are superspirit beings, unlimited and boundless personalities. They are of an entirely different order of personality as compared with Solitary Messengers." P. 347.

10. **Definition of linear gravity.**

"Linear-gravity response is a quantitative measure of nonspirit energy. All mass—organized energy—is subject to this grasp except as motion and mind act upon it. Linear gravity is the short-range cohesive force of the macrocosmos somewhat as the forces of intra-atomic cohesion are the short-range forces of the microcosmos. Physical materialized energy, organized as so-called matter, cannot traverse space without affecting linear-gravity response. Although such gravity response is directly proportional to mass, it is so modified by intervening space that the final result is no more than roughly approximated when expressed as inversely according to the square of the distance. Space eventually conquers linear gravitation because of the presence therein of the antigravity influences of numerous supermaterial forces which operate to neutralize gravity action and all responses thereto." P. 482.

Section Two
FORCE, ENERGY, POWER, MATTER

I. Physical Energy

"*Physical energy* is a term denoting all phases and forms of phenomenal motion, action, and potential.

"In discussing physical-energy manifestations, we generally use the terms cosmic force, emergent energy, and universe power. These are often employed as follows:

"1. *Cosmic force* embraces all energies deriving from the Unqualified Absolute but which are as yet unresponsive to Paradise gravity.

"2. *Emergent energy* embraces those energies which are responsive to Paradise gravity but are as yet unresponsive to local or linear gravity. This is the pre-electronic level of energy-matter.

"3. *Universe power* includes all forms of energy which, while still responding to Paradise gravity, are directly responsive to linear gravity. This is the electronic level of energy-matter and all subsequent evolutions thereof." P. 9.

A. The source of all physical energy.

1. "As a physical controller in the material universe of universes, the First Source and Center functions in the patterns of the eternal Isle of Paradise, and through this absolute gravity center the eternal God exercises cosmic overcontrol of the physical level equally in the central universe and throughout the universe of universes." P. 24.

2. "The foundation of the universe is material in the sense that energy is the basis of all existence, and pure energy is controlled by the Universal Father." P. 467.

    "The manipulation of universe energy is ever in accordance with the personal will and the all-wise mandates of the Universal Father." P. 467.

3. **All reality is Deity-derived. The ultimaton has Paradise as its nucleus.**

    "Matter—energy—for they are but diverse manifestations of the same cosmic reality, as a universe phenomenon is inherent in the Universal Father. 'In him all things consist.' Matter may appear to manifest inherent energy and to exhibit self-contained powers, but the lines of gravity involved in the energies concerned in all these physical phenomena are derived from, and are dependent on, Paradise. The ultimaton, the first measurable form of energy, has Paradise as its nucleus." P. 467.

PART III — *Physics and Chemistry*

4. **All original force-energy proceeds from Paradise.**
   "The bestowal of cosmic force, the domain of cosmic gravity, is the function of the Isle of Paradise. All original force-energy proceeds from Paradise, and the matter for the making of untold universes now circulates throughout the master universe in the form of a supergravity presence which constitutes the force-charge of pervaded space." P. 139.

5. **Physical energy is always obedient to universal law—only volitional mind deviates from the divine plan.**
   "Whatever the transformations of force in the outlying universes, having gone out from Paradise, it journeys on subject to the never-ending, ever-present, unfailing pull of the eternal Isle, obediently and inherently swinging on forever around the eternal space paths of the universes. Physical energy is the one reality which is true and steadfast in its obedience to universal law. Only in the realms of creature volition has there been deviation from the divine paths and the original plans. Power and energy are the universal evidences of the stability, constancy, and eternity of the central Isle of Paradise." P. 139.

6. **Numerous unpredictable and unfathomable phenomena of primal force and mind may be due to activity of the Ultimate and the Absolutes.**
   "All phases of primordial force, nascent spirit, and other nonpersonal ultimates appear to react in accordance with certain relatively stable but unknown laws and are characterized by a latitude of performance and an elasticity of response which are often disconcerting when encountered in the phenomena of a circumscribed and isolated situation. What is the explanation of this unpredictable freedom of reaction disclosed by these emerging universe actualities? These unknown, unfathomable unpredictables—whether pertaining to the behavior of a primordial unit of force, the reaction of an unidentified level of mind, or the phenomenon of a vast preuniverse in the making in the domains of outer space—probably disclose the activities of the Ultimate and the presence-performances of the Absolutes, which antedate the function of all universe Creators." P. 136.

7. **No future discovery will prove matter to be self-existent or natural laws to be operated apart from the technique of Paradise and the motivating purpose of the Universal Father.**

"There is innate in matter and present in universal space a form of energy not known on Urantia. When this discovery is finally made, then will physicists feel that they have solved, almost at least, the mystery of matter. And so will they have approached one step nearer the Creator; so will they have mastered one more phase of the divine technique; but in no sense will they have found God, neither will they have established the existence of matter or the operation of natural laws apart from the cosmic technique of Paradise and the motivating purpose of the Universal Father." P. 467.

B. Physical-energy circuits.

1. **There are two energy emanations from Paradise—the cosmic-energy work of the Master Spirits and the force functions of the Unqualified Absolute.**

   "We are unable to trace any personal connection between the cosmic-energy work of the Master Spirits and the force functions of the Unqualified Absolute. The energy manifestations under the jurisdiction of the Master Spirits are all directed from the periphery of Paradise; they do not appear to be in any direct manner associated with the force phenomena identified with the nether surface of Paradise." P. 189.

2. **Energy is eternal, not infinite.**

   "Energy is eternal but not infinite; it ever responds to the all-embracing grasp of Infinity. Forever force and energy go on; having gone out from Paradise, they must return thereto, even if age upon age be required for the completion of the ordained circuit. That which is of Paradise Deity origin can have only a Paradise destination or a Deity destiny." P. 468.

C. Physical energies.

1. **Force has a Deity origin and, regardless of endless transformation, it is indestructible.**

   "Force derived from self-existent Deity is in itself ever existent. Force-energy is imperishable, indestructible; these manifestations of the Infinite may be subject to unlimited transmutation, endless transformation, and eternal metamorphosis; but in no sense or degree, not even to the slightest imaginable extent, could they or ever shall they suffer extinction. But energy, though springing from the Infinite, is not infinitely manifest; there are outer limits to the presently conceived master universe." P. 468.

PART III — *Physics and Chemistry*

2. Classification and metamorphosis of cosmic force, emergent energy, and universe power.

"I will, however, endeavor to lessen conceptual confusion by suggesting the advisability of adopting the following classification for cosmic force, emergent energy, and universe power—physical energy:

"1. *Space potency.* This is the unquestioned free space presence of the Unqualified Absolute. The extension of this concept connotes the universe force-space potential inherent in the functional totality of the Unqualified Absolute, while the intension of this concept implies the totality of cosmic reality—universes—which emanated eternitywise from the never-beginning, never-ending, never-moving, never-changing Isle of Paradise.

"The phenomena indigenous to the nether side of Paradise probably embrace three zones of absolute force presence and performance: the fulcral zone of the Unqualified Absolute, the zone of the Isle of Paradise itself, and the intervening zone of certain unidentified equalizing and compensating agencies or functions. These triconcentric zones are the centrum of the Paradise cycle of cosmic reality.

"Space potency is a prereality; it is the domain of the Unqualified Absolute and is responsive only to the personal grasp of the Universal Father, notwithstanding that it is seemingly modifiable by the presence of the Primary Master Force Organizers.

"On Uversa, space potency is spoken of as ABSOLUTA.

"2. *Primordial force.* This represents the first basic change in space potency and may be one of the nether Paradise functions of the Unqualified Absolute. We know that the space presence going out from nether Paradise is modified in some manner from that which is incoming. But regardless of any such possible relationships, the openly recognized transmutation of space potency into primordial force is the primary differentiating function of the tension-presence of the living Paradise force organizers.

"Passive and potential force becomes active and primordial in response to the resistance afforded by the space presence of the Primary Eventuated Master Force Organizers. Force is now emerging from the exclusive domain of the Unqualified Absolute into the realms of multiple response—response to certain primal motions initiated by the God of Action and thereupon to certain compensating motions emanating from the Universal Absolute. Primordial force is seemingly reactive to transcendental causation in proportion to absoluteness. "Primordial force is sometimes spoken of as *pure energy*; on Uversa we refer to it as SEGREGATA.

"3. *Emergent energies.* The passive presence of the primary force organizers is sufficient to transform space potency into primordial force, and it is upon such an activated space field that these same force organizers begin their initial and active operations. Primordial force is destined to pass through two distinct phases of transmutation in the realms of energy manifestation before appearing as universe power. These two levels of emerging energy are:

"a. *Puissant energy.* This is the powerful-directional, mass-movemented, mighty-tensioned, and forcible-reacting energy—gigantic energy systems set in motion by the activities of the primary force organizers. This primary or puissant energy is not at first definitely responsive to the Paradise-gravity pull though probably yielding an aggregate-mass or space-directional response to the collective group of absolute influences operative from the nether side of Paradise. When energy emerges to the level of initial response to the circular and absolute-gravity grasp of Paradise, the primary force organizers give way to the functioning of their secondary associates.

"b. *Gravity energy.* The now-appearing gravity-responding energy carries the potential of universe power and becomes the active ancestor of all universe matter. This secondary or gravity energy is the product of the energy elaboration resulting from the pressure-presence and the tension-trends set up by the Associate Transcendental Master Force Organizers. In response to the work of these force manipulators, space-energy rapidly passes from the puissant to the gravity stage, thus becoming directly responsive to the circular grasp of Paradise (absolute) gravity while disclosing a certain potential for sensitivity to the linear-gravity pull inherent in the soon appearing material mass of the

Part III — *Physics and Chemistry*

electronic and the postelectronic stages of energy and matter. Upon the appearance of gravity response, the Associate Master Force Organizers may retire from the energy cyclones of space provided the Universe Power Directors are assignable to that field of action.

"We are quite uncertain regarding the exact causes of the early stages of force evolution, but we recognize the intelligent action of the Ultimate in both levels of emergent-energy manifestation. Puissant and gravity energies, when regarded collectively, are spoken of on Uversa as ULTIMATA.

"4. *Universe power.* Space-force has been changed into space-energy and thence into the energy of gravity control. Thus has physical energy been ripened to that point where it can be directed into channels of power and made to serve the manifold purposes of the universe Creators. This work is carried on by the versatile directors, centers, and controllers of physical energy in the grand universe—the organized and inhabited creations. These Universe Power Directors assume the more or less complete control of twenty-one of the thirty phases of energy constituting the present energy system of the seven superuniverses. This domain of power-energy-matter is the realm of the intelligent activities of the Sevenfold, functioning under the time-space overcontrol of the Supreme.

"On Uversa we refer to the realm of universe power as GRAVITA.

"5. *Havona energy.* In concept this narrative has been moving Paradiseward as transmuting space-force has been followed, level by level, to the working level of the energy-power of the universes of time and space. Continuing Paradiseward, there is next encountered a pre-existent phase of energy which is characteristic of the central universe. Here the evolutionary cycle seems to turn back upon itself; energy-power now seems to begin to swing back towards force, but force of a nature very unlike that of space potency and primordial force. Havona energy systems are not dual; they are triune. This is the existential energy domain of the Conjoint Actor, functioning in behalf of the Paradise Trinity.

"On Uversa these energies of Havona are known as TRIATA.

"6. *Transcendental energy*. This energy system operates on and from the upper level of Paradise and only in connection with the absonite peoples. On Uversa it is denominated TRANOSTA.

"7. *Monota*. Energy is close of kin to divinity when it is Paradise energy. We incline to the belief that monota is the living, nonspirit energy of Paradise—an eternity counterpart of the living, spirit energy of the Original Son—hence the nonspiritual energy system of the Universal Father.

"We cannot differentiate the *nature* of Paradise spirit and Paradise monota; they are apparently alike. They have different names, but you can hardly be told very much about a reality whose spiritual and whose nonspiritual manifestations are distinguishable only by *name*." P. 469-71.

D. **Energy and matter transmutations.**

1. **The various forms of energy and matter are all one and the same thing.**

   "Light, heat, electricity, magnetism, chemism, energy, and matter are—in origin, nature, and destiny—one and the same thing, together with other material realities as yet undiscovered on Urantia." P. 472.

2. **Energy and matter may undergo endless transformations but they swing ever true to the circle of eternity and are always responsive to their Infinite source.**

   "We do not fully comprehend the almost endless changes to which physical energy may be subject. In one universe it appears as light, in another as light plus heat, in another as forms of energy unknown on Urantia; in untold millions of years it may reappear as some form of restless, surging electrical energy or magnetic power; and still later on it may again appear in a subsequent universe as some form of variable matter, going through a series of metamorphoses, to be followed by its outward physical disappearance in some great cataclysm of the realms. And then, after countless ages and almost endless wandering through numberless universes, again may this same energy re-emerge and many times change its form and potential; and so do these transformations continue through successive ages and throughout countless realms. Thus matter sweeps on, undergoing the transmutations of time but

Part III — *Physics and Chemistry*

swinging ever true to the circle of eternity; even if long prevented from returning to its source, it is ever responsive thereto, and it ever proceeds in the path ordained by the Infinite Personality who sent it forth." P. 472.

3. **Power centers and physical controllers are masters of energy before it attains the atomic level.**
"The power centers and their associates are much concerned in the work of transmuting the ultimaton into the circuits and revolutions of the electron. These unique beings control and compound power by their skillful manipulation of the basic units of materialized energy, the ultimatons. They are masters of energy as it circulates in this primitive state. In liaison with the physical controllers they are able to effectively control and direct energy even after it has transmuted to the electrical level, the so-called electronic stage. But their range of action is enormously curtailed when electronically organized energy swings into the whirls of the atomic systems. Upon such materialization, these energies fall under the complete grasp of the drawing power of linear gravity." P. 473.

4. **Power centers and physical controllers exert only a negative influence on gravity—their antigravity endowments.**
"Gravity acts positively on the power lanes and energy channels of the power centers and the physical controllers, but these beings have only a negative relation to gravity—the exercise of their anti-gravity endowments." P. 473.

5. **Throughout space, cold and other influences are organizing ultimatons into electrons.**
"Throughout all space, cold and other influences are at work creatively organizing ultimatons into electrons. Heat is the measurement of electronic activity, while cold merely signifies absence of heat—comparative energy rest—the status of the universal force-charge of space provided neither emergent energy nor organized matter were present and responding to gravity." P. 473.

6. **Energy activities prevent absolute zero in interstellar space. Space is not empty. Nebadon's most empty space contains one electron in each cubic inch.**
"Gravity presence and action is what prevents the appearance of the theoretical absolute zero, for interstellar space does not have the temperature of absolute zero. Throughout all organized

space there are gravity-responding energy currents, power circuits, and ultimatonic activities, as well as organizing electronic energies. Practically speaking, space is not empty. Even the atmosphere of Urantia thins out increasingly until at about three thousand miles it begins to shade off into the average space matter in this section of the universe. The most nearly empty space known in Nebadon would yield about one hundred ultimatons—the equivalent of one electron—in each cubic inch. Such scarcity of matter is regarded as practically empty space." P. 473.

7. **Heat and cold are secondary only to gravity in the evolution of energy and matter.**

   "Temperature—heat and cold—is secondary only to gravity in the realms of energy and matter evolution. Ultimatons are humbly obedient to temperature extremes. Low temperatures favor certain forms of electronic construction and atomic assembly, while high temperatures facilitate all sorts of atomic breakup and material disintegration." P. 473.

8. **Intense solar heat can largely overcome gravity, but cannot convert ultimatons into puissant energy.**

   "When subjected to the heat and pressure of certain internal solar states, all but the most primitive associations of matter may be broken up. Heat can thus largely overcome gravity stability. But no known solar heat or pressure can convert ultimatons back into puissant energy." P. 473.

9. **Blazing suns transform matter into energy, but the influences of outer space convert energy into matter.**

   "The blazing suns can transform matter into various forms of energy, but the dark worlds and all outer space can slow down electronic and ultimatonic activity to the point of converting these energies into the matter of the realms. Certain electronic associations of a close nature, as well as many of the basic associations of nuclear matter, are formed in the exceedingly low temperatures of open space, being later augmented by association with larger accretions of materializing energy." P. 473.

10. **Many influences, including force organizers and power directors are concerned in the transmutations of energy and matter.**

    "Throughout all of this never-ending metamorphosis of energy and matter we must reckon with the influence of gravity pressure and with the antigravity behavior of the ultimatonic energies under certain conditions of temperature, velocity, and revolution. Temperature, energy currents, distance, and the presence of the living force organizers and the power directors also have a bearing on all transmutation phenomena of energy and matter." P. 473.

11. **Increase of mass in matter is equal to the increase of energy divided by the square of the velocity of light.**
"The increase of mass in matter is equal to the increase of energy divided by the square of the velocity of light. In a dynamic sense the work which resting matter can perform is equal to the energy expended in bringing its parts together from Paradise minus the resistance of the forces overcome in transit and the attraction exerted by the parts of matter on one another." P. 474.

12. **Multiple atomic weights indicate loss of radioactive energy.**
"The existence of pre-electronic forms of matter is indicated by the two atomic weights of lead. The lead of original formation weighs slightly more than that produced through uranium disintegration by way of radium emanations; and this difference in atomic weight represents the actual loss of energy in the atomic breakup." P. 474.

13. **Matter can absorb or release energy only in exact amounts—quanta.**
"The relative integrity of matter is assured by the fact that energy can be absorbed or released only in those exact amounts which Urantia scientists have designated quanta. This wise provision in the material realms serves to maintain the universes as going concerns." P. 474.

14. **Wavelike behavior of quanta is due to many factors. Such energy ripples are 860 times the diameters of the material particles concerned.**
"The quantity of energy taken in or given out when electronic or other positions are shifted is always a 'quantum' or some multiple thereof, but the vibratory or wavelike behavior of such units of energy is wholly determined by the dimensions of the material structures concerned. Such wavelike energy ripples are 860 times the diameters of the ultimatons, electrons, atoms, or other units thus performing. The never-ending confusion attending the observation of the wave mechanics of quantum behavior is due to the superimposition of energy

waves: Two crests can combine to make a double-height crest, while a crest and a trough may combine, thus producing mutual cancellation." P. 474.

E. **Forms of energy.**

"In the superuniverse of Orvonton there are one hundred octaves of wave energy. Of these one hundred groups of energy manifestations, sixty-four are wholly or partially recognized on Urantia. The sun's rays constitute four octaves in the superuniverse scale, the visible rays embracing a single octave, number forty-six in this series. The ultraviolet group comes next, while ten octaves up are the X rays, followed by the Y rays of radium. Thirty-two octaves above the visible light of the sun are the outer-space energy rays so frequently commingled with their associated highly energized minute particles of matter. Next downward from visible sunlight appear the infrared rays, and thirty octaves below are the radio transmission group." P. 474.

1. **Wavelike energy may be classified in ten groups.**

"Wavelike energy manifestations—from the standpoint of twentieth-century Urantia scientific enlightenment—may be classified into the following ten groups:

"1. *Infraultimatonic rays*—the borderland revolutions of ultimatons as they begin to assume definite form. This is the first stage of emergent energy in which wavelike phenomena can be detected and measured.

"2. *Ultimatonic rays*. The assembly of energy into the minute spheres of the ultimatons occasions vibrations in the content of space which are discernible and measurable. And long before physicists ever discover the ultimaton, they will undoubtedly detect the phenomena of these rays as they shower in upon Urantia. These short and powerful rays represent the initial activity of the ultimatons as they are slowed down to that point where they veer towards the electronic organization of matter. As the ultimatons aggregate into electrons, condensation occurs with a consequent storage of energy.

"3. *The short space rays*. These are the shortest of all purely electronic vibrations and represent the preatomic stage of this form of matter. These rays require extraordinarily high or low temperatures for their production. There are two sorts of these space rays: one attendant upon the birth of

Part III — *Physics and Chemistry*

atoms and the other indicative of atomic disruption. They emanate in the largest quantities from the densest plane of the superuniverse, the Milky Way, which is also the densest plane of the outer universes.

"4. *The electronic stage.* This stage of energy is the basis of all materialization in the seven superuniverses. When electrons pass from higher to lower energy levels of orbital revolution, quanta are always given off. Orbital shifting of electrons results in the ejection or the absorption of very definite and uniform measurable particles of light-energy, while the individual electron always gives up a particle of light-energy when subjected to collision. Wavelike energy manifestations also attend upon the performances of the positive bodies and the other members of the electronic stage.

"5. *Gamma rays*—those emanations which characterize the spontaneous dissociation of atomic matter. The best illustration of this form of electronic activity is in the phenomena associated with radium disintegration.

"6. *The X-ray group.* The next step in the slowing down of the electron yields the various forms of solar X rays together with artificially generated X rays. The electronic charge creates an electric field; movement gives rise to an electric current; the current produces a magnetic field. When an electron is suddenly stopped, the resultant electromagnetic commotion produces the X ray; the X ray is that disturbance. The solar X rays are identical with those which are mechanically generated for exploring the interior of the human body except that they are a trifle longer.

"7. *The ultraviolet* or chemical rays of sunlight and the various mechanical productions.

"8. *The white light*—the whole visible light of the suns.

"9. *Infrared rays*—the slowing down of electronic activity still nearer the stage of appreciable heat.

"10. *Hertzian waves*—those energies utilized on Urantia for broadcasting.

"Of all these ten phases of wavelike energy activity, the human eye can react to just one octave, the whole light of ordinary sunlight." P. 474-5.

2. **The ether is not real. Light and other forms of energy proceed in direct lines and consist of definite energy particles. Wavelike phenomena result from the action of gravity and other intervening influences.**

   "The so-called ether is merely a collective name to designate a group of force and energy activities occurring in space. Ultimatons, electrons, and other mass aggregations of energy are uniform particles of matter, and in their transit through space they really proceed in direct lines. Light and all other forms of recognizable energy manifestations consist of a succession of definite energy particles which proceed in direct lines except as modified by gravity and other intervening forces. That these processions of energy particles appear as wave phenomena when subjected to certain observations is due to the resistance of the undifferentiated force blanket of all space, the hypothetical ether, and to the intergravity tension of the associated aggregations of matter. The spacing of the particle-intervals of matter, together with the initial velocity of the energy beams, establishes the undulatory appearance of many forms of energy-matter.

   "The excitation of the content of space produces a wavelike reaction to the passage of rapidly moving particles of matter, just as the passage of a ship through water initiates waves of varying amplitude and interval." P. 475-6.

3. **Space is not empty—it is an ocean of outspread force-energy.**

   "Primordial-force behavior does give rise to phenomena which are in many ways analogous to your postulated ether. Space is not empty; the spheres of all space whirl and plunge on through a vast ocean of outspread force-energy; neither is the space content of an atom empty. Nevertheless there is no ether, and the very absence of this hypothetical ether enables the inhabited planet to escape falling into the sun and the encircling electron to resist falling into the nucleus." P. 476.

F. **Energy control and regulation.**

1. **Superuniverse headquarters spheres—the energy regulators and directionizers of energy to the local universes.**

   "The headquarters spheres of the superuniverses are so constructed that they are able to function as efficient power-energy regulators for their various sectors, serving as focal points for the directionization of energy to their component local universes. They exert a powerful influence over the balance and control of the physical energies circulating through organized space." P. 175.

Part III — *Physics and Chemistry*

2. **Additional regulative functions as performed by the superuniverse power centers and physical controllers.**
"Further regulative functions are performed by the superuniverse power centers and physical controllers, living and semiliving intelligent entities constituted for this express purpose. These power centers and controllers are difficult of understanding; the lower orders are not volitional, they do not possess will, they do not choose, their functions are very intelligent but apparently automatic and inherent in their highly specialized organization. The power centers and physical controllers of the superuniverses assume direction and partial control of the thirty energy systems which comprise the gravita domain. The physical-energy circuits administered by the power centers of Uversa require a little over 968 million years to complete the encirclement of the superuniverse." P. 175.

3. **Laws governing the relations of mass and energy.**
"Evolving energy has substance; it has weight, although weight is always relative, depending on revolutionary velocity, mass, and antigravity. Mass in matter tends to retard velocity in energy; and the anywhere-present velocity of energy represents: the initial endowment of velocity, minus retardation by mass encountered in transit, plus the regulatory function of the living energy controllers of the superuniverse and the physical influence of nearby highly heated or heavily charged bodies." P. 175.

4. **Plan for maintenance of equilibrium between matter and energy.**
"The universal plan for the maintenance of equilibrium between matter and energy necessitates the everlasting making and unmaking of the lesser material units. The Universe Power Directors have the ability to condense and detain, or to expand and liberate, varying quantities of energy." P. 175.

5. **Factors which prevent gravity from converting all energy into matter.**
"Given a sufficient duration of retarding influence, gravity would eventually convert all energy into matter were it not for two factors: First, because of the antigravity influences of the energy controllers, and second, because organized matter tends to disintegrate under certain conditions found in very hot

stars and under certain peculiar conditions in space near highly energized cold bodies of condensed matter." P. 175.

6. **The never-ending struggle between energy and matter and the many influences contributing to the maintenance of balance.**

   "When mass becomes over aggregated and threatens to unbalance energy, to deplete the physical power circuits, the physical controllers intervene unless gravity's own further tendency to over materialize energy is defeated by the occurrence of a collision among the dead giants of space, thus in an instant completely dissipating the cumulative collections of gravity. In these collisional episodes enormous masses of matter are suddenly converted into the rarest form of energy, and the struggle for universal equilibirum is begun anew. Eventually the larger physical systems become stabilized, become physically settled, and are swung into the balanced and established circuits of the superuniverses. Subsequent to this event no more collisions or other devastating catastrophes will occur in such established systems." P. 176.

7. **The continuing struggle between plus energy and minus energy states.**

   "During the times of plus energy there are power disturbances and heat fluctuations accompanied by electrical manifestations. During times of minus energy there are increased tendencies for matter to aggregate, condense, and to get out of control in the more delicately balanced circuits, with resultant tidal or collisional adjustments which quickly restore the balance between circulating energy and more literally stabilized matter. To forecast and otherwise to understand such likely behavior of the blazing suns and the dark islands of space is one of the tasks of the celestial star observers." P. 176.

8. **Difficulties encountered in proceeding outward from Paradise in predicting all physical phenomena because of the unfathomable effect of the Absolutes and the experiential Deities.**

   "We are able to recognize most of the laws governing universe equilibrium and to predict much pertaining to universe stability. Practically, our forecasts are reliable, but we are always confronted by certain forces which are not wholly amenable to the laws of energy control and matter behavior known to us. The predictability of all physical phenomena becomes increasingly difficult as we proceed outward in the universes from Paradise. As we pass beyond the borders of the personal administration of the Paradise Rulers, we are confronted with increasing inability to reckon in accordance with the standards established and the experience acquired in connection with observations having exclusively to do with the physical phenomena of the near-by astronomic systems. Even in the realms of the seven superuniverses we are living in the midst of force actions and energy reactions which pervade all our domains and extend in unified equilibrium on through all regions of outer space.

"The farther out we go, the more certainly we encounter those variational and unpredictable phenomena which are so unerringly characteristic of the unfathomable presence-performances of the Absolutes and the experiential Deities. And these phenomena must be indicative of some universal overcontrol of all things." P. 176.

9. **Power directors and force organizers—the secret of control and direction, preventing universes from running down.**

"The superuniverse of Orvonton is apparently now running down; the outer universes seem to be winding up for unparalleled future activities; the central Havona universe is eternally stabilized. Gravity and absence of heat (cold) organize and hold matter together; heat and antigravity disrupt matter and dissipate energy. The living power directors and force organizers are the secret of the special control and intelligent direction of the endless metamorphoses of universe making, unmaking, and remaking. Nebulae may disperse, suns burn out, systems vanish, and planets perish, but the universes do not run down." P. 176.

II. Suns

A. Solar radiation.

1. The ease with which light escapes from a sun indicates lack of density. Opacity would retain light and result in explosions. "That the suns of space are not very dense is proved by the steady streams of escaping light-energies. Too great a density would retain light by opacity until the light-energy pressure reached the explosion point. There is a tremendous light or gas pressure within a sun to cause it to shoot forth such a stream of energy as to penetrate space for millions upon millions of miles to energize, light, and heat the distant planets. Fifteen feet of surface of the density of Urantia would effectually prevent the escape of

all X rays and light-energies from a sun until the rising internal pressure of accumulating energies resulting from atomic dismemberment overcame gravity with a tremendous outward explosion." P. 460.

2. **Light is explosive at high temperatures and under pressure. Sunlight would be economical at a million dollars a pound.**

   "Light, in the presence of the propulsive gases, is highly explosive when confined at high temperatures by opaque retaining walls. Light is real. As you value energy and power on your world, sunlight would be economical at a million dollars a pound.

   "The interior of your sun is a vast X-ray generator. The suns are supported from within by the incessant bombardment of these mighty emanations." P. 460.

3. **It requires half a million years for an electron to escape from the center of a sun to enter upon its varied adventures in space.**

   "It requires more than one-half million years for an X-ray-stimulated electron to work its way from the very center of an average sun up to the solar surface, whence it starts out on its space adventure, maybe to warm an inhabited planet, to be captured by a meteor, to participate in the birth of an atom, to be attracted by a highly charged dark island of space, or to find its space flight terminated by a final plunge into the surface of a sun similar to the one of its origin." P. 460.

4. **The energy required for an electron to escape from a sun is sufficient to carry it through vast distances of space.**

   "The X rays of a sun's interior charge the highly heated and agitated electrons with sufficient energy to carry them out through space, past the hosts of detaining influences of intervening matter and, in spite of divergent gravity attractions, on to the distant spheres of the remote systems. The great energy of velocity required to escape the gravity clutch of a sun is sufficient to insure that the sunbeam will travel on with unabated velocity until it encounters considerable masses of matter; whereupon it is quickly transformed into heat with the liberation of other energies." P. 461.

5. **Energy moves through space in a straight line except as modified by gravity and other influences.**

   "Energy, whether as light or in other forms, in its flight through space moves straight forward. The actual particles of material

PART III — *Physics and Chemistry*

existence traverse space like a fusillade. They go in a straight and unbroken line or procession except as they are acted on by superior forces, and except as they ever obey the linear-gravity pull inherent in material mass and the circular-gravity presence of the Isle of Paradise." P. 461.

6. **The wave behavior is due to the action of diverse coexistent influences.**

    "Solar energy may seem to be propelled in waves, but that is due to the action of coexistent and diverse influences. A given form of organized energy does not proceed in waves but in direct lines. The presence of a second or a third form of force-energy may cause the stream under observation to appear to travel in wavy formation, just as, in a blinding rainstorm accompanied by a heavy wind, the water sometimes appears to fall in sheets or to descend in waves. The raindrops are coming down in a direct line of unbroken procession, but the action of the wind is such as to give the visible appearance of sheets of water and waves of raindrops." P. 461.

7. **Wave behavior of light and its division into definite particles results from the action of many influences, some known, others unknown.**

    "The action of certain secondary and other undiscovered energies present in the space regions of your local universe is such that solar-light emanations appear to execute certain wavy phenomena as well as to be chopped up into infinitesimal portions of definite length and weight. And, practically considered, that is exactly what happens. You can hardly hope to arrive at a better understanding of the behavior of light until such time as you acquire a clearer concept of the interaction and interrelationship of the various space-forces and solar energies operating in the space regions of Nebadon. Your present confusion is also due to your incomplete grasp of this problem as it involves the interassociated activities of the personal and nonpersonal control of the master universe—the presences, the performances, and the co-ordination of the Conjoint Actor and the Unqualified Absolute." P. 461.

8. **Spectral analyses show only sun-surface compositions.**

    "It should be remembered that spectral analyses show only sun-surface compositions. For example: Solar spectra exhibit many iron lines, but iron is not the chief element in the sun. This phenomenon is almost wholly due to the present temperature of the sun's surface, a little less than 6,000 degrees, this temperature being very favorable to the registry of the iron spectrum." P. 462.

B. **Sources of solar energy.**

1. **There are seven sources of the enormous expenditure of solar energies.**

   "All of these phenomena are indicative of enormous energy expenditure, and the sources of solar energy, named in the order of their importance, are:

   "1. Annihilation of atoms and, eventually, of electrons.

   "2. Transmutation of elements, including the radioactive group of energies thus liberated.

   "3. The accumulation and transmission of certain universal space-energies.

   "4. Space matter and meteors which are incessantly diving into the blazing suns.

   "5. Solar contraction; the cooling and consequent contraction of a sun yields energy and heat sometimes greater than that supplied by space matter.

   "6. Gravity action at high temperatures transforms certain circuitized power into radiative energies.

   "7. Receptive light and other matter which are drawn back into the sun after having left it, together with other energies having extrasolar origin." P. 463.

2. **Suns have a regulating gas blanket which stabilizes heat loss. The internal temperature remains at 35,000,000 degrees.**

   "There exists a regulating blanket of hot gases (sometimes millions of degrees in temperature) which envelops the suns, and which acts to stabilize heat loss and otherwise prevent hazardous fluctuations of heat dissipation. During the active life of a sun the internal temperature of 35,000,000 degrees remains about the same quite regardless of the progressive fall of the external temperature." P. 463.

3. **Thirty-five million degrees is the electronic boiling point. While atoms are shattered, ultimatons are not broken up.**

   "You might try to visualize 35,000,000 degrees of heat, in association with certain gravity pressures, as the electronic boiling point. Under such pressure and at such temperature all atoms are degraded and broken up into their electronic and other ancestral components; even the electrons and other associations of ultimatons may be broken up, but the suns are not able to degrade the ultimatons." P. 463.

PART III — *Physics and Chemistry*

C. **Solar energies.**
1. **The largest amount of solar energy is derived from the hydrogen-carbon-helium reaction.**
   "In those suns which are encircuited in the space-energy channels, solar energy is liberated by various complex nuclear-reaction chains, the most common of which is the hydrogen-carbon-helium reaction. In this metamorphosis, carbon acts as an energy catalyst since it is in no way actually changed by this process of converting hydrogen into helium. Under certain conditions of high temperature the hydrogen penetrates the carbon nuclei. Since the carbon cannot hold more than four such protons, when this saturation state is attained, it begins to emit protons as fast as new ones arrive. In this reaction the ingoing hydrogen particles come forth as a helium atom." P. 464.
2. **Exhaustion of hydrogen results in producing a highly condensed white dwarf star.**
   "Reduction of hydrogen content increases the luminosity of a sun. In the suns destined to burn out, the height of luminosity is attained at the point of hydrogen exhaustion. Subsequent to this point, brilliance is maintained by the resultant process of gravity contraction. Eventually, such a star will become a so-called white dwarf, a highly condensed sphere." P. 464.
3. **Conditions which lead to the sudden collapse of a giant nova.**
   "In large suns—small circular nebulae—when hydrogen is exhausted and gravity contraction ensues, if such a body is not sufficiently opaque to retain the internal pressure of support for the outer gas regions, then a sudden collapse occurs. The gravity-electric changes give origin to vast quantities of tiny particles devoid of electric potential, and such particles readily escape from the solar interior, thus bringing about the collapse of a gigantic sun within a few days. It was such an emigration of these 'runaway particles' that occasioned the collapse of the giant nova of the Andromeda nebula about fifty years ago. This vast stellar body collapsed in forty minutes of Urantia time." P. 464.
4. **Conditions leading to stabilization of solar behavior. Our sun radiates one hundred billion tons of matter annually.**
   "Your own solar center radiates almost one hundred billion tons of actual matter annually, while the giant suns lose matter

at a prodigious rate during their earlier growth, the first billion years. A sun's life becomes stable after the maximum of internal temperature is reached, and the subatomic energies begin to be released. And it is just at this critical point that the larger suns are given to convulsive pulsations." P. 465.

6. **Our sun is now functioning through a period of great economy—will so continue for twenty-five billion years.**

"Your own sun has long since attained relative equilibrium between its expansion and contraction cycles, those disturbances which produce the gigantic pulsations of many of the younger stars. Your sun is now passing out of its six billionth year. At the present time it is functioning through the period of greatest economy. It will shine on as of present efficiency for more than twenty-five billion years. It will probably experience a partially efficient period of decline as long as the combined periods of its youth and stabilized function." P. 465.

Part III — *Physics and Chemistry*

Section Three
PHYSICAL-ENERGY CONTROLLERS AND REGULATORS

Little has been known of power directors, and their associates, but three groups are revealed.

"Of all the universe personalities concerned in the regulation of interplanetary and interuniverse affairs, the power directors and their associates have been the least understood on Urantia. While your races have long known of the existence of angels and similar orders of celestial beings, little information concerning the controllers and regulators of the physical domain has ever been imparted. Even now I am permitted fully to disclose only the last of the following three groups of living beings having to do with force control and energy regulation in the master universe:

"1. Primary Eventuated Master Force Organizers.

"2. Associate Transcendental Master Force Organizers.

"3. Universe Power Directors." P. 319.

I. Eventuated Transcendental Beings

A. Force organizers.

1. **Preuniverse manipulation of space-force is the work of Paradise Master Force Organizers.**
   "The preuniverse manipulations of space-force and the primordial energies are the work of the Paradise Master Force Organizers; but in the superuniverse domains, when emergent energy becomes responsive to local or linear gravity, they retire in favor of the power directors of the superuniverse concerned." P. 357.

2. **Master Force Organizers mobilize the space energies which are later organized into inhabited universes.**
   "The Master Force Organizers go out into space and mobilize its energies to become gravity responsive to the Paradise pull of the Universal Father; and subsequently there come the Creator Sons, who organize these gravity-responding forces into inhabited universes and therein evolve intelligent creatures who receive unto themselves the spirit of the Paradise Father and subsequently ascend to the Father to become like him in all possible divinity attributes." P. 645.

3. **There is an unending expansion of Paradise creative forces throughout all space attended by the multiplication of varied intelligent beings.**

"The ceaseless and expanding march of the Paradise creative forces through space seems to presage the ever-extending domain of the gravity grasp of the Universal Father and the never-ending multiplication of varied types of intelligent creatures who are able to love God and be loved by him, and who, by thus becoming God-knowing, may choose to be like him, may elect to attain Paradise and find God." P. 645.

4. **The two divisions of Paradise force organizers work under the supervision of the Architects of the Master Universe.**

    "The force organizers are resident on Paradise, but they function throughout the master universe, more particularly in the domains of unorganized space. These extraordinary beings are neither creators nor creatures, and they comprise two grand divisions of service:

    "1. Primary Eventuated Master Force Organizers.

    "2. Associate Transcendental Master Force Organizers.

    "These two mighty orders of primordial-force manipulators work exclusively under the supervision of the Architects of the Master Universe, and at the present time they do not function extensively within the boundaries of the grand universe." P. 329.

5. **Primary Master Force Organizers manipulate primordial space-force; they are nebulae creators. They transfer energy from the exclusive grasp of the Unqualified Absolute to the grasp of Paradise gravity.**

    "Primary Master Force Organizers are the manipulators of the primordial or basic space-forces of the Unqualified Absolute; they are nebulae creators. They are the living instigators of the energy cyclones of space and the early organizers and directionizers of these gigantic manifestations. These force organizers transmute *primordial force* (pre-energy not responsive to direct Paradise gravity) into primary or *puissant energy*, energy transmuting from the exclusive grasp of the Unqualified Absolute to the gravity grasp of the Isle of Paradise. They are thereupon succeeded by the associate force organizers, who continue the process of energy transmutation from the primary through the secondary or *gravity-energy* stage." P. 329.

II. Universe Power Directors

A. Classification and general description.

Part III — *Physics and Chemistry*

1. **Power directors function in four grand divisions.**
   "Though I deem it impossible to portray the individuality of the various groups of directors, centers, and controllers of universe power, I hope to be able to explain something about the domain of their activities. They are a unique group of living beings having to do with the intelligent regulation of energy throughout the grand universe. Including the supreme directors, they embrace the following major divisions:
   "1. The Seven Supreme Power Directors.
   "2. The Supreme Power Centers.
   "3. The Master Physical Controllers.
   "4. The Morontia Power Supervisors." P. 319.

2. **The Universe Power Directors direct the modified energies of nether Paradise into constructive channels.**
   "All energy is circuited in the Paradise cycle, but the Universe Power Directors *direct* the force-energies of nether Paradise as they find them modified in the space functions of the central and superuniverses, converting and directing these energies into channels of useful and constructive application. There is a difference between Havona energy and the energies of the superuniverses." P. 321.

3. **The power charge of a superuniverse consists of three phases of ten segregations each.**
   "The power charge of a superuniverse consists of three phases of energy of ten segregations each. This threefold energy charge spreads throughout the space of the grand universe; it is like a vast moving ocean of energy which engulfs and bathes the whole of each of the seven supercreations." P. 321.

4. **Function of power directors during early phases of universe organization.**
   "These power directors function alone in the prematerial and post-force phases of a local universe creation. There is no opportunity for a Creator Son to begin universe organization until the power directors have effected the mobilization of the space-energies sufficiently to provide a material foundation—literal suns and material spheres—for the emerging universe." P. 357.

5. **The power directors function somewhat as catalyzers—their work is something of a mystery.**
   "These power directors themselves are energy catalyzers; that is, they cause energy to segment, organize, or assemble in unit

formation by their presence. And all this implies that there must be something inherent in energy which causes it thus to function in the presence of these power entities. The Nebadon Melchizedeks long since denominated the phenomenon of the transmutation of cosmic force into universe power as one of the seven 'infinities of divinity.' And that is as far as you will advance on this point during your local universe ascension." P. 471.

B. The Seven Supreme Power Directors.

1. **Origin and function of Supreme Power Directors and their associates.**
   "The Supreme Power Directors and Centers have existed from the near times of eternity, and as far as we know, no more beings of these orders have been created. The Seven Supreme Directors were personalized by the Seven Master Spirits, and then they collaborated with their parents in the production of more than ten billion associates. Before the days of the power directors the energy circuits of space outside of the central universe were under the intelligent supervision of the Master Force Organizers of Paradise." P. 319.

2. **Origin, nature, and function of the Seven Supreme Power Directors.**
   "The Seven Supreme Power Directors are the physical-energy regulators of the grand universe. Their creation by the Seven Master Spirits is the first recorded instance of the derivation of semimaterial progeny from true spirit ancestry. When the Seven Master Spirits create individually, they bring forth highly spiritual personalities on the angelic order; when they create collectively, they sometimes produce these high types of semimaterial beings. But even these quasi-physical beings would be invisible to the short-range vision of Urantia mortals." P. 320.

3. **The Seven Supreme Power Directors, stationed on peripheral Paradise, regulate the power-energy of a superuniverse.**
   "The Seven Supreme Power Directors are stationed on peripheral Paradise, where their slowly circulating presences indicate the whereabouts of the force-focal headquarters of the Master Spirits. These power directors function singly in the power-energy regulation of the superuniverses but collectively in the administration of the central creation. They operate from Paradise but maintain themselves as effective power centers in all divisions of the grand universe." P. 320.

PART III — *Physics and Chemistry*

4. **The Supreme Power Directors are the ancestors of power centers and physical controllers.**
   "These mighty beings are the physical ancestors of the vast host of the power centers and, through them, of the physical controllers scattered throughout the seven superuniverses. Such subordinate physical-control organisms are basically uniform, identical except for the differential toning of each superuniverse corps. In order to change in superuniverse service, they would merely have to return to Paradise for retoning. The physical creation is fundamentally uniform in administration." P. 320.

C. **The Supreme Power Centers.**
   1. **Nature, origin, and function of the Seven Supreme Power Centers.**
      "The Seven Supreme Power Directors are not able individually, to reproduce themselves, but collectively, and in association with the Seven Master Spirits, they can and do reproduce—create—other beings like themselves. Such is the origin of the Supreme Power Centers of the grand universe, who function in the following seven groups:
      "1. Supreme Center Supervisors.
      "2. Havona Centers.
      "3. Superuniverse Centers.
      "4. Local Universe Centers.
      "5. Constellation Centers.
      "6. System Centers.
      "7. Unclassified Centers." P. 320.
   2. **Power centers utilize material mechanisms in addition to their one million units of truly kaleidoscopic associative possibilities.**
      "The power centers utilize vast mechanisms and co-ordinations of a material order in liaison with the living mechanisms of the various segregated energy concentrations. Each individual power center is constituted in exactly one million units of functional control, and these energy-modifying units are not stationary as are the vital organs of man's physical body; these 'vital organs' of power regulation are mobile and truly kaleidoscopic in associative possibilities." P. 323.
   3. **Power centers work with the physical energies of organized space, not with the forces in outer space.**

"The power centers and their subordinate controllers are assigned to the working of all of the physical energies of organized space. They work with the three basic currents of ten energies each. That is the energy charge of organized space; and organized space is their domain. The Universe Power Directors have nothing whatever to do with those tremendous actions of force which are now taking place outside the present boundaries of the seven superuniverses." P. 323-4.

4. **Power centers and controllers exert perfect control over seven of the ten forms of basic universe energy.**

"The power centers and controllers exert perfect control over only seven of the ten forms of energy contained in each basic universe current; those forms which are partly or wholly exempt from their control must represent the unpredictable realms of energy manifestation dominated by the Unqualified Absolute. If they exert an influence upon the primordial forces of this Absolute, we are not cognizant of such functions, though there is some slight evidence which would warrant the opinion that certain of the physical controllers are sometimes automatically reactive to certain impulses of the Universal Absolute.

"These living power mechanisms are not consciously related to the master universe energy overcontrol of the Unqualified Absolute, but we surmise that their entire and almost perfect scheme of power direction is in some unknown manner subordinated to this supergravity presence. In any local energy situation the centers and controllers exert near-supremacy, but they are always conscious of the superenergy presence and the unrecognizable performance of the Unqualified Absolute." P. 324.

5. **The electronic forces of a superuniverse function in seven phases with varying response to linear gravity.**

"The electronic organization of universe power functions in seven phases and discloses varying response to local or linear gravity. This sevenfold circuit proceeds from the superuniverse power centers and pervades each supercreation. Such specialized currents of time and space are definite and localized energy movements initiated and directed for specific purposes, much as the Gulf Stream functions as a circumscribed phenomenon in the midst of the Atlantic Ocean." P. 321.

PART III — *Physics and Chemistry*

6. **One hundred Supreme Power Centers regulate the energy systems of a local universe. They are not concerned with local energy upheavals—such as sun spots.**
   "One hundred Supreme Power Centers of the fourth order are permanently assigned to our local universe. These beings receive the incoming lines of power from the third-order centers of Uversa and relay the down-stepped and modified circuits to the power centers of our constellations and systems. These power centers, in association, function to produce the living system of control and equalization which operates to maintain the balance and distribution of otherwise fluctuating and variable energies. Power centers are not, however, concerned with transient and local energy upheavals, such as sun spots and system electric disturbances; light and electricity are not the basic energies of space; they are secondary and subsidiary manifestations." P. 456.

7. **One Supreme Power Center functions on a dark island of space at the astronomic center of the system of Satania.**
   "One Supreme Power Center of the sixth order is stationed at the exact gravity focus of each local system. In the system of Satania the assigned power center occupies a dark island of space located at the astronomic center of the system. Many of these dark islands are vast dynamos which mobilize and directionize certain space-energies, and these natural circumstances are effectively utilized by the Satania Power Center, whose living mass functions as a liaison with the higher centers, directing the streams of more materialized power to the Master Physical Controllers on the evolutionary planets of space." P. 456.

8. **Power centers and physical controllers never play. They are thoroughly businesslike in all their reactions.**
   "Having no ascendant past to revert to in memory, power centers and physical controllers never play; they are thoroughly businesslike in all their actions. They are always on duty; there is no provision in the universal scheme for the interruption of the physical lines of energy; never for a fraction of a second can these beings relinquish their direct supervision of the energy circuits of time and space." P. 323.

D. **Master Physical Controllers.**

   1. **These mobile subordinates of the Supreme Power Centers are capable of individual metamorphosis that permits them to travel at unusual velocities.**

"These beings are the mobile subordinates of the Supreme Power Centers. The physical controllers are endowed with capabilities of individuality metamorphosis of such a nature that they can engage in a remarkable variety of autotransport, being able to traverse local space at velocities approaching the flight of Solitary Messengers. But like all other space traversers they require the assistance of both their fellows and certain other types of beings in overcoming the action of gravity and the resistance of inertia in departing from a material sphere." P. 324.

2. **There are seven groups of the Master Physical Controllers.**
"The Master Physical Controllers are the direct offspring of the Supreme Power Centers, and their numbers include the following:
"1. Associate Power Directors.
"2. Mechanical Controllers.
"3. Energy Transformers.
"4. Energy Transmitters.
"5. Primary Associators.
"6. Secondary Dissociators.
"7. The Frandalanks and Chronoldeks." P. 324-5.

3. **Physical controllers are largely occupied with the adjustment of energies unknown on Urantia.**
"The physical controllers are chiefly occupied in the adjustment of basic energies undiscovered on Urantia. These unknown energies are very essential to the interplanetary system of transport and to certain techniques of communication. When we lay lines of energy for the purpose of conveying sound equivalents or of extending vision, these undiscovered forms of energy are utilized by the living physical controllers and their associates. These same energies are also, on occasion, used by the midway creatures in their routine work." P. 325.

4. **Problems in controlling the Urantia energy circuits.**
"Urantia is in the lines of tremendous energies, a small planet in the circuit of enormous masses, and the local controllers sometimes employ enormous numbers of their order in an effort to equalize these lines of energy. They do fairly well with regard to the physical circuits of Satania but have trouble insulating against the powerful Norlatiadek currents." P. 458.

5. **Associate Power Directors assign and dispatch all orders of the Master Physical Controllers.**

Part III — *Physics and Chemistry*

"*Associate Power Directors.* These marvelously efficient beings are intrusted with the assignment and dispatch of all orders of the Master Physical Controllers in accordance with the ever-shifting needs of the constantly changing energy status of the realms. The vast reserves of the physical controllers are maintained on the headquarters worlds of the minor sectors, and from these concentration points they are periodically dispatched by the associate power directors to the headquarters of the universes, constellations, and systems, and to the individual planets. When thus assigned, the physical controllers are provisionally subject to the orders of the divine executioners of the conciliating commissions but are otherwise solely amenable to their associate directors and to the Supreme Power Centers." P. 325.

6. **Function of the mechanical controllers in the regulation of interplanetary energy circuits.**

 "The mechanical controllers are competent to directionize the flow of energy and to facilitate its concentration into the specialized currents or circuits. These mighty beings have much to do with the segregation, directionization, and intensification of the physical energies and with the equalization of the pressures of the interplanetary circuits. They are expert in the manipulation of twenty-one of the thirty physical energies of space, constituting the power charge of a superuniverse. They are also able to accomplish much towards the management and control of six of the nine more subtle forms of physical energy. By placing these controllers in proper technical relationship to each other and to certain of the power centers, the associate power directors are enabled to effect unbelievable changes in power adjustment and energy control." P. 326.

7. **Nature, origin, and function of the versatile energy transformers.**

 "*Energy Transformers.* The number of these beings in a superuniverse is unbelievable. There are almost one million in Satania alone, and the usual quota is one hundred for each inhabited world.

 "The energy transformers are the conjoint creation of the Seven Supreme Power Directors and the Seven Central Supervisors. They are among the more personal orders of physical controllers, and except when an associate power director is present on an inhabited world, the transformers are in command. They are the planetary inspectors of all departing seraphic transports. All classes of celestial life can utilize the less personal orders of the physical controllers only by liaison with the more personal orders of the associate directors and the energy transformers." P. 326.

8. **Function of energy transformers in storing and liberating energy, thus maintaining universal energy balance and power equilibrium.**

"These transformers are powerful and effective living switches, being able to dispose themselves for or against a given power disposition or directionization. They are also skillful in their efforts to insulate the planets against the powerful energy streams passing between gigantic planetary and starry neighbors. Their energy-transmutive attributes render them most serviceable in the important task of maintaining universal energy balance, or power equilibrium. At one time they seem to consume or store energy; at other times they appear to exude or liberate energy. The transformers are able to increase or to diminish the 'storage-battery' potential of the living and dead energies of their respective realms. But they deal only with physical and semimaterial energies, they do not directly function in the domain of life, neither do they change the forms of living beings." P. 326.

9. **The transformers, possibly the most remarkable and mysterious of semimaterial creatures, can and do change the physical form of the energies of space.**

"In some respects the energy transformers are the most remarkable and mysterious of all semimaterial living creatures. They are in some unknown manner physically differentiated, and by varying their liaison relationships, they are able to exert a profound influence upon the energy which passes through their associated presences. The status of the physical realms seems to undergo a transformation under their skillful manipulation. *They can and do change the physical form of the energies of space.* With the aid of their fellow controllers they are actually able to change the form and potential of twenty-seven of the thirty physical energies of the superuniverse power charge. That three of these energies are beyond their control proves that they are not instrumentalities of the Unqualified Absolute." P. 327.

PART III — *Physics and Chemistry*

10. **Function of energy transmitters.**
    These beings dispatch energy to inhabited worlds. They are living superconductors for more than half of the thirty forms of physical energy.
    "Energy transmitters can function with regard to all forms of communicable perception; they can render a distant scene 'visible' as well as a distant sound 'audible.' They provide the emergency lines of communication in the local systems and on the individual planets. These services must be used by practically all creatures for purposes of communication outside of the regularly established circuits." P. 327.

11. **Primary associators are energy custodians—they store energy. They hold it in a state unknown on Urantia.**
    "*Primary Associators.* These interesting and invaluable entities are masterly energy conservators and custodians. Somewhat as a plant stores solar light, so do these living organisms store energy during times of plus manifestations. They work on a gigantic scale, converting the energies of space into a physical state not known on Urantia. They are also able to carry forward these transformations to the point of producing some of the primitive units of material existence. These beings simply act by their presence. They are in no way exhausted or depleted by this function; they act like living catalytic agents." P. 328.

12. **The associators manipulate all forms of energy and release energy in times of need.**
    "During seasons of minus manifestations they are empowered to release these accumulated energies. But your knowledge of energy and matter is not sufficiently advanced to make it possible to explain the technique of this phase of their work. They always labor in compliance with universal law, handling and manipulating atoms, electrons, and ultimatons much as you maneuver adjustable type to make the same alphabetical symbols tell vastly different stories." P. 328.

13. **The secondary dissociators have enormous antigravity powers and can thus turn matter into energy.**
    "*Secondary Dissociators.* Compared with the primary associators, these beings of enormous antigravity endowment are the reverse workers. There is never any danger that the special or modified forms of physical energy on the local worlds or in the local systems will be exhausted, for these living organizations are endowed with the unique power of evolving limitless supplies of

energy. They are chiefly concerned with the evolution of a form of energy which is hardly known on Urantia from a form of matter which is recognized still less. They are truly the alchemists of space and the wonder-workers of time. But in all the wonders they work, they never transgress the mandates of Cosmic Supremacy." P. 328.

14. **Frandalanks and chronoldeks function as living gauges.**
   "*The Frandalanks.* These beings are the joint creation of all three orders of energy-control beings: the primary and secondary force organizers and the power directors. Frandalanks are the most numerous of all the Master Physical Controllers; the number functioning in Satania alone is beyond your numerical concept. They are stationed on all inhabited worlds and are always attached to the higher orders of physical controllers. They function interchangeably in the central and superuniverses and in the domains of outer space.
   "The frandalanks are created in thirty divisions, one for each form of basic universe force, and they function exclusively as living and automatic presence, pressure, and velocity gauges. These living barometers are solely concerned with the automatic and unerring registration of the status of all forms of force-energy. They are to the physical universe what the vast reflectivity mechanism is to the minded universe. The frandalanks that register time in addition to quantitative and qualitative energy presence are called *chronoldeks*." P. 328.

E. **Morontia Power Supervisors.**

1. **Function of Morontia Power Supervisors.**
   "These unique beings are exclusively concerned with the supervision of those activities which represent a working combination of spiritual and physical or semimaterial energies. They are exclusively devoted to the ministry of morontia progression. Not that they so much minister to mortals during the transition experience, but they rather make possible the transition environment for the progressing morontia creatures. They are the channels of morontia power which sustain and energize the morontia phases of the transition worlds." P. 542.

2. **Morontia Power Supervisors can unite material and spiritual energies. They provide morontians with 570 morontia forms:**
   - 8   *in the local system.*
   - 71 *in the constellation.*
   - 491 *on the Salvington spheres.*

PART III — *Physics and Chemistry*

"The Morontia Power Supervisors are able to effect a union of material and of spiritual energies, thereby organizing a morontia form of materialization which is receptive to the superimposition of a controlling spirit. When you traverse the morontia life of Nebadon, these same patient and skillful Morontia Power Supervisors will successively provide you with 570 morontia bodies, each one a phase of your progressive transformation. From the time of leaving the material worlds until you are constituted a first-stage spirit on Salvington, you will undergo just 570 separate and ascending morontia changes. Eight of these occur in the system, seventy-one in the constellation, and 491 during the sojourn on the spheres of Salvington." P. 542.

3. **Summary of the types and functions of Morontia Power Supervisors.**

   These beings are the offspring of the local universe Mother Spirit.

   a. *Circuit regulators transform physical and spiritual energies into materials that are woven into the bodies and life activities of ascending mortals.*

   b. *System co-ordinators effect the necessary changes in morontia bodies when ascenders advance from one morontia sphere to another.*

   c. *Planetary custodians grant material for and authorize changes in morontia form as ascenders proceed to succeeding spheres.*

   d. *Combined controllers deal with physical, spiritual, and morontia energies.*

   e. *Liaison stabilizers make possible the conversion of morontia energy into morontia material.*

   f. *Selective assorters re-key ascenders to keep them in progressive synchrony with the morontia life.*

   g. *Associate registrars keep records on morontia worlds. (P. 542, 543, 544, 545)*

F. **Physical-energy manipulators.**

1. **Physical-energy manipulators are recruited or volunteer celestial artisans who are concerned with physical energy.**

   "The physical-energy manipulators serve for long periods with the power directors and are experts in the manipulation and control of many phases of physical energy. They are conversant with the three basic currents and the thirty subsidiary energy segregations of the superuniverses. These beings are of inestimable assistance to the Morontia Power Supervisors of the transition worlds. They are the persistent students of the cosmic projections of Paradise." P. 504.

Part III — *Physics and Chemistry*

Section Four
CHEMICAL PHENOMENA

I. Matter

"Matter in all universes, excepting in the central universe, is identical. Matter in its physical properties depends on the revolutionary rates of its component members, the number and size of the revolving members, their distance from the nuclear body or the space content of matter, as well as on the presence of certain forces as yet undiscovered on Urantia." P. 471.

A. General classification.

1. **The ten grand divisions of matter.**
   "In the varied suns, planets, and space bodies there are ten grand divisions of matter:
   "1. Ultimatonic matter—the prime physical units of material existence, the energy particles which go to make up electrons.
   "2. Subelectronic matter—the explosive and repellent stage of the solar supergases.
   "3. Electronic matter—the electrical stage of material differentiation—electrons, protons, and various other units entering into the varied constitution of the electronic groups.
   "4. Subatomic matter—matter existing extensively in the interior of the hot suns.
   "5. Shattered atoms—found in the cooling suns and throughout space.
   "6. Ionized matter—individual atoms stripped of their outer (chemically active) electrons by electrical, thermal, or X-ray activities and by solvents.
   "7. Atomic matter—the chemical stage of elemental organization, the component units of molecular or visible matter.
   "8. The molecular stage of matter—matter as it exists on Urantia in a state of relatively stable materialization under ordinary conditions.
   "9. Radioactive matter—the disorganizing tendency and activity of the heavier elements under conditions of moderate heat and diminished gravity pressure.
   "10. Collapsed matter—the relatively stationary matter found in the interior of the cold or dead suns. This form of matter is not really stationary; there is still some ultimatonic even electronic activity, but these units are in

very close proximity, and their rates of revolution are greatly diminished.

"The foregoing classification of matter pertains to its organization rather than to the forms of its appearance to created beings. Neither does it take into account the pre-emergent stages of energy nor the eternal materializations on Paradise and in the central universe." P. 471-2.

B. **Ultimatons, electrons, and atoms.**

1. **The space charge is homogeneous and undifferentiated, but matter consists of particles of definite weight.**

   "While the space charge of universal force is homogeneous and undifferentiated, the organization of evolved energy into matter entails the concentration of energy into discrete masses of definite dimensions and established weight—precise gravity reaction." P. 476.

2. **Local or linear gravity becomes operative on the atomic form of matter.**

   "Local or linear gravity becomes fully operative with the appearance of the atomic organization of matter. Preatomic matter becomes slightly gravity responsive when activated by X ray and other similar energies, but no measurable linear-gravity pull is exerted on free, unattached, and uncharged electronic-energy particles or on unassociated ultimatons." P. 476.

3. **Ultimatons respond only to Paradise gravity. Without assistance they cannot return to puissant energy, except in terminal sun disruptions.**

   "Ultimatons function by mutual attraction, responding only to the circular Paradise-gravity pull. Without linear-gravity response they are thus held in the universal space drift. Ultimatons are capable of accelerating revolutionary velocity to the point of partial antigravity behavior, but they cannot, independent of force organizers or power directors, attain the critical escape velocity of deindividuation, return to the puissant-energy stage. In nature, ultimatons escape the status of physical existence only when participating in the terminal disruption of a cooled-off and dying sun." P. 476.

4. **The varieties of motion of ultimatons.**

   "The ultimatons, unknown on Urantia, slow down through many phases of physical activity before they attain the revolutionary-energy prerequisites to electronic organization.

PART III — *Physics and Chemistry*

Ultimatons have three varieties of motion: mutual resistance to cosmic force, individual revolutions of antigravity potential, and the intraelectronic positions of the one hundred mutually

5. **There are never more than one hundred ultimatons in a typical electron.**
    "Mutual attraction holds one hundred ultimatons together in the constitution of the electron; and there are never more nor less than one hundred ultimatons in a typical electron. The loss of one or more ultimatons destroys typical electronic identity, thus bringing into existence one of the ten modified forms of the electron." P. 476.

6. **Electron size and type are determined by ultimatonic behavior.**
    "Ultimatons do not describe orbits or whirl about in circuits within the electrons, but they do spread or cluster in accordance with their axial revolutionary velocities, thus determining the differential electronic dimensions. This same ultimatonic velocity of axial revolution also determines the negative or positive reactions of the several types of electronic units. The entire segregation and grouping of electronic matter, together with the electric differentiation of negative and positive bodies of energy-matter, result from these various functions of the component ultimatonic interassociation." P. 476.

7. **Size of atoms and electrons.**
    "Each atom is a trifle over 1/100,000,000th of an inch in diameter, while an electron weighs a little less than 1/2,000th of the smallest atom, hydrogen. The positive proton, characteristic of the atomic nucleus, while it may be no larger than a negative electron, weighs from two to three thousand times more." P. 477.

8. **Comparison of mass and volume of electrons and protons.**
    "If the mass of matter should be magnified until that of an electron equaled one tenth of an ounce, then were size to be proportionately magnified, the volume of such an electron would become as large as that of the earth. If the volume of a proton—eighteen hundred times as heavy as an electron—should be magnified to the size of the head of a pin, then, in comparison, a pin's head would attain a diameter equal to that of the earth's orbit around the sun." P. 477.

C. **Atomic matter.**
1. **All matter is formed on the order of the solar system—central nucleus surrounded by whirling units.**
   "The formation of all matter is on the order of the solar system. There is at the center of every minute universe of energy a relatively stable, comparatively stationary, nuclear portion of material existence. This central unit is endowed with a threefold possibility of manifestation. Surrounding this energy center there whirl, in endless profusion but in fluctuating circuits, the energy units which are faintly comparable to the planets encircling the sun of some starry group like your own solar system. P. 477.
2. **In the atom the electrons revolve around the proton with the comparative room the planets have in revolving around the sun.**
   "Within the atom the electrons revolve about the central proton with about the same comparative room the planets have as they revolve about the sun in the space of the solar system. There is the same relative distance, in comparison with actual size, between the atomic nucleus and the inner electronic circuit as exists between the inner planet, Mercury, and your sun." P. 477.
3. **Subatomic particle velocities are beyond human imagination.**
   "The electronic axial revolutions and their orbital velocities about the atomic nucleus are both beyond the human imagination, not to mention the velocities of their component ultimatons. The positive particles of radium fly off into space at the rate of ten thousand miles a second, while the negative particles attain a velocity approximating that of light." P. 477.
4. **The universe is of decimal construction. There are just 100 types of the atom.**
   "The local universes are of decimal construction. There are just one hundred distinguishable atomic materializations of space-energy in a dual universe; that is the maximum possible organization of matter in Nebadon. These one hundred forms of matter consist of a regular series in which from one to one hundred electrons revolve around a central and relatively compact nucleus. It is this orderly and dependable association of various energies that constitutes matter." P. 477.

5. **All of the one hundred elements are not always found on the surface of a planet.**
   "Not every world will show one hundred recognizable elements at the surface, but they are somewhere present, have been present, or are in process of evolution. Conditions surrounding the origin and subsequent evolution of a planet determine how many of the one hundred atomic types will be observable. The heavier atoms are not found on the surface of many worlds. Even on Urantia the known heavier elements manifest a tendency to fly to pieces, as is illustrated by radium behavior." P. 477.
6. **Atomic stability is dependent on the neutrons; chemical activity on the electrons.**
   "Stability of the atom depends on the number of electrically inactive neutrons in the central body. Chemical behavior is wholly dependent on the activity of the freely revolving electrons." P. 477.
7. **More than one hundred electrons in an atom induces disruption with energy dispersion.**
   "In Orvonton it has never been possible naturally to assemble over one hundred orbital electrons in one atomic system. When one hundred and one have been artificially introduced into the orbital field, the result has always been the instantaneous disruption of the central proton with the wild dispersion of the electrons and other liberated energies." P. 478.
8. **Only outer electrons revolve in distinct orbits—the inner ones are more diffuse.**
   "While atoms may contain from one to one hundred orbital electrons, only the outer ten electrons of the larger atoms revolve about the central nucleus as distinct and discrete bodies, intactly and compactly swinging around on precise and definite orbits. The thirty electrons nearest the center are difficult of observation or detection as separate and organized bodies. This same comparative ratio of electronic behavior in relation to nuclear proximity obtains in all atoms regardless of the number of electrons embraced. The nearer the nucleus, the less there is of electronic individuality. The wavelike energy extension of an electron may so spread out as to occupy the whole of the lesser atomic orbits; especially is this true of the electrons nearest the atomic nucleus." P. 478.

9. **Description of the four zones of atomic organization and behavior.**

   "The thirty innermost orbital electrons have individuality, but their energy systems tend to intermingle, extending from electron to electron and well-nigh from orbit to orbit. The next thirty electrons constitute the second family, or energy zone, and are of advancing individuality, bodies of matter exerting a more complete control over their attendant energy systems. The next thirty electrons, the third energy zone, are still more individualized and circulate in more distinct and definite orbits. The last ten electrons, present in only the ten heaviest elements, are possessed of the dignity of independence and are, therefore, able to escape more or less freely from the control of the mother nucleus. With a minimum variation in temperature and pressure, the members of this fourth and outermost group of electrons will escape from the grasp of the central nucleus, as is illustrated by the spontaneous disruption of uranium and kindred elements." P. 478.

10. **The unpredictability of atomic behavior is due to many influences.**

    "The first twenty-seven atoms, those containing from one to twenty-seven orbital electrons, are more easy of comprehension than the rest. From twenty-eight upward we encounter more and more of the unpredictability of the supposed presence of the Unqualified Absolute. But some of this electronic unpredictability is due to differential ultimatonic axial revolutionary velocities and to the unexplained 'huddling' proclivity of ultimatons. Other influences—physical, electrical, magnetic, and gravitational—also operate to produce variable electronic behavior. Atoms therefore are similar to persons as to predictability. Statisticians may announce laws governing a large number of either atoms or persons but not for a single individual atom or person." P. 478.

D. **Atomic cohesion.**

   1. **Atoms are held together by gravity and an unknown force.**

      "While gravity is one of several factors concerned in holding together a tiny atomic energy system, there is also present in and among these basic physical units a powerful and unknown energy, the secret of their basic constitution and ultimate behavior, a force which remains to be discovered on Urantia. This universal influence permeates all the space embraced within this tiny energy organization." P. 478.

Part III — *Physics and Chemistry*

2. **Atomic interelectronic space is not empty. The unpredictability of the atom may be due to the space-force reaction of the Unqualified Absolute.**

   "The interelectronic space of an atom is not empty. Throughout an atom this interelectronic space is activated by wavelike manifestations which are perfectly synchronized with electronic velocity and ultimatonic revolutions. This force is not wholly dominated by your recognized laws of positive and negative attraction; its behavior is therefore sometimes unpredictable. This unnamed influence seems to be a space-force reaction of the Unqualified Absolute." P. 478.

3. **Size and function of the mesotron.**

   "The charged protons and the uncharged neutrons of the nucleus of the atom are held together by the reciprocating function of the mesotron, a particle of matter 180 times as heavy as the electron. Without this arrangement the electric charge carried by the protons would be disruptive of the atomic nucleus." P. 479.

4. **Technique of the mesotron in maintaining the integrity of the atomic nucleus.**

   "As atoms are constituted, neither electric nor gravitational forces could hold the nucleus together. The integrity of the nucleus is maintained by the reciprocal cohering function of the mesotron, which is able to hold charged and uncharged particles together because of superior force-mass power and by the further function of causing protons and neutrons constantly to change places. The mesotron causes the electric charge of the nuclear particles to be incessantly tossed back and forth between protons and neutrons. At one infinitesimal part of a second a given nuclear particle is a charged proton and the next an uncharged neutron. And these alternations of energy status are so unbelievably rapid that the electric charge is deprived of all opportunity to function as a disruptive influence. Thus does the mesotron function as an 'energy-carrier' particle which mightily contributes to the nuclear stability of the atom." P. 479.

5. **Explanation of excess radiation in atomic disruption.**

   "The presence and function of the mesotron also explains another atomic riddle. When atoms perform radioactively, they emit far more energy than would be expected. This excess of radiation is derived from the breaking up of the mesotron 'energy carrier,' which thereby becomes a mere electron. The mesotronic disintegration is also accompanied by the emission of certain small uncharged particles." P. 479.

6. **The mesotron does not explain all of the cohesive properties of the atomic nucleus. There is present an undiscovered force.**

"The mesotron explains 'certain cohesive properties of the atomic nucleus, but it does not account for the cohesion of proton to proton nor for the adhesion of neutron to neutron. The paradoxical and powerful force of atomic cohesive integrity is a form of energy as yet undiscovered on Urantia.
"These mesotrons are found abundantly in the space rays which so incessantly impinge upon your planet." 479.

E. **Classification of elements.**

1. **Seven is characteristic of the spiritual world, but ten is basic to the material creation.**

"The number seven is basic to the central universe and the spiritual system of inherent transmissions of character, but the number ten, the decimal system, is inherent in energy, matter, and the material creation. Nevertheless the atomic world does display a certain periodic characterization which recurs in groups of seven—a birthmark carried by this material world indicative of its far-distant spiritual origin." P. 479

2. **The sevenfold periodic system of chemistry indicates the sevenphase creative origin of the material realms. There are just seven colors in the spectrum.**

"This sevenfold persistence of creative constitution is exhibited in the chemical domains as a recurrence of similar physical and chemical properties in segregated periods of seven when the basic elements are arranged in the order of their atomic weights. When the Urantia chemical elements are thus arranged in a row, any given quality or property tends to recur by sevens. This periodic change by sevens recurs diminishingly and with variations throughout the entire chemical table, being most markedly observable in the earlier or lighter atomic groupings. Starting from any one element, after noting some one property, such a quality will change for six consecutive elements, but on reaching the eighth, it tends to reappear, that is, the eighth chemically active element resembles the first, the ninth the second, and so on. Such a fact of the physical world unmistakably points to the sevenfold constitution of ancestral energy and is indicative of the fundamental reality of the sevenfold diversity of the creations of time and space. Man should also note that there are seven colors in the natural spectrum." P. 480.

3. **Spectral phenomena are modified by numerous shattered atoms wandering through space.**

    "In deciphering spectral phenomena, it should be remembered that space is not empty; that light, in traversing space, is sometimes slightly modified by the various forms of energy and matter which circulate in all organized space. Some of the lines indicating unknown matter which appear in the spectra of your sun are due to modifications of well-known elements which are floating throughout space in shattered form, the atomic casualties of the fierce encounters of the solar elemental battles. Space is pervaded by these wandering derelicts, especially sodium and calcium." P. 461.

F. **Calcium.**

1. **The reason why calcium is so prevalent throughout the universes.**

    "Calcium is, in fact, the chief element of the matter-permeation of space throughout Orvonton. Our whole superuniverse is sprinkled with minutely pulverized stone. Stone is literally the basic building matter for the planets and spheres of space. The cosmic cloud, the great space blanket, consists for the most part of the modified atoms of calcium. The stone atom is one of the most prevalent and persistent of the elements. It not only endures solar ionization—splitting—but persists in an associative identity even after it has been battered by the destructive X rays and shattered by the high solar temperatures. Calcium possesses an individuality and a longevity excelling all of the more common forms of matter." P. 461.

2. **Further discussion of the escape of the calcium atom from the solar photosphere.**

    "As your physicists have suspected, these mutilated remnants of solar calcium literally ride the light beams for varied distances and thus their widespread dissemination throughout space is tremendously facilitated. The sodium atom, under certain modifications, is also capable of light and energy locomotion. The calcium feat is all the more remarkable since this element has almost twice the mass of sodium. Local space-permeation by calcium is due to the fact that it escapes from the solar photosphere, in modified form, by literally riding the outgoing sunbeams. Of all the solar elements, calcium, notwithstanding its comparative bulk—containing as it does twenty revolving electrons—is the most successful in escaping from the solar interior to the realms of space. This explains why there is a calcium layer, a gaseous stone surface, on the sun six thousand miles thick; and this despite the fact that nineteen lighter elements and numerous heavier ones, are underneath." P. 462.

3. **The technique of calcium escape from the sun—the loss of electron twenty and the agility of number nineteen.**
"Calcium is an active and versatile element at solar temperatures. The stone atom has two agile and loosely attached electrons in the two outer electronic circuits, which are very close together. Early in the atomic struggle it loses its outer electron; whereupon it engages in a masterful act of juggling the nineteenth electron back and forth between the nineteenth and twentieth circuits of electronic revolution. By tossing this nineteenth electron back and forth between its own orbit and that of its lost companion more than twenty-five thousand times a second, a mutilated stone atom is able partially to defy gravity and thus successfully to ride the emerging streams of light and energy, the sunbeams, to liberty and adventure. This calcium atom moves outward by alternate jerks of forward propulsion, grasping and letting go the sunbeam about twenty-five thousand times each second. And this is why stone is the chief component of the worlds of space. Calcium is the most expert solar-prison escaper." P. 462.

4. **The phenomenal performances of electron nineteen of the calcium atom.**
"The agility of this acrobatic calcium electron is indicated by the fact that, when tossed by the temperature-X-ray solar forces to the circle of the higher orbit, it only remains in that orbit for about one one-millionth of a second; but before the electric-gravity power of the atomic nucleus pulls it back into its old orbit, it is able to complete one million revolutions about the atomic center." P. 462.

5. **The sun has lost much calcium—most of its present supply is now in the outer solar crust.**
"Your sun has parted with an enormous quantity of its calcium, having lost tremendous amounts during the times of its

PART III — *Physics and Chemistry*

convulsive eruptions in connection with the formation of the solar system. Much of the solar calcium is now in the outer crust of the sun." P. 462.

G. **Other chemical phenomena.**
1. **Factors concerned in the origin of space rays.**
   During early times of universe materialization the space regions are interspersed with vast hydrogen clouds, which later through disruption produce a powerful short space ray. Several factors affect the origin of these rays including the shape of the orbits in matter and also the direction of electron spin. (P. 666-7)
2. **The relation of hydrogen clouds and various space energies to the inheritance factors of living beings.**
   "The vast hydrogen clouds are veritable cosmic chemical laboratories, harboring all phases of evolving energy and metamorphosing matter. Great energy actions also occur in the marginal gases of the great binary stars which so frequently overlap and hence extensively commingle. But none of these tremendous and far-flung energy activities of space exerts the least influence upon the phenomena of organized life—the germ plasm of living things and beings. These energy conditions of space are germane to the essential environment of life establishment but they are not effective in the subsequent modification of the inheritance factors of the germ plasm as are some of the longer rays of radiant energy. The implanted life of the Life Carriers is fully resistant to all of this amazing flood of the short space rays of universe energy." P. 667.
3. **There are over one million basic chemical formulas concerned in the organization and transmission of life.**
   "There are over one million fundamental or cosmic chemical formulas which constitute the parent patterns and the numerous basic functional variations of life manifestations. Satellite number one of the life-planning sphere is the realm of the universe physicists and electrochemists who serve as technical assistants to the Life Carriers in the work of capturing, organizing, and manipulating the essential units of energy which are employed in building up the material vehicles of life transmission, the so-called germ plasm." P. 398.
4. **In the blood stream of man there exists the possibility of over fifteen million chemical reactions.**

"But many seemingly mysterious adjustments of living organisms are purely chemical, wholly physical. At any moment of time, in the blood stream of any human being there exists the possibility of upward of 15,000,000 chemical reactions between the hormone output of a dozen ductless glands." P. 737.

Part III — *Physics and Chemistry*

Section Five
PHYSICAL ASPECTS OF THE GRAND UNIVERSE

I. The Central Universe

A. Havona realities.

1. **Havona energies are threefold and unlike the physical organization of the evolutionary universes.**

   "The physical realities of Havona represent an order of energy organization radically different from any prevailing in the evolutionary universes of space. Havona energies are threefold; superuniverse units of energy-matter contain a twofold energy charge, although one form of energy exists in negative and positive phases. The creation of the central universe is threefold (Trinity); the creation of a local universe (directly) is twofold, by a Creator Son and a Creative Spirit." P. 154.

2. **Havona reality consists of one thousand elements, and seven forms of basic energies. Havoners respond to forty-nine special sensations.**

   "The material of Havona consists of the organization of exactly one thousand basic chemical elements and the balanced function of the seven forms of Havona energy. Each of these basic energies manifests seven phases of excitation, so that the Havona natives respond to forty-nine differing sensation stimuli. In other words, viewed from a purely physical standpoint, the natives of the central universe possess forty-nine specialized forms of sensation. The morontia senses are seventy, and the higher spiritual orders of reaction response vary in different types of beings from seventy to two hundred and ten." P. 154.

3. **The threefold energies of Havona are under perfect control. All cosmic realities are in perfect balance.**

   "All natural law is co-ordinated on a basis entirely different than in the dual-energy systems of the evolving creations. The entire central universe is organized in accordance with the threefold system of perfect and symmetrical control. Throughout the whole Paradise-Havona system there is maintained a perfect balance between all cosmic realities and all spiritual forces. Paradise, with an absolute grasp of material creation, perfectly regulates and maintains the physical energies of this central universe; the Eternal Son, as a part of his all-embracing spirit grasp, most perfectly sustains the spiritual status of all who indwell Havona. On Paradise nothing is experimental, and the Paradise-Havona system is a unit of creative perfection." P. 154.

II. The Superuniverses

"The physical systems of time and space are all evolutionary in origin." P. 360.

"Except in the central universe, perfection is a progressive attainment." P. 360.

A. Architectural worlds of the superuniverses.

"While each superuniverse government presides near the center of the evolutionary universes of its space segment, it occupies a world made to order and is peopled by accredited personalities. These headquarters worlds are architectural spheres, space bodies specifically constructed for their special purpose. While sharing the light of near-by suns, these spheres are independently lighted and heated. Each has a sun which gives forth light without heat, like the satellites of Paradise, while each is supplied with heat by the circulation of certain energy currents near the surface of the sphere. These headquarters worlds belong to one of the greater systems situated near the astronomical center of their respective superuniverses." P. 174.

B. Architectural worlds of the local universe.

"Architectural spheres, such as Salvington, Edentia, and Jerusem, are lighted, heated, and energized by methods which make them quite independent of the suns of space. These spheres were constructed—made to order—by the power centers and physical controllers and were designed to exert a powerful influence over energy distribution. Basing their activities on such focal points of energy control, the power centers, by their living presences, directionize and channelize the physical energies of space." P. 456.

C. Edentia.

1. Topography.

"Edentia abounds in fascinating highlands, extensive elevations of physical matter crowned with morontia life and overspread with spiritual glory, but there are no rugged mountain ranges such as appear on Urantia. There are tens of thousands of sparkling lakes and thousands upon thousands of interconnecting streams, but there are no great oceans nor torrential rivers. Only the highlands are devoid of these surface streams." P. 485-86

PART III — *Physics and Chemistry*

2. **Water.**
"The water of Edentia and similar architectural spheres is no different from the water of the evolutionary planets. The water systems of such spheres are both surface and subterranean, and the moisture is in constant circulation. Edentia can be circumnavigated via these various water routes, though the chief channel of transportation is the atmosphere. Spirit beings would naturally travel above the surface of the sphere, while the morontia and material beings make use of material and semimaterial means to negotiate atmospheric passage." P. 486.

3. **Atmosphere.**
"Edentia and its associated worlds have a true atmosphere, the usual three-gas mixture which is characteristic of such architectural creations, and which embodies the two elements of Urantian atmosphere plus that morontia gas suitable for the respiration of morontia creatures. But while this atmosphere is both material and morontial, there are no storms or hurricanes; neither is there summer nor winter. This absence of atmospheric disturbances and of seasonal variation makes it possible to embellish all outdoors on these especially created worlds." P. 486.

D. **Satania.**

1. **Heating of headquarters worlds.**
"The energy of Jerusem is superbly controlled and circulates about the sphere in the zone channels, which are directly fed from the energy charges of space and expertly administered by the Master Physical Controllers. The natural resistance to the passage of these energies through the physical channels of conduction yields the heat required for the production of the equable temperature of Jerusem. The full-light temperature is maintained at about 70 degrees Fahrenheit, while during the period of light recession it falls to a little lower than 50 degrees." P. 519.

2. **Lighting system of Jerusem.**
"The lighting system of Jerusem should not be so difficult for you to comprehend. There are no days and nights, no seasons of heat and cold. The power transformers maintain one hundred thousand centers from which rarefied energies are projected upward through the planetary atmosphere, undergoing certain changes, until they reach the electric air-ceiling of

the sphere; and then these energies are reflected back and down as a gentle, sifting, and even light of about the intensity of Urantia sunlight when the sun is shining overhead at ten o'clock in the morning." P. 519.

3. **Because of this gentle sifting light the headquarters worlds are not luminous in space.**

   "Under such conditions of lighting, the light rays do not seem to come from one place; they just sift out of the sky, emanating equally from all space directions. This light is very similar to natural sunlight except that it contains very much less heat. Thus it will be recognized that such headquarters worlds are not luminous in space; if Jerusem were very near Urantia, it would not be visible." P. 520.

4. **Light is reflected by ionosphere gases much as such gases reflect broadcast waves on Urantia.**

   "The gases which reflect this light-energy from the Jerusem upper ionosphere back to the ground are very similar to those in the Urantia upper air belts which are concerned with the auroral phenomena of your so-called northern lights, although these are produced by different causes. On Urantia it is this same gas shield which prevents the escape of the terrestrial broadcast waves, reflecting them earthward when they strike this gas belt in their direct outward flight. In this way broadcasts are held near the surface as they journey through the air around your world." P. 520.

5. **The Jerusem worlds are lighted seventy-five per cent of the day—the recession light is like full moon on Urantia.**

   "This lighting of the sphere is uniformly maintained for seventy-five per cent of the Jerusem day, and then there is a gradual recession until, at the time of minimum illumination, the light is about that of your full moon on a clear night. This is the quiet hour for all Jerusem. Only the broadcast-receiving stations are in operation during this period of rest and rehabilitation." P. 520.

6. **All of the Jerusem worlds receive faint sunlight—like bright starlight—but are not disturbed by sun disturbances.**

   "Jerusem receives faint light from several near-by suns—a sort of brilliant starlight—but it is not dependent on them; worlds like Jerusem are not subject to the vicissitudes of sun disturbances, neither are they confronted with the problem of a cooling or dying sun.

PART III — *Physics and Chemistry*

"The seven transitional study worlds and their forty-nine satellites are heated, lighted, energized, and watered by the Jerusem technique." P. 520.

7. **Architectural worlds have two hundred elements—one hundred material and one hundred morontial.**

"All of these worlds are architectural spheres, and they have just double the number of elements of the evolved planets. Such made-to-order worlds not only abound in the heavy metals and crystals, having one hundred physical elements, but likewise have exactly one hundred forms of a unique energy organization called *morontia material*. The Master Physical Controllers and the Morontia Power Supervisors are able so to modify the revolutions of the primary units of matter and at the same time so to transform these associations of energy as to create this new substance." P. 541.

8. **The Jerusem landscape and other variations of topography.**

"On Jerusem you will miss the rugged mountain ranges of Urantia and other evolved worlds since there are neither earthquakes nor rainfalls, but you will enjoy the beauteous highlands and other unique variations of topography and landscape. Enormous areas of Jerusem are preserved in a 'natural state,' and the grandeur of such districts is quite beyond the powers of human imagination." P. 520.

9. **Jerusem climatic conditions and the system of water circulation. The interconnecting lakes.**

"There are thousands upon thousands of small lakes but no raging rivers nor expansive oceans. There is no rainfall, neither storms nor blizzards, on any of the architectural worlds, but there is the daily precipitation of the condensation of moisture during the time of lowest temperature attending the light recession. (The dew point is higher on a three-gas world than on a two-gas planet like Urantia.) The physical plant life and the morontia world of living things both require moisture, but this is largely supplied by the subsoil system of circulation which extends all over the sphere, even up to the very tops of the highlands. This water system is not entirely subsurface, for there are many canals interconnecting the sparkling lakes of Jerusem." P. 520.

10. **The three-gas atmosphere of Jerusem.**

"The atmosphere of Jerusem is a three-gas mixture. This air is very similar to that of Urantia with the addition of a gas adapted to the respiration of the morontia order of life. This third gas in no way unfits the air for the respiration of animals or plants of the material orders." P. 520.

E. **Urantia.**

1. **The earth receives only one two-billionths of the sun's light emanations; at two cents a kilowatt-hour, Chicago's light bill would be one hundred million dollars a day.**

   "The planetary atmosphere filters through to the earth about one two-billionths of the sun's total light emanation. If the light falling upon North America were paid for at the rate of two cents per kilowatt-hour, the annual light bill would be upward of 800 quadrillion dollars. Chicago's bill for sunshine would amount to considerably over 100 million dollars a day. And it should be remembered that you receive from the sun other forms of energy—light is not the only solar contribution reaching your atmosphere. Vast solar energies pour in upon Urantia embracing wave lengths ranging both above and below the recognition range of human vision." P. 665.

2. **The nature and function of the ozone layer about ten miles above the earth's surface.**

   "The earth's atmosphere is all but opaque to much of the solar radiation at the extreme ultraviolet end of the spectrum. Most of these short wave lengths are absorbed by a layer of ozone which exists throughout a level about ten miles above the surface of the earth, and which extends spaceward for another ten miles. The ozone permeating this region, at conditions prevailing on the earth's surface, would make a layer only one tenth of an inch thick; nevertheless, this relatively small and apparently insignificant amount of ozone protects Urantia inhabitants from the excess of these dangerous and destructive ultraviolet radiations present in sunlight. But were this ozone layer just a trifle thicker, you would be deprived of the highly important and health-giving ultraviolet rays which now reach the earth's surface, and which are ancestral to one of the most essential of your vitamins." P. 665.

3. **The midwayers present over fifty thousand facts of physics and chemistry proving that the cosmos is not just an accident. They catalogue over a hundred thousand other findings.**

   "And yet some of the less imaginative of your mortal mechanists insist on viewing material creation and human evolution as an accident. The Urantia midwayers have assembled over fifty

Part III — *Physics and Chemistry*

thousand facts of physics and chemistry which they deem to be incompatible with the laws of accidental chance, and which they contend unmistakably demonstrate the presence of intelligent purpose in the material creation. And all of this takes no account of their catalogue of more than one hundred thousand findings outside the domain of physics and chemistry which they maintain prove the presence of mind in the planning, creation, and maintenance of the material cosmos." P. 665.

4. **The nature and function of the earth's atmosphere, ionosphere, and stratosphere.**

"The lower five or six miles of the earth's atmosphere is the troposphere; this is the region of winds and air currents which provide weather phenomena. Above this region is the inner ionosphere and next above is the stratosphere. Ascending from the surface of the earth, the temperature steadily falls for six or eight miles, at which height it registers around 70 degrees below zero F. This temperature range of from 65 to 70 degrees below zero F. is unchanged in the further ascent for forty miles; this realm of constant temperature is the stratosphere. At a height of forty-five or fifty miles, the temperature begins to rise, and this increase continues until, at the level of the auroral displays, a temperature of 1200° F. is attained, and it is this intense heat that ionizes the oxygen. But temperature in such a rarefied atmosphere is hardly comparable with heat reckoning at the surface of the earth. Bear in mind that one half of all your atmosphere is to be found in the first three miles. The height of the earth's atmosphere is indicated by the highest auroral streamers—about four hundred miles." P. 666.

5. **The relation of auroral phenomena to sunspots and other solar disturbances.**

"Auroral phenomena are directly related to sunspots, those solar cyclones which whirl in opposite directions above and below the solar equator, even as do the terrestrial tropical hurricanes. Such atmospheric disturbances whirl in opposite directions when occurring above or below the equator.

"The power of sunspots to alter light frequencies shows that these solar storm centers function as enormous magnets. Such magnetic fields are able to hurl charged particles from the sunspot craters out through space to the earth's outer atmosphere, where their ionizing influence produces such spectacular auroral displays. Therefore do you have the greatest auroral phenomena when sunspots are at their height—or soon thereafter—at which time the spots are more generally equatorially situated." P. 666

6. **Relation of solar activities to the behavior of the compass.**

"Even the compass needle is responsive to this solar influence since it turns slightly to the east as the sun rises and slightly to the west as the sun nears setting. This happens every day, but during the height of sunspot cycles this variation of the compass is twice as great. These diurnal wanderings of the compass are in response to the increased ionization of the upper atmosphere, which is produced by the sunlight." P. 666.

7. **Relation of the superstratosphere to broadcasting disturbances.**

"It is the presence of two different levels of electrified conducting regions in the superstratosphere that accounts for the long-distance transmission of your long- and short-wave radiobroadcasts. Your broadcasting is sometimes disturbed by the terrific storms which occasionally rage in the realms of these outer ionospheres." P. 666.

CONCLUSION

"There is a great and glorious purpose in the march of the universes through space. All of your mortal struggling is not in vain. We are all part of an immense plan, a gigantic enterprise, and it is the vastness of the undertaking that renders it impossible to see very much of it at any one time and during any one life. We are all a part of an eternal project which the Gods are supervising and outworking. The whole marvelous and universal mechanism moves on majestically through space to the music of the meter of the infinite thought and the eternal purpose of the First Great Source and Center." P. 364.

PART IV — BIOLOGY

Introduction
THE SOURCE OF LIFE

1. "The Universal Father is the God of all creation, the First Source and Center of all things and beings." P. 21.

2. "The myriads of planetary systems were all made to be eventually inhabited by many different types of intelligent creatures, beings who could know God, receive the divine affection, and love him in return. The universe of universes is the work of God and the dwelling place of his diverse creatures. 'God created the heavens and formed the earth; he established the universe and created this world not in vain; he formed it to be inhabited.'" P. 21.

3. "The Father unceasingly pours forth energy, light, and life." P. 55.

4. "Therefore, nature', as mortal man understands it, presents the underlying foundation and fundamental background of a changeless Deity and his immutable laws, modified by, fluctuating because of, and experiencing upheavals through, the working of the local plans, purposes, patterns, and conditions which have been inaugurated and are being carried out by the local universe, constellation, system, and planetary forces and personalities. For example: As God's laws have been ordained in Nebadon, they are modified by the plans established by the Creator Son and Creative Spirit of this local universe; and in addition to all this the operation of these laws has been further influenced by the errors, defaults, and insurrections of certain beings resident upon your planet and belonging to your immediate planetary system of Satania." P. 56.

    "Nature is the perfection of Paradise divided by the incompletion, evil, and sin of the unfinished universes. This quotient is thus expressive of both the perfect and the partial, of both the eternal and the temporal. Continuing evolution modifies nature by augmenting the content of Paradise perfection and by diminishing the content of the evil, error, and disharmony of relative reality." P. 57.

5. "The Creator Sons go out from Paradise into the universes of time and, with the co-operation of the controlling and creative agencies of the Third Source and Center, complete the organization of the local universes of progressive evolution." P. 88.

6. "Since the personalization of the Third Source, the First Source no more personally participates in universe creation. The Universal Father delegates everything possible to his Eternal Son; likewise does the

Eternal Son bestow all possible authority and power upon the Conjoint Creator.

"The Eternal Son and the Conjoint Creator have, as partners and through their co-ordinate personalities, planned and fashioned every post-Havona universe which has been brought into existence. The Spirit sustains the same personal relation to the Son in all subsequent creation that the Son sustains to the Father in the first and central creation.

"A Creator Son of the Eternal Son and a Creative Spirit of the Infinite Spirit created you and your universe; and while the Father in faithfulness upholds that which they have organized, it devolves upon this Universe Son and this Universe Spirit to foster and sustain their work as well as to minister to the creatures of their own making." P. 93.

7. "It is highly probable, though we cannot offer definite proof, that the Master Spirit of Orvonton exerts a decided influence in the following spheres of activity:

   "1. The life-initiation procedures of the local universe Life Carriers.

   "2. The life activations of the adjutant mind-spirits bestowed upon the worlds by a local universe Creative Spirit." P. 190.

8. "The Creator Sons are the makers and rulers of the local universes of time and space." P. 234.

9. "Among these limitations to the otherwise all-powerful creator prerogatives of a local universe Father are the following: ...

   "2. *Creature designs and types* are controlled by the Eternal Son. Before a Creator Son may engage in the creation of any new type of being, any new design of creature, he must secure the consent of the Eternal and Original Mother Son." P. 236.

Section One
THE LOCAL UNIVERSE
THE CREATIVE DOMAIN OF A CREATOR SON

I. THE CREATION OF LIFE IN THE LOCAL UNIVERSE

A. Function of the Creator Son and Creative Spirit.

1. **The projection of the plan of life creation by the Creator Son and Creative Spirit is followed by the creation of the Bright and Morning Star.**
   "Presently, the physical plan of a universe is completed, and the Creator Son, in association with the Creative Spirit, projects his plan of life creation; whereupon does this representation of the

Infinite Spirit begin her universe function as a distinct creative personality. When this first creative act is formulated and personal associate of the Creator Son, one like him in all aspects of character, though markedly limited in the attributes of divinity." P. 359.

2. **After the creation of Gabriel, there ensues the creation of a vast array of diverse creatures, including mortal man.**

    "And now that the right-hand helper and chief executive of the Creator Son has been provided, there ensues the bringing into existence of a vast and wonderful array of diverse creatures. The sons and daughters of the local universe are forthcoming, and soon thereafter the government of such a creation is provided, extending from the supreme councils of the universe to the fathers of the constellations and the sovereigns of the local systems—the aggregations of those worlds which are designed subsequently to become the homes of the varied mortal races of will creatures; and each of these worlds will be presided over by a Planetary Prince.

    "And then, when such a universe has been so completely organized and so repletely manned, does the Creator Son enter into the Father's proposal to create mortal man in their divine image." P. 359.

3. **The Creative Spirit is coresponsible with the Creator Son in producing the creatures of the worlds.**

    "The Creative Spirit is coresponsible with the Creator Son in producing the creatures of the worlds and never fails the Son in all efforts to uphold and conserve these creations. Life is ministered and maintained through the agency of the Creative Spirit. 'You send forth your Spirit, and they are created. You renew the face of the earth.'

    "In the creation of a universe of intelligent creatures the Creative Mother Spirit functions first in the sphere of universe perfection, collaborating with the Son in the production of the Bright and Morning Star. Subsequently the offspring of the Spirit increasingly approach the order of created beings on the planets, even as the Sons grade downward from the Melchizedeks to the Material Sons, who actually contact with the mortals of the realms. In the later evolution of mortal creatures the Life Carrier Sons provide the physical body, fabricated out of the existing organized material of the realm, while the Universe Spirit contributes the 'breath of life.'" P. 376.

B. The nature of creatures of the superuniverses.
1. Except Deity-origin beings, all creatures are of progressive evolutionary nature. There is no limit to the progress of Thought Adjuster-endowed creatures.
"Excepting perfect beings of Deity origin, all will creatures in the superuniverses are of evolutionary nature, beginning in lowly estate and climbing ever upward, in reality inward. Even highly spiritual personalities continue to ascend the scale of life by progressive translations from life to life and from sphere to sphere. And in the case of those who entertain the Mystery Monitors, there is indeed no limit to the possible heights of their spiritual ascent and universe attainment." P. 361.
2. The fact of evolutionary origin is not a stigma. All the more honor for those who climb from the bottom to the top.
"The fact of animal evolutionary origin does not attach stigma to any personality in the sight of the universe as that is the exclusive method of producing one of the two basic types of finite intelligent will creatures. When the heights of perfection and eternity are attained, all the more honor to those who began at the bottom and joyfully climbed the ladder of life, round by round, and who, when they do reach the heights of glory, will have gained a personal experience which embodies an actual knowledge of every phase of life from the bottom to the top." P. 361.
C. Biologic headquarters of the local universe.
1. Life Carrier World No. 1 is devoted to the study of universal life and life planning. Here are the central emplacements of the adjutant mind-spirits.
"World Number One, the headquarters sphere, together with its six tributary satellites, is devoted to the study of universal life, life in all of its known phases of manifestation. Here is located the college of life planning, wherein function teachers and advisers from Uversa and Havona, even from Paradise. And I am permitted to reveal that the seven central emplacements of the adjutant mindspirits are situated on this world of the Life Carriers." P. 397.
2. The second world is the life-designing sphere.
"The Second World is the life-designing sphere; here all new modes of life organization are worked out. While the original life designs are provided by the Creator Son, the actual

outworking of these plans is intrusted to the Life Carriers and their associates. When the general life plans for a new world have been formulated, they are transmitted to the headquarters sphere, where they are minutely scrutinized by the supreme council of the senior Life Carriers in collaboration with a corps of consulting Melchizedeks. If the plans are a departure from previously accepted formulas, they must be passed upon, and endorsed by, the Creator Son. The chief of Melchizedeks often represents the Creator Son in these deliberations." P. 397.

3. **A whole world is devoted to the study and elaboration of basic life patterns. On Urantia, life is reproduced in a pattern of twenty-four units.**

    "World Number Three is devoted to the conservation of life. Here various modes of life protection and preservation are studied and developed by the assistants and custodians of the Life Carrier corps. The life plans for every new world always provide for the early establishment of the life-conservation commission, consisting of custodian specialists in the expert manipulation of the basic life patterns. On Urantia there were twenty-four such custodian commissioners, two for each fundamental or parent pattern of the architectural organization of the life material. On planets such as yours the highest form of life is reproduced by a life-carrying bundle which possesses twenty-four pattern units. (And since the intellectual life grows out of, and upon the foundation of, the physical, there come into existence the four and twenty basic orders of psychic organization.)" P. 398.

4. **The original life plasm contains the potentials of all future variations of organic evolution.**

    Sphere Number Four and its tributary satellites are devoted to the study of the evolution of creature life in general and to the evolutionary antecedents of any one life level in particular. The original life plasm of an evolutionary world must contain the full potential for all future developmental variations and for all subsequent evolutionary changes and modifications. The provision for such far-reaching projects of life metamorphosis may require the appearance of many apparently useless forms of animal and vegetable life. Such by-products of planetary evolution, foreseen or unforeseen, appear upon the stage of action only to disappear, but in and through all this long process there runs the thread of the wise and intelligent formulations of the original designers of the planetary life plan and species scheme. The manifold by-products of biologic evolution are all essential to the final and full function of the higher intelligent forms of life, notwithstanding that great outward disharmony may prevail from time to time in the long upward struggle of the higher creatures to effect the mastery of the lower forms of life, many of which are sometimes so antagonistic to the peace and comfort of the evolving will creatures." P. 398.

D. **Function of the Life Carriers.**

1. **The Life Carriers either import life or formulate its patterns on the local worlds.**

    "Life does not originate spontaneously. Life is constructed according to plans formulated by the (unrevealed) Architects of Being and appears on the inhabited planets either by direct importation or as a result of the operations of the Life Carriers of the local universes. These carriers of life are among the most interesting and versatile of the diverse family of universe Sons. They are intrusted with designing and carrying creature life to the planetary spheres. And after planting this life on such new worlds, they remain there for long periods to foster its development." P. 396.

2. **Life does not spontaneously appear in the universes.**

    "Life does not spontaneously appear in the universes; the Life Carriers must initiate it on the barren planets. They are the carriers, disseminators, and guardians of life as it appears on the evolutionary worlds of space. All life of the order and forms known on Urantia arises with these Sons, though not all forms of planetary life are existent on Urantia." P. 399.

3. **Life Carriers may carry actual life plasms to a new world, or organize life patterns after arriving in accordance with approved formulas.**

    "The corps of Life Carriers commissioned to plant life upon a new world usually consists of one hundred senior carriers, one hundred assistants, and one thousand custodians. The Life Carriers often carry actual life plasm to a new world, but not always. They sometimes organize the life patterns after arriving on the planet of assignment in accordance with formulas previously approved for a new adventure in life establishment. Such was the origin of the planetary life of Urantia." P. 399.

4. **Life Carriers catalyze the lifeless material, and the vital spark from the Mother Spirit is imparted through them. From the Universe Mother Spirit comes the vital spark which enlivens the body and presages the mind.**
"When, in accordance with approved formulas, the physical patterns have been provided, then do the Life Carriers catalyze this lifeless material, imparting through their persons the vital spirit spark; and forthwith do the inert patterns become living matter.

"The vital spark—the mystery of life—is bestowed through the Life Carriers, not by them. They do indeed supervise such transactions, they formulate the life plasm itself, but it is the Universe Mother Spirit who supplies the essential factor of the living plasm. From the Creative Daughter of the Infinite Spirit comes that energy spark which enlivens the body and presages the mind." P. 399.

5. **It is the spirit of God who really contributes the vital spark.**
"When the Life Carriers have designed the patterns of life, after they have organized the energy systems, there must occur an additional phenomenon; the 'breath of life' must be imparted to these lifeless forms. The Sons of God can construct the forms of life, but it is the Spirit of God who really contributes the vital spark. And when the life thus imparted is spent, then again the remaining material body becomes dead matter. When the bestowed life is exhausted, the body returns to the bosom of the material universe from which it was borrowed by the Life Carriers to serve as a transient vehicle for that life endowment which they conveyed to such a visible association of energy-matter." P. 404.

6. **Life Carriers are living catalytic presences.**
"In the bestowal of life the Life Carriers transmit nothing of their personal natures, not even on those spheres where new orders of life are projected. At such times they simply initiate and transmit the spark of life, start the required revolutions of matter in accord with the physical, chemical, and electrical specifications of the ordained plans and patterns. Life Carriers are living catalytic presences which agitate, organize, and vitalize the otherwise inert elements of the material order of existence." P. 399.

7. **Life Carriers are given a certain period to establish life on a new world, after which nothing new may be added by them.**

Until the emergence of human beings they may directionize the course of evolution. The Life Carriers of a planetary corps are given a certain period in which to establish life on a new world, approximately one-half million years of the time of that planet. At the termination of this period, indicated by certain developmental attainments of the planetary life, they cease implantation efforts, and they may not subsequently add any thing new or supplemental to the life of that planet

"During the ages intervening between life establishment and the emergence of human creatures of moral status, the Life Carriers are permitted to manipulate the life environment and otherwise favorably directionize the course of biologic evolution. And this they do for long periods of time." P. 400.

8. **While Life Carriers can organize living forms—such life is devoid of two powers—mind and reproductive powers.**

"Things material may enjoy an independent existence, but life springs only from life. Mind can be derived only from pre-existent mind. Spirit takes origin only from spirit ancestors. The creature may produce the forms of life, but only a creator personality or a creative force can supply the activating living spark.

"Life Carriers can organize the material forms, or physical patterns, of living beings, but the Spirit provides the initial spark of life and bestows the endowment of mind. Even the living forms of experimental life which the Life Carriers organize on their Salvington worlds are always devoid of reproductive powers. When the life formulas and the vital patterns are correctly assembled and properly organized, the presence of a Life Carrier is sufficient to initiate life, but all such living organisms are lacking in two essential attributes—mind endowment and reproductive powers. Animal mind and human mind are gifts of the local universe Mother Spirit, functioning through the seven adjutant mindspirits, while creature ability to reproduce is the specific and personal impartation of the Universe Spirit to the ancestral life plasm inaugurated by the Life Carriers." P. 403.

9. **There is a mystery connected with the impartation of life. But we do know that concept is inherent in the Father, expression in the Son, and life realization in the Spirit.**

"There are some things connected with the elaboration of life on the evolutionary planets which are not altogether clear to us. We fully comprehend the physical organization of the electrochemical formulas of the Life Carriers, but we do not wholly understand the nature and source of the *life-activation spark*. We know that life flows from the Father through the Son and *by* the Spirit. It is more than possible that the Master Spirits are the sevenfold channel of the river of life which is poured out upon all creation. But we do not comprehend the technique whereby the supervising Master Spirit participates in the initial episode of life bestowal on a new planet. The Ancients of Days, we are confident, also have some part in this inauguration of life on a new world, but we are wholly ignorant of the nature thereof. We do know that the Universe Mother Spirit actually vitalizes the lifeless patterns and imparts to such activated plasm the prerogatives of organismal reproduction. We observe that these three are the levels of God the Sevenfold, sometimes designated as the Supreme Creators of time and space; but otherwise we know little more than Urantia mortals—simply that concept is inherent in the Father, expression in the Son, and life realization in the Spirit." P. 404.

E. **Function of the adjutant mind circuits.**

1. **The seven adjutant mind-spirits determine the course of organic evolution.**
   "It is the presence of the seven adjutant mind-spirits on the primitive worlds that conditions the course of organic evolution; that explains why evolution is purposeful and not accidental. These adjutants represent that function of the mind ministry of the Infinite Spirit which is extended to the lower orders of intelligent life through the operations of a local universe Mother Spirit. The adjutants are the children of the Universe Mother Spirit and constitute her personal ministry to the material minds of the realms. Wherever and whenever such mind is manifest, these spirits are variously functioning." P. 401.

2. **Names and function of the seven adjutant mind-spirits.**
   "The seven adjutant mind-spirits are called by names which are the equivalents of the following designations: intuition, understanding, courage, knowledge, counsel, worship, and wisdom. These mindspirits send forth their influence into all the inhabited worlds as a differential urge, each seeking receptivity capacity for manifestation quite apart from the

degree to which its fellows may find reception and opportunity for function." P. 401.

F. **Control and function of life energies.**

1. **We know but little about the mobilization and transmutation of universal energy.**

    "Life has inherent capacity for the mobilization and transmutation of universal energy. You are familiar with the action of vegetable life in transforming the material energy of light into the varied manifestations of the vegetable kingdom. You also know something of the method whereby this vegetative energy can be converted into the phenomena of animal activities, but you know practically nothing of the technique of the power directors and the physical controllers, who are endowed with ability to mobilize, transform, directionize, and concentrate the manifold energies of space." P. 457.

2. **Science will never create matter, energy or life.**

    "Subsequent to even still greater progress and further discoveries, after Urantia has advanced immeasurably in comparison with present knowledge, though you should gain control of the energy revolutions of the electrical units of matter to the extent of modifying their physical manifestations—even after all such possible progress, forever will scientists be powerless to create one atom of matter or to originate one flash of energy or ever to add to matter that which we call life." P. 468.

3. **Life is both mechanistic and vitalistic—but it is not inherent in matter.**

    "Life is both mechanistic and vitalistic—material and spiritual. Ever will Urantia physicists and chemists progress in their understanding of the protoplasmic forms of vegetable and animal life, but never will they be able to produce living organisms. Life is something different from all energy manifestations; even the material life of physical creatures is not inherent in matter." P. 403.

4. **Life after death.**

    "The life bestowed upon plants and animals by the Life Carriers does not return to the Life Carriers upon the death of plant or animal. The departing life of such a living thing possesses neither identity nor personality; it does not individually survive death. During its existence and the time of its sojourn in the body of matter, it has undergone a change; it has

Part IV — *Biology*

undergone energy evolution and survives only as a part of the cosmic forces of the universe; it does not survive as individual life. The survival of mortal creatures is wholly predicated on the evolvement of an immortal soul within the mortal mind." P. 404.

II. Biology of the Architectural Worlds

A. Description of the constellation headquarters worlds.

1. **The architectural worlds enjoy ten forms of life.**
   "The architectural worlds enjoy ten forms of life of the material order. On Urantia there is plant and animal life, but on such a world as Edentia there are ten divisions of the material orders of life. Were you to view these ten divisions of Edentia life, you would quickly classify the first three as vegetable and the last three as animal, but you would be utterly unable to comprehend the nature of the intervening four groups of prolific and fascinating forms of life." P. 492.

2. **The biologic beautification of the architectural worlds.**
   "Being endowed with ten divisions of physical life, not to mention the morontia variations, these architectural worlds provide tremendous possibilities for the biologic beautification of the landscape and of the material and the morontia structures. The celestial artisans direct the native spornagia in this extensive work of botanic decoration and biologic embellishment. Whereas your artists must resort to inert paint and lifeless marble to portray their concepts, the celestial artisans and the univitatia more frequently utilize living materials to represent their ideas and to capture their ideals." P. 492.

3. **The material growth is green, the morontia violet or orchid. Morontial growth is purely energy—has no residue.**
   "The vegetable life is also very different from that of Urantia, consisting of both material and morontia varieties. The material growths have a characteristic green coloration, but the morontia equivalents of vegetative life have a violet or orchid tinge of varying hue and reflection. Such morontia vegetation is purely an energy growth; when eaten there is no residual portion." P. 492.

4. **There is floral grandeur and botanic beauty in the supernal gardens of Eden.**
   "If you enjoy the flowers, shrubs, and trees of Urantia, then will you feast your eyes upon the botanical beauty and the

floral grandeur of the supernal gardens of Edentia. But it is beyond my powers of description to undertake to convey to the mortal mind an adequate concept of these beauties of the heavenly worlds. Truly, eye has not seen such glories as await your arrival on these worlds of the mortal-ascension adventure." P. 493.

5. **The animal life of Edentia is manifold—but there are no carnivorous creatures.**

   "Even the distinctively animal life is very different from that of the evolutionary worlds, so different that it is quite impossible to portray to mortal minds the unique character and affectionate nature of these nonspeaking creatures. There are thousands upon thousands of living creatures which your imagination could not possibly picture. The whole animal creation is of an entirely different order from the gross animal species of the evolutionary planets. But all this animal life is most intelligent and exquisitely serviceable, and all the various species are surprisingly gentle and touchingly companionable. There are no carnivorous creatures on such architectural worlds; there is nothing in all Edentia to make any living being afraid." P. 492.

B. **Description of Jerusem.**

1. **There are beauteous highlands and "natural" parks.**

   "On Jerusem you will miss the rugged mountain ranges of Urantia and other evolved worlds since there are neither earthquakes nor rainfalls, but you will enjoy the beauteous highlands and other unique variations of topography and landscape. Enormous areas of Jerusem are preserved in a 'natural state,' and the grandeur of such districts is quite beyond the powers of human imagination.

   "There are thousands upon thousands of small lakes but no raging rivers nor expansive oceans. There is no rainfall, neither storms nor blizzards, on any of the architectural worlds, but there is the daily precipitation of the condensation of moisture during the time of lowest temperature attending the light recession." P. 520.

2. **The system headquarters worlds are endowed with ten divisions of physical life—which foreshadows the beauty of the central universe.**

   "Jerusem and its associated worlds are endowed with the ten standard divisions of physical life characteristic of the architec tural spheres of Nebadon. And since there is no organic evolution on Jerusem, there are no conflicting forms of life, no struggle for existence, no survival of the fittest. Rather is there a creative adaptation which foreshadows the beauty, the harmony, and the perfection of the eternal worlds of the central and divine universe. And in all this creative perfection there is the most amazing intermingling of physical and of morontia life, artistically contrasted by the celestial artisans and their fellows." P. 521.

C. **Spornagia.**

1. **Spornagia do not have Adjusters—they do not possess survival souls, but they do have long lives.**

   "Spornagia are not Adjuster indwelt. They do not possess survival souls, but they do enjoy long lives, sometimes to the extent of forty to fifty thousand standard years. Their number is legion, and they afford physical ministry to all orders of universe personalities requiring material service." P. 528.

2. **Spornagia experience reincarnation. They are the only beings in the universe who do have this experience.**

   "Although spornagia neither possess nor evolve survival souls, though they do not have personality, nevertheless, they do evolve an individuality which can experience reincarnation. When, with the passing of time, the physical bodies of these unique creatures deteriorate from usage and age, their creators, in collaboration with the Life Carriers, fabricate new bodies in which the old spornagia re-establish their residences.
   "Spornagia are the only creatures in all the universe of Nebadon who experience this or any other sort of reincarnation. They are only reactive to the first five of the adjutant mind-spirits; they are not responsive to the spirits of worship and wisdom. But the five adjutant mind equivalates to a totality or sixth reality level, and it is this factor which persists as an experiential identity." P. 528.

3. **In a future age, spornagia may escape the animal level of existence.**

   "There are those who believe that, in a future universe age, these faithful spornagia will escape from their animal level of existence and attain a worthy evolutionary destiny of progressive intellectual growth and even spiritual achievement." P. 528.

D. **Material Sons.**
1. **Material Sons are sustained by both material and cosmic energies.**
 "The Material Sons enjoy a dual nutrition; they are really dual in nature and constitution, partaking of materialized energy much as do the physical beings of the realm, while their immortal existence is fully maintained by the direct and automatic intake of certain sustaining cosmic energies." P. 581.
2. **In case of sin, Material Sons are degraded and become subject to physical death.**
 "Should they fail on some mission of assignment or even consciously and deliberately rebel, this order of Sons becomes isolated, cut off from connection with the universe source of light and life. Thereupon they become practically material beings, destined to take the course of material life on the world of their assignment and compelled to look to the universe magistrates for adjudication. Material death will eventually terminate the planetary career of such an unfortunate and unwise Material Son or Daughter." P. 581.

PART IV — *Biology*

SECTION TWO
URANTIA BIOLOGY

I. RELATION OF MIND TO EVOLUTIONARY STAGES

A. Three mind levels.

1. **There are three distinct levels of life production and evolution.**
    "There are, then, three distinct levels of life production and evolution:
    "1. The physical-energy domain—mind-capacity production.
    "2. The mind ministry of the adjutant spirits—impinging upon spirit capacity.
    "3. The spirit endowment of mortal mind—culminating in Thought Adjuster bestowal." P. 730.

2. **Progression through the three mind levels.**
    "Living mind, prior to the appearance of capacity to learn from experience, is the ministry domain of the Master Physical Controllers. Creature mind, before acquiring the ability to recognize divinity and worship Deity, is the exclusive domain of the adjutant spirits. With the appearance of the spiritual response of the creature intellect, such created minds at once become superminded, being instantly encircuited in the spirit cycles of the local universe Mother Spirit." P. 403.

3. **The three evolutionary mind levels.**
    "The universal nonspiritual energies are reassociated in the living systems of non-Creator minds on various levels, certain of which may be depicted as follows:
    "1. *Preadjutant-spirit minds.* This level of mind is nonexperiencing and on the inhabited worlds is ministered by the Master Physical Controllers. This is mechanical mind, the nonteachable intellect of the most primitive forms of material life, but the nonteachable mind functions on many levels beside that of primitive planetary life.
    "2. *Adjutant-spirit minds.* This is the ministry of a local universe Mother Spirit functioning through her seven adjutant mind-spirits on the teachable (nonmechanical) level of material mind. On this level material mind is experiencing: as subhuman (animal) intellect in the first five adjutants; as human (moral) intellect in the seven adjutants; as superhuman (midwayer) intellect in the last two adjutants.
    "3. *Evolving morontia minds*—the expanding consciousness of evolving personalities in the local universe ascending

careers. This is the bestowal of the local universe Mother Spirit in liaison with the Creator Son. This mind level connotes the organization of the morontia type of life vehicle, a synthesis of the material and the spiritual which is effected by the Morontia Power Supervisors of a local universe. Morontia mind functions differentially in response to the 570 levels of morontia life, disclosing increasing associative capacity with the cosmic mind on the higher levels of attainment. This is the evolutionary course of mortal creatures, but mind of a nonmorontia order is also bestowed by a Universe Son and a Universe Spirit upon the nonmorontia children of the local creations." P. 480-1.

B. **The physical-energy domain.**
  1. **There is a threefold creativity concerned in the production of mind mechanisms.**
     "Basic evolutionary material life—premind life—is the formulation of the Master Physical Controllers and the life-impartation ministry of the Seven Master Spirits in conjunction with the active ministration of the ordained Life Carriers. As a result of the coordinate function of this threefold creativity there develops organismal physical capacity for mind—material mechanisms for intelligent reaction to external environmental stimuli and, later on, to internal stimuli, influences taking origin in the organismal mind itself." P. 730.
  2. **Nature and control of the prehuman levels of mind function.**
     "The mechanical-nonteachable levels of organismal environmental response are the domains of the physical controllers. The adjutant mind-spirits activate and regulate the adaptative or nonmechanicalteachable types of mind—those response mechanisms of organisms capable of learning from experience. And as the spirit adjutants thus manipulate mind potentials, so do the Life Carriers exercise considerable discretionary control over the environmental aspects of evolutionary processes right up to the time of the appearance of human will—the ability to know God and the power of choosing to worship him." P. 730.

C. **Mind ministry of the Adjutant Spirits.**
  1. **Analogy of adjutant spirits to power centers.**

Part IV — Biology

"These mind-adjutants of a local universe Mother Spirit are related to creature life of intelligence status much as the power centers and physical controllers are related to the nonliving forces of the universe. They perform invaluable service in the mind circuits on the inhabited worlds and are effective collaborators with the Master Physical Controllers, who also serve as controllers and directors of the preadjutant mind levels, the levels of nonteachable or mechanical mind." P. 403.

2. **Function of the adjutant mind-spirits on the animal level.**

"The acquisition of the potential of the ability to *learn* from experience marks the beginning of the functioning of the adjutant spirits, and they function from the lowliest minds of primitive and invisible existences up to the highest types in the evolutionary scale of human beings. They are the source and pattern for the otherwise more or less mysterious behavior and incompletely understood quick reactions of mind to the material environment. Long must these faithful and always dependable influences carry forward their preliminary ministry before the animal mind attains the human levels of spirit receptivity." P. 739.

3. **The difference between animal instinctive response and human insight.**

"The selective response of an animal is limited to the motor level of behavior. The supposed insight of the higher animals is on a motor level and usually appears only after the experience of motor trial and error. Man is able to exercise scientific, moral, and spiritual insight prior to all exploration or experimentation." P. 193.

4. **Only a personality can possess insight in advance of experience.**

"Only a personality can know what it is doing before it does it; only personalities possess insight in advance of experience. A personality can look before it leaps and can therefore learn from looking as well as from leaping. A nonpersonal animal ordinarily learns only by leaping." P. 193.

5. **A moral being can discriminate between both ends and their means of attainment.**

"As a result of experience an animal becomes able to examine the different ways of attaining a goal and to select an approach based on accumulated experience. But a personality can also examine the goal itself and pass judgment on its worthwhileness, its value. Intelligence alone can discriminate as to the best means of attaining indiscriminate ends, but a moral being possesses an insight which enables him to discriminate between ends as well as between means. And a moral being in choosing virtue is nonetheless intelligent. He knows what he is doing, why he is doing it, where he is going, and how he will get there." P. 193.

6. **When man fails to discriminate moral goals he descends to the animal level of thinking.**

"When man fails to discriminate the ends of his mortal striving, he finds himself functioning on the animal level of existence. He has failed to avail himself of the superior advantages of that material acumen, moral discrimination, and spiritual insight which are an integral part of his cosmic-mind endowment as a personal being." P. 193.

D. **Cosmic mind.**

1. **The cosmic mind is the mind of the finite level.**

"*The cosmic mind.* This is the sevenfold diversified mind of time and space, one phase of which is ministered by each of the Seven Master Spirits to one of the seven superuniverses. The cosmic mind encompasses all finite-mind levels and co-ordinates experientially with the evolutionary-deity levels of the Supreme Mind and transcendentally with the existential levels of absolute mind—the direct circuits of the Conjoint Actor." P. 481.

E. **Absolute mind.**

1. **The absolute mind of Paradise and the mind-gravity grasp of the Conjoint Actor.**

"On Paradise, mind is absolute; in Havona, absonite; in Orvonton, finite. Mind always connotes the presence-activity of living ministry plus varied energy systems, and this is true of all levels and of all kinds of mind. But beyond the cosmic mind it becomes increasingly difficult to portray the relationships of mind to nonspiritual energy. Havona mind is subabsolute but superevolutionary; being existential-experiential, it is nearer the absonite than any other concept revealed to you. Paradise mind is beyond human understanding; it is existential, nonspatial, and nontemporal. Nevertheless, all of these levels of mind are overshadowed by the universal presence of the Conjoint Actor—by the mind-gravity grasp of the God of mind on Paradise." P. 481.

II. Life Implantation by the Life Carriers

"When the Life Carriers make ready to engage in life implantation, and after they have selected the sites for such an undertaking, they summon the archangel commission of Life Carrier transmutation. This group consists of ten orders of diverse personalities, including the physical controllers and their associates, and is presided over by the chief of archangels, who acts in this capacity by the mandate of Gabriel and with the permission of the Ancients of Days. When these beings are properly encircuited, they can effect such modifications in the Life Carriers as will enable them immediately to function on the physical levels of electrochemistry." P. 731

A. Conditions necessary for formulation of life on Urantia.

1. **Life can be initiated only in suitable environment.**
   "It should be made clear that Life Carriers cannot initiate life until a sphere is ripe for the inauguration of the evolutionary cycle. Neither can we provide for a more rapid life development than can be supported and accommodated by the physical progress of the planet." P. 664.

2. **The Urantia life is a sodium chloride type.**
   "The Satania Life Carriers had projected a sodium chloride pattern of life; therefore no steps could be taken toward planting it until the ocean waters had become sufficiently briny. The Urantia type of protoplasm can function only in a suitable salt solution. All ancestral life—vegetable and animal—evolved in a salt-solution habitat. And even the more highly organized land animals could not continue to live did not this same essential salt solution circulate throughout their bodies in the blood stream which freely bathes, literally submerses, every tiny living cell in this 'briny deep.'" P. 664.

3. **Primitive life circulated in the salty ocean; today this same solution circulates in the animal body.**
   "Your primitive ancestors freely circulated about in the salty ocean; today, this same oceanlike salty solution freely circulates about in your bodies, bathing each individual cell with a chemical liquid in all essentials comparable to the salt water which stimulated the first protoplasmic reactions of the first living cells to function on the planet." P. 664.

B. **Three simultaneous life implantations.**

1. **Life was not brought to Urantia. It was formulated on the planet and is unique.**
   "That we are called Life Carriers should not confuse you. We can and do carry life to the planets, but we brought no life to Urantia. Urantia life is unique, original with the planet. This sphere is a life-modification world; all life appearing hereon was formulated by us right here on the planet; and there is no other world in all Satania, even in all Nebadon, that has a life existence just like that of Urantia." P. 667.

2. **Three life implantations were made to accompany the separating continents.**
   "We had planted the primitive form of marine life in the sheltered tropic bays of the central seas of the east-west cleavage of the breaking-up continental land mass. Our purpose in making three marine life implantations was to insure that each great land mass would carry this life with it, in its warm-water seas, as the land subsequently separated. We foresaw that in the later era of the emergence of land life large oceans of water would separate these drifting continental land masses." P. 668.

III. Biologic History of Urantia

A. **Chronology of Urantia biology.**

1. **The five major biologic eras.**
   "We reckon the history of Urantia as beginning about one billion years ago and extending through five major eras:

   "1. *The prelife era* extends over the initial four hundred and fifty million years, from about the time the planet attained its present size to the time of life establishment. Your students have designated this period as the *Archeozoic*.

   "2. *The life-dawn era* extends over the next one hundred and fifty million years. This epoch intervenes between the preceding prelife or cataclysmic age and the following period of more highly developed marine life. This era is known to your researchers as the *Proterozoic*.

   "3. *The marine-life era* covers the next two hundred and fifty million years and is best known to you as the *Paleozoic*.

   "4. *The early land-life era* extends over the next one hundred million years and is known as the *Mesozoic*.

   "5. *The mammalian era* occupies the last fifty million years. This recent-times era is known as the *Cenozoic*." P. 672.

PART IV — *Biology*

B. **The life-dawn era.**
1. **Life was implanted simultaneously in three marine locations on Urantia 550,000,000 years ago.**
   "*550,000,000* years ago the Life Carrier corps returned to Urantia. In co-operation with spiritual powers and superphysical forces we organized and initiated the original life patterns of this world and planted them in the hospitable waters of the realm. All planetary life (aside from extraplanetary personalities) down to the days of Caligastia, the Planetary Prince, had its origin in our three original, identical, and simultaneous marine-life implantations. These three life implantations have been designated as: the *central* or Eurasian-African, the *eastern* or Australasian, and the *western*, embracing Greenland and the Americas." P. 667.
2. **Half a billion years ago, marine vegetable life was well established.**
   "*500,000,000* years ago primitive marine vegetable life was well established on Urantia. Greenland and the arctic land mass, together with North and South America, were beginning their long and slow westward drift. Africa moved slightly south, creating an east and west trough, the Mediterranean basin, between itself and the mother body. Antarctica, Australia, and the land indicated by the islands of the Pacific broke away on the south and east and have drifted far away since that day." P. 668.
3. **The transition from marine vegetable to animal life was gradual. It took place 450,000,000 years ago.**
   "*450,000,000* years ago the *transition from vegetable to animal life* occurred. This metamorphosis took place in the shallow waters of the sheltered tropic bays and lagoons of the extensive shore lines of the separating continents. And this development, all of which was inherent in the original life patterns, came about gradually. There were many transitional stages between the early primitive vegetable forms of life and the later well-defined animal organisms. Even today the transition slime molds persist, and they can hardly be classified either as plants or as animals." P. 669.
4. **Few species that participated in the transition from vegetable to animal types exist today.**

"Very few species of the early types of marine vegetation that participated in those epochal changes which resulted in the animallike borderland organisms are in existence today. The sponges are the survivors of one of these early midway types, those organisms through which the *gradual* transition from the vegetable to the animal took place. These early transition forms, while not identical with modern sponges, were much like them; they were true borderline organisms—neither vegetable nor animal—but they eventually led to the development of the true animal forms of life." P. 731.

5. **The nature, evolution, and retrogression of bacteria.**
"The bacteria, simple vegetable organisms of a very primitive nature, are very little changed from the early dawn of life; they even exhibit a degree of retrogression in their parasitic behavior. Many of the fungi also represent a retrograde movement in evolution, being plants which have lost their chlorophyll-making ability and have become more or less parasitic. The majority of disease-causing bacteria and their auxiliary virus bodies really belong to this group of renegade parasitic fungi. During the intervening ages all of the vast kingdom of plant life has evolved from ancestors from which the bacteria have also descended." P. 732.

6. **Changes from one great division of the animal kingdom to another and from prehuman animal types to dawn men occurred suddenly. "Missing links" never existed.**
"Although the evolution of vegetable life can be traced into animal life, and though there have been found graduated series of plants and animals which progressively lead up from the most simple to the most complex and advanced organisms, you will not be able to find such connecting links between the great divisions of the animal kingdom nor between the highest of the prehuman animal types and the dawn men of the human races. These so-called 'missing links' will forever remain missing, for the simple reason that they never existed.

"From era to era radically new spees of animal life arise. They do not evolve as the result of the gradual accumulation of small variations; they appear as full-fledged and new orders of life, and they appear *suddenly*.

"The *sudden* appearance of new species and diversified orders of living organisms is wholly biologic, strictly natural. There is nothing supernatural connected with these genetic mutations." P. 669.

7. **The adjustment of animal life to both salt water and fresh water.**
   "At the proper degree of saltiness in the oceans animal life evolved, and it was comparatively simple to allow the briny waters to circulate through the animal bodies of marine life. But when the oceans were contracted and the percentage of salt was greatly increased, these same animals evolved the ability to reduce the saltiness of their body fluids just as those organisms which learned to live in fresh water acquired the ability to maintain the proper degree of sodium chloride in their body fluids by ingenious techniques of salt conservation." P. 669.

8. **The never-ending adjustment of life to its changing environment.**
   "Study of the rock-embraced fossils of marine life reveals the early adjustment struggles of these primitive organisms. Plants and animals never cease to make these adjustment experiments. Ever the environment is changing, and always are living organisms striving to accommodate themselves to these never-ending fluctuations." P. 669.

9. **"Survival of the fittest."**
   "Through almost endless cycles of gains and losses, adjustments and readjustments, all living organisms swing back and forth from age to age. Those that attain cosmic unity persist, while those that fall short of this goal cease to exist." P. 670.

10. **The most important factors in plant evolution were chlorophyll and seeds.**
    "The most important step in plant evolution was the development of chlorophyll-making ability, and the second greatest The spore is most efficient as a reproductive agent, but it lacks the potentials of variety and versatility inherent in the seed." P. 737.

C. **The marine-life era.**

1. **The marine-life era is divided into six periods and covers one quarter of planetary history.**
   "The marine-life era thus covers about one quarter of your planetary history. It may be subdivided into six long periods, each characterized by certain well-defined developments in advance was the evolution of the spore into the complex seed. both the geologic realms and the biologic domains." P. 672.

2. **The widespread distribution of marine vegetable and animal life.**

   "As this era begins, the sea bottoms, the extensive continental shelves, and the numerous shallow near-shore basins are covered with prolific vegetation. The more simple and primitive forms of animal life have already developed from preceding vegetable organisms, and the early animal organisms have gradually made their way along the extensive coast lines of the various land masses until the many inland seas are teeming with primitive marine life. Since so few of these early organisms had shells, not many have been preserved as fossils. Nevertheless the stage is set for the opening chapters of that great 'stone book' of the life-record preservation which was so methodically laid down during the succeeding ages." P. 672.

3. **In North America, marine-life fossils are found in two segregated strata.**

   "The continent of North America is wonderfully rich in the fossilbearing deposits of the entire marine-life era. The very first and oldest layers are separated from the later strata of the preceding period by extensive erosion deposits which clearly segregate these two stages of planetary development." P. 672.

4. **Ameba are typical survivors of the early animal life.**

   "By the dawn of this period of relative quiet on the earth's surface, life is confined to the various inland seas and the oceanic shore line; as yet no form of land organism has evolved. Primitive marine animals are well established and are prepared for the next evolutionary development. Ameba are typical survivors of this initial stage of animal life, having made their appearance toward the close of the preceding transition period." P. 673.

5. **The ameba represents a primitive type of animal which failed to develop.**

   "The higher protozoan type of animal life soon appeared, and appeared *suddenly*. And from these far-distant times the ameba, the typical single-celled animal organism, has come on down but little modified. He disports himself today much as he did when he was the last and greatest achievement in life evolution. This minute creature and his protozoan cousins are to the animal creation what bacteria are to the plant kingdom; they represent the survival of the first early evolutionary steps in life differentiation together with *failure of subsequent development*." P. 732.

6. **The beginnings of land life.**
"400,000,000 years ago marine life, both vegetable and animal, is fairly well distributed over the whole world. The world climate grows slightly warmer and becomes more equable. There is a general inundation of the seashores of the various continents, particularly of North and South America. New oceans appear, and the older bodies of water are greatly enlarged.

"Vegetation now for the first time crawls out upon the land and soon makes considerable progress in adaptation to a nonmarine habitat.

"*Suddenly* and without gradation ancestry the first multicellular animals make their appearance. The trilobites have evolved, and for ages they dominate the seas. From the standpoint of marine life this is the trilobite age." P. 673.

7. **Marine life during the trilobite age—the Cambrian Period.**
"The marine life was much alike the world over and consisted of the seaweeds, one-celled organisms, simple sponges, trilobites, and other crustaceans—shrimps, crabs, and lobsters. Three thousand varieties of brachiopods appeared at the close of this period, only two hundred of which have survived. These animals represent a variety of early life which has come down to the present time practically unchanged.

"But the trilobites were the dominant living creatures. They were sexed animals and existed in many forms; being poor swimmers, they sluggishly floated in the water or crawled along the sea bottoms, curling up in self-protection when attacked by their later appearing enemies. They grew in length from two inches to one foot and developed into four distinct groups: carnivorous, herbivorous, omnivorous, and 'mud eaters.' The ability of the latter group largely to subsist on inorganic matter—being the last multicelled animal that could—explains their great increase and long survival." P. 674.

8. **Evolutionary developments during the invertebrate—animal age—the Ordovician Period.**
"This was the great age of individual animal organismal evolution, though many of the basic changes, such as the transition from plant to animal, had previously occurred. The marine fauna developed to the point where every type of life

below the vertebrate scale was represented in the fossils of those rocks which were laid down during these times. But all of these animals were marine organisms. No land animals had yet appeared except a few types of worms which burrowed along the seashores, nor had the land plants yet overspread the continents; there was still too much carbon dioxide in the air to permit of the existence of air breathers. Primarily, all animals except certain of the more primitive ones are directly or indirectly dependent on plant life for their existence.

"The trilobites were still prominent. These little animals existed in tens of thousands of patterns and were the predecessors of modern crustaceans. Some of the trilobites had from twenty-five to four thousand tiny eyelets; others had aborted eyes. As this period closed, the trilobites shared domination of the seas with several other forms of invertebrate life. But they utterly perished during the beginning of the next period.

"Lime-secreting algae were widespread. There existed thousands of species of the early ancestors of the corals. Sea worms were abundant, and there were many varieties of jellyfish which have since become extinct. Corals and the later types of sponges evolved. The cephalopods were well developed, and they have survived as the modern pearly nautilus, octopus, cuttlefish, and squid.

"There were many varieties of shell animals, but their shells were not then so much needed for defensive purposes as in subsequent ages. The gastropods were present in the waters of the ancient seas, and they included single-shelled drills, periwinkles, and snails. The bivalve gastropods have come on down through the intervening millions of years much as they then existed and embrace the muscles, clams, oysters, and scallops. The valve-shelled organisms also evolved, and these brachiopods lived in those ancient waters much as they exist today; they even had hinged, notched, and other sorts of protective arrangements of their valves." P. 675-6.

9. **The Silurian period—the coral period—the brachiopod age.**

"The trilobites rapidly declined, and the center of the stage was occupied by the larger mollusks, or cephalopods. These animals grew to be fifteen feet long and one foot in diameter and became masters of the seas. This species of animal appeared *suddenly* and assumed dominance of sea life." P. 677.

"Toward the close of the final Silurian submergence there is a great increase in the echinoderms—the stone lilies—as is evidenced by the crinoid limestone deposits. The trilobites have nearly disappeared, and the mollusks continue monarchs of the seas; coral-reef formation increases greatly. During this age, in the more favorable locations the primitive water scorpions first evolve. Soon thereafter, and *suddenly*, the true scorpions—actual air breathers—make their appearance." P. 677-78.

10. **The Devonian period—the vegetative land-life period—the age of fishes.**

   a. *The appearance of vertebrates.*

   "The marine life of this age was very diverse due to the early species segregation, but later on there was free commingling and association of all these different types. The brachiopods early reached their climax, being succeeded by the arthropods, and barnacles made their first appearance. But the greatest event of all was the sudden appearance of the fish family. This became the age of fishes, that period of the world's history characterized by the *vertebrate* type of animal." P. 678.

   "One of the most serviceable and complex episodes in the evolution of the higher types of animals consisted in the development of the ability of the iron in the circulating blood cells to perform in the double role of oxygen carrier and carbon dioxide remover. And this performance of the red blood cells illustrates how evolving organisms are able to adapt their functions to varying or changing environment. The higher animals, including man, oxygenate their tissues by the action of the iron of the red blood cells, which carries oxygen to the living cells and just as efficiently removes the carbon dioxide. But other metals can be made to serve the same purpose. The cuttlefish employs copper for this function, and the sea squirt utilizes vanadium." P. 737.

   "*250,000,000* years ago witnessed the appearance of the fish family, the vertebrates, one of the most important steps in all prehuman evolution.

   "The arthropods, or crustaceans, were the ancestors of the first vertebrates. The forerunners of the fish family were two modified arthropod ancestors; one had a long body connecting a head and tail, while the other was a backboneless, jawless prefish. But these preliminary types were quickly destroyed when the fishes, the first vertebrates of the animal world, made their *sudden* appearance from the north.

"Many of the largest true fish belong to this age, some of the teeth-bearing varieties being twenty-five to thirty feet long; the present-day sharks are the survivors of these ancient fishes. The lung and armored fishes reached their evolutionary apex, and before this epoch had ended, fishes had adapted to both fresh and salt waters.

"Veritable bone beds of fish teeth and skeletons may be found in the deposits laid down toward the close of this period, and rich fossil beds are situated along the coast of California since many sheltered bays of the Pacific Ocean extended into the land of that region." P. 679.

    b.   *The appearance of ferns.*

"The earth was being rapidly overrun by the new orders of land vegetation. Heretofore few plants grew on land except about the water's edge. Now, and *suddenly*, the prolific *fern family* appeared and quickly spread over the face of the rapidly rising land in all parts of the world. Tree types, two feet thick and forty feet high, soon developed; later on, leaves evolved, but these early varieties had only rudimentary foliage. There were many smaller plants, but their fossils are not found since they were usually destroyed by the still earlier appearing bacteria." P. 679.

"The elevation of the continents proceeded, and the atmosphere was becoming enriched with oxygen. The earth was overspread by vast forests of ferns one hundred feet high and by the peculiar trees of those days, silent forests; not a sound was heard, not even the rustle of a leaf, for such trees had no leaves." P. 680.

11. The Carboniferous period—the age of frogs.

    a.   *The age of ferns.*

"*220,000,000* years ago many of the continental land areas, including most of North America, were above water. The land was overrun by luxurious vegetation; this was indeed the *age of ferns*. Carbon dioxide was still present in the atmosphere but in lessening degree." P. 680.

    b.   *The age of frogs and insects.*

"When the seas were at their height, a new evolutionary

development *suddenly* occurred. Abruptly, the first of the land animals appeared. There were numerous species of these animals that were able to live on land or in water. These airbreathing amphibians developed from the arthropods, whose swim bladders had evolved into lungs. "From the briny waters of the seas there crawled out upon the land snails, scorpions, and frogs. Today frogs still lay their eggs in water, and their young first exist as little fishes, tadpoles. This period could well be known as the *age of frogs*.

"Very soon thereafter the insects first appeared and, together with spiders, scorpions, cockroaches, crickets, and locusts, soon overspread the continents of the world. Dragon flies measured thirty inches across. One thousand species of cockroaches developed, and some grew to be four inches long." P. 680.

c. *Marine life continues to evolve.*

"Two groups of echinoderms became especially well developed, and they are in reality the guide fossils of this epoch. The large shell-feeding sharks were also highly evolved, and for more than five million years they dominated the oceans. The climate was still mild and equable; the marine life was little changed. Fresh-water fish were developing and the trilobites were nearing extinction. Corals were scarce, and much of the limestone was being made by the crinoids. The finer building limestones were laid down during this epoch." P. 680-1.

d. *The formation of coal.*

"The land was periodically going up and down due to the shifting sea level occasioned by activities on the ocean bottoms. This crustal uneasiness—the settling and rising of the land-in connection with the prolific vegetation of the coastal swamps, contributed to the production of extensive coal deposits, which have caused this period to be known as the *Carboniferous*. And the climate was still mild the world over.

"The coal layers alternate with shale, stone, and conglomerate. These coal beds over central and eastern United States vary in thickness from forty to fifty feet. But many of these deposits were washed away during subsequent land elevations. In some parts of North America and Europe the coal-bearing strata are 18,000 feet in thickness.

"The presence of roots of trees as they grew in the clay underlying the present coal beds demonstrates that coal was formed exactly where it is now found. Coal is the water-preserved and pressure-modified remains of the rank vegetation growing in the bogs and on the swamp shores of this faraway age. Coal layers often hold both gas and oil. Peat beds, the remains of past vegetable growth, would be converted into a type of coal if subjected to proper pressure and heat. Anthracite has been subjected to more pressure and heat than other coal." P. 681.

"The plants of these times were spore bearing, and the wind was able to spread them far and wide. The trunks of the Carboniferous trees were commonly seven feet in diameter and often one hundred and twenty-five feet high. The modern ferns are truly relics of these bygone ages." P. 682.

12. **The Permian period—the seed-plant period—the age of biologic tribulation.**

   a. *The climatic transition stage.*

   "This period marks the end of pivotal evolutionary development in marine life and the opening of the transition period leading to the subsequent ages of land animals.

   "This age was one of great life impoverishment. Thousands of marine species perished, and life was hardly yet established on land. This was a time of biologic tribulation, the age when life nearly vanished from the face of the earth and from the depths of the oceans. Toward the close of the long marine-life era there were more than one hundred thousand species of living things on earth. At the close of this period of transition less than five hundred had survived.

   "The peculiarities of this new period were not due so much to the cooling of the earth's crust or to the long absence of volcanic action as to an unusual combination of common place and preexisting influences—restrictions of the seas and increasing elevation of enormous land masses. The mild marine climate of former times was disappearing,

b. *Development of seed plants.*
"Throughout these times of climatic change, great variations also occurred in the land plants. The *seed plants* first appeared, and they afforded a better food supply for the subsequently increased land-animal life. The insects underwent a radical change. The *resting stages* evolved to meet the demands of suspended animation during winter and drought." P. 683.

c. *Beginning of the marine-life-adversity age.*
"The gradual cooling of the ocean waters contributed much to the destruction of oceanic life. The marine animals of those ages took temporary refuge in three favorable retreats: the present Gulf of Mexico region, the Ganges Bay of India, and the Sicilian Bay of the Mediterranean basin. And it was from these three regions that the new marine species, born to adversity, later went forth to replenish the seas." P. 683.

d. *Changes during the life-adversity period—the marine-life crisis.*
"Among the land animals the frogs reached their climax in the preceding age and rapidly declined, but they survived because they could long live even in the drying-up pools and ponds of these far-distant and extremely trying times. During this declining frog age, in Africa, the first step in the evolution of the frog into the reptile occurred. And since the land masses were still connected, this prereptilian creature, an air breather, spread over all the world. By this time the atmosphere had been so changed that it served admirably to support animal respiration. It was soon after the arrival of these prereptilian frogs that North America was temporarily isolated, cut off from Europe, Asia, and South America." P. 683.

e. *The ending of the life-adversity age.*
"160,000,000 years ago the land was largely covered with vegetation adapted to support land-animal life, and the atmosphere had become ideal for animal respiration. Thus ends the period of marine-life curtailment and those testing times of biologic adversity which eliminated all forms of life except such as had survival value, and which

were therefore entitled to function as the ancestors of the more rapidly developing and highly differentiated life of the ensuing ages of planetary evolution." P. 683.

"The ending of this period of biologic tribulation, known to your students as the *Permian*, also marks the end of the long *Paleozoic* era, which covers one quarter of the planetary history, two hundred and fifty million years." P. 684.

    f. *The primary era of marine life diminishes while the second stage of evolution begins to unfold on land.*

"The vast oceanic nursery of life on Urantia has served its purpose. During the long ages when the land was unsuited to support life, before the atmosphere contained sufficient oxygen to sustain the higher land animals, the sea mothered and nurtured the early life of the realm. Now the biologic importance of the sea progressively diminishes as the second stage of evolution begins to unfold on the land." P. 684.

D. The early land-life era.

"The era of exclusive marine life has ended. Land elevation, cooling crust and cooling oceans, sea restriction and consequent deepening, together with a great increase of land in northern latitudes, all conspired greatly to change the world's climate in all regions far removed from the equatorial zone.

"The closing epochs of the preceding era were indeed the age of frogs, but these ancestors of the land vertebrates were no longer dominant, having survived in greatly reduced numbers. Very few types outlived the rigorous trials of the preceding period of biologic tribulation. Even the spore-bearing plants were nearly extinct." P. 685.

1. **The Triassic period—the early reptilian age.**
    a. *The land-life period begins.*

    "*150,000,000* years ago the early land-life periods of the world's history began. Life, in general, did not fare well but did better than at the strenuous and hostile close of the marinelife era." P. 686.

    b. *The sudden appearance of the reptiles.*

    "*140,000,000* years ago, *suddenly* and with only the hint of the two prereptilian ancestors that developed in Africa during the preceding epoch, the reptiles appeared in full-fledged form. They developed rapidly, soon yielding crocodiles, scaled reptiles, and eventually both sea serpents and flying reptiles. Their transition ancestors speedily disappeared." P. 686.

 c. *The age of the dinosaurs.*
"These rapidly evolving reptilian dinosaurs soon became the monarchs of this age. They were egg layers and are distinguished from all animals by their small brains, having brains weighing less than one pound to control bodies later weighing as much as forty tons. But earlier reptiles were smaller, carnivorous, and walked kangaroolike on their hind legs. They had hollow avian bones and subsequently developed only three toes on their hind feet, and many of their fossil footprints have been mistaken for those of giant birds. Later on, the herbivorous dinosaurs evolved. They walked on all fours, and one branch of this group developed a protective armor." P. 686.

 d. *Failure of the nonplacental mammals.*
"Several million years later the first mammals appeared. They were nonplacental and proved a speedy failure; none survived. This was an experimental effort to improve mammalian types, but it did not succeed on Urantia." P. 686.

2. **The Jurassic period—the later reptilian age.**

 a. *The later reptilian age.*
"120,000,000 years ago a new phase of the reptilian age began. The great event of this period was the evolution and decline of the dinosaurs. Land-animal life reached its greatest development, in point of size, and had virtually perished from the face of the earth by the end of this age. The dinosaurs evolved in all sizes from a species less than two feet long up to the huge noncarnivorous dinosaurs, seventy-five feet long, that have never since been equaled in bulk by any living creature.

"The largest of the dinosaurs originated in western North America. These monstrous reptiles are buried throughout the Rocky Mountain regions, along the whole of the Atlantic coast of North America, over western Europe, South Africa, and India, but not in Australia."

"These massive creatures became less active and strong as they grew larger and larger; but they required such an enormous amount of food and the land was so overrun by them that they literally starved to death and became extinct—they lacked the intelligence to cope with the situation." P. 687.

b. *The flora of this age.*
"The flora of this age was much like that of the preceding. Ferns persisted, while conifers and pines became more and more like the present-day varieties. Some coal was still being formed along the northern Mediterranean shores." P. 687.

c. *Marine life continues to evolve and some dinosaurs return to the sea.*
"110,000,000 years ago the potentials of marine life were continuing to unfold. The sea urchin was one of the outstanding mutations of this epoch. Crabs, lobsters, and the modern types of crustaceans matured. Marked changes occurred in the fish family, a sturgeon type first appearing, but the ferocious sea serpents, descended from the land reptiles, still infested all the seas, and they threatened the destruction of the entire fish family.
"This continued to be, pre-eminently, the age of the dinosaurs. They so overran the land that two species had taken to the water for sustenance during the preceding period of sea encroachment. These sea serpents represent a backward step in evolution. While some new species are progressing, certain strains remain stationary and others gravitate backward, reverting to a former state. And this is what happened when these two types of reptiles forsook the land." P. 688.

d. *The failure of several species—the survival of one species.*
"As time passed, the sea serpents grew to such size that they became very sluggish and eventually perished because they did not have brains large enough to afford protection for their immense bodies. Their brains weighed less than two ounces notwithstanding the fact that these huge ichthyosaurs sometimes grew to be fifty feet long, the majority being over thirty-five feet in length. The marine crocodilians were also a reversion from the land type of reptile, but unlike the sea serpents, these animals always returned to the land to lay their eggs.

"Soon after two species of dinosaurs migrated to the water in a futile attempt at self-preservation, two other types were driven to the air by the bitter competition of life on land. But these flying pterosaurs were not the ancestors of the true birds of subsequent ages. They evolved from the hollow-boned leaping dinosaurs, and their wings were of bat like formation with a spread of twenty to twenty-five feet. These ancient flying reptiles grew to be ten feet long, and they had separable jaws much like those of modern snakes. For a time these flying reptiles appeared to be a success, but they failed to evolve along lines which would enable them to survive as air navigators. They represent the nonsurviving strains of bird ancestry.

"Turtles increased during this period, first appearing in North America. Their ancestors came over from Asia by way of the northern land bridge." P. 688.

    e.   *The decline of the dinosaurs.*

"One hundred million years ago the reptilian age was drawing to a close. The dinosaurs, for all their enormous mass, were all but brainless animals, lacking the intelligence to provide sufficient food to nourish such enormous bodies. And so did these sluggish land reptiles perish in ever-increasing numbers. Henceforth, evolution will follow the growth of brains, not physical bulk, and the development of brains will characterize each succeeding epoch of animal evolution and planetary progress." P. 688.

3.   **The Cretaceous period—the flowering plant—the age of birds.**

    a.   *The angiosperms suddenly appear on land and overrun the continents.*

"90,000,000 years ago the angiosperms emerged from these early Cretaceous seas and soon overran the continents. These land plants *suddenly* appeared along with fig trees, magnolias, and tulip trees. Soon after this time fig trees, breadfruit trees, and palms overspread Europe and the western plains of North America. No new land animals appeared." P. 689.

    b.   Bering Strait is closed and marine life is modified.

"85,000,000 years ago Bering Strait closed, shutting off the cooling waters of the northern seas. Theretofore the marine life of the Atlantic-Gulf waters and that of the Pacific Ocean had differed greatly, owing to the temperature variations of these two bodies of water, which now became uniform." P. 689.

c. *Present-day trees appear, together with cereals, grasses, and flowering plants.*

"Great plant-life evolution was taking place. Among the land plants the angiosperms predominated, and many present-day trees first appeared, including beech, birch, oak, walnut, sycamore, maple, and modern palms. Fruits, grasses, and cereals were abundant, and these seed-bearing grasses and trees were to the plant world what the ancestors of man were to the animal world—they were second in evolutionary importance only to the appearance of man himself. *Suddenly* and without previous gradation, the great family of flowering plants mutated. And this new flora soon overspread the entire world." P. 690-1.

d. *The dinosaurs still rule the land as the stage is set for the appearance of birds.*

"60,000,000 years ago, though the land reptiles were on the decline, the dinosaurs continued as monarchs the smaller leaping kangaroo varieties of the carnivorous dinosaurs. But some time previously there had appeared new types of the herbivorous dinosaurs, whose rapid increase was due to the appearance of the grass family of land plants. One of these new grass-eating dinosaurs was a true quadruped having two horns and a capelike shoulder flange. The land type of turtle, twenty feet across, appeared as did also the modern crocodile and true snakes of the modern type. Great changes were also occurring among the fishes and other forms of marine life.

"The wading and swimming prebirds of earlier ages had not been a success in the air, nor had the flying dinosaurs. They were a short-lived species, soon becoming extinct. They, too, were subject to the dinosaur doom, destruction, because of having too little brain substance in comparison with body size. This second attempt to produce animals that could navigate the atmosphere failed, as did the abortive attempt to produce mammals during this and a preceding age." 691.

    e. *The birds suddenly appear as the reptiles decline.*
       "55,000,000 years ago the evolutionary march was from the earlier types of toothed land birds. And so this becomes known as the *age of birds* as well as the decling age of reptiles." P. 691.

    f. *The close of the Cretaceous period and the Mesozoic era.*
       "Biologically as well as geologically this was an eventful and active age on land and under water. Sea urchins increased while corals and crinoids decreased. The ammonites, of preponderant influence during a previous age, also rapidly declined. On land the fern forests were largely replaced by pine and other modern trees, including the gigantic redwoods. By the end of this period, while the placental mammal has not yet evolved, the biologic stage is fully set for the appearance, in a subsequent age, of the early ancestors of the future mammalian types." P. 692.

E. The mammalian era.

"The era of mammals extends from the times of the origin of placental mammals to the end of the ice age, covering a little less than fifty million years.

"During this Cenozoic age the world's landscape presented an attractive appearance—rolling hills, broad valleys, wide rivers, and great forests. Twice during this sector of time the Panama Isthmus went up and down; three times Bering Strait land bridge did the same. The animal types were both many and varied. The trees swarmed with birds, and the whole world was an animal paradise, notwithstanding the incessant struggle of the evolving animal species for supremacy." P. 693.

1. The Eocene—the age of early mammals.
    a. *Mammalian life suddenly appears in North America.*
       "50,000,000 years ago the land areas of the world were very generally above water or only slightly submerged. The formations and deposits of this period are both land and marine, but chiefly land. For a considerable time the land gradually rose but was simultaneously washed down to the lower levels and toward the seas.

       "Early in this period and in North America the placental type of mammals *suddenly* appeared, and they constituted the most important evolutionary development up to this time. Previous orders of nonplacental mammals had existed, but this new type sprang directly and *suddenly* from the pre-existent reptilian ancestor whose descendants had persisted on down through the times of dinosaur decline. The father of the placental mammals was a small, highly active, carnivorous, springing type of dinosaur." P. 693.

b. *Mammalian survival advantages.*

"Basic mammalian instincts began to be manifested in these primitive mammalian types. Mammals possess an immense survival advantage over all other forms of animal life in that they can:

"1.   Bring forth relatively mature and well-developed offspring.
"2.   Nourish, nurture, and protect their offspring with affectionate regard.
"3.   Employ their superior brain power in self-perpetuation.
"4.   Utilize increased agility in escaping from enemies.
"5.   Apply superior intelligence to environmental adjustment and adaptation." P. 693.

c. *Diversification of mammals.*

"45,000,000 years ago the continental backbones were elevated in association with a very general sinking of the coast lines. Mammalian life was evolving rapidly. A small reptilian, egg-laying type of mammal flourished, and the ancestors of the later kangaroos roamed Australia. Soon there were small horses, fleet-footed rhinoceroses, tapirs with proboscises, primitive pigs, squirrels, lemurs, opossums, and several tribes of monkeylike animals. They were all small, primitive, and best suited to living among the forests of the mountain regions. A large ostrichlike land bird developed to a height of ten feet and laid an egg nine by thirteen inches. These were the ancestors of the later gigantic passenger birds that were so highly intelligent, and that onetime transported human beings through the air. "The mammals of the early Cenozoic lived on land, under the water, in the air, and among the treetops. They had from one to eleven pairs of mammary glands, and all were covered with considerable hair. In common with the later appearing orders, they developed two successive sets of teeth and possessed large brains in comparison to body size. But among them all no modern forms existed." P. 694.

PART IV — *Biology*

2. **The Oligocene—the age of advanced mammals.**
    a. *Development of herbivorous and omnivorous animals.*
    "This period was characterized by the further and rapid evolution of placental mammals, the more progressive forms of mammalian life developing during these times.
    "Although the early placental mammals sprang from carnivorous ancestors, very soon herbivorous branches developed, and, ere long, omnivorous mammalian families also sprang up. The angiosperms were the principal food of the rapidly increasing mammals, the modern land flora, including the majority of present-day plants and trees, having appeared during earlier periods." P. 694-5.
    b. *Mammals begin to dominate the world.*
    "35,000,000 years ago marks the beginning of the age of placental mammalian world domination. The southern land bridge was extensive, reconnecting the then enormous Antarctic continent with South America, South Africa, and Australia. In spite of the massing of land in high latitudes, the world climate remained relatively mild because of the enormous increase in the size of the tropic seas, nor was the land elevated sufficiently to produce glaciers. Extensive lava flows occurred in Greenland and Iceland, some coal being deposited between these layers." P. 695.
    c. *Mammals dominate the earth as dinosaurs decline.*
    "On land this was pre-eminently the age of mammalian renovation and expansion. Of the earlier and more primitive mammals, over one hundred species were extinct before this period ended. Even the mammals of large size and small brain soon perished. Brains and agility had replaced armor and size in the progress of animal survival. And with the dinosaur family on the decline, the mammals slowly assumed domination of the earth, speedily and completely destroying the remainder of their reptilian ancestors.
    "Along with the disappearance of the dinosaurs, other and great changes occurred in the various branches of thesaurian family. The surviving members of the early reptilian families are turtles, snakes, and crocodiles, together with the venerable frog, the only remaining

group representative of man's earlier ancestors. "Various groups of mammals had their origin in a unique animal now extinct. This carnivorous creature was something of a cross between a cat and a seal; it could live on land or in water and was highly intelligent and very active. In Europe the ancestor of the canine family evolved, soon giving rise to many species of small dogs. About the same time the gnawing rodents, including beavers, squirrels, gophers, mice, and rabbits, appeared and soon became a notable form of life, very little change having since occurred in this family. The later deposits of this period contain the fossil remains of dogs, cats, coons, and weasels in ancestral form." P. 695.

d. *A great variety of mammals continues to evolve.*
"*30,000,000* years ago the modern types of mammals began to make their appearance. Formerly the mammals had lived for the greater part in the hills, being of the mountainous types; *suddenly* there began the evolution of the plains or hoofed type, the grazing species, as differentiated from the clawed flesh eaters. These grazers sprang from an undifferentiated ancestor having five toes and forty-four teeth, which perished before the end of the age. Toe evolution did not progress beyond the three-toed stage throughout this period.

"The horse, an outstanding example of evolution, lived during these times in both North America and Europe, though his development was not fully completed until the later ice age. While the rhinoceros family appeared at the close of this period, it underwent its greatest expansion subsequently. A small hoglike creature also developed which became the ancestor of the many species of swine, peccaries, and hippopotamuses. Camels and llamas had their origin in North America about the middle of this period and overran the western plains. Later, the llamas migrated to South America, the camels to Europe, and soon both were extinct in North America, though a few camels survived up to the ice age." P. 695-6.

e. *In North America, the ancestors of the true lemurs appear.*
"About this time a notable thing occurred in western North America: The early ancestors of the ancient lemurs first made their appearance. While this family cannot be

regarded as true lemurs, their coming marked the establishment of the line from which the true lemurs subsequently sprang." P. 696.

3. The Miocene—age of the elephant and the horse.
   a.   *Evolution of the grazing type of mammals.*
       "There was a great increase in the varieties of grasses, and the teeth of many mammalian species gradually altered to conform to the present-day grazing type." P. 696.
   b.   *The golden age of mammals.*
       "20,000,000 years ago was indeed the golden age of mammals. Bering Strait land bridge was up, and many groups of animals migrated to North America from Asia, including the four-tusked mastodons, short-legged rhinoceroses, and many varieties of the cat family.
       "The first deer appeared, and North America was soon overrun by ruminants—deer, oxen, camels, bison, and several species of rhinoceroses—but the giant pigs, more than six feet tall, became extinct.
       "The huge elephants of this and subsequent periods possessed large brains as well as large bodies, and they soon overran the entire world except Australia. For once the world was dominated by a huge animal with a brain sufficiently large to enable it to carry on. Confronted by the highly intelligent life of these ages, no animal the size of an elephant could have survived unless it had possessed a brain of large size and superior quality. In intelligence and adaptation the elephant is approached only by the horse and is surpassed only by man himself. Even so, of the fifty species of elephants in existence at the opening of this period, only two have survived." P. 696-7.
   c.   *The age of horses and elephants.*
       "Mammalian life continued to evolve. Enormous herds of horses joined the camels on the western plains of North America; this was truly the age of horses as well as of elephants. The horse's brain is next in animal quality to that of the elephant, but in one respect it is decidedly inferior, for the horse never fully overcame the deep-seated propensity to flee when frightened. The horse lacks the emotional control of the elephant, while the elephant is greatly handicapped by size and lack of agility. During this period an animal evolved which was somewhat like

both the elephant and the horse, but it was soon destroyed by the rapidly increasing cat family.

"As Urantia is entering the so-called 'horseless age,' you should pause and ponder what this animal meant to your ancestors. Men first used horses for food, then for travel, and later in agriculture and war. The horse has long served mankind and has played an important part in the development of human civilization." P. 697.

    d. *Evolution of types of monkeys.*

"The biologic developments of this period contributed much toward the setting of the stage for the subsequent appearance of man. In central Asia the true types of both the primitive monkey and the gorilla evolved, having a common ancestor, now extinct. But neither of these species is concerned in the line of living beings which were, later on, to become the ancestors of the human race." P. 697.

    e. *The dog and cat family.*

"The dog family was represented by several groups, notably wolves and foxes; the cat tribe, by panthers and large saber-toothed tigers, the latter first evolving in North America. The modern cat and dog families increased in numbers all over the world. Weasels, martins, otters, and raccoons thrived and developed throughout the northern latitudes." P. 697.

4. **The Pliocene—the last great mammalian migration.**

    a. *World-wide animal migration*

"For a short time all the land of the world was again joined excepting Australia, and the last great world-wide animal migration took place. North America was connected with both South America and Asia, and there was a free exchange of animal life. Asiatic sloths, armadillos, antelopes, and bears entered North America, while North American camels went to China. Rhinoceroses migrated over the whole world except Australia and South America, but they were extinct in the Western Hemisphere by the close of this period..

"In general, the life of the preceding period continued to evolve and spread. The cat family dominated the animal life, and marine life was almost at a standstill.

Many of the horses were still three-toed, but the modern types were arriving; llamas and giraffelike camels mingled with the horses on the grazing plains. The giraffe appeared in Africa, having just as long a neck then as now. In South America sloths, armadillos, anteaters, and the South American type of primitive monkeys evolved. Before the continents were finally isolated, those massive animals, the mastodons, migrated everywhere except to Australia." P. 698.

    b. *The horse appears in North America.*
"5,000,000 years ago the horse evolved as it now is and from North America migrated to all the world. But the horse had become extinct on the continent of its origin long before the red man arrived." P. 698.

5. **The Pleistocene—the ice age.**

    a. *North American animals during early epochs of the ice age.*
"These first two ice invasions were not extensive in Eurasia. During these early epochs of the ice age North America was overrun with mastodons, woolly mammoths, horses, camels, deer, musk oxen, bison, ground sloths, giant beavers, saber-toothed tigers, sloths as large as elephants, and many groups of the cat and dog families. But from this time forward they were rapidly reduced in numbers by the increasing cold of the glacial period. Toward the close of the ice age the majority of these
animal species were extinct in North America." P. 699-700.

    b. *The appearance of ancestors of the human race.*
"The great event of this glacial period was the evolution of primitive man. Slightly to the west of India, on land now under water and among the offspring of Asiatic migrants of the older North American lemur types, the dawn mammals *suddenly* appeared. These small animals walked mostly on their hind legs, and they possessed large brains in proportion to their size and in comparison with the brains of other animals. In the seventieth generation of this order of life a new and higher group of animals *suddenly*

differentiated. These new mid-mammals—almost twice the size and height of their ancestors and possessing proportionately increased brain power—had only well established themselves when the Primates, the third vital mutation, *suddenly* appeared. (At this same time, a retrograde development within the mid-mammal stock gave origin to the simian ancestry; and from that day to this the human branch has gone forward by progressive evolution, while the simian tribes have remained stationary or have actually retrogressed.)" P. 700.

c. *The appearance of man.*
"1,000,000 years ago Urantia was registered as an *inhabited world*. A mutation within the stock of the progressing Primates *suddenly* produced two primitive human beings, the actual ancestors of mankind." P. 700.

d. *The effects of the ice age.*
"This event occurred at about the time of the beginning of the third glacial advance; thus it may be seen that your early ancestors were born and bred in a stimulating, invigorating, and difficult environment. And the sole survivors of these Urantia aborigines, the Eskimos, even now prefer to dwell in frigid northern climes.

"Human beings were not present in the Western Hemisphere until near the close of the ice age. But during the interglacial epochs they passed westward around the Mediterranean and soon overran the continent of Europe. In the caves of western Europe may be found human bones mingled with the remains of both tropic and arctic animals, testifying that man lived in these regions throughout the later epochs of the advancing and retreating glaciers." P. 700.

IV. Overview of Evolution.

A. The evolutionary panorama.

"The story of man's ascent from seaweed to the lordship of earthly creation is indeed a romance of biologic struggle and mind survival. Man's primordial ancestors were literally the slime and ooze of the ocean bed in the sluggish and warm-water bays and lagoons of the vast shore lines of the ancient inland seas, those very waters in which the Life Carriers established the three independent life implantations on Urantia." P. 731.

PART IV — *Biology*

1. **Few early marine vegetable species still exist.**
"Very few species of the early types of marine vegetation that participated in those epochal changes which resulted in the animallike borderland organisms are in existence today. The sponges are the survivors of one of these early midway types, those organisms through which the *gradual* transition from the vegetable to the animal took place. These early transition forms, while not identical with modern sponges, were much like them; they were true borderline organisms—neither vegetable nor animal—but they eventually led to the development of the true animal forms of life." P. 731.

2. **Single-celled animal types associated into communities and later evolved into more complex forms.**
"Before long the early single-celled animal types associated themselves in communities, first on the plan of the Volvox and presently along the lines of the Hydra and jellyfish. Still later there evolved the starfish, stone lilies, sea urchins, sea cucumbers, centipedes, insects, spiders, crustaceans, and the closely related groups of earthworms and leeches, soon followed by the mollusks-the oyster, octopus, and snail. Hundreds upon hundreds of species intervened and perished; mention is made only of those which survived the long, long struggle. Such nonprogressive specimens, together with the later appearing fish family, today represent the stationary types of early and lower animals, branches of the tree of life which failed to progress." P. 732.

3. **Development of vertebrates, amphibians, reptiles, birds.**
"The stage was thus set for the appearance of the first backboned animals, the fishes. From this fish family there sprang two unique modifications, the frog and the salamander. And it was the frog which began that series of progressive differentiations in animal life that finally culminated in man himself.

"The frog is one of the earliest of surviving human-race ancestors, but it also failed to progress, persisting today much as in those remote times. The frog is the only species ancestor of the early dawn races now living on the face of the earth. The human race has no surviving ancestry between the frog and the Eskimo.

"The frogs gave rise to the Reptilia, a great animal family which is virtually extinct, but which, before passing out of existence, gave origin to the whole bird family and the numerous orders of mammals.

"Probably the greatest single leap of all prehuman evolution was executed when the reptile became a bird. The bird types of today eagles, ducks, pigeons, and ostriches—all descended from the enormous reptiles of long, long ago.

"The kingdom of reptiles, descended from the frog family, is today represented by four surviving divisions: two nonprogressive, snakes and lizards, together with their cousins, alligators and turtles; one partially progressive, the bird family, and the fourth, the ancestors of mammals and the direct line of descent of the human species. But though long departed, the massiveness of the passing Reptilia found echo in the elephant and mastodon, while their peculiar forms were perpetuated in the leaping kangaroos." P. 732.

4. **Development of placental mammals and prehuman types.**

"It was from an agile little reptilian dinosaur of carnivorous habits but having a comparatively large brain that the placental mammals *suddenly* sprang. These mammals developed rapidly and in many different ways, not only giving rise to the common modern varieties but also evolving into marine types, such as whales and seals, and into air navigators like the bat family.

"Man thus evolved from the higher mammals derived principally from the *western implantation* of life in the ancient east-west sheltered seas. The *eastern* and *central groups* of living organisms were early progressing favorably toward the attainment of prehuman levels of animal existence. But as the ages passed, the eastern focus of life emplacement failed to attain a satisfactory level of intelligent prehuman status, having suffered such repeated and irretrievable losses of its highest types of germ plasm that it was forever shorn of the power to rehabilitate human potentialities." P. 733.

PART IV — *Biology*

5. **Manipulation of favorable prehuman strains toward the evolution of man.**

   "Since the quality of the mind capacity for development in this eastern group was so definitely inferior to that of the other two groups, the Life Carriers, with the consent of their superiors, so manipulated the environment as further to circumscribe these inferior prehuman strains of evolving life. To all outward appearances the elimination of these inferior groups of creatures was accidental, but in reality it was altogether purposeful.

   "Later in the evolutionary unfolding of intelligence, the lemur ancestors of the human species were far more advanced in North America than in other regions; and they were therefore led to migrate from the arena of western life implantation over the Bering land bridge and down the coast to southwestern Asia, where they continued to evolve and to benefit by the addition of certain strains of the central life group. Man thus evolved out of certain western and central life strains but in the central to near-eastern regions.

   "In this way the life that was planted on Urantia evolved until the ice age, when man himself first appeared and began his eventful planetary career. And this appearance of primitive man on earth during the ice age was not just an accident; it was by design. The rigors and climatic severity of the glacial era were in every way adapted to the purpose of fostering the production of a hardy type of human being with tremendous survival endowment." P. 733.

B. **Various aspects or repercussions of evolution.**

   1. Change in nature and function of the Life Carriers upon the appearance of will creatures—human beings.

      "After the life patterns have been formulated and the material organizations have been duly completed, the supermaterial forces concerned in life propagation become forthwith active, and life is existent. Whereupon the Life Carriers are immediately returned to their normal mid-phase of personality existence, in which estate they can manipulate the living units and maneuver the evolving organisms, even though they are shorn of all ability to organize-create—new patterns of living matter.

      "After organic evolution has run a certain course and free will of the human type has appeared in the highest evolving organisms, the Life Carriers must either leave the planet or take renunciation vows; that is, they must pledge themselves to refrain from all attempts further to influence the course of organic evolution. And when such vows are voluntarily taken by those Life Carriers who choose to remain on the planet as future advisers to those who shall be intrusted with the fostering of the newly evolved will creatures, there is summoned a commission of twelve, presided over by the chief of the Evening Stars, acting by authority of the System Sovereign and with permission of Gabriel; and forthwith these Life Carriers are transmuted to the third phase of personality existence—the semispiritual level of being. And I have functioned on Urantia in this third phase of existence ever since the times of Andon and Fonta." P. 731.

2. **The biologic bacterial regression and the Adamic default in relation to human diseases.**

   "But throughout all of this biologic adventure our greatest disappointment grew out of the reversion of certain primitive plant life to the prechlorophyll levels of parasitic bacteria on such an extensive and unexpected scale. This eventuality in plant-life evolution caused many distressful diseases in the higher mammals, particularly in the more vulnerable human species. When we were confronted with this perplexing situation, we somewhat discounted the difficulties involved because we knew that the subsequent admixture of the Adamic life plasm would so reinforce the resisting powers of the resulting blended race as to make it practically immune to all diseases produced by the vegetable type of organism. But our hopes were doomed to disappointment owing to the misfortune of the Adamic default." P. 736.

3. **The inexorable progress of evolution.**

   "You have been informed that Urantia mortals evolved by way of primitive frog development, and that this ascending strain, carried in potential in a single frog, narrowly escaped extinction on a certain occasion. But it should not be inferred that the evolution of mankind would have been terminated by an accident at this juncture. At that very moment we were observing and fostering no less than one thousand different and remotely situated mutating strains of life which could have been directed into various different patterns of prehuman development. This particular ancestral frog represented our third selection, the two prior life strains having perished in spite of all our efforts toward their conservation.

"Even the loss of Andon and Fonta before they had offspring, though delaying human evolution, would not have prevented it. Subsequent to the appearance of Andon and Fonta and before the mutating human potentials of animal life were exhausted, there evolved no less than seven thousand favorable strains which could have achieved some sort of human type of development. And many of these better stocks were subsequently assimilated by the various branches of the expanding human species.

"Long before the Material Son and Daughter, the biologic uplifters, arrive on a planet, the human potentials of the evolving animal species have been exhausted. This biologic status of animal life is disclosed to the Life Carriers by the phenomenon of the third phase of adjutant spirit mobilization, which automatically occurs concomitantly with the exhaustion of the capacity of all animal life to give origin to the mutant potentials of prehuman individuals." P. 733-4.

4. **Unique features of Urantia life experiment.**

"There were many unique features of the Urantia life experiment, but the two outstanding episodes were the appearance of the Andonic race prior to the evolution of the six colored peoples and the later simultaneous appearance of the Sangik mutants in a single family. Urantia is the first world in Satania where the six colored races sprang from the same human family. They ordinarily arise in diversified strains from independent mutations within the prehuman animal stock and usually appear on earth one at a time and successively over long periods of time, beginning with the red man and passing on down through the colors to indigo.

"Another outstanding variation of procedure was the late arrival of the Planetary Prince. As a rule, the prince appears on a planet about the time of will development; and if such a plan had been followed, Caligastia might have come to Urantia even during the lifetimes of Andon and Fonta instead of almost five hundred thousand years later, simultaneously with the appearance of the six Sangik races." P. 735.

5. **The enigma of evolution.**

"But many seemingly mysterious adjustments of living organisms are purely chemical, wholly physical. At any moment of time, in the blood stream of any human being there exists the possibility of upward of 15,000,000 chemical reactions between the hormone output of a dozen ductless glands." P. 737.

"Physics and chemistry alone cannot explain how a human being evolved out of the primeval protoplasm of the early seas. The ability to learn, memory and differential response to environment, is the endowment of mind. The laws of physics are not responsive to training; they are immutable and unchanging. The reactions of chemistry are not modified by education; they are uniform and dependable. Aside from the presence of the Unqualified Absolute, electrical and chemical reactions are predictable. But mind can profit from experience, can learn from reactive habits of behavior in response to repetition of stimuli." P. 738.

6. **Reasons for the apparent slow progress of evolution.**

"If spending so much time in effecting the evolutionary changes of life development occasions perplexity, I would say that we cannot time the life processes to unfold any faster than the physical metamorphoses of a planet will permit. We must wait upon the natural, physical development of a planet; we have absolutely no control over geologic evolution. If the physical conditions would allow, we could arrange for the completed evolution of life in considerably less than one million years. But we are all under the jurisdiction of the Supreme Rulers of Paradise, and time is nonexistent on Paradise.

"The individual's yardstick for time measurement is the length of his life. All creatures are thus time conditioned, and therefore do they regard evolution as being a long-drawn-out process. To those of us whose life span is not limited by a temporal existence, evolution does not seem to be such a protracted transaction. On Paradise, where time is nonexistent, these things are all *present* in the mind of Infinity and the acts of Eternity." P. 739.

PART IV — *Biology*

CONCLUSION

"The fact of animal evolutionary origin does not attach stigma to any personality in the sight of the universe as that is the exclusive method of producing one of the two basic types of finite intelligent will creatures. When the heights of perfection and eternity are attained, all the more honor to those who began at the bottom and joyfully climbed the ladder of life, round by round, and who, when they do reach the heights of glory, will have gained a personal experience which embodies an actual knowledge of every phase of life from the bottom to the top.

"In all this is shown the wisdom of the Creators. It would be just as easy for the Universal Father to make all mortals perfect beings, to impart perfection by his divine word. But that would deprive them of the wonderful experience of the adventure and training associated with the long and gradual inward climb, an experience to be had only by those who are so fortunate as to begin at the very bottom of living existence." P. 361-2.

"Nature is a time-space resultant of two cosmic factors: first, the immutability, perfection, and rectitude of Paradise Deity, and second, the experimental plans, executive blunders, insurrectionary errors, incompleteness of development, and imperfection of wisdom of the extra-Paradise creatures, from the highest to the lowest. Nature therefore carries a uniform, unchanging, majestic, and marvelous thread of perfection from the circle of eternity; but in each universe, on each planet, and in each individual life, this nature is modified, qualified, and perchance marred by the acts, the mistakes, and the disloyalties of the creatures of the evolutionary systems and universes; and therefore must nature ever be of a changing mood, whimsical withal, though stable underneath, and varied in accordance with the operating procedures of a local universe." P. 56-7.

"The apparent defects of the natural world are not indicative of any such corresponding defects in the character of God. Rather are such observed imperfections merely the inevitable stop-moments in the exhibition of the evermoving reel of infinity picturization. It is these very defect-interruptions of perfection-continuity which make it possible for the finite mind of material man to catch a fleeting glimpse of divine reality in time and space. The material manifestations of divinity appear defective to the evolutionary mind of man only because mortal man persists in viewing the phenomena of nature through natural eyes, human vision unaided by morontia mota or by revelation, its compensatory substitute on the worlds of time." P. 57.

"But the inhabitants of Urantia are to find deliverance from these ancient errors and pagan superstitions respecting the nature of the Universal Father. The revelation of the truth about God is appearing, and the human race is destined to know the Universal Father in all that beauty of character and loveliness of attributes so magnificently portrayed by the Creator Son who sojourned on Urantia as the Son of Man and the Son of God." P. 60-1.

"Be not discouraged; human evolution is still in progress, and the revelation of God to the world, in and through Jesus, shall not fail." P. 2097.

PART V — ANTHROPOLOGY

Section One
COMPONENTS AND ATTRIBUTES OF URANTIA MORTALS

I. Mind Dominance of Matter

A. Cosmic mind.

1. **Source of the cosmic mind.**
   "The Master Spirits are the sevenfold source of the cosmic mind, the intellectual potential of the grand universe. This cosmic mind is a subabsolute manifestation of the mind of the Third Source and Center and, in certain ways, is functionally related to the mind of the evolving Supreme Being." P. 191.

2. **Influence of the Master Spirits on Urantians.**
   "On a world like Urantia we do not encounter the direct influence of the Seven Master Spirits in the affairs of the human races. You live under the immediate influence of the Creative Spirit of Nebadon. Nevertheless these same Master Spirits dominate the basic reactions of all creature mind because they are the actual sources of the intellectual and spiritual potentials which have been specialized in the local universes for function in the lives of those individuals who inhabit the evolutionary worlds of time and space." P. 191.

3. **The cosmic mind responds to three levels of universe reality.**
   "The cosmic mind unfailingly responds (recognizes response) on three levels of universe reality. These responses are self-evident to clear-reasoning and deep-thinking minds. These levels of reality are:

   "1. *Causation*—the reality domain of the physical senses, the scientific realms of logical uniformity, the differentiation of the factual and the nonfactual, reflective conclusions based on cosmic response. This is the mathematical form of the cosmic discrimination.

   "2. *Duty*—the reality domain of morals in the philosophic realm, the arena of reason, the recognition of relative right and wrong. This is the judicial form of the cosmic discrimination.

   "3. *Worship*—the spiritual domain of the reality of religious experience, the personal realization of divine fellowship, the

PART V — *Anthropology*

recognition of spirit values, the assurance of eternal survival, the ascent from the status of servants of God to the joy and liberty of the sons of God. This is the highest insight of the cosmic mind, the reverential and worshipful form of the cosmic discrimination." P. 192.

4. **These scientific, moral, and spiritual insights are innate in the minds of all will creatures.**

   "These scientific, moral, and spiritual insights, these cosmic responses, are innate in the cosmic mind, which endows all will creatures. The experience of living never fails to develop these three cosmic intuitions; they are constitutive in the self-consciousness of reflective thinking. But it is sad to record that so few persons on Urantia take delight in cultivating these qualities of courageous and independent cosmic thinking." P. 192.

5. **The creative mind is dominant and always functions in seven directions.**

   "The evolution of mechanisms implies and indicates the concealed presence and dominance of creative mind. The ability of the mortal intellect to conceive, design, and create automatic mechanisms demonstrates the superior, creative, and purposive qualities of man's mind as the dominant influence on the planet. Mind always reaches out towards:

   "1. Creation of material mechanisms.
   "2. Discovery of hidden mysteries.
   "3. Exploration of remote situations.
   "4. Formulation of mental systems.
   "5. Attainment of wisdom goals.
   "6. Achievement of spirit levels.
   "7. The accomplishment of divine destinies—supreme, ultimate, and absolute." P. 483.

6. **Function of creative mind in producing a mechanism of identity.**

   "Mind is always creative. The mind endowment of an individual animal, mortal, morontian, spirit ascender, or finality attainer is always competent to produce a suitable and serviceable body for the living creature identity. But the presence phenomenon of a personality or the pattern of an identity, as such, is not a manifestation of energy, either physical, mindal, or spiritual. The personality form is the *pattern* aspect of a living being; it connotes the *arrangement* of energies, and this, plus life and motion, is the *mechanism* of creature existence." P. 483.

7. **There are four inherent reality realisations in the self-conscious mind.**

    "Self-consciousness is in essence a communal consciousness: God and man, Father and son, Creator and creature. In human self-consciousness four universe-reality realizations are latent and inherent:

    "1. The quest for knowledge, the logic of science.
    "2. The quest for moral values, the sense of duty.
    "3. The quest for spiritual values, the religious experience.
    "4. The quest for personality values, the ability to recognize the reality of God as a personality and the concurrent realization of our fraternal relationship with fellow personalities." P. 196.

8. **The liaison of cosmic mind and adjutant mind-spirits evolves a suitable physical tabernacle. Morontia mind individualizes the morontia form.**

    "The liaison of the cosmic mind and the ministry of the adjutant mind-spirits evolve a suitable physical tabernacle for the evolving human being. Likewise does the morontia mind individualize the morontia form for all mortal survivors. As the mortal body is personal and characteristic for every human being, so will the morontia form be highly individual and adequately characteristic of the creative mind which dominates it. No two morontia forms are any more alike than any two human bodies. The Morontia Power Supervisors sponsor, and the attending seraphim provide, the undifferentiated morontia material wherewith the morontia life can begin to work. And after the morontia life it will be found that spirit forms are equally diverse, personal, and characteristic of their respective spirit-mind indwellers." P. 483.

B. **The seven adjutant mind-spirits.**

   1. **Adjutant mind-spirits condition the course of organic evolution.**

        "It is the presence of the seven adjutant mind-spirits on the primitive worlds that conditions the course of organic evolution; that explains why evolution is purposeful and not accidental. These adjutants represent that function of the mind ministry of the Infinite Spirit which is extended to the lower orders of intelligent life through the operations of a local universe Mother Spirit. The adjutants are the children of the Universe Mother Spirit and constitute her personal ministry to the material minds of the realms. Wherever and whenever such mind is manifest, these spirits are variously functioning." P. 401.

2. **Mind levels on evolutionary worlds.**
"Living mind, prior to the appearance of capacity to learn from experience, is the ministry domain of the Master Physical Controllers. Creature mind, before acquiring the ability to recognize divinity and worship Deity, is the exclusive domain of the adjutant spirits. With the appearance of the spiritual response of the creature intellect, such created minds at once become superminded, being instantly encircuited in the spirit cycles of the local universe Mother Spirit." P. 403.

3. **The Sons of God can construct the forms of life, but it is the Spirit of God who really contributes the vital spark.**
"When the Life Carriers have designed the patterns of life, after they have organized the energy systems, there must occur an additional phenomenon; the 'breath of life' must be imparted to these lifeless forms. The Sons of God can construct the forms of life, but it is the Spirit of God who really contributes the vital spark. And when the life thus imparted is spent, then again the remaining material body becomes dead matter. When the bestowed life is exhausted, the body returns to the bosom of the material universe from which it was borrowed by the Life Carriers to serve as a transient vehicle for that life endowment which they conveyed to such a visible association of energy-matter." P. 404.

II. PERSONALITY

A. Function of personality.

1. **Personality is original, unique, diverse, and is independent of and antecedent to the bestowal of the Thought Adjuster.**
"Personality is a unique endowment of original nature whose existence is independent of, and antecedent to, the bestowal of the Thought Adjuster. Nevertheless, the presence of the Adjuster does augment the qualitative manifestation of personality. Thought Adjusters, when they come forth from the Father, are identical in nature, but personality is diverse, original, and exclusive; and the manifestation of personality is further conditioned and qualified by the nature and qualities of

the associated energies of a material, mindal, and spiritual nature which constitute the organismal vehicle for personality manifestation." P. 194.

2. **Personality is the part of an individual we know—it is his identity.**

    "Personalities may be similar, but they are never the same. Persons of a given series, type, order, or pattern may and do resemble one another, but they are never identical. Personality is that feature of an individual which we know, and which enables us to identify such a being at some future time regardless of the nature and extent of changes in form, mind, or spirit status. Personality is that part of any individual which enables us to recognize and positively identify that person as the one we have previously known, no matter how much he may have changed because of the modification of the vehicle of expression and manifestation of his personality." P. 194.

3. **Creature personality is distinguished by self-consciousness and relative free will.**

    "Creature personality is distinguished by two self-manifesting and characteristic phenomena of mortal reactive behavior: self-consciousness and associated relative free will." P. 194.

4. **The function and range of self-consciousness.**

    "Self-consciousness consists in intellectual awareness of personality actuality; it includes the ability to recognize the reality of other personalities. It indicates capacity for individualized experience in and with cosmic realities, equivatating to the attainment of identity status in the personality relationships of the universe. Self-consciousness connotes recognition of the actuality of mind ministration and the realization of relative independence of creative and determinative free will." P. 194.

5. **Personality confers the dignity of cosmic citizenship and is reactive to the three basic realities of the cosmos.**

    "The Urantia type of human personality may be viewed as functioning in a physical mechanism consisting of the planetary modification of the Nebadon type of organism belonging to the electrochemical order of life activation and endowed with the Nebadon order of the Orvonton series of the cosmic mind of parental reproductive pattern. The bestowal of the divine gift of personality upon such a mind-endowed mortal mechanism confers the dignity of cosmic citizenship and enables such a mortal creature forthwith to become reactive to the constitutive recognition of the three basic mind realities of the cosmos:

PART V — *Anthropology*

"1. The mathematical or logical recognition of the uniformity of physical causation.

"2. The reasoned recognition of the obligation of moral conduct.

"3. The faith-grasp of the fellowship worship of Deity, associated with the loving service of humanity." P. 195.

6. **Personality leads to realization of Deity kinship and responds to the personality gravity circuit of the Universal Father.**

   "The full function of such a personality endowment is the beginning realization of Deity kinship. Such a selfhood, indwelt by a prepersonal fragment of God the Father, is in truth and in fact a spiritual son of God. Such a creature not only discloses capacity for the reception of the gift of the divine presence but also exhibits reactive response to the personality-gravity circuit of the Paradise Father of all personalities." P. 195.

B. **Attributes of personality.**

1. **Personalities of different stages and in varied beings are able to recognize both spirit and material beings.**

   "There are certain types of beings who are capable of discerning the reality of the creatures of both the spirit and the material worlds. Belonging to this class are the so-called fourth creatures of the Havona Servitals and the fourth creatures of the conciliators. The angels of time and space are endowed with the ability to discern both spirit and material beings as also are the ascending mortals subsequent to deliverance from the life in the flesh. After attainment of the higher spirit levels the ascenders are able to recognize material, morontia, and spirit realities." P. 498.

2. **Ascending personalities never lose the ability to recognize those they have known on previous levels of existence.**

   "There is also here with me a Mighty Messenger from Uversa, an ascendant Adjuster-fused, onetime mortal being, and he perceives you as you are, and at the same time he visualizes the Solitary Messenger, the supernaphim, and other celestial beings present. Never in your long ascendancy will you lose the power to recognize your associates of former existences. Always, as you ascend inward in the scale of life, will you retain the ability to recognize and fraternize with the fellow beings of your previous and lower levels of experience. Each new translation or resurrection will add one more group of spirit beings to your vision range without in the least depriving you of the ability to recognize your friends and fellows of former estates." P. 498.

III. Spirit Dominance

A. Relation of physical, spiritual, and mindal energies.

1. **Each type of energy is dominant in different situations.**
   "Physical, spiritual, and mindal energies, as such and in their pure states, do not fully interact as actuals of the phenomenal universes. On Paradise the three energies are co-ordinate, in Havona co-ordinated, while in the universe levels of finite activities there must be encountered all ranges of material, mindal, and spiritual dominance. In nonpersonal situations of time and space, physical energy seems to predominate, but it also appears that the more nearly spirit-mind function approaches divinity of purpose and supremacy of action, the more nearly does the spirit phase become dominant; that on the ultimate level spirit-mind may become all but completely dominant. On the absolute level spirit certainly is dominant. And from there on out through the realms of time and space, wherever a divine spirit reality is present, whenever a real spirit-mind is functioning, there always tends to be produced a material or physical counterpart of that spirit reality." P. 484.

2. **The spirit is the creative reality.**
   "The spirit is the creative reality; the physical counterpart is the time-space reflection of the spirit reality, the physical repercussion of the creative action of spirit-mind." P. 484.

3. **Mind dominates matter, and in turn is controlled by spirit.**
   "Mind universally dominates matter, even as it is in turn responsive to the ultimate overcontrol of spirit. And with mortal man, only that mind which freely submits itself to the spirit direction can hope to survive the mortal time-space existence as an immortal child of the eternal spirit world of the Supreme, the Ultimate, and the Absolute: the Infinite." P. 484.

4. **Spirit identification, Adjuster fusion, is the secret of survival and Paradise attainment.**
   "Spirit identification constitutes the secret of personal survival and determines the destiny of spiritual ascension." P. 445.
   "It is the Adjuster who creates within man that unquenchable yearning and incessant longing to be like God, to attain

Paradise, and there before the actual person of Deity to worship the infinite source of the divine gift. The Adjuster is the living presence which actually links the mortal son with his Paradise Father and draws him nearer and nearer to the Father. The Adjuster is our compensatory equalization of the enormous universe tension which is created by the distance of man's removal from God and by the degree of his partiality in contrast with the universality of the eternal Father.

"The Adjuster is an absolute essence of an infinite being imprisoned within the mind of a finite creature which, depending on the choosing of such a mortal, can eventually consummate this temporary union of God and man and veritably actualize a new order of being for unending universe service. The Adjuster is the divine universe reality which factualizes the truth that God is man's Father. The Adjuster is man's infallible cosmic compass, always and unerringly pointing the soul Godward." P. 1176.

Science In *The Urantia Book*

Section Two
PREHUMAN MAMMALS

"About one million years ago the immediate ancestors of mankind made their appearance by three successive and sudden mutations stemming from early stock of the lemur type of placental mammal. The dominant factors of these early lemurs were derived from the western or later American group of the evolving life plasm. But before establishing the direct line of human ancestry, this strain was reinforced by contributions from the central life implantation evolved in Africa. The eastern life group contributed little or nothing to the actual production of the human species." P. 703.

I. The Early Lemur Types

    A. Derivation and migration of early lemur types.

        1. **The lemur ancestors of the human species are not directly related to present-day lemurs.**
"The early lemurs concerned in the ancestry of the human species were not directly related to the pre-existent tribes of gibbons and apes then living in Eurasia and northern Africa, whose progeny have survived to the present time. Neither were they the offspring of the modern type of lemur, though springing from an ancestor common to both but long since extinct." P. 703.

        2. **Migration of North American lemurs to southwestern Asia where the human race had its origin.**
"While these early lemurs evolved in the Western Hemisphere, the establishment of the direct mammalian ancestry of mankind took place in southwestern Asia, in the original area of the central life implantation but on the borders of the eastern regions. Several million years ago the North American type lemurs had migrated westward over the Bering land bridge and had slowly made their way southwestward along the Asiatic coast. These migrating tribes finally reached the salubrious region lying between the then expanded Mediterranean Sea and the elevating mountainous regions of the Indian peninsula. In these lands to the west of India they united with other and favorable strains, thus establishing the ancestry of the human race." P. 703.

II. The Dawn Mammals

    A. Appearance and physical characteristics.

        1. One million years ago the dawn mammals suddenly appeared.
"A little more than one million years ago the Mesopotamian

dawn mammals, the direct descendants of the North American lemur type of placental mammal, *suddenly* appeared. They were active little creatures, almost three feet tall; and while they did not habitually walk on their hind legs, they could easily stand erect. They were hairy and agile and chattered in monkeylike fashion, but unlike the simian tribes, they were flesh eaters. They had a primitive opposable thumb as well as a highly useful grasping big toe. From this point onward the prehuman species successively developed the opposable thumb while they progressively lost the grasping power of the great toe. The alter ape tribes retained the grasping big toe but never developed the human type of thumb. "These dawn mammals attained full growth when three or four years of age, having a potential life span, on the average, of about twenty years. As a rule offspring were born singly, although twins were occasional." P. 703-4.

B. **Instincts, emotions, habits.**

1. **Many humanlike emotions were manifested in the behavior of these dawn mammals.**
   "The members of this new species had the largest brains for their size of any animal that had theretofore existed on earth. They experienced many of the emotions and shared numerous instincts which later characterized primitive man, being highly curious and exhibiting considerable elation when successful at any undertaking. Food hunger and sex craving were well developed, and a definite sex selection was manifested in a crude form of courtship and choice of mates. They would fight fiercely in defense of their kindred and were quite tender in family associations, possessing a sense of self-abasement bordering on shame and remorse. They were very affectionate and touchingly loyal to their mates, but if circumstances separated them, they would choose new partners." P. 704.

2. **They built treetop homes and developed a great fear capacity.**
   "Being small of stature and having keen minds to realize the dangers of their forest habitat, they developed an extraordinary fear which led to those wise precautionary measures that so enormously contributed to survival, such as their construction of crude shelters in the high treetops which eliminated many of the perils of ground life. The beginning of the fear tendencies of mankind more specifically dates from these days." P. 704.

3. **They were gregarious, bellicose, and pugnacious. They destroyed their inferior neighbors.**

   "These dawn mammals developed more of a tribal spirit than had ever been previously exhibited. They were, indeed, highly gregarious but nevertheless exceedingly pugnacious when in any way disturbed in the ordinary pursuit of their routine life, and they displayed fiery tempers when their anger was fully aroused. Their bellicose natures, however, served a good purpose; superior groups did not hesitate to make war on their inferior neighbors, and thus, by selective survival, the species was progressively improved. They very soon dominated the life of the smaller creatures of this region, and very few of the older noncarnivorous monkeylike tribes survived." P. 704.

4. **In seventy generations suddenly appeared the ancestors of the next step in the evolution of the human race.**

   "These aggressive little animals multiplied and spread over the Mesopotamian peninsula for more than one thousand years, constantly improving in physical type and general intelligence. And it was just seventy generations after this new tribe had taken origin from the highest type of lemur ancestor that the next epoch-making development occurred—the *sudden* differentiation of the ancestors of the next vital step in the evolution of human beings on Urantia." P. 704.

C. **Extinction.**

1. **Mid-mammals eventually destroyed all the dawn mammals.**

   "When the numbers of this new and superior group grew great, war, relentless war, broke out; and when the terrible struggle was over, not a single individual of the pre-existent and ancestral race of dawn mammals remained alive. The less numerous but more powerful and intelligent offshoot of the species had survived at the expense of their ancestors." P. 705.

III. THE MID-MAMMALS

A. **Appearance and characteristics.**

1. **The mid-mammal twins are born.**

   "Early in the career of the dawn mammals, in the treetop abode of a superior pair of these agile creatures, twins were born, one male and one female. Compared with their ancestors, they were really handsome little creatures. They had little hair on their bodies, but this was no disability as they lived in a warm and equable climate." P. 704.

PART V — Anthropology

2. **Physical characteristics of the mid-mammals.**
   "These children grew to be a little over four feet in height. They were in every way larger than their parents, having longer legs and shorter arms. They had almost perfectly opposable thumbs, just about as well adapted for diversified work as the present human thumb. They walked upright, having feet almost as well suited for walking as those of the later human races." P. 705.

B. **Instincts, emotions, habits.**

1. **Mid-mammals became the terror of their part of the world.**
   "And now, for almost fifteen thousand years (six hundred generations), this creature became the terror of this part of the world. All of the great and vicious animals of former times had perished. The large beasts native to these regions were not carnivorous, and the larger species of the cat family, lions and tigers, had not yet invaded this peculiarly sheltered nook of the earth's surface. Therefore did these mid-mammals wax valiant and subdue the whole of their corner of creation." P. 705.

2. **Their life span was twenty-five years; near-human traits appeared.**
   "Compared with the ancestral species, the mid-mammals were an improvement in every way. Even their potential life span was longer, being about twenty-five years. A number of rudimentary human traits appeared in this new species. In addition to the innate propensities exhibited by their ancestors, these mid-mammals were capable of showing disgust in certain repulsive situations. They further possessed a well-defined hoarding instinct; they would hide food for subsequent use and were greatly given to the collection of smooth round pebbles and certain types of round stones suitable for defensive and offensive ammunition." P. 705.

3. **Mental and social endowments of the mid-mammals.**
   "Their brains were inferior to, and smaller than, those of human beings but very superior to, and comparatively much larger than, those of their ancestors. The twins early displayed superior intelligence and were soon recognized as the heads of the whole tribe of dawn mammals, really instituting a primitive form of social organization and a crude economic division of labor. This brother and sister mated and soon enjoyed the

society of twenty-one children much like themselves, all more than four feet tall and in every way superior to the ancestral species. This new group formed the nucleus of the mid-mammals." P. 705.

4. **The mid-mammals were the first to construct ground dwellings.**
"These mid-mammals were the first to exhibit a definite construction propensity, as shown in their rivalry in the building of both treetop homes and their many-tunneled subterranean retreats; they were the first species of mammals ever to provide for safety in both arboreal and underground shelters. They largely forsook the trees as places of abode, living on the ground during the day and sleeping in the treetops at night." P. 705.

5. **Near extinction.**
"As time passed, the natural increase in numbers eventually resulted in serious food competition and sex rivalry, all of which culminated in a series of internecine battles that nearly destroyed the entire species. These struggles continued until only one group of less than one hundred individuals was left alive. But peace once more prevailed, and this lone surviving tribe built anew its treetop bedrooms and once again resumed a normal and semipeaceful existence." P. 705.

IV. THE PRIMATES

A. Appearance and characteristics.

1. **Birth of the Primates twins.**
"Soon after the completion of their home, this couple, veterans of so many struggles, found themselves the proud parents of twins, the most interesting and important animals ever to have been born into the world up to that time, for they were the first of the new species of *Primates* constituting the next vital step in prehuman evolution." P. 706.

2. **Physical characteristics.**
"Going back to the birth of the superior twins, one male and one female, to the two leading members of the mid-mammal tribe: These animal babies were of an unusual order; they had still less hair on their bodies than their parents and, when very young, insisted on walking upright. Their ancestors had always learned to walk on their hind legs, but these Primates twins stood erect from the beginning. They attained a height of over

five feet, and their heads grew larger in comparison with others among the tribe. While early learning to communicate with each other by means of signs and sounds, they were never able to make their people understand these new symbols." P. 706.

3. **Flight to Mesopotamia.**
"When about fourteen years of age, they fled from the tribe, going west to raise their family and establish the new species of Primates. And these new creatures are very properly denominated *Primates* since they were the direct and immediate animal ancestors of the human family itself.

"Thus it was that the Primates came to occupy a region on the west coast of the Mesopotamian peninsula as it then projected into the southern sea, while the less intelligent and closely related tribes lived around the peninsula point and up the eastern shore line." P. 707.

4. **Improvements in characteristics of Primates over their ancestors.**
"The Primates were more human and less animal than their mid-mammal predecessors. The skeletal proportions of this new species were very similar to those of the primitive human races. The human type of hand and foot had fully developed, and these creatures could walk and even run as well as any of their later-day human descendants. They largely abandoned tree life, though continuing to resort to the treetops as a safety measure at night, for like their earlier ancestors, they were greatly subject to fear. The increased use of their hands did much to develop inherent brain power, but they did not yet possess minds that could really be called human.

"Although in emotional nature the Primates differed little from their forebears, they exhibited more of a human trend in all of their propensities. They were, indeed, splendid and superior animals, reaching maturity at about ten years of age and having a natural life span of about forty years. That is, they might have lived that long had they died natural deaths, but in those early days very few animals ever died a natural death; the struggle for existence was altogether too intense." P. 707.

B. **Origin of the human race on Urantia.**

1. **The Primates gave birth to the first true human beings.**
"And now, after almost nine hundred generations of development, covering about twenty-one thousand years from the

origin of the dawn mammals, the Primates *suddenly* gave birth to two remarkable creatures, the first true human beings.

"Thus it was that the dawn mammals, springing from the North American lemur type, gave origin to the mid-mammals, and these mid-mammals in turn produced the superior Primates, who became the immediate ancestors of the primitive human race. The Primates tribes were the last vital link in the evolution of man, but in less than five thousand years not a single individual of these extraordinary tribes was left." P. 707.

V. Recapitulation

A. Evolutionary history of prehuman mammals.

1. **Mutations occur suddenly.**

    "The great event of this glacial period was the evolution of primitive man. Slightly to the west of India, on land now under water and among the offspring of Asiatic migrants of the older North American lemur types, the dawn mammals *suddenly* appeared. These small animals walked mostly on their hind legs, and they possessed large brains in proportion to their size and in comparison with the brains of other animals. In the seventieth generation of this order of life a new and higher group of animals *suddenly* differentiated. These new mid-mammals—almost twice the size and height of their ancestors and possessing proportionately increased brain power—had only well established themselves when the Primates, the third vital mutation, *suddenly* appeared. (At this same time, a retrograde development within the mid-mammal stock gave origin to the simian ancestry; and from that day to this the human branch has gone forward by progressive evolution, while the simian tribes have remained stationary or have actually retrogressed.)" P. 700.

2. **Dangers that threatened the course of evolution.**

    "You can hardly realize by what narrow margins your prehuman ancestors missed extinction from time to time. Had the ancestral frog of all humanity jumped two inches less on a certain occasion, the whole course of evolution would have been markedly changed. The immediate lemurlike mother of the dawn-mammal species escaped death no less than five times by mere hairbreadth margins before she gave birth to the father of the new and higher mammalian order. But the closest call of all was when lightning struck the tree in which the

PART V — *Anthropology*

prospective mother of the Primates twins was sleeping. Both of these mid-mammal parents were severely shocked and badly burned; three of their seven children were killed by this bolt from the skies. These evolving animals were almost superstitious. This couple whose treetop home had been struck were really the leaders of the more progressive group of the midmammal species; and following their example, more than half the tribe, embracing the more intelligent families, moved about two miles away from this locality and began the construction of new treetop abodes and new ground shelters—their transient retreats in time of sudden danger." P. 705.

B. **Origin of simian tribes.**

1. **Separation of the superior and inferior strains of the Primates.**
   "Contemporaneously with the birth of these Primates twins, another couple—a peculiarly retarded male and female of the mid-mammal tribe, a couple that were both mentally and physically inferior-also gave birth to twins. These twins, one male and one female, were indifferent to conquest; they were concerned only with obtaining food and, since they would not eat flesh, soon lost all interest in seeking prey. These retarded twins became the founders of the modern simian tribes. Their descendants sought the warmer southern regions with their mild climates and an abundance of tropical fruits, where they have continued much as of that day except for those branches which mated with the earlier types of gibbons and apes and have greatly deteriorated in consequence." P. 706.

2. **Relation of modern man to the simian tribes.**
   "And so it may be readily seen that man and the ape are related only in that they sprang from the mid-mammals, a tribe in which there occurred the contemporaneous birth and subsequent segregation of two pairs of twins: the inferior pair destined to produce the modern types of monkey, baboon, chimpanzee, and gorilla; the superior pair destined to continue the line of ascent which evolved into man himself.
   "Modern man and the simians did spring from the same tribe and species but not from the same parents. Man's ancestors are descended from the superior strains of the selected remnant of this mid-mammal tribe, whereas the modern simians (excepting certain pre-existent types of lemurs, gibbons, apes, and other monkeylike creatures) are the descendants of the most

inferior couple of this mid-mammal group, a couple who only survived by hiding themselves in a subterranean food-storage retreat for more than two weeks during the last fierce battle of their tribe, emerging only after the hostilities were well over." P. 706.

Part V — *Anthropology*

Section Three
HUMAN BEINGS

I. **Evolution of Man**

  A. **The first human beings.**

  1. **In A.D. 1934, the human race was 993,419 years old.**
     "From the year A.D. 1934 back to the birth of the first two human beings is just 993,419 years." P. 707.

  2. **The first human beings appeared during the third glacier. Their sole survivors are the Eskimos.**
     "*1,000,000* years ago Urantia was registered as an *inhabited world*. A mutation within the stock of the progressing Primates *suddenly* produced two primitive human beings, the actual ancestors of mankind.
     "This event occurred at about the time of the beginning of the third glacial advance; thus it may be seen that your early ancestors were born and bred in a stimulating, invigorating, and difficult environment. And the sole survivors of these Urantia aborigines, the Eskimos, even now prefer to dwell in frigid northern climes." P. 700.

  3. **Physical characteristics and life span.**
     "These two remarkable creatures were true human beings. They possessed perfect human thumbs, as had many of their ancestors, while they had just as perfect feet as the present-day human races. They were walkers and runners, not climbers; the grasping function of the big toe was absent, completely absent. When danger drove them to the treetops, they climbed just like the humans of today would. They would climb up the trunk of a tree like a bear and not as would a chimpanzee or a gorilla, swinging up by the branches.
     "These first human beings (and their descendants) reached full maturity at twelve years of age and possessed a potential life span of about seventy-five years." P. 707-8.

  4. **Emotions and feelings.**
     "Many new emotions early appeared in these human twins. They experienced admiration for both objects and other beings and exhibited considerable vanity. But the most remarkable advance in emotional development was the sudden appearance of a new group of really human feelings, the worshipful group, embracing awe, reverence, humility, and even a primitive form of gratitude. Fear, joined with ignorance of natural phenomena, is about to give birth to primitive religion.

"Not only were such human feelings manifested in these primitive humans, but many more highly evolved sentiments were also present in rudimentary form. They were mildly cognizant of pity, shame, and reproach and were acutely conscious of love, hate, and revenge, being also susceptible to marked feelings of jealousy." P. 708.

5. **The early life of the first two human beings.**

"These first two humans—the twins—were a great trial to their Primates parents. They were so curious and adventurous that they nearly lost their lives on numerous occasions before they were eight years old. As it was, they were rather well scarred up by the time they were twelve.

"Very early they learned to engage in verbal communication; by the age of ten they had worked out an improved sign and word language of almost half a hundred ideas and had greatly improved and expanded the crude communicative technique of their ancestors. But try as hard as they might, they were able to teach only a few of their new signs and symbols to their parents." P. 708.

6. **The noontide tryst—the decision of the twins to flee from home, to found the human race.**

"When about nine years of age, they journeyed off down the river one bright day and held a momentous conference. Every celestial intelligence stationed on Urantia, including myself, was present as an observer of the transactions of this noontide tryst. On this eventful day they arrived at an understanding to live with and for each other, and this was the first of a series of such agreements which finally culminated in the decision to flee from their inferior animal associates and to journey northward, little knowing that they were thus to found the human race." P. 708.

7. **Migration of the twins northward with the guidance of Life Carriers to escape biologic degradation by admixture with their inferior relatives.**

"While we were all greatly concerned with what these two little savages were planning, we were powerless to control the working of their minds; we did not—could not—arbitrarily influence their decisions. But within the permissible limits of planetary function, we, the Life Carriers, together with our associates, all conspired to lead the human twins northward and far from their hairy and partially tree-dwelling people. And

PART V — *Anthropology*

so, by reason of their own intelligent choice, the twins did *migrate*, and because of our supervision they migrated *northward* to a secluded region where they escaped the possibility of biologic degradation through admixture with their inferior relatives of the Primates tribes." P. 708.

8. **The sacrifice of the mother to save the twins.**
"Shortly before their departure from the home forests they lost their mother in a gibbon raid. While she did not possess their intelligence, she did have a worthy mammalian affection of a high order for her offspring, and she fearlessly gave her life in the attempt to save the wonderful pair. Nor was her sacrifice in vain, for she held off the enemy until the father arrived with reinforcements and put the invaders to rout." P. 708.

9. **The tragic end of the father of the human twins.**
"Soon after this young couple forsook their associates to found the human race, their Primates father became disconsolate— he was heartbroken. He refused to eat, even when food was brought to him by his other children. His brilliant offspring having been lost, life did not seem worth living among his ordinary fellows; so he wandered off into the forest, was set upon by hostile gibbons and beaten to death." P. 709.

B. **Evolution of the human mind.**
1. **Successive functioning of the first five adjutant spirits.**
"At first only the *spirit of intuition* could function in the instinctive and reflex behavior of the primordial animal life. With the differentiation of higher types, the *spirit of understanding* was able to endow such creatures with the gift of spontaneous association of ideas. Later on we observed the *spirit of courage* in operation; evolving animals really developed a crude form of protective self-consciousness. Subsequent to the appearance of the mammalian groups, we beheld the *spirit of knowledge* manifesting itself in increased measure. And the evolution of the higher mammals brought the function of the *spirit of counsel*, with the resulting growth of the herd instinct and the beginnings of primitive social development." P. 709.

2. **The first functioning of the adjutant spirits of worship and wisdom.**
"Increasingly, on down through the dawn mammals, the midmammals, and the Primates, we had observed the augmented

service of the first five adjutants. But never had the remaining two, the highest mind ministers, been able to function in the Urantia type of evolutionary mind.

"Imagine our joy one day—the twins were about ten years old-when the *spirit of worship* made its first contact with the mind of the female twin and shortly thereafter with the male. We knew that something closely skin to human mind was approaching culmination; and when, about a year later, they finally resolved, as a result of meditative thought and purposeful decision, to flee from home and journey north, then did the *spirit of wisdom* begin to function on Urantia and in these two now recognized human minds.

"There was an immediate and new order of mobilization of the seven adjutant mind-spirits. We were alive with expectation; we realized that the long-waited-for hour was approaching; we knew we were upon the threshold of the realization of our protracted effort to evolve will creatures on Urantia." P. 709.

C. **Recognition as an inhabited world.**

1. **The recognition of Urantia as an inhabited planet.**
   "We did not have to wait long. At noon, the day after the runaway of the twins, there occurred the initial test flash of the universe circuit signals at the planetary reception-focus of Urantia. We were, of course, all astir with the realization that a great event was impending; but since this world was a life-experiment station, we had not the slightest idea of just how we would be apprised of the recognition of intelligent life on the planet. But we were not long in suspense. On the third day after the elopement of the twins, and before the Life Carrier corps departed, there arrived the Nebadon archangel of initial planetary circuit establishment." P. 709.

2. **Message to the Life Carriers in recognition of the existence of human mind on Urantia.**
   "It was an eventful day on Urantia when our small group gathered about the planetary pole of space communication and received the first message from Salvington over the newly established mind circuit of the planet. And this first message, dictated by the chief of the archangel corps, said:

   "'To the Life Carriers on Urantia—Greetings! We transmit assurance of great pleasure on Salvington, Edentia, and Jerusem in honor of the registration on the headquarters of Nebadon of the signal of the existence on Urantia of mind of will dignity. The purposeful decision of the twins to flee northward and segregate their offspring from their inferior ancestors has been noted. This is the first decision of mind—the human type of mind—on Urantia and automatically establishes the circuit of communication over which this initial message of acknowledgment is transmitting.'" P. 710.

3. **Instructions to the Life Carriers on Urantia concerning their future relation to the human race.**

"Next over this new circuit came the greetings of the Most Highs of Edentia, containing instructions for the resident Life Carriers forbidding us to interfere with the pattern of life we had established. We were directed not to intervene in the affairs of human progress. It should not be inferred that Life Carriers ever arbitrarily and mechanically interfere with the natural outworking of the planetary evolutionary plans, for we do not. But up to this time we had been permitted to manipulate the environment and shield the life plasm in a special manner, and it was this extraordinary, but wholly natural, supervision that was to be discontinued." P. 710.

4. **The Lucifer message to the Life Carriers in acceptance of their work.**

"And no sooner had the Most Highs left off speaking than the beautiful message of Lucifer, then sovereign of the Satania system, began to planetize. Now the Life Carriers heard the welcome words of their own chief and received his permission to return to Jerusem. This message from Lucifer contained the official acceptance of the Life Carriers' work on Urantia and absolved us from all future criticism of any of our efforts to improve the life patterns of Nebadon as established in the Satania system." P. 710.

5. **It was—from A.D. 1934—993,408 years ago that Urantia was recognized as an inhabited planet.**

"It is just 993,408 years ago (from the year A.D. 1934) that Urantia was formally recognized as a planet of human habitation in the universe of Nebadon. Biologic evolution had once again achieved the human levels of will dignity; man had arrived on planet 606 of Satania." P. 710.

7. **Urantia was recognized when the twins were eleven years old and they were named Andon and Fonta.**

"Urantia was registered as an inhabited world when the first two human beings—the twins—were eleven years old, and before they had become the parents of the first-born of the second generation of actual human beings. And the archangel message from Salvington, on this occasion of formal planetary recognition, closed with these words:

"'Man-mind has appeared on 606 of Satania, and these parents of the new race shall be called *Andon* and *Fonta*. And all archangels pray that these creatures may speedily be endowed with the personal indwelling of the gift of the spirit of the Universal Father." P. 711.

7. **Andon and Fonta called each other Sonta-an and Sonta-en.**
"Andon is the Nebadon name which signifies 'the first Fatherlike creature to exhibit human perfection hunger.' Fonta signifies 'the first Sonlike creature to exhibit human perfection hunger.' Andon and Fonta never knew these names until they were bestowed upon them at the time of fusion with their Thought Adjusters. Throughout their mortal sojourn on Urantia they called each other Sonta-an and Sonta-en, Sonta-an meaning 'loved by mother,' Sonta-en signifying 'loved by father.' They gave themselves these names, and the meanings are significant of their mutual regard and affection." P. 711.

II. THE FIRST HUMAN FAMILY

A. Andon and Fonta.

"In many respects, Andon and Fonta were the most remarkable pair of human beings that have ever lived on the face of the earth. This wonderful pair', the actual parents of all mankind, were in every way superior to many of their immediate descendants, and they were radically different from all of their ancestors, both immediate and remote." P. 711.

1. **Their weapons.**
"While still living with his parents, Andon had fastened a sharp piece of flint on the end of a club, using animal tendons for this purpose, and on no less than a dozen occasions he made good use of such a weapon in saving both his own life and that of his equally adventurous and inquisitive sister, who unfailingly accompanied him on all of his tours of exploration." P. 711.

2. **Effect of personality and Thought Adjusters.**
"The decision of Andon and Fonta to flee from the Primates tribes implies a quality of mind far above the baser intelligence which characterized so many of their later descendants who

PART V — *Anthropology*

stooped to mate with their retarded cousins of the simian tribes. But their vague feeling of being something more than mere animals was due to the possession of personality and was augmented by the indwelling presence of the Thought Adjusters." P. 711.

3. **Their relation with their Primates cousins.**
"After Andon and Fonta had decided to flee northward, they succumbed to their fears for a time, especially the fear of displeasing their father and immediate family. They envisaged being set upon by hostile relatives and thus recognized the possibility of meeting death at the hands of their already jealous tribesmen. As youngsters, the twins had spent most of their time in each other's company and for this reason had never been overly popular with their animal cousins of the Primates tribe. Nor had they improved their standing in the tribe by building a separate, and a very superior, tree home.
"And it was in this new home among the treetops, one night after they had been awakened by a violent storm, and as they held each other in fearful and fond embrace, that they finally and fully made up their minds to flee from the tribal habitat and the home treetops." P. 712.

4. **Preparations for their eventide elopement.**
"They had already prepared a crude treetop retreat some half-day's journey to the north. This was their secret and safe hiding place for the first day away from the home forests. Notwithstanding that the twins shared the Primates' deathly fear of being on the ground at nighttime, they sallied forth shortly before nightfall on their northern trek. While it required unusual courage for them to undertake this night journey, even with a full moon, they correctly concluded that they were less likely to be missed and pursued by their tribesmen and relatives. And they safely made their previously prepared rendezvous shortly after midnight." P. 712.

5. **Discovery of the use of flint in making fire.**
"On their northward journey they discovered an exposed flint deposit and, finding many stones suitably shaped for various uses, gathered up a supply for the future. In attempting to chip these flints so that they would be better adapted for certain purposes, Andon discovered their sparking quality and conceived the idea of building fire. But the notion did not take firm hold of him at the time as the climate was still salubrious and there was little need of fire.

"But the autumn sun was getting lower in the sky, and as they journeyed northward, the nights grew cooler and cooler. Already they had been forced to make use of animal skins for warmth. Before they had been away from home one moon, Andon signified to his mate that he thought he could make fire with the flint. They tried for two months to utilize the flint spark for kindling a fire but only met with failure. Each day this couple would strike the flints and endeavor to ignite the wood. Finally, one evening about the time of the setting of the sun, the secret of the technique was unraveled when it occurred to Fonta to climb a near-by tree to secure an abandoned bird's nest. The nest was dry and highly inflammable and consequently flared right up into a full blaze the moment the spark fell upon it. They were so surprised and startled at their success that they almost lost the fire, but they saved it by the addition of suitable fuel, and then began the first search for firewood by the parents of all mankind.

"This was one of the most joyous moments in their short but eventful lives. All night long they sat up watching their fire burn, vaguely realizing that they had made a discovery which would make it possible for them to defy climate and thus forever to be independent of their animal relatives of the southern lands. After three days' rest and enjoyment of the fire, they journeyed on." P. 712.

6. **They learn to make use of different materiials in starting fire.**

"The Primates ancestors of Andon had often replenished fire which had been kindled by lightning, but never before had the creatures of earth possessed a methoof starting fire at will. But it was a long time before the twins learned that dry moss and other materials would kindle fire just as well as birds' nests." P. 712.

B. **Andon's family.**

1. **The birth of Sontad.**

"It was almost two years from the night of the twins' departure from home before their first child was born. They named him Sontad; and Sontad was the first creature to be born on Urantia who was wrapped in protective coverings at the time of birth. The human race had begun, and with this new evolution there appeared the instinct properly to care for the increasingly enfeebled infants which would characterize the progressive development of mind of the intellectual order as contrasted with the more purely animal type." P. 713.

2. **The children and grandchildren of Andon and Fonta.**
"Andon and Fonta had nineteen children in all, and they lived to enjoy the association of almost half a hundred grandchildren and half a dozen great-grandchildren. The family was domiciled in four adjoining rock shelters, or semicaves, three of which were interconnected by hallways which had been excavated in the soft limestone with flint tools devised by Andon's children." P. 713.

3. **The early Andonites were a clannish people.**
"These early Andonites evinced a very marked clannish spirit; they hunted in groups and never strayed very far from the homesite. They seemed to realize that they were an isolated and unique group of living beings and should therefore avoid becoming separated. This feeling of intimate kinship was undoubtedly due to the enhanced mind ministry of the adjutant spirits." P. 713.

4. **The tragic death of Andon and Fonta.**
"Andon and Fonta labored incessantly for the nurture and uplift of the clan. They lived to the age of forty-two, when both were killed at the time of an earthquake by the falling of an overhanging rock. Five of their children and eleven grandchildren perished with them, and almost a score of their descendants suffered serious injuries." P. 713.

5. **Sontad became head of the clan and it held together for twenty generations.**
"Upon the death of his parents, Sontad, despite a seriously injured foot, immediately assumed the leadership of the clan and was ably assisted by his wife, his eldest sister. Their first task was to roll up stones to effectively entomb their dead parents, brothers, sisters, and children. Undue significance should not attach to this act of burial. Their ideas of survival after death were very vague and indefinite, being largely derived from their fantastic and variegated dream life.

"This family of Andon and Fonta held together until the twentieth generation, when combined food competition and social friction brought about the beginning of dispersion." P. 713.

6. **Physical characteristics of the Andonites.**

   "Primitive man—the Andonites—had black eyes and a swarthy complexion, something of a cross between yellow and red. Melanin is a coloring substance which is found in the skins of all human beings. It is the original Andonic skin pigment. In general appearance and skin color these early Andonites more nearly resembled the present-day Eskimo than any other type of living human beings. They were the first creatures to use the skins of animals as a protection against cold; they had little more hair on their bodies than present-day humans." P. 713.

7. **The survival of Andon and Fonta.**

   "Andon and Fonta, the splendid founders of the human race, received recognition at the time of the adjudication of Urantia upon the arrival of the Planetary Prince, and in due time they emerged from the regime of the mansion worlds with citizenship status on Jerusem. Although they have never been permitted to return to Urantia, they are cognizant of the history of the race they founded. They grieved over the Caligastia betrayal, sorrowed because of the Adamic failure, but rejoiced exceedingly when announcement was received that Michael had selected their world as the theater for his final bestowal.

   "On Jerusem both Andon and Fonta were fused with their Thought Adjusters, as also were several of their children, including Sontad, but the majority of even their immediate descendants only achieved Spirit fusion." P. 717.

8. **Andon and Fonta join the reception committee on the first mansion world.**

   "Andon and Fonta, shortly after their arrival on Jerusem, received permission from the System Sovereign to return to the first mansion world to serve with the morontia personalities who welcome the pilgrims of time from Urantia to the heavenly spheres. And they have been assigned indefinitely to this service. They sought to send greetings to Urantia in connection with these revelations, but this request was wisely denied them.

   "And this is the recital of the most heroic and fascinating chapter in all the history of Urantia, the story of the evolution, life struggles, death, and eternal survival of the unique parents of all mankind." P. 717.

III. The Andonic Tribes

A. General characteristics.

1. **Social conventions developed, humor was lacking, and Andonites were less sensitive than later races.**
   "The tribal life of the animal ancestors of these early men had foreshadowed the beginnings of numerous social conventions, and with the expanding emotions and augmented brain powers of these beings, there was an immediate development in social organization and a new division of clan labor. They were exceedingly imitative, but the play instinct was only slightly developed, and the sense of humor was almost entirely absent. Primitive man smiled occasionally, but he never indulged in hearty laughter. Humor was the legacy of the later Adamic race. These early human beings were not so sensitive to pain nor so reactive to unpleasant situations as were many of the later evolving mortals. Childbirth was not a painful or distressing ordeal to Fonta and her immediate progeny." P. 713-4.

2. **The Andonites had tribal patriotism, but they were deficient in altruism.**
   "They were a wonderful tribe. The males would fight heroically for the safety of their mates and their offspring; the females were affectionately devoted to their children. But their patriotism was wholly limited to the immediate clan. They were very loyal to their families; they would die without question in defense of their children, but they were not able to grasp the idea of trying to make the world a better place for their grandchildren. Altruism was as yet unborn in the human heart, notwithstanding that all of the emotions essential to the birth of religion were already present in these Urantia aborigines." P. 714.

3. **Many noble human traits were foreshadowed in these primitive people.**
   "These early men possessed a touching affection for their comrades and certainly had a real, although crude, idea of friendship. It was a common sight in later times, during their constantly recurring battles with the inferior tribes, to see one of these primitive men valiantly fighting with one hand while he struggled on, trying to protect and save an injured fellow warrior. Many of the most noble and highly human traits of subsequent evolutionary development were touchingly foreshadowed in these primitive peoples." P. 714.

4. **A well-developed language evolved.**

   "Before the extensive dispersion of the Andonic clans a welldeveloped language had evolved from their early efforts to intercommunicate. This language continued to grow, and almost daily additions were made to it because of the new inventions and adaptations to environment which were developed by these active, restless, and curious people. And this language became the word of Urantia, the tongue of the early human family, until the later appearance of the colored races." P. 714.

B. **Dispersion of the Andonites.**

1. **Friction developed and wars threatened the extinction of primitive civilization.**

   "As time passed, the Andonic clans grew in number, and the contact of the expanding families developed friction and misunderstandings. Only two things came to occupy the minds of these peoples: hunting to obtain food and fighting to avenge themselves against some real or supposed injustice or insult at the hands of the neighboring tribes.

   "Family feuds increased, tribal wars broke out, and serious losses were sustained among the very best elements of the more able and advanced groups. Some of these losses were irreparable; some of the most valuable strains of ability and intelligence were forever lost to the world. This early race and its primitive civilization were threatened with extinction by this incessant warfare of the clans.

   "It is impossible to induce such primitive beings long to live together in peace. Man is the descendant of fighting animals, and when closely associated, uncultured people irritate and offend each other. The Life Carriers know this tendency among evolutionary creatures and accordingly make provision for the eventual separation of developing human beings into at least three, and more often six, distinct and separate races." P. 714.

2. **The Andonic tribes migrated northward and westward—overrunning Europe.**

   "The early Andon races did not penetrate very far into Asia, and they did not at first enter Africa. The geography of those times pointed them north, and farther and farther north these people journeyed until they were hindered by the slowly advancing ice of the third glacier.

   "Before this extensive ice sheet reached France and the British

PART V — *Anthropology*

Isles, the descendants of Andon and Fonta had pushed on westward over Europe and had established more than one thousand separate settlements along the great rivers leading to the then warm waters of the North Sea." P. 715.

3. **In large numbers they lived along the rivers of France.**
"These Andonic tribes were the early river dwellers of France; they lived along the river Somme for tens of thousands of years. The Somme is the one river unchanged by the glaciers, running down to the sea in those days much as it does today. And that explains why so much evidence of the Andonic descendants is found along the course of this river valley." P. 715.

4. **They regularly dwelt in cliffs and grottoes and were clever in building stone huts.**
"These aborigines of Urantia were not tree dwellers, though in emergencies they still betook themselves to the treetops. They regularly dwelt under the shelter of overhanging cliffs along the rivers and in hillside grottoes which afforded a good view of the approaches and sheltered them from the elements. They could thus enjoy the comfort of their fires without being too much inconvenienced by the smoke. They were not really cave dwellers either, though in subsequent times the later ice sheets came farther south and drove their descendants to the caves. They preferred to camp near the edge of a forest and beside a stream.

"They very early became remarkably clever in disguising their partially sheltered abodes and showed great skill in constructing stone sleeping chambers, dome-shaped stone huts, into which they crawled at night. The entrance to such a hut was closed by rolling a stone in front of it, a large stone which had been placed inside for this purpose before the roof stones were finally put in place." P. 715.

C. **Development of primitive culture.**

1. **Their use of weapons and tools.**
"The Andonites were fearless and successful hunters and, with the exception of wild berries and certain fruits of the trees, lived exclusively on flesh. As Andon had invented the stone ax, so his descendants early discovered and made effective use of the throwing stick and the harpoon. At last a tool-creating mind was functioning in conjunction with an implement-using

hand, and these early humans became highly skillful in the fashioning of flint tools. They traveled far and wide in search of flint, much as present-day humans journey to the ends of the earth in quest of gold, platinum, and diamonds.

"And in many other ways these Andon tribes manifested a degree of intelligence which their retrogressing descendants did not attain in half a million years, though they did again and again rediscover various methods of kindling fire." P. 715.

2. **Development of art.**

"The Andonites early developed a fear of the elements—thunder, lightning, rain, snow, hail, and ice. But hunger was the constantly recurring urge of these early days, and since they largely subsisted on animals, they eventually evolved a form of animal worship. To Andon, the larger food animals were symbols of creative might and sustaining power. From time to time it became the custom to designate various of these larger animals as objects of worship. During the vogue of a particular animal, crude outlines of it would be drawn on the walls of the caves, and later on, as continued progress was made in the arts, such an animal god was engraved on various ornaments." P. 716.

3. **Physical conditions controlling Andonic migrations.**

"Primitive man made his evolutionary appearance on earth a little less than one million years ago, and he had a vigorous experience. He instinctively sought to escape the danger of mingling with the inferior simian tribes. But he could not migrate eastward because of the arid Tibetan land elevations, 30,000 feet above sea level; neither could he go south nor west because of the expanded Mediterranean Sea, which then extended eastward to the Indian Ocean; and as he went north, he encountered the advancing ice. But even when further migration was blocked by the ice, and though the dispersing tribes became increasingly hostile, the more intelligent groups never entertained the idea of going southward to live among their hairy tree-dwelling cousins of inferior intellect." P. 718.

4. **Religious emotions were born of man's geographic shut-in environment.**

"Many of man's earliest religious emotions grew out of his feeling of helplessness in the shut-in environment of this geographic situation—mountains to the right, water to the left, and ice in front. But these progressive Andonites would not turn back to their inferior tree-dwelling relatives in the south." P. 718.

PART V — *Anthropology*

5. **The Andonites avoided the forests and remained in northern climes.**
   "These Andonites avoided the forests in contrast with the habits of their nohuman relatives. In the forests man has always deteriorated; human evolution has made progress only in the open and in the higher latitudes. The cold and hunger of the open lands stimulate action, invention, and resourcefulness. While these Andonic tribes were developing the pioneers of the present human race amidst the hardships and privations of these rugged northern climes, their backward cousins were luxuriating in the southern tropical forests of the land of their early common origin." P. 718.

D. **Growth of religion.**

1. **Development of sacrifices.**
   "Very early the Andonic peoples formed the habit of refraining from eating the flesh of the animal of tribal veneration. Presently, in order more suitably to impress the minds of their youths, they evolved a ceremony of reverence which was carried out about the body of one of these venerated animals; and still later on, this primitive performance developed into the more elaborate sacrificial ceremonies of their descendants. And this is the origin of sacrifices as a part of worship. This idea was elaborated by Moses in the Hebrew ritual and was preserved, in principle, by the Apostle Paul as the doctrine of atonement for sin by 'the shedding of blood.'" P. 716.

2. **Onagar assumed leadership of the Andonites, bringing peace and religion.**
   "As the Andonic dispersion extended, the cultural and spiritual status of the clans retrogressed for nearly ten thousand years until the days of Onagar, who assumed the leadership of these tribes, brought peace among them, and for the first time, led all of them in the worship of the 'Breath Giver to men and animals.'" P. 715.

3. **Andon had a confused philosophy. He reverenced fire, but failed to become a sun worshiper.**
   "Andon's philosophy had been most confused; he had barely escaped becoming a fire worshiper because of the great comfort derived from his accidental discovery of fire. Reason,

however, directed him from his own discovery to the sun as a superior and more aweinspiring source of heat and light, but it was too remote, and so he failed to become a sun worshiper." P. 716.

4. **From his headquarters at Oban, near the Caspian Sea, Onagar sent missionaries far and wide.**

   "Onagar maintained headquarters on the northern shores of the ancient Mediterranean in the region of the present Caspian Sea at a settlement called Oban, the tarrying place on the westward turning of the travel trail leading up northward from the Mesopotamian southland. From Oban he sent out teachers to the remote settlements to spread his new doctrines of one Deity and his concept of the hereafter, which he called the Great Beyond. These emissaries of Onagar were the world's first missionaries; they were also the first human beings to cook meat, the first regularly to use fire in the preparation of food. They cooked flesh on the ends of sticks and also on hot stones; later on they roasted large pieces in the fire, but their descendants almost entirely reverted to the use of raw flesh." P. 716.

5. **Onagar organized a real society and introduced a superior religion. Many were indwelt by Thought Adjusters.**

   "Onagar was born 983,323 years ago (from A.D. 1934), and he lived to be sixty-nine years of age. The record of the achievements of this master mind and spiritual leader of the pre-Planetary Prince days is a thrilling recital of the organization of these primitive peoples into a real society. He instituted an efficient tribal government, the like of which was not attained by succeeding generations in many millenniums. Never again, until the arrival of the Planetary Prince, was there such a high spiritual civilization on earth. These simple people had a real though primitive religion, but it was subsequently lost to their deteriorating descendants.

   "Although both Andon and Fonta had received Thought Adjusters, as had many of their descendants, it was not until the days of Onagar that the Adjusters and guardian seraphim came in great numbers to Urantia. This was, indeed, the golden age of primitive man." P. 716-7.

PART V — *Anthropology*

IV. LATER MIGRATIONS OF THE ANDONITES

A. Java man.

1. **The Andonites penetrated to England on the west and Java on the east. The Java man was an Andonite.**
"950,000 years ago the descendants of Andon and Fonta had migrated far to the east and to the west. To the west they passed over Europe to France and England. In later times they penetrated eastward as far as Java, where their bones were so recently found — the so-called Java man — and then journeyed on to Tasmania." P. 719.

2. **Deterioration and threatened extinction of Andonic people.**
"The groups going west became less contaminated with the backward stocks of mutual ancestral origin than those going east, who mingled so freely with their retarded animal cousins. These unprogressive individuals drifted southward and presently mated with the inferior tribes. Later on, increasing numbers of their mongrel descendants returned to the north to mate with the rapidly expanding Andonic peoples, and such unfortunate unions unfailingly deteriorated the superior stock. Fewer and fewer of the primitive settlements maintained the worship of the Breath Giver. This early dawn civilization was threatened with extinction.
"And thus it has ever been on Urantia. Civilizations of great promise have successively deteriorated and have finally been extinguished by the folly of allowing the superior freely to procreate with the inferior." P. 719.

B. Heidelberg race.

1. **The widespread decline of Onagar's civilization.**
"900,000 years ago the arts of Andon and Fonta and the culture of Onagar were vanishing from the face of the earth; culture, religion, and even flintworking were at their lowest ebb.
"These were the times when large numbers of inferior mongrel groups were arriving in England from southern France. These tribes were so largely mixed with the forest apelike creatures that they were scarcely human. They had no religion but were crude flintworkers and possessed sufficient intelligence to kindle fire." P. 719.

2. **The Heidelberg race appears, while the Foxhall people of England and the Badonan tribes maintain the remnants of Onagar's culture.**
"They were followed in Europe by a somewhat superior and prolific people, whose descendants soon spread over the entire

continent from the ice in the north to the Alps and Mediterranean in the south. These tribes are the so-called *Heidelberg race*.
"During this long period of cultural decadence the Foxhall peoples of England and the Badonan tribes northwest of India continued to hold on to some of the traditions of Andon and certain remnants of the culture of Onagar." P. 719.

C. The Foxhall peoples.

1. **The Foxhall people retained much of Onagar's culture and transmitted it to the ancestors of the ancient Eskimos.**
   "The Foxhall peoples were farthest west and succeeded in retaining much of the Andonic culture; they also preserved their knowledge of flintworking, which they transmitted to their descendants, the ancient ancestors of the Eskimos." P. 719.

2. **The Foxhall people were the first human inhabitants of England, but most of their settlements are now under the waters of the English Channel and the North Sea.**
   "Though the remains of the Foxhall peoples were the last to be discovered in England, these Andonites were really the first human beings to live in those regions. At that time the land bridge still connected France with England; and since most of the early settlements of the Andon descendants were located along the rivers and seashores of that early day, they are now under the waters of the English Channel and the North Sea, but some three or four are still above water on the English coast." P. 719.

3. **The Foxhall people became admixed with other stocks and survive as the present-day Eskimos.**
   "Many of the more intelligent and spiritual of the Foxhall peoples maintained their racial superiority and perpetuated their primitive religious customs. And these people, as they were later admixed with subsequent stocks, journeyed on west from England after a later ice visitation and have survived as the present-day Eskimos." P. 720.

B. The Badonan tribes.

1. **Story of the Badonan people.**
   "Besides the Foxhall peoples in the west, another struggling center of culture persisted in the east. This group was located in the foothills of the northwestern Indian highlands among

PART V — *Anthropology*

the tribes of Badonan, a great-great-grandson of Andon. These people were the only descendants of Andon who never practiced human sacrifice.

"These highland Badonites occupied an extensive plateau surrounded by forests, traversed by streams, and abounding in game. Like some of their cousins in Tibet, they lived in crude stone huts, hillside grottoes, and semiunderground passages.

"While the tribes of the north grew more and more to fear the ice, those living near the homeland of their origin became exceedingly fearful of the water. They observed the Mesopotamian peninsula gradually sinking into the ocean, and though it emerged several times, the traditions of these primitive races grew up around the dangers of the sea and the fear of periodic engulfment. And this fear, together with their experience with river floods, explains why they sought out the highlands as a safe place in which to live." P. 720.

2. **Out of the Badonan tribes comes the later Neanderthal race.**

"*850,000* years ago the superior Badonan tribes began a warfare of extermination directed against their inferior and animalistic neighbors. In less than one thousand years most of the borderland animal groups of these regions had been either destroyed or driven back to the southern forests. This campaign for the extermination of inferiors brought about a slight improvement in the hill tribes of that age. And the mixed descendants of this improved Badonite stock appeared on the stage of action as an apparently new people—the *Neanderthal race*." P. 720.

E. **The Neanderthal races.**

1. **The Neanderthalers spread east, west, and south and dominated the world for half a million years.**

"The Neanderthalers were excellent fighters, and they traveled extensively. They gradually spread from the highland centers in northwest India to France on the west, China on the east, and even down into northern Africa. They dominated the world for almost half a million years until the times of the migration of the evolutionary races of color.

"*800,000* years ago game was abundant; many species of deer, as well as elephants and hippopotamuses, roamed over Europe. Cattle were plentiful; horses and wolves were everywhere. The Neanderthalers were great hunters, and the tribes in France were the first to adopt the practice of giving the most successful hunters the choice of women for wives." P. 720.

2. **The fourth glacier forced Neanderthalers south, but the human species had so differentiated there was little danger of mingling with simian stock.**

"750,000 years ago the fourth ice sheet was well on its way south. With their improved implements the Neanderthalers made holes in the ice covering the northern rivers and thus were able to spear the fish which came up to these vents. Ever these tribes retreated before the advancing ice, which at this time made its most extensive invasion of Europe.

"In these times the Siberian glacier was making its southernmost march, compelling early man to move southward, back toward the lands of his origin. But the human species had so differentiated that the danger of further mingling with its nonprogressive simian relatives was greatly lessened." P. 721.

3. **The fifth glacier witnessed the further spread of Neanderthal culture, but little progress was made and a period of spiritually dark ages occurred and continued until the origin of the colored races.**

"550,000 years ago the advancing glacier again pushed man and the animals south. But this time man had plenty of room in the wide belt of land stretching northeast into Asia and lying between the ice sheet and the then greatly expanded Black Sea extension of the Mediterranean.

"These times of the fourth and fifth glaciers witnessed the further spread of the crude culture of the Neanderthal races. But there was so little progress that it truly appeared as though the attempt to produce a new and modified type of intelligent life on Urantia was about to fail. For almost a quarter of a million years these primitive peoples drifted on, hunting and fighting, by spells improving in certain directions, but, on the whole, steadily retrogressing as compared with their superior Andonic ancestors.

"During these spiritually dark ages the culture of superstitious mankind reached its lowest levels. The Neanderthalers really had no religion beyond a shameful superstition. They were deathly afraid of clouds, more especially of mists and fogs. A primitive religion of the fear of natural forces gradually developed, while animal worship declined as improvement in tools, with abundance of game, enabled these people to live with lessened anxiety about food; the sex rewards of the chase tended greatly to improve hunting skill. This new religion of fear led to attempts to placate the invisible forces behind these natural elements and culminated, later on, in the sacrificing of humans to appease these invisible and unknown physical forces. And this terrible practice of human sacrifice has been perpetuated by the more backward peoples of Urantia right on down to the twentieth century." P. 721-22.

Section Four
THE EVOLUTIONARY RACES

I. Urantia a Life-Experiment World

A. Life Carrier supervision of the sixtieth Satania experiment.

1. **Urantia is a life-experiment world. At least 28 life improvements have been made.**

    "Do not overlook the fact that Urantia was assigned to us as a life-experiment world. On this planet we made our sixtieth attempt to modify and, if possible, improve the Satania adaptation of the Nebadon life designs, and it is of record that we achieved numerous beneficial modifications of the standard life patterns. To be specific, on Urantia we worked out and have satisfactorily demonstrated not less than twenty-eight features of life modification which will be of service to all Nebadon throughout all future time.

    "But the establishment of life on no world is ever experimental in the sense that something untried and unknown is attempted. The evolution of life is a technique ever progressive, differential, and variable, but never haphazard, uncontrolled, nor wholly experimental, in the accidental sense." P. 734-5.

2. **Organic evolution is not a cosmic accident. Wound healing evidences mind planning.**

    "Many features of human life afford abundant evidence that the phenomenon of mortal existence was intelligently planned, that organic evolution is not a mere cosmic accident. When a living cell is injured, it possesses the ability to elaborate certain chemical substances which are empowered so to stimulate and activate the neighboring normal cells that they immediately begin the secretion of certain substances which facilitate healing processes in the wound; and at the same time these normal and uninjured cells begin to proliferate—they actually start to work creating new cells to replace any fellow cells which may have been destroyed by the accident." P. 735.

3. **Urantia type of wound healing results from half a million experiments in developing a formula embracing one hundred thousand possible chemical reactions and biologic repercussions.**

    "This chemical action and reaction concerned in wound healing and cell reproduction represents the choice of the Life Carriers of a formula embracing over one hundred thousand phases and features of possible chemical reactions and biologic

PART V — *Anthropology*

repercussions. More than half a million specific experiments were made by the Life Carriers in their laboratories before they finally settled upon this formula for the Urantia life experiment." P. 735.

4. **Better understanding of healing chemicals will improve the treatment of certain diseases.**

   "When Urantia scientists know more of these healing chemicals, they will become more efficient in the treatment of injuries, and indirectly they will know more about controlling certain serious diseases." P. 735.

5. **Urantia experience has resulted in the improvement of healing techniques.**

   "Since life was established on Urantia, the Life Carriers have improved this healing technique as it has been introduced on another Satania world, in that it affords more pain relief and exercises better control over the proliferation capacity of the associated normal cells." P. 735.

B. **Unique features of Urantia experiment.**

1. **The Andonic race appeared before the six colored races and these six mutants simultaneously appeared in one family.**

   "There were many unique features of the Urantia life experiment, but the two outstanding episodes were the appearance of the Andonic race prior to the evolution of the six colored peoples and the later simultaneous appearance of the Sangik mutants in a single family. Urantia is the first world in Satania where the six colored races sprang from the same human family. They ordinarily arise in diversified strains from independent mutations within the prehuman animal stock and usually appear on earth one at a time and successively over long periods of time, beginning with the red man and passing on down through the colors to indigo." P. 735.

   "It was our intention to produce an early manifestation of will in the evolutionary life of Urantia, and we succeeded. Ordinarily, will does not emerge until the colored races have long been in existence, usually first appearing among the superior types of the red man. Your world is the only planet in Satania where the human type of will has appeared in a precolored race." P. 736.

2. **The Planetary Prince appeared five hundred thousand years later than on ordinary worlds.**

   "Another outstanding variation of procedure was the late arrival of the Planetary Prince. As a rule, the prince appears on a planet about the time of will development; and if such a plan had been followed, Caligastia might have come to Urantia even during the lifetimes of Andon and Fonta instead of almost five hundred thousand years later, simultaneously with the appearance of the six Sangik races.

"On an ordinary inhabited world a Planetary Prince would have been granted on the request of the Life Carriers at, or sometime after, the appearance of Andon and Fonta. But Urantia having been designated a life-modification planet, it was by preagreement that the Melchizedek observers, twelve in number, were sent as advisers to the Life Carriers and as overseers of the planet until the subsequent arrival of the Planetary Prince. These Melchizedeks came at the time Andon and Fonta made the decisions which enabled Thought Adjusters to indwell their mortal minds." P. 735-6.

3. **Many useless forms of life were produced.**

"On Urantia the endeavors of the Life Carriers to improve the Satania life patterns necessarily resulted in the production of many apparently useless forms of transition life. But the gains already accrued are sufficient to justify the Urantia modifications of the standard life designs." P. 736.

"But in our effort to provide for that combination and association of inheritance factors which finally gave rise to the mammalian ancestors of the human race, we were confronted with the necessity of permitting hundreds and thousands of other and comparatively useless combinations and associations of inheritance factors to take place. Many of these seemingly strange by-products of our efforts are certain to meet your gaze as you dig back into the planetary past, and I can well understand how puzzling some of these things must be to the limited human viewpoint." P. 736.

4. **Man evolves from mammals derived from the western life implantation.**

"Man thus evolved from the higher mammals derived principally from the *western implantation* of life in the ancient east-west sheltered seas. The *eastern* and *central groups* of living organisms were early progressing favorably toward the attainment of prehuman levels of animal existence. But as the ages passed, the eastern focus of life emplacement failed to attain a satisfactory level of intelligent prehuman status, having

Part V — *Anthropology*

suffered such repeated and irretrievable losses of its highest types of germ plasm that it was forever shorn of the power to rehabilitate human potentialities." P. 733.

II. Evolution of Man on Nonexperimental Worlds

A. The six evolutionary races.

1. **On inhabited worlds the red man usually appears first—soon followed by the other colored races.**

   "The race of dominance during the early ages of the inhabited worlds is the red man, who ordinarily is the first to attain human levels of development. But while the red man is the senior race of the planets, the succeeding colored peoples begin to make their appearances very early in the age of mortal emergence.

   "The earlier races are somewhat superior to the later: the red man stands far above the indigo—black—race. The Life Carriers impart the full bestowal of the living energies to the initial or red race, and each succeeding evolutionary manifestation of a distinct group of mortals represents variation at the expense of the original endowment. Even mortal stature tends to decrease from the red man down to the indigo race, although on Urantia unexpected strains of giantism appeared among the green and orange peoples." P. 584.

2. **The red, yellow, and blue races are the superior peoples among the colored races.**

   "On those worlds having all six evolutionary races the superior peoples are the first, third, and fifth races—the red, the yellow, and the blue. The evolutionary races thus alternate in capacity for intellectual growth and spiritual development, the second, fourth, and sixth being somewhat less endowed. These secondary races are the peoples that are missing on certain worlds; they are the ones that have been exterminated on many others. It is a misfortune on Urantia that you so largely lost your superior blue men, except as they persist in your amalgamated 'white race.' The loss of your orange and green stocks is not of such serious concern." P. 584.

3. **Advantage of racial variety and the amalgamation of the colored races.**

   "The evolution of six—or of three—colored races, while seeming to deteriorate the original endowment of the red man, provides certain very desirable variations in mortal types and affords an otherwise unattainable expression of diverse human potentials. These modifications are beneficial to the progress of mankind as a whole provided they are subsequently upstepped by the imported Adamic or violet race. On Urantia this usual plan of amalgamation was not extensively carried out, and this failure to execute the plan of race evolution makes it impossible for you to understand very much about the status of these peoples on an average inhabited planet by observing the remnants of these early races on your world.

"In the early days of racial development there is a slight tendency for the red, the yellow, and the blue man to interbreed; there is a similar tendency for the orange, green, and indigo races to intermingle." P. 584-5.

4. **Subjugation of the secondary races and the origin of slavery.**

"The more backward humans are usually employed as laborers by the more progressive races. This accounts for the origin of slavery on the planets during the early ages. The orange men are usually subdued by the red and reduced to the status of servants—sometimes exterminated. The yellow and red men often fraternize, but not always. The yellow race usually enslaves the green, while the blue man subdues the indigo. These races of primitive men think no more of utilizing the services of their backward fellows in compulsory labor than Urantians would of buying and selling horses and cattle." P. 585.

5. **On normal worlds slavery does not survive the dispensation of the Planetary Prince.**

"On most normal worlds involuntary servitude does not survive the dispensation of the Planetary Prince, although mental defectives and social delinquents are often still compelled to perform involuntary labor. But on all normal spheres this sort of primitive slavery is abolished soon after the arrival of the imported violet or Adamic race." P. 585.

6. **Problem of eliminating defective stocks before upstepping by the Adamic race.**

"These six evolutionary races are destined to be blended and exalted by amalgamation with the progeny of the Adamic uplifters. But before these peoples are blended, the inferior and unfit are largely eliminated. The Planetary Prince and the Material Son, with other suitable planetary authorities, pass upon the fitness of the reproducing strains. The difficulty of

PART V — *Anthropology*

executing such a radical program on Urantia consists in the absence of competent judges to pass upon the biologic fitness or unfitness of the individuals of your world races. Notwithstanding this obstacle, it seems that you ought to be able to agree upon the biologic disfellowshiping of your more markedly unfit, defective, degenerate, and antisocial stocks." P. 585.

B. **General description of primitive man.**

1. **Order of appearance of the primitive colored races.**
"From the time of man's emergence from the animal level—when he can choose to worship the Creator—to the arrival of the Planetary Prince, mortal will creatures are called *primitive men*. There are six basic types or races of primitive men, and these early peoples successively appear in the order of the spectrum colors, beginning with the red. The length of time consumed in this early life evolution varies greatly on the different worlds, ranging from one hundred and fifty thousand years to over one million years of Urantia time.
"The evolutionary races of color—red, orange, yellow, green, blue, and indigo—begin to appear about the time that primitive man is developing a simple language and is beginning to exercise the creative imagination. By this time man is well accustomed to standing erect." P. 589.

2. **Primitive men are hunters and fighters—it is the age of the survival of the fittest.**
"Primitive men are mighty hunters and fierce fighters. The law of this age is the physical survival of the fittest; the government of these times is wholly tribal. During the early racial struggles on many worlds some of the evolutionary races are obliterated, as occurred on Urantia. Those who survive are usually subsequently blended with the later imported violet race, the Adamic peoples." P. 589.

3. **The long struggle of primitive man will be more fully understood as man goes forward in the Paradise path.**
"In the light of subsequent civilization, this era of primitive man is a long, dark, and bloody chapter. The ethics of the jungle and the morals of the primeval forests are not in keeping with the standards of later dispensations of revealed religion and higher spiritual development. On normal and nonexperimental worlds this epoch is very different from the prolonged and

extraordinarily brutal struggles which characterized this age on Urantia. When you have emerged from your first world experience, you will begin to see why this long and painful struggle on the evolutionary worlds occurs, and as you go forward in the Paradise path, you will increasingly understand the wisdom of these apparently strange doings. But notwithstanding all the vicissitudes of the early ages of human emergence, the performances of primitive man represent a splendid, even a heroic, chapter in the annals of an evolutionary world of time and space." P. 589-90.

4. **A view of early evolutionary man.**
"Early evolutionary man is not a colorful creature. In general, these primitive mortals are cave dwellers or cliff residents. They also build crude huts in the large trees. Before they acquire a high order of intelligence, the planets are sometimes overrun with the larger types of animals. But early in this era mortals learn to kindle and maintain fire, and with the increase of inventive imagination and the improvement in tools, evolving man soon vanquishes the larger and more unwieldy animals. The early races also make extensive use of the larger flying animals. These enormous birds are able to carry one or two average-sized men for a nonstop flight of over five hundred miles. On some planets these birds are of great service since they possess a high order of intelligence, often being able to speak many words of the languages of the realm. These birds are most intelligent, very obedient, and unbelievably affectionate. Such passenger birds have been long extinct on Urantia, but your early ancestors enjoyed their services." P. 590.

5. **Arrival of the Planetary Prince.**
"Within one hundred thousand years from the time man acquires erect posture, the Planetary Prince usually arrives, having been dispatched by the System Sovereign upon the report of the Life Carriers that will is functioning, even though comparatively few individuals have thus developed. Primitive mortals usually welcome the Planetary Prince and his visible staff; in fact, they often look upon them with awe and reverence, almost with worshipfulness, if they are not restrained." P. 590.

PART V — *Anthropology*

III. Evolution of the Colored Races on Urantia

A. The Sangik family.

1. **The Sangik family appears in one of the Badonan tribes.**
   "500,000 years ago the Badonan tribes of the northwestern highlands of India became involved in another great racial struggle. For more than one hundred years this relentless warfare raged, and when the long fight was finished, only about one hundred families were left. But these survivors were the most intelligent and desirable of all the then living descendants of Andon and Fonta.
   "And now, among these highland Badonites there was a new and strange occurrence. A man and woman living in the northeastern part of the then inhabited highland region began *suddenly* to produce a family of unusually intelligent children. This was the *Sangik family*, the ancestors of all of the six colored races of Urantia." P. 722.

2. **Nineteen colored children are born in this Sangik family.**
   "These Sangik children, nineteen in number, were not only intelligent above their fellows, but their skins manifested a unique tendency to turn various colors upon exposure to sunlight. Among these nineteen children were five red, two orange, four yellow, two green, four blue, and two indigo. These colors became more pronounced as the children grew older, and when these youths later mated with their fellow tribesmen, all of their offspring tended toward the skin color of the Sangik parent.
   "And now I interrupt the chronological narrative, after calling attention to the arrival of the Planetary Prince at about this time, while we separately consider the six Sangik races of Urantia." P. 722.

3. **On an average world the colored races appear one at a time—the red man coming first. On no other world in Satania has a race evolved before the colored races.**
   "On an average evolutionary planet the six evolutionary races of color appear one by one; the red man is the first to evolve, and for ages he roams the world before the succeeding colored races make their appearance. The simultaneous emergence of all six races on Urantia, *and in one family*, was most unusual." P. 722.
   "The appearance of the earlier Andonites on Urantia was also something new in Satania. On no other world in the local system has such a race of will creatures evolved in advance of the evolutionary races of color." P. 723.

B. **The six Sangik races of Urantia.**
1. **The story of the red man.**
   "1. *The red man.* These peoples were remarkable specimens of the human race, in many ways superior to Andon and Fonta. They were a most intelligent group and were the first of the Sangik children to develop a tribal civilization and government. They were always monogamous; even their mixed descendants seldom practiced plural mating.

   "In later times they had serious and prolonged trouble with their yellow brethren in Asia. They were aided by their early invention of the bow and arrow, but they had unfortunately inherited much of the tendency of their ancestors to fight among themselves, and this so weakened them that the yellow tribes were able to drive them off the Asiatic continent.

   "About eighty-five thousand years ago the comparatively pure remnants of the red race went en masse across to North America, and shortly thereafter the Bering land isthmus sank, thus isolating them. No red man ever returned to Asia. But throughout Siberia, China, central Asia, India, and Europe they left behind much of their stock blended with the other colored races.

   "When the red man crossed over into America, he brought along much of the teachings and traditions of his early origin. His immediate ancestors had been in touch with the later activities of the world headquarters of the Planetary Prince. But in a short time after reaching the Americas, the red men began to lose sight of these teachings, and there occurred a great decline in intellectual and spiritual culture. Very soon these people again fell to fighting so fiercely among themselves that it appeared that these tribal wars would result in the speedy extinction of this remnant of the comparatively pure red race.

   "Because of this great retrogression the red men seemed doomed when, about sixty-five thousand years ago, Onamonalonton appeared as their leader and spiritual deliverer. He brought temporary peace among the American red men and revived their worship of the 'Great Spirit.' Onamonalonton lived to be ninety-six years of age and maintained his headquarters among the great redwood trees of California. Many of his later descendants have come down to modern times among the Blackfoot Indians.

"As time passed, the teachings of Onamonalonton became hazy traditions. Internecine wars were resumed, and never after the days of this great teacher did another leader succeed in bringing universal peace among them. Increasingly the more intelligent strains perished in these tribal struggles; otherwise a great civilization would have been built upon the North American continent by these able and intelligent red men.

"After crossing over to America from China, the northern red man never again came in contact with other world influences (except the Eskimo) until he was later discovered by the white man. It was most unfortunate that the red man almost completely missed his opportunity of being upstepped by the admixture of the later Adamic stock. As it was, the red man could not rule the white man, and he would not willingly serve him. In such a circumstance, if the two races do not blend, one or the other is doomed." P. 723.

2. **The story of the orange man.**

"2. *The orange man.* The outstanding characteristic of this race was their peculiar urge to build, to build anything and everything, even to the piling up of vast mounds of stone just to see which tribe could build the largest mound. Though they were not a progressive people, they profited much from the schools of the Prince and sent delegates there for instruction.

"The orange race was the first to follow the coast line southward toward Africa as the Mediterranean Sea withdrew to the west. But they never secured a favorable footing in Africa and were wiped out of existence by the later arriving green race.

"Before the end came, this people lost much cultural and spiritual ground. But there was a great revival of higher living as a result of the wise leadership of *Porshunta*, the master mind of this unfortunate race, who ministered to them when their headquarters was at Armageddon some three hundred thousand years ago.

"The last great struggle between the orange and the green men occurred in the region of the lower Nile valley in Egypt. This long-drawn-out battle was waged for almost one hundred years, and at its close very few of the orange race were left alive. The shattered remnants of these people were absorbed by the green and by the later arriving indigo men. But as a race the orange man ceased to exist about one hundred thousand years ago." P. 723-4.

3. **The story of the yellow man.**

"3. *The yellow man.* The primitive yellow tribes were the first to abandon the chase, establish settled communities, and develop a home life based on agriculture. Intellectually they were somewhat inferior to the red man, but socially and collectively they proved themselves superior to all of the Sangik peoples in the matter of fostering racial civilization. Because they developed a fraternal spirit, the various tribes learning to live together in relative peace, they were able to drive the red race before them as they gradually expanded into Asia.

"They traveled far from the influences of the spiritual headquarters of the world and drifted into great darkness following the Caligastia apostasy; but there occurred one brilliant age among this people when Singlangton, about one hundred thousand years ago, assumed the leadership of these tribes and proclaimed the worship of the 'One Truth.'

"The survival of comparatively large numbers of the yellow race is due to their intertribal peacefulness. From the days of Singlangton to the times of modern China, the yellow race has been numbered among the more peaceful of the nations of Urantia. This race received a small but potent legacy of the later imported Adamic stock." P. 724.

4. **The story of the green man.**

"4. *The green man.* The green race was one of the less able groups of primitive men, and they were greatly weakened by extensive migrations in different directions. Before their dispersion these tribes experienced a great revival of culture under the leadership of Fantad, some three hundred and fifty thousand years ago.

"The green race split into three major divisions: The northern tribes were subdued, enslaved, and absorbed by the yellow and blue races. The eastern group were amalgamated with the Indian peoples of those days, and remnants still persist among them. The southern nation entered Africa, where they destroyed their almost equally inferior orange cousins.

"In many ways both groups were evenly matched in this struggle since each carried strains of the giant order, many of

PART V — *Anthropology*

their leaders being eight and nine feet in height. These giant strains of the green man were mostly confined to this southern or Egyptian nation.

"The remnants of the victorious green men were subsequently absorbed by the indigo race, the last of the colored peoples to develop and emigrate from the original Sangik center of race dispersion." P. 724-5.

5. **The story of the blue man.**

"5. *The blue man*. The blue men were a great people. They early invented the spear and subsequently worked out the rudiments of many of the arts of modern civilization. The blue man had the brain power of the red man associated with the soul and sentiment of the yellow man. The Adamic descendants preferred them to all of the later persisting colored races.

"The early blue men were responsive to the persuasions of the teachers of Prince Caligastia's staff and were thrown into great confusion by the subsequent perverted teachings of those traitorous leaders. Like other primitive races they never fully recovered from the turmoil produced by the Caligastia betrayal, nor did they ever completely overcome their tendency to fight among themselves.

"About five hundred years after Caligastia's downfall a widespread revival of learning and religion of a primitive sort—but none the less real and beneficial—occurred. Orlandof became a great teacher among the blue race and led many of the tribes back to the worship of the true God under the name of the "Supreme Chief." This was the greatest advance of the blue man until those later times when this race was so greatly upstepped by the admixture of the Adamic stock.

"The European researches and explorations of the Old Stone Age have largely to do with unearthing the tools, bones, and artcraft of these ancient blue men, for they persisted in Europe until recent times. The so-called *white races* of Urantia are the descendants of these blue men as they were first modified by slight mixture with yellow and red, and as they were later greatly upstepped by assimilating the greater portion of the violet race." P. 725.

6. **The story of the indigo race.**

"6. *The indigo race*. As the red men were the most advanced of all the Sangik peoples, so the black men were the least progressive.

They were the last to migrate from their highland homes. They journeyed to Africa, taking possession of the continent, and have ever since remained there except when they have been forcibly taken away, from age to age, as slaves.

"Isolated in Africa, the indigo peoples, like the red man, received little or none of the race elevation which would have been derived from the infusion of the Adamic stock. Alone in Africa, the indigo race made little advancement until the days of Orvonon, when they experienced a great spiritual awakening. While they later almost entirely forgot the "God of Gods" proclaimed by Orvonon, they did not entirely lose the desire to worship the Unknown; at least they maintained a form of worship up to a few thousand years ago.

"Notwithstanding their backwardness, these indigo peoples have exactly the same standing before the celestial powers as any other earthly race." P. 725.

7. **There are at least five reasons for evolving different colored races.**

"There are many good and sufficient reasons for the plan of evolving either three or six colored races on the worlds of space.

"Though Urantia mortals may not be in a position fully to appreciate all of these reasons, we would call attention to the following:

"1. Variety is indispensable to opportunity for the wide functioning of natural selection, differential survival of superior strains.

"2. Stronger and better races are to be had from the interbreeding of diverse peoples when these different races are carriers of superior inheritance factors. And the Urantia races would have benefited by such an early amalgamation provided such a conjoint people could have been subsequently effectively upstepped by a thorough going admixture with the superior Adamic stock. The attempt to execute such an experiment on Urantia under present racial conditions would be highly disastrous.

"3. Competition is healthfully stimulated by diversification of races.

"4. Differences in status of the races and of groups within each race are essential to the development of human tolerance and altruism.

PART V — *Anthropology*

"5. Homogeneity of the human race is not desirable until the peoples of an evolving world attain comparatively high levels of spiritual development." P. 726.

C. **Dispersion of the colored races.**

1. **Natural conditions prevented extensive dispersion for one hundred thousand years.**

    "When the colored descendants of the Sangik family began to multiply, and as they sought opportunity for expansion into adjacent territory, the fifth glacier, the third of geologic count, was well advanced on its southern drift over Europe and Asia. These early colored races were extraordinarily tested by the rigors and hardships of the glacial age of their origin. This glacier was so extensive in Asia that for thousands of years migration to eastern Asia was cut off. And not until the later retreat of the Mediterranean Sea, consequent upon the elevation of Arabia, was it possible for them to reach Africa.

    "Thus it was that for almost one hundred thousand years these Sangik peoples spread out around the foothills and mingled together more or less, notwithstanding the peculiar but natural antipathy which early manifested itself between the different races." P. 726.

2. **Migrations of the red, yellow, and blue men and the "melting pot" of India.**

    "Between the times of the Planetary Prince and Adam, India became the home of the most cosmopolitan population ever to be found on the face of the earth. But it was unfortunate that this mixture came to contain so much of the green, orange, and indigo races. These secondary Sangik peoples found existence more easy and agreeable in the southlands, and many of them subsequently migrated to Africa. The primary Sangik peoples, the superior races, avoided the tropics, the red man going northeast to Asia, closely followed by the yellow man, while the blue race moved northwest into Europe." P 726-27.

3. **The red man enters North America**

    "The red men early began to migrate to the northeast, on the heels of the retreating ice, passing around the highlands of India and occupying all of northeastern Asia. They were closely followed by the yellow tribes, who subsequently drove them out of Asia into North America." P. 727.

4. **Mongrel red races establish the civilizations of Mexico, Central America, and South America.**

   "When the relatively pure-line remnants of the red race forsook Asia, there were eleven tribes, and they numbered a little over seven thousand men, women, and children. These tribes were accompanied by three small groups of mixed ancestry, the largest of these being a combination of the orange and blue races. These three groups never fully fraternized with the red man and early journeyed southward to Mexico and Central America, where they were later joined by a small group of mixed yellows and reds. These peoples all intermarried and founded a new and amalgamated race, one which was much less warlike than the pure-line red men. Within five thousand years this amalgamated race broke up into three groups, establishing the civilizations respectively of Mexico, Central America, and South America. The South American offshoot did receive a faint touch of the blood of Adam." P. 727.

5. **The brown races were derived from a mixture of the red and yellow peoples.**

   "To a certain extent the early red and yellow men mingled in Asia, and the offspring of this union journeyed on to the east and along the southern seacoast and, eventually, were driven by the rapidly increasing yellow race onto the peninsulas and near-by islands of the sea. They are the present-day brown men." P. 727.

6. **The yellow races survived in Asia. The red, green, and orange races almost destroyed themselves by racial wars.**

   "The yellow race has continued to occupy the central regions of eastern Asia. Of all the six colored races they have survived in greatest numbers. While the yellow men now and then engaged in racial war, they did not carry on such incessant and relentless wars of extermination as were waged by the red, green, and orange men. These three races virtually destroyed themselves before they were finally all but annihilated by their enemies of other races." P. 727.

7. **As Sangik tribes, particularly the blue men, invaded Europe they mingled with and upstepped the Neanderthalers, who subsequently were extended from England to India.**

   "Since the fifth glacier did not extend so far south in Europe, the way was partially open for these Sangik peoples to migrate to the northwest; and upon the retreat of the ice the blue men, together

PART V — *Anthropology*

with a few other small racial groups, migrated westward along the old trails of the Andon tribes. They invaded Europe in successive waves, occupying most of the continent.

"In Europe they soon encountered the Neanderthal descendants of their early and common ancestor, Andon. These older European Neanderthalers had been driven south and east by the glacier and thus were in position quickly to encounter and absorb their invading cousins of the Sangik tribes.

"In general and to start with, the Sangik tribes were more intelligent than, and in most ways far superior to, the deteriorated descendants of the early Andonic plainsmen; and the mingling of these Sangik tribes with the Neanderthal peoples led to the immediate improvement of the older race. It was this infusion of Sangik blood, more especially that of the blue man, which produced that marked improvement in the Neanderthal peoples exhibited by the successive waves of increasingly intelligent tribes that swept over Europe from the east.

"During the following interglacial period this new Neanderthal race extended from England to India. The remnant of the blue race left in the old Persian peninsula later amalgamated with certain others, primarily the yellow; and the resultant blend, subsequently somewhat upstepped by the violet race of Adam, has persisted as the swarthy nomadic tribes of modern Arabs." P. 727.

8. **The ultimate destiny of the Sangik tribes must take into account the later admixture of Adamic blood.**

    "All efforts to identify the Sangik ancestry of modern peoples must take into account the later improvement of the racial strains by the subsequent admixture of Adamic blood." P. 728.

9. **The primary Sangiks sought the temperate climes while the secondary moved southward.**

    "The superior races sought the northern or temperate climes, while the orange, green, and indigo races successively gravitated to Africa over the newly elevated land bridge which separated the westward retreating Mediterranean from the Indian Ocean." P. 728.

10. **The mass migration of the indigo peoples into Africa.**
"The last of the Sangik peoples to migrate from their center of race origin was the indigo man. About the time the green man was killing off the orange race in Egypt and greatly weakening himself in so doing, the great black exodus started south through Palestine along the coast; and later, when these physically strong indigo peoples overran Egypt, they wiped the green man out of existence by sheer force of numbers. These indigo races absorbed the remnants of the orange man and much of the stock of the green man, and certain of the indigo tribes were considerably improved by this racial amalgamation." P. 728.

11. **The racial history of early Egypt.**
"And so it appears that Egypt was first dominated by the orange man, then by the green, followed by the indigo (black) man, and still later by a mongrel race of indigo, blue, and modified green men. But long before Adam arrived, the blue men of Europe and the mixed races of Arabia had driven the indigo race out of Egypt and far south on the African continent." P. 728.

12. **Distribution of the colored races at the end of the Sangik migrations.**
"As the Sangik migrations draw to a close, the green and orange races are gone, the red man holds North America, the yellow man eastern Asia, the blue man Europe, and the indigo race has gravitated to Africa. India harbors a blend of the secondary Sangik races, and the brown man, a blend of the red and yellow, holds the islands off the Asiatic coast. An amalgamated race of rather superior potential occupies the highlands of South America. The purer Andonites live in the extreme northern regions of Europe and in Iceland, Greenland, and northeastern North America." P. 728.

13. **Fear of glaciers produced the first marine adventurers.**
"During the periods of farthest glacial advance the westernmost of the Andon tribes came very near being driven into the sea. They lived for years on a narrow southern strip of the present island of England. And it was the tradition of these repeated glacial advances that drove them to take to the sea when the sixth and last glacier finally appeared. They were the first marine

PART V — *Anthropology*

adventurers. They built boats and started in search of new lands which they hoped might be free from the terrifying ice invasions. And some of them reached Iceland, others Greenland, but the vast majority perished from hunger and thirst on the open sea." P. 728.

14. **Arrival of the red man and the Eskimos in North America.**

    "A little more than eighty thousand years ago, shortly after the red man entered northwestern North America, the freezing over of the north seas and the advance of local ice fields on Greenland drove these Eskimo descendants of the Urantia aborigines to seek a better land, a new home; and they were successful, safely crossing the narrow straits which then separated Greenland from the northeastern land masses of North America. They reached the continent about twenty-one hundred years after the red man arrived in Alaska. Subsequently some of the mixed stock of the blue man journeyed westward and amalgamated with the later-day Eskimos, and this union was slightly beneficial to the Eskimo tribes." P. 728.

15. **The courage and devotion of early man often bordered on grandeur and sublimity.**

    "The struggles of these early ages were characterized by courage, bravery, and even heroism. And we all regret that so many of those sterling and rugged traits of your early ancestors have been lost to the later-day races. While we appreciate the value of many of the refinements of advancing civilization, we miss the magnificent persistency and superb devotion of your early ancestors, which oftentimes bordered on grandeur and sublimity." P. 729.

D. **Secondary Sangik races in Africa.**

1. **Climatic and geologic changes caused the dwellers of Sahara to disperse.**

    "The early expansion of the violet race into Europe was cut short by certain rather sudden climatic and geologic changes. With the retreat of the northern ice fields the water-laden winds from the west shifted to the north, gradually turning the great open pasture regions of Sahara into a barren desert. This drought dispersed the smaller-statured brunets, dark-eyed but long-headed dwellers of the great Sahara plateau.

"The purer indigo elements moved southward to the forests of central Africa, where they have ever since remained. The more mixed groups spread out in three directions: The superior tribes to the west migrated to Spain and thence to adjacent parts of Europe, forming the nucleus of the later Mediterranean long-headed brunet races. The least progressive division to the east of the Sahara plateau migrated to Arabia and thence through northern Mesopotamia and India to faraway Ceylon. The central group moved north and east to the Nile valley and into Palestine.

"It is this secondary Sangik substratum that suggests a certain degree of kinship among the modern peoples scattered from the Deccan through Iran, Mesopotamia, and along both shores of the Mediterranean Sea." P. 890.

E. **The red man and yellow man.**

1. **The red man and yellow man escaped admixture with the Neanderthalers. The red man reigned supreme in eastern Asia until population pressure caused the yellow race to move northward. Warfare resulted and after two hundred thousand years the red man was driven across the Bering isthmus into North America.**

   "While the story of India is that of Andite conquest and eventual submergence in the older evolutionary peoples, the narrative of eastern Asia is more properly that of the primary Sangiks, particularly the red man and the yellow man. These two races largely escaped that admixture with the debased Neanderthal strain which so greatly retarded the blue man in Europe, thus preserving the superior potential of the primary Sangik type.

   "While the early Neanderthalers were spread out over the entire breadth of Eurasia, the eastern wing was the more contaminated with debased animal strains. These subhuman types were pushed south by the fifth glacier, the same ice sheet which so long blocked Sangik migration into eastern Asia. And when the red man moved northeast around the highlands of India, he found northeastern Asia free from these subhuman types. The tribal organization of the red races was formed earlier than that of any other peoples, and they were the first to migrate from the central Asian focus of the Sangiks. The inferior Neanderthal strains were destroyed or driven off the mainland by the later migrating yellow tribes. But the red man had reigned supreme in eastern Asia for almost one hundred thousand years before the yellow tribes arrived.

"More than three hundred thousand years ago the main body of the yellow race entered China from the south as coastwise migrants. Each millennium they penetrated farther and farther inland, but they did not make contact with their migrating Tibetan brethren until comparatively recent times.

"Growing population pressure caused the northward-moving yellow race to begin to push into the hunting grounds of the red man. This encroachment, coupled with natural racial antagonism, culminated in increasing hostilities, and thus began the crucial struggle for the fertile lands of farther Asia.

"The story of this agelong contest between the red and yellow races is an epic of Urantia history. For over two hundred thousand years these two superior races waged bitter and unremitting warfare. In the earlier struggles the red men were generally successful, their raiding parties spreading havoc among the yellow settlements. But the yellow man was an apt pupil in the art of warfare, and he early manifested a marked ability to live peaceably with his compatriots; the Chinese were the first to learn that in union there is strength. The red tribes continued their internecine conflicts, and presently they began to suffer repeated defeats at the aggressive hands of the relentless Chinese, who continued their inexorable march northward.

"One hundred thousand years ago the decimated tribes of the red race were fighting with their backs to the retreating ice of the last glacier, and when the land passage to the west, over the Bering isthmus, became passable, these tribes were not slow in forsaking the inhospitable shores of the Asiatic continent. It is eighty-five thousand years since the last of the pure red men departed from Asia, but the long struggle left its genetic imprint upon the victorious yellow race. The northern Chinese peoples, together with the Andonite Siberians, assimilated much of the red stock and were in considerable measure benefited thereby." P. 883.

2. **The North American Indians never came in contact with the descendants of Adam and Eve since the last to migrate to North America arrived 85,000 years ago.**

   "The North American Indians never came in contact with even the Andite offspring of Adam and Eve, having been dispossessed of their Asiatic homelands some fifty thousand years before the coming of Adam. During the age of Andite migrations the pure red strains were spreading out over North America as nomadic tribes, hunters who practiced agriculture to a small extent. These races and cultural groups remained almost completely isolated from the remainder of the world from their arrival in the Americas down to the end of the first millennium of the Christian era, when they were discovered by the white races of Europe. Up to that time the Eskimos were the nearest to white men the northern tribes of red men had ever seen.

   "The red and the yellow races are the only human stocks that ever achieved a high degree of civilization apart from the influences of the Andites. The oldest Amerindian culture was the Onamonalonton center in California, but this had long since vanished by 35,000 B.C. In Mexico, Central America, and in the mountains of South America the later and more enduring civilizations were founded by a race predominantly red but containing a considerable admixture of the yellow, orange, and blue." P. 884.

3. **Movement of races in southeastern Asia.**

   "Sometime after driving the red man across to North America, the expanding Chinese cleared the Andonites from the river valleys of eastern Asia, pushing them north into Siberia and west into Turkestan, where they were soon to come in contact with the superior culture of the Andites.

   "In Burma and the peninsula of Indo-China the cultures of India and China mixed and blended to produce the successive civilizations of those regions. Here the vanished green race has persisted in larger proportion than anywhere else in the world.

   "Many different races occupied the islands of the Pacific. In general, the southern and then more extensive islands were occupied by peoples carrying a heavy percentage of green and indigo blood. The northern islands were held by Andonites and, later on, by races embracing large proportions of the

PART V — *Anthropology*

yellow and red stocks. The ancestors of the Japanese people were not driven off the mainland until 12,000 B.C., when they were dislodged by a powerful southern-coastwise thrust of the northern Chinese tribes. Their final exodus was not so much due to population pressure as to the initiative of a chieftain whom they came to regard as a divine personage.

"Like the peoples of India and the Levant, victorious tribes of the yellow man established their earliest centers along the coast and up the rivers. The coastal settlements fared poorly in later years as the increasing floods and the shifting courses of the rivers made the lowland cities untenable.

"Twenty thousand years ago the ancestors of the Chinese had built up a dozen strong centers of primitive culture and learning, especially along the Yellow River and the Yangtze. And now these centers began to be reinforced by the arrival of a steady stream of superior blended peoples from Sinkiang and Tibet. The migration from Tibet to the Yangtze valley was not so extensive as in the north, neither were the Tibetan centers so advanced as those of the Tarim basin. But both movements carried a certain amount of Andite blood eastward to the river settlements." P. 884-5.

F. **The Cro-Magnoid blue man.**

1. **The ancient centers of blue man culture were located along the rivers of Europe.**

"The ancient centers of the culture of the blue man were located along all the rivers of Europe, but only the Somme now flows in the same channel which it followed during preglacial times." P. 891.

2. **The European culture of the blue man was a blend of many races.**

"While we speak of the blue man as pervading the European continent, there were scores of racial types. Even thirty-five thousand years ago the European blue races were already a highly blended people carrying strains of both red and yellow, while on the Atlantic coastlands and in the regions of present-day Russia they had absorbed a considerable amount of Andonite blood and to the south were in contact with the Saharan peoples. But it would be fruitless to attempt to enumerate the many racial groups." P. 891.

3. **The post-Adamic culture of the Cro-Magnoids was a blend of the blue man and the Adamites.**

"The European civilization of this early post-Adamic period was a unique blend of the vigor and art of the blue men with the creative imagination of the Adamites. The blue men were a race of great vigor, but they greatly deteriorated the cultural and spiritual status of the Adamites. It was very difficult for the latter to impress their religion upon the Cro-Magnoids because of the tendency of so many to cheat and to debauch the maidens. For ten thousand years religion in Europe was at a low ebb as compared with the developments in India and Egypt." P. 891.

4. **The culture and civilization of the blue man.**
"The blue men were perfectly honest in all their dealings and were wholly free from the sexual vices of the mixed Adamites. They respected maidenhood, only practicing polygamy when war produced a shortage of males.

"These Cro-Magnon peoples were a brave and farseeing race. They maintained an efficient system of child culture. Both parents participated in these labors, and the services of the older children were fully utilized. Each child was carefully trained in the care of the caves, in art, and in flint making. At an early age the women were well versed in the domestic arts and in crude agriculture, while the men were skilled hunters and courageous warriors.

"The blue men were hunters, fishers, and food gatherers; they were expert boat builders. They made stone axes, cut down trees, erected log huts, partly below ground and roofed with hides. And there are peoples who still build similar huts in Siberia. The southern Cro-Magnons generally lived in caves and grottoes." P. 891.

5. **The Cro-Magnons were courageous; later, with the infusion of Adamic blood, they became artistic.**
"It was not uncommon during the rigors of winter for their sentinels standing on night guard at cave entrances to freeze to death. They had courage, but above all they were artists; the Adamic mixture suddenly accelerated creative imagination. The height of the blue man's art was about fifteen thousand years ago, before the days when the darker-skinned races came north from Africa through Spain." P. 892.

6. **Climatic changes resulted in cultural advances, but caused certain biologic retrogressions.**
"About fifteen thousand years ago the Alpine forests were

spreading extensively. The European hunters were being driven to the river valleys and to the sea shores by the same climatic coercion that had turned the world's happy hunting grounds into dry and barren deserts. As the rain winds shifted to the north, the great open grazing lands of Europe became covered by forests. These great and relatively sudden climatic modifications drove the races of Europe to change from open-space hunters to herders, and in some measure to fishers and tillers of the soil.

"These changes, while resulting in cultural advances, produced certain biologic retrogressions. Duriing the previous hunting era the superior tribes had intermarried with the higher types of war captives and had unvaryingly destroyed those whom they deemed inferior. But as they commenced to establish settlements and engage in agriculture and commerce, they began to save many of the mediocre captives as slaves. And it was the progeny of these slaves that subsequently so greatly deteriorated the whole CroMagnon type. This retrogression of culture continued until it received a fresh impetus from the east when the final and en masse invasion of the Mesopotamians swept over Europe, quickly absorbing the Cro-Magnon type and culture and initiating the civilization of the white races." P. 892.

Science In *The Urantia Book*

Section Five
SECOND AND THIRD PLANETARY MORTAL EPOCHS
I. The Planetary Prince Dispensation
A. Post-Planetary Prince man on a normal planet.
1. **Description of advances made during Planetary Prince dispensation.**
   "With the arrival of the Planetary Prince a new dispensation begs. Government appears on earth, and the advanced tribal epoch is attained. Great social strides are made during a few thousand years of this regime. Under normal conditions mortals attain a high state of civilization during this age. They do not struggle so long in barbarism as did the Urantia races. But life on an inhabited world is so changed by rebellion that you can have little or no idea of such a regime on a normal planet.
   "The average length of this dispensation is around five hundred thousand years, some longer, some shorter. During this era the planet is established in the circuits of the system, and a full quota of seraphic and other celestial helpers is assigned to its administration. The Thought Adjusters come in increasing numbers, and the seraphic guardians amplify their regime of mortal supervision.
   "When the Planetary Prince arrives on a primitive world, the evolved religion of fear and ignorance prevails. The prince and his staff make the first revelations of higher truth and universe organization. These initial presentations of revealed religion are very simple, and they usually pertain to the affairs of the local system. Religion is wholly an evolutionary process prior to the arrival of the Planetary Prince. Subsequently, religion progresses by graduated revelation as well as by evolutionary growth. Each dispensation, each mortal epoch, receives an enlarged presentation of spiritual truth and religious ethics. The evolution of the religious capacity of receptivity in the inhabitants of a world largely determines their rate of spiritual advancement and the extent of religious revelation." P. 591.
2. **Wars continue, but national life begins to replace tribal organization, and there is an emergence of family life.**
   "But the Planetary Prince is not 'the Prince of Peace.' Racial struggles and tribal wars continue over into this dispensation but with diminishing frequency and severity. This is the great age of racial dispersion, and it culminates in a period of intense nationalism. Color is the basis of tribal and national groupings,

PART V — *Anthropology*

and the different races often develop separate languages. Each expanding group of mortals tends to seek isolation. This segregation is favored by the existence of many languages. Before the unification of the several races their relentless warfare sometimes results in the obliteration of whole peoples; the orange and green men are particularly subject to such extinction.

"On average worlds, during the latter part of the prince's rule, national life begins to replace tribal organization or rather to be superimposed upon the existing tribal groupings. But the great social achievement of the prince's epoch is the emergence of family life. Heretofore, human relationships have been chiefly tribal; now, the home begins to materialize.

"This is the dispensation of the realization of sex equality. On some planets the male may rule the female; on others the reverse prevails. During this age normal worlds establish full equality of the sexes, this being preliminary to the fuller realization of the ideals of home life. This is the dawn of the golden age of the home. The idea of tribal rule gradually gives way to the dual concept of national life and family life.

"During this age agriculture makes its appearance. The growth of the family idea is incompatible with the roving and unsettled life of the hunter. Gradually the practices of settled habitations and the cultivation of the soil become established. The domestication of animals and the development of home arts proceed space. Upon reaching the apex of biologic evolution, a high level of civilization has been attained, but there is little development of a mechanical order; invention is the characteristic of the succeeding age." P. 591-2.

3. The beginning of race purification is one of the great achievements of this age.

    "One of the great achievements of the age of the prince is this restriction of the multiplication of mentally defective and socially unfit individuals. Long before the times of the arrival of the second Sons, the Adams, most worlds seriously address themselves to the tasks of race purification, something which the Urantia peoples have not even yet seriously undertaken." P. 592.

4. When primitive man attains the height of evolutionary development the biologic uplifters arrive—Adam and Eve.

    "During the dispensation of a Planetary Prince, primitive man reaches the limit of natural evolutionary development, and this biologic attainment signals the System Sovereign to dispatch to such a world the second order of sonship, the biologic uplifters. These Sons, for there are two of them—the Material Son and Daughter—are usually known on a planet as Adam and Eve. The original Material Son of Satania is Adam, and those who go to the system worlds as biologic uplifters always carry the name of this first and original Son of their unique order." P. 580.

B. Staff of the Planetary Prince on Urantia.

1. The Prince's corporeal staff of one hundred.

"The planetary staff included a large number of angelic co-operators and a host of other celestial beings assigned to advance the interests and promote the welfare of the human races. But from your standpoint the most interesting group of all were the corporeal members of the Prince's staff—sometimes referred to as *the Caligastia one hundred*.

"These one hundred rematerialized members of the Prince's staff were chosen by Caligastia from over 785,000 ascendant citizens of Jerusem who volunteered for embarkation on the Urantia adventure. Each one of the chosen one hundred was from a different planet, and none of them were from Urantia.

"These Jerusemite volunteers were brought by seraphic transport direct from the system capital to Urantia, and upon arrival they were held enseraphimed until they could be provided with personality forms of the dual nature of special planetary service, literal bodies consisting of flesh and blood but also attuned to the life circuits of the system." P. 742.

2. Implantation of the life plasm of one hundred Urantia humans into the new bodies of the Prince's staff.

"Sometime before the arrival of these one hundred Jerusem citizens, the two supervising Life Carriers resident on Urantia, having previously perfected their plans, petitioned Jerusem and Edentia for permission to transplant the life plasm of one hundred selected survivors of the Andon and Fonta stock into the material bodies to be projected for the corporeal members of the Prince's staff. The request was granted on Jerusem and approved on Edentia.

"Accordingly, fifty males and fifty females of the Andon and Fonta posterity, representing the survival of the best strains of

Part V — Anthropology

that unique race, were chosen by the Life Carriers. With one or two exceptions these Andonite contributors to the advancement of the race were strangers to one another. They were assembled from widely separated places by co-ordinated Thought Adjuster direction and seraphic guidance at the threshold of the planetary headquarters of the Prince. Here the one hundred human subjects were given into the hands of the highly skilled volunteer commission from Avalon, who directed the material extraction of a portion of the life plasm of these Andon descendants. This living material was then transferred to the material bodies constructed for the use of the one hundred Jerusemite members of the Prince's staff. Meantime, these newly arrived citizens of the system capital were held in the sleep of seraphic transport." P. 742.

3. **These transactions covered ten days and gave rise to numerous myths and legends.**

   "These transactions, together with the literal creation of special bodies for the Caligastia one hundred, gave origin to numerous legends, many of which subsequently became confused with the later traditions concerning the planetary installation of Adam and Eve.

   "The entire transaction of repersonalization, from the time of the arrival of the seraphic transports bearing the one hundred Jerusem volunteers until they became conscious, threefold beings of the realm, consumed exactly ten days." P. 742-3.

4. **There were no offspring of the Prince's corporeal staff before isolation of the Satania life currents. The staff followed the Andonic race in skin color and language.**

   "These special beings therefore had little or no idea as to what type of material creature would be produced by their sexual union. And they never did know; before the time for such a step in the prosecution of their world work the entire regime was upset by rebellion, and those who later functioned in the parental role had been isolated from the life currents of the system.

   "In skin color and language these materialized members of Caligastia's staff followed the Andonic race. They partook of food as did the mortals of the realm with this difference: The recreated bodies of this group were fully satisfied by a nonflesh diet. This was one of the considerations which determined their residence in a warm region abounding in fruits and nuts. The practice of subsisting on a nonflesh diet dates from the times of the Caligastia one hundred, for this custom spread near and far to affect the eating habits of many surrounding tribes, groups of origin in the once exclusively meat-eating evolutionary races." P. 744.

5. **Certain changes were also made in the bodies of the one hundred Andonites.**

    "It should be explained in this connection that, at the time the one hundred Andonites contributed their human germ plasm to the members of the Prince's staff, the Life Carriers introduced into their mortal bodies the complement of the system circuits; and thus were they enabled to live on concurrently with the staff, century after century, in defiance of physical death.

    "Eventually the one hundred Andonites were made aware of their contribution to the new forms of their superiors, and these same one hundred children of the Andon tribes were kept at headquarters as the personal attendants of the Prince's corporeal staff." P. 745.

6. **Nature and function of the Prince's corporeal staff.**

    "2. The one hundred were material but superhuman beings, having been reconstituted on Urantia as unique men and women of a high and special order.

    "This group, while enjoying provisional citizenship on Jerusem, volunteered and were accepted for planetary service in liaison with the descending orders of sonship, their Adjusters were detached. But these Jerusemites were superhuman beings—they possessed souls of ascendant growth. During the mortal life in the flesh the soul is of embryonic estate; it is born (resurrected) in the morontia life and experiences growth through the successive morontia worlds. And the souls of the Caligastia one hundred had thus expanded through the progressive experiences of the seven mansion worlds to citizenship status on Jerusem." P. 744.

    "The Life Carriers, the architects of form, provide such volunteers with new physical bodies, which they occupy for the periods of their planetary sojourn. These personality forms, while exempt from the ordinary diseases of the realms, are, like the early morontia bodies, subject to certain accidents of a mechanical nature." P. 574.

Part V — *Anthropology*

7. **Two classes of offspring result from the sex mating of the Prince's staff.**
"These assistants to the Planetary Prince seldom mate with the world races, but they do always mate among themselves. Two classes of beings result from these unions: the primary type of midway creatures and certain high types of material beings who remain attached to the prince's staff after their parents have been removed from the planet at the time of the arrival of Adam and Eve. These children do not mate with the mortal races except in certain emergencies and then only by direction of the Planetary Prince. In such an event, their children—the grandchildren of the corporeal staff—are in status as of the superior races of their day and generation. All the offspring of these semimaterial assistants of the Planetary Prince are Adjuster indwelt." P. 574.

"In conformity to their instructions the staff did not engage in sexual reproduction, but they did painstakingly study their personal constitutions, and they carefully explored every imaginable phase of intellectual (mind) and morontia (soul) liaison. And it was during the thirty-third year of their sojourn in Dalamatia, long before the wall was completed, that number two and number seven of the Danite group accidentally discovered a phenomenon attendant upon the liaison of their morontia selves (supposedly nonsexual and nonmaterial); and the result of this adventure proved to be the first of the primary midway creatures. This new being was wholly visible to the planetary staff and to their celestial associates but was not visible to the men and women of the various human tribes. Upon authority of the Planetary Prince the entire corporeal staff undertook the production of similar beings, and all were successful, following the instructions of the pioneer Danite pair. Thus did the Prince's staff eventually bring into being the original corps of 50,000 primary midwayers." P. 744.

8. **The Caligastia one hundred were kept immortal by fruit from the tree of life.**
"3. The Caligastia one hundred were personally immortal, or undying. There circulated through their material forms the antidotal complements of the life currents of the system; and had they not lost contact with the life circuits through rebellion, they would have lived on indefinitely until the arrival of a subsequent Son of God, or until their sometime later release to resume the interrupted journey to Havona and Paradise.

"These antidotal complements of the Satania life currents were derived from the fruit of the tree of life, a shrub of Edentia which was sent to Urantia by the Most Highs of Norlatiadek at the time of Caligastia's arrival. In the days of Dalamatia this tree grew in the central courtyard of the temple of the unseen Father, and it was the fruit of the tree of life that enabled the material and otherwise mortal beings of the Prince's staff to live on indefinitely as long as they had access to it. "While of no value to the evolutionary races, this supersustenance was quite sufficient to confer continuous life upon the Caligastia one hundred and also upon the one hundred modified Andonites who were associated with them." P. 745.

C. **The Prince's reign.**

1. **Each of the ten commissions set about slowly to advance the primitive races.**

    "The Caligastia one hundred—graduates of the Satania mansion worlds—well knew the arts and culture of Jerusem, but such knowledge is nearly valueless on a barbaric planet populated by primitive humans. These wise beings knew better than to undertake the *sudden* transformation, or the en masse uplifting, of the primitive races of that day. They well understood the slow evolution of the human species, and they wisely refrained from any radical attempts at modifying man's mode of life on earth. "Each of the ten planetary commissions set about *slowly* and naturally to advance the interests intrusted to them. Their plan consisted in attracting the best minds of the surrounding tribes and, after training them, sending them back to their people as emissaries of social uplift." P. 749.

2. **They used natives of the tribes or races to uplift the mores of the races**

    "Foreign emissaries were never sent to a race except upon the specific request of that people. Those who labored for the uplift and advancement of a given tribe or race were always natives of that tribe or race. The one hundred would not attempt to impose the habits and mores of even a superior race upon another tribe. Always they patiently worked to uplift and advance the time-tried mores of each race. The simple folk of Urantia brought their social customs to Dalamatia, not to exchange them for new and better practices, but to have them uplifted by contact with a higher culture and by association with superior minds. The process was slow but very effectual." P. 749.

3. **They attempted to accelerate normal and natural evolution.**
   "The Dalamatia teachers sought to add conscious social selection to the purely natural selection of biologic evolution. They did not derange human society, but they did markedly accelerate its normal and natural evolution. Their motive was progression by evolution and not revolution by revelation. The human race had spent ages in acquiring the little religion and morals it had, and these supermen knew better than to rob mankind of these few advances by the confusion and dismay which always result when enlightened and superior beings undertake to uplift the backward races by overteaching and overenlightenment." P. 750.

4. **Civilization progressed normally for about 300,000 years.**
   "From the arrival of Prince Caligastia, planetary civilization progressed in a fairly normal manner for almost three hundred thousand years. Aside from being a life-modification sphere and therefore subject to numerous irregularities and unusual episodes of evolutionary fluctuation, Urantia progressed very satisfactorily in its planetary career up to the times of the Lucifer rebellion and the concurrent Caligastia betrayal. All subsequent history has been definitely modified by this catastrophic blunder as well as by the later failure of Adam and Eve to fulfill their planetary mission." P. 752.

5. **Calagastia joined Lucifer in rebellion.**
   "The Prince of Urantia went into darkness at the time of the Lucifer rebellion, thus precipitating the long confusion of the planet. He was subsequently deprived of sovereign authority by the coordinate action of the constellation rulers and other universe authorities. He shared the inevitable vicissitudes of isolated Urantia down to the time of Adam's sojourn on the planet and contributed something to the miscarriage of the plan to uplift the mortal races through the infusion of the lifeblood of the new violet race—the descendants of Adam and Eve." P. 752.

D. **Results of the rebellion.**

   1. **Great confusion reigned in Dalamatia and before long society sank to its old biologic level.**

"Great confusion reigned in Dalamatia and thereabout for almost fifty years after the instigation of rebellion. The complete and radical reorganization of the whole world was attempted; revolution displaced evolution as the policy of cultural advancement and racial improvement. Among the superior and partially trained sojourners in and near Dalamatia there appeared a sudden advancement in cultural status, but when these new and radical methods were attempted on the outlying peoples, indescribable confusion and racial pandemonium was the immediate result. Liberty was quickly translated into license by the half-evolved primitive men of those days.

"Very soon after the rebellion the entire staff of sedition were engaged in energetic defense of the city against the hordes of semisavages who besieged its walls as a result of the doctrines of liberty which had been prematurely taught them. And years before the beautiful headquarters went down beneath the southern waves, the misled and mistaught tribes of the Dalamatia hinterland had already swept down in semisavage assault on the splendid city, driving the secession staff and their associates northward.

"The Caligastia scheme for the immediate reconstruction of human society in accordance with his ideas of individual freedom and group liberties, proved a swift and more or less complete failure. Society quickly sank back to its old biologic level, and the forward struggle began all over, starting not very far in advance of where it was at the beginning of the Caligastia regime, this upheaval having left the world in confusion worse confounded." P. 758-59.

2. **The Caligastia downfall had little effect upon biologic evolution, and ultimately the developmental progress of the Urantia races neared its apex.**

"The cultural decadence and spiritual poverty resulting from the Caligastia downfall and consequent social confusion had little effect on the physical or biologic status of the Urantia peoples. Organic evolution proceeded apace, quite regardless of the cultural and moral setback which so swiftly followed the disaffection of Caligastia and Daligastia. And there came a time in the planetary history, almost forty thousand years ago, when the Life Carriers on duty took note that, from a purely biologic standpoint, the developmental progress of the Urantia races was nearing its apex. The Melchizedek receivers, concurring in this opinion, readily agreed to join the Life Carriers in a petition to the Most Highs of Edentia asking that Urantia be inspected with a view to authorizing the dispatch of biologic uplifters, a Material Son and Daughter." P. 821.

E. **The Nodites and the Amadonites.**

1. **When the rebel members of the Prince's staff realized they were degraded to the status of mortal beings, they resorted to sexual reproduction.**

   "The sixty members of the planetary staff who went into rebellion chose Nod as their leader. They worked wholeheartedly for the rebel Prince but soon discovered that they were deprived of the sustenance of the system life circuits. They awakened to the fact that they had been degraded to the status of mortal beings. They were indeed superhuman but, at the same time, material and mortal. In an effort to increase their numbers, Daligastia ordered immediate resort to sexual reproduction, knowing full well that the original sixty and their forty-four modified Andonite associates were doomed to suffer extinction by death, sooner or later. After the fall of Dalamatia the disloyal staff migrated to the north and the east. Their descendants were long known as the Nodites, and their dwelling place as 'the land of Nod.'" P. 757.

2. **Derivation of the Nodites and Amadonites.**

   "The *Nodites* were the descendants of the rebel members of the Prince's staff, their name deriving from their first leader, Nod, onetime chairman of the Dalamatia commission on industry and trade. The *Amadonites* were the descendants of those Andonites who chose to remain loyal with Van and Amadon. 'Amadonite' is more of a cultural and religious designation than a racial term; racially considered the Amadonites were essentially *Andonites*. 'Nodite' is both a cultural and racial term, for the Nodites themselves constituted the eighth race of Urantia." P. 821.

3. **The Nodites were a superior race because of unexpected modification of the life plasms from the Andonite contributors.**

   "Since the one hundred corporeal members of the Prince's staff carried germ plasm of the Andonic human strains, it would naturally be expected that, if they engaged in sexual reproduction, their progeny would altogether resemble the offspring of other Andonite parents. But when the sixty rebels of the staff, the followers of Nod, actually engaged in sexual reproduction, their children proved to be far superior in almost every way to both the Andonite and the Sangik peoples. This unexpected excellence characterized not only physical and intellectual qualities but also spiritual capacities.

"These mutant traits appearing in the first Nodite generation resulted from certain changes which had been wrought in the configuration and in the chemical constituents of the inheritance factors of the Andonic germ plasm. These changes were caused by the presence in the bodies of the staff members of the powerful life maintenance circuits of the Satania system. These life circuits caused the chromosomes of the specialized Urantia pattern to reorganize more after the patterns of the standardized Satania specialization of the ordained Nebadon life manifestation. The technique of this germ plasm metamorphosis by the action of the system life currents is not unlike those procedures whereby Urantia scientists modify the germ plasm of plants and animals by the use of X rays.

"Thus did the Nodite peoples arise out of certain peculiar and unexpected modifications occurring in the life plasm which had been transferred from the bodies of the Andonite contributors to those of the corporeal staff members by the Avalon surgeons.

"It will be recalled that the one hundred Andonite germ plasm contributors were in turn made possessors of the organic complement of the tree of life so that the Satania life currents likewise invested their bodies. The forty-four modified Andonites who followed the staff into rebellion also mated among themselves and made a great contribution to the better strains of the Nodite people.

"These two groups, embracing 104 individuals who carried the modified Andonite germ plasm, constitute the ancestry of the Nodites, the eighth race to appear on Urantia. And this new feature of human life on Urantia represents another phase of the outworking of the original plan of utilizing this planet as a life-modification world, except that this was one of the unforeseen developments." P. 857.

PART V — *Anthropology*

4. **Division of the Nodites.**
"Shortly after the destruction of Dalamatia the followers of Nod became divided into three major groups. The central group remained in the immediate vicinity of their original home near the headwaters of the Persian Gulf. The eastern group migrated to the highland regions of Elam just east of the Euphrates valley. The western group was situated on the northeastern Syrian shores of the Mediterranean and in adjacent territory." P. 822.

5. **Nodites and Amadonites became the most advanced races on earth.**
"These Nodites had freely mated with the Sangik races and had left behind an able progeny. And some of the descendants of the rebellious Dalamatians subsequently joined Van and his loyal followers in the lands north of Mesopotamia. Here, in the vicinity of Lake Van and the southern Caspian Sea region, the Nodites mingled and mixed with the Amadonites, and they were numbered among the 'mighty men of old.'
"Prior to the arrival of Adam and Eve these groups—Nodites and Amadonites—were the most advanced and cultured races on earth." P. 822.

6. **Deterioration of the Nodites.**
"The pure-line Nodites were a magnificent race, but they gradually mingled with the evolutionary peoples of earth, and before long great deterioration had occurred. Ten thousand years after the rebellion they had lost ground to the point where their average length of life was little more than that of the evolutionary races." P. 857.
After the submergence of Dalamatia the Nodites founded Dilmun as their headquarters city. They planned a tower as a monument to their race.
"After the submergence of Dalamatia the Nodites moved north and east, presently founding the new city of Dilmun as their racial and cultural headquarters. And about fifty thousand years after the death of Nod, when the offspring of the Prince's staff had become too numerous to find subsistence in the lands immediately surrounding their new city of Dilmun, and after they had reached out to intermarry with the Andonite and Sangik tribes adjoining their borders, it occurred to their leaders that something should be done to preserve their racial unity. Accordingly a council of the tribes was called, and after much deliberation the plan of Bablot, a descendant of Nod, was indorsed.

"Bablot proposed to erect a pretentious temple of racial glorification at the center of their then occupied territory. This temple was to have a tower the like of which the world had never seen. It was to be a monumental memorial to their passing greatness. There were many who wished to have this monument erected in Dilmun, but others contended that such a great structure should be placed a safe distance from the dangers of the sea, remembering the traditions of the engulfment of their first capital, Dalamatia." P. 858.

8. **Different views as to the purpose of the tower caused dissension and dispersion.**

"But the Nodites were still somewhat divided in sentiment as to the plans and purposes of this undertaking. Neither were their leaders altogether agreed concerning either construction plans or usage of the buildings after they should be completed. After four and one-half years of work a great dispute arose about the object and motive for the erection of the tower. The contentions became so bitter that all work stopped. The food carriers spread the news of the dissension, and large numbers of the tribes began to forgather at the building site. Three differing views were propounded as to the purpose of building the tower.

"1. The largest group, almost one half, desired to see the tower built as a memorial of Nodite history and racial superiority. They thought it ought to be a great and imposing structure which would challenge the admiration of all future generations.

"2. The next largest faction wanted the tower designed to commemorate the Dilmun culture. They foresaw that Bablot would become a great center of commerce, art, and manufacture.

"3. The smallest and minority contingent held that the erection of the tower presented an opportunity for making atonement for the folly of their progenitors in participating in the Caligastia rebellion. They maintained that the tower should be devoted to the worship of the Father of all, that the whole purpose of the new city should be to take the place of Dalamatia—to function as the cultural and religious center for the surrounding barbarians.

PART V — *Anthropology*

"The religious group were promptly voted down. The majority rejected the teaching that their ancestors had been guilty of rebellion; they resented such a racial stigma. Having disposed of one of the three angles to the dispute and failing to settle the other two by debate, they fell to fighting. The religionists, the noncombatants, fled to their homes in the south, while their fellows fought until well-nigh obliterated." P. 858-59.

F. **Nodite centers of civilization.**

1. **The dispersion of the Nodites led to the establishment of four centers of Nodite culture.**

    "The dispersion of the Nodites was an immediate result of the internecine conflict over the tower of Babel. This internal war greatly reduced the numbers of the purer Nodites and was in many ways responsible for their failure to establish a great pre-Adamic civilization. From this time on Nodite culture declined for over one hundred and twenty thousand years until it was upstepped by Adamic infusion. But even in the times of Adam the Nodites were still an able people. Many of their mixed descendants were numbered among the Garden builders, and several of Van's group captains were Nodites. Some of the most capable minds serving on Adam's staff were of this race.

    "Three out of the four great Nodite centers were established immediately following the Bablot conflict:

    "1. *The western or Syrian Nodites.* The remnants of the nationalistic or racial memorialists journeyed northward, uniting with the Andonites to found the later Nodite centers to the northwest of Mesopotamia. This was the largest group of the dispersing Nodites, and they contributed much to the later appearing Assyrian stock.

    "2. *The eastern or Elamite Nodites.* The culture and commerce advocates migrated in large numbers eastward into Elam and there united with the mixed Sangik tribes. The Elamites of thirty to forty thousand years ago had become largely Sangik in nature, although they continued to maintain a civilization superior to that of the surrounding barbarians.

    "After the establishment of the second garden it was customary to allude to this near-by Nodite settlement as 'the land of Nod'; and during the long period of relative peace between this Nodite group and the Adamites, the two races were greatly blended, for it became more and more the custom for the Sons of God (the Adamites) to intermarry with the daughters of men (the Nodites).

"3. *The central or pre-Sumerian Nodites.* A small group at the mouth of the Tigris and Euphrates rivers maintained more of their racial integrity. They persisted for thousands of years and eventually furnished the Nodite ancestry which blended with the Adamites to found the Sumerian peoples of historic times.

"And all this explains how the Sumerians appeared so suddenly and mysteriously on the stage of action in Mesopotamia. Investigators will never be able to trace out and follow these tribes back to the beginning of the Sumerians, who had their origin two hundred thousand years ago after the submergence of Dalamatia. Without a trace of origin elsewhere in the world, these ancient tribes suddenly loom upon the horizon of civilization with a full-grown and superior culture, embracing temples, metal-work, agriculture, animals, pottery, weaving, commercial law, civil codes, religious ceremonial, and an old system of writing. At the beginning of the historical era they had long since lost the alphabet of Dalamatia, having adopted the peculiar writing system originating in Dilmun. The Sumerian language, though virtually lost to the world, was not Semitic; it had much in common with the so-called Aryan tongues.

"The elaborate records left by the Sumerians describe the site of a remarkable settlement which was located on the Persian Gulf near the earlier city of Dilmun. The Egyptians called this city of ancient glory Dilmat, while the later Adamized Sumerians confused both the first and second Nodite cities with Dalamatia and called all three Dilmun. And already have archaeologists found these ancient Sumerian clay tablets which tell of this earthly paradise 'where the Gods first blessed mankind with the example of civilized and cultured life.' And these tablets, descriptive of Dilmun, the paradise of men and God, are now silently resting on the dusty shelves of many museums.

"The Sumerians well knew of the first and second Edens but, despite extensive intermarriage with the Adamites, continued to regard the garden dwellers to the north as an alien race. Sumerian pride in the more ancient Nodite culture led them to ignore these later vistas of glory in favor of the grandeur and paradisiacal traditions of the city of Dilmun.

"4. *The northern Nodites and Amadonites—the Vanites.* This group arose prior to the Bablot conflict. These northernmost Nodites were descendants of those who had forsaken the leadership of Nod and his successors for that of Van and Amadon.

"Some of the early associates of Van subsequently settled about the shores of the lake which still bears his name, and their traditions grew up about this locality. Ararat became their sacred mountain, having much the same meaning to laterday Vanites that Sinai had to the Hebrews. Ten thousand years ago the Vanite ancestors of the Assyrians taught that their moral law of seven commandments had been given to Van by the Gods upon Mount Ararat. They firmly believed that Van and his associate Amadon were taken alive from the planet while they were up on the mountain engaged in worship.

"Mount Ararat was the sacred mountain of northern Mesopotamia, and since much of your tradition of these ancient times was acquired in connection with the Babylonian story of the flood, it is not surprising that Mount Ararat and its region were woven into the later Jewish story of Noah and the universal flood.

"About 35,000 B.C. Adamson visited one of the easternmost of the old Vanite settlements to found his center of civilization." P. 859-60.

II. THE ADAMIC DISPENSATION

A. Post-Adamic man on a normal planet.

1. **When man reaches the limit of evolutionary development biologic uplifters are sent.**

   "When the original impetus of evolutionary life has run its biologic course, when man has reached the apex of animal development, there arrives the second order of sonship, and the second dispensation of grace and ministry is inaugurated. This is true on all evolutionary worlds. When the highest possible level of evolutionary life has been attained, when primitive man has ascended as far as possible in the biologic scale, a Material Son and Daughter always appear on the planet, having been dispatched by the System Sovereign." P. 592.

2. **Accomplishments of the Material Son and Daughter dispensation.**

"It is the prime purpose of the Adamic regime to influence evolving man to complete the transit from the hunter and herder stage of civilization to that of the agriculturist and horticulturist, to be later supplemented by the appearance of the urban and industrial adjuncts to civilization. Ten thousand years of this dispensation of the biologic uplifters is sufficient to effect a marvelous transformation. Twenty-five thousand years of such an administration of the conjoint wisdom of the Planetary Prince and the Material Sons usually ripens the sphere for the advent of a Magisterial Son.

"This age usually witnesses the completion of the elimination of the unfit and the still further purification of the racial strains; on normal worlds the defective bestial tendencies are very nearly eliminated from the reproducing stocks of the realm.

"The Adamic progeny never amalgamate with the inferior strains of the evolutionary races. Neither is it the divine plan for the Planetary Adam or Eve to mate, personally, with the evolutionary peoples. This race-improvement project is the task of their progeny. But the offspring of the Material Son and Daughter are mobilized for generations before the racial-amalgamation ministry is inaugurated.

"The result of the gift of the Adamic life plasm to the mortal races is an immediate upstepping of intellectual capacity and an acceleration of spiritual progress. There is usually some physical improvement also. On an average world the post-Adamic dispensation is an age of great invention, energy control, and mechanical development. This is the era of the appearance of multiform manufacture and the control of natural forces; it is the golden age of exploration and the final subduing of the planet. Much of the material progress of a world occurs during this time of the inauguration of the development of the physical sciences, just such an epoch as Urantia is now experiencing. Your world is a full dispensation and more behind the average planetary schedule." P. 593.

"The post-Adamic epoch is the dispensation of internationalism. With the near completion of the task of race blending, nationalism wanes, and the brotherhood of man really begins to materialize. Representative government begins to take the

PART V — *Anthropology*

place of the monarchial or paternal form of rulership. The educational system becomes world-wide, and gradually the languages of the races give way to the tongue of the violet people. Universal peace and cooperation are seldom attained until the races are fairly well blended, and until they speak a common language.

"During the closing centuries of the post-Adamic age there develops new interest in art, music, and literature, and this world-wide awakening is the signal for the appearance of a Magisterial Son. The crowning development of this era is the universal interest in intellectual realities, true philosophy. Religion becomes less nationalistic, becomes more and more a planetary affair. New revelations of truth characterize these ages, and the Most Highs of the constellations begin to rule in the affairs of men. Truth is revealed up to the administration of the constellations.

"Great ethical advancement characterizes this era; the brotherhood of man is the goal of its society. World-wide peace—the cessation of race conflict and national animosity—is the indicator of planetary ripeness for the advent of the third order of sonship, the Magisterial Son." P. 594.

B. Adam and Eve on Urantia.

1. Van transplants the tree of life to the center of the Garden of Eden.
    "In the center of the Garden temple Van planted the long-guarded tree of life, whose leaves were for the 'healing of the nations,' and whose fruit had so long sustained him on earth. Van well knew that Adam and Eve would also be dependent on this gift of Edentia for their life maintenance after they once appeared on Urantia in material form.
    "The Material Sons on the system capitals do not require the tree of life for sustenance. Only in the planetary repersonalization are they dependent on this adjunct to physical immortality." P. 825.

2. The "tree of the knowledge of good and evil" may be a figure of speech, but the "tree of life" was real.
    "The 'tree of the knowledge of good and evil' may be a figure of speech, a symbolic designation covering a multitude of human experiences, but the 'tree of life' was not a myth; it was real and for a long time was present on Urantia. When the Most Highs

of Edentia approved the commission of Caligastia as Planetary Prince of Urantia and those of the one hundred Jerusem citizens as his administrative staff, they sent to the planet, by the Melchizedeks, a shrub of Edentia, and this plant grew to be the tree of life on Urantia. This form of nonintelligent life is native to the constellation headquarters spheres, being also found on the headquarters worlds of the local and superuniverses as well as on the Havona spheres, but not on the system capitals." P. 825.

3. **The Melchizedeks instructed Adam and Eve concerning their planetary mission.**

   "The Melchizedeks counseled Adam not to initiate the program of racial uplift and blending until his own family had numbered onehalf million. It was never intended that the Garden should be the permanent home of the Adamites. They were to become emissaries of a new life to all the world; they were to mobilize for unselfish bestowal upon the needy races of earth.

   "The instructions given Adam by the Melchizedeks implied that he was to establish racial, continental, and divisional headquarters to be in charge of his immediate sons and daughters, while he and Eve were to divide their time between these various world capitals as advisers and co-ordinators of the world-wide ministry of biologic uplift, intellectual advancement, and moral rehabilitation." P. 827.

4. **No Material Sons of Nebadon had a more difficult task than those of Urantia, but patience would have led to success.**

   "Probably no Material Sons of Nebadon were ever faced with such a difficult and seemingly hopeless task as confronted Adam and Eve in the sorry plight of Urantia. But they would have sometime met with success had they been more farseeing and *patient*. Both of them, especially Eve, were altogether too impatient; they were not willing to settle down to the long, long endurance test. They wanted to see some immediate results, and they did, but the results thus secured proved most disastrous both to themselves and to their world." P. 840.

5. **Adam and Eve defaulted, but still contributed much to the races of Urantia.**

   "Adam and Eve did fall from their high estate of material sonship down to the lowly status of mortal man. But that was not the fall of man. The human race has been uplifted despite the immediate consequences of the Adamic default. Although the divine plan of giving the violet race to the Urantia peoples miscarried, the mortal races have profited enormously from the limited contribution which Adam and his descendants made to the Urantia races.

"There has been no 'fall of man.' The history of the human race is one of progressive evolution, and the Adamic bestowal left the world peoples greatly improved over their previous biologic condition. The more superior stocks of Urantia now contain inheritance factors derived from as many as four separate sources: Andonite, Sangik, Nodite, and Adamic.

"Adam should not be regarded as the cause of a curse on the human race. While he did fail in carrying forward the divine plan, while he did transgress his covenant with Deity, while he and his mate were most certainly degraded in creature status, notwithstanding all this, their contribution to the human race did much to advance civilization on Urantia." P. 845-6.

6. **The great value of patience. The miscarriage of the Adamic mission on Urantia was largely due to impatience.**

"In estimating the results of the Adamic mission on your world, justice demands the recognition of the condition of the planet. Adam was confronted with a well-nigh hopeless task when, with his beautiful mate, he was transported from Jerusem to this dark and confused planet. But had they been guided by the counsel of the Melchizedeks and their associates, and *had they been more patient*, they would have eventually met with success. But Eve listened to the insidious propaganda of personal liberty and planetary freedom of action. She was led to experiment with the life plasm of the material order of sonship in that she allowed this life trust to become prematurely commingled with that of the then mixed order of the original design of the Life Carriers which had been previously combined with that of the reproducing beings once attached to the staff of the Planetary Prince.

"Never, in all your ascent to Paradise, will you gain anything by impatiently attempting to circumvent the established and divine plan by short cuts, personal inventions, or other devices for improving on the way of perfection, to perfection, and for eternal perfection." P. 846.

7. **In evolutionary universes perfection is our goal, not our origin. This is not a mechanistic universe.**

"All in all, there probably never was a more disheartening miscarriage of wisdom on any planet in all Nebadon. But it is not surprising that these missteps occur in the affairs of the evolutionary universes. We are a part of a gigantic creation, and it is not strange that everything does not work in perfection; our universe was not created in perfection. Perfection is our eternal goal, not our origin.

"If this were a mechanistic universe, if the First Great Source and Center were only a force and not also a personality, if all creation were a vast aggregation of physical matter dominated by precise laws characterized by unvarying energy actions, then might perfection obtain, even despite the incompleteness of universe status. There would be no disagreement; there would be no friction. But in our evolving universe of relative perfection and imperfection we rejoice that disagreement and misunderstanding are possible, for thereby is evidenced the fact and the act of personality in the universe. And if our creation is an existence dominated by personality, then can you be assured of the possibilities of personality survival, advancement, and achievement; we can be confident of personality growth, experience, and adventure. What a glorious universe, in that it is personal and progressive, not merely mechanical or even passively perfect!" P. 846.

8. **In spite of the default, Adam contributed much to Urantia culture. The people make a civilization. Civilization does not make the people.**

"And thus ends the story of the Planetary Adam and Eve of Urantia, a story of trial, tragedy, and triumph, at least personal triumph for your well-meaning but deluded Material Son and Daughter and undoubtedly, in the end, a story of ultimate triumph for their world and its rebellion-tossed and evil-harassed inhabitants. When all is summed up, Adam and Eve made a mighty contribution to the speedy civilization and accelerated biologic progress of the human race. They left a great culture on earth, but it was not possible for such an advanced civilization to survive in the face of the early dilution and the eventual submergence of the Adamic inheritance. It is the people who make a civilization; civilization does not make the people." P. 854.

PART V — *Anthropology*

C. **The violet race.**
1. **Plan for the marriage of Adam's children to the superior evolutionary races.**
"Usually the violet peoples do not begin to amalgamate with the planetary natives until their own group numbers over one million. But in the meantime the staff of the Planetary Prince proclaims that the children of the Gods have come down, as it were, to be one with the races of men; and the people eagerly look forward to the day when announcement will be made that those who have qualified as belonging to the superior racial strains may proceed to the Garden of Eden and be there chosen by the sons and daughters of Adam as the evolutionary fathers and mothers of the new and blended order of mankind." P. 585.
2. **On normal worlds the Planetary Prince's staff supervise the mating of the Adamites and the evolutionary peoples.**
"On normal worlds the Planetary Adam and Eve never mate with the evolutionary races. This work of biologic betterment is a function of the Adamic progeny. But these Adamites do not go out among the races; the prince's staff bring to the Garden of Eden the superior men and women for voluntary mating with the Adamic offspring. And on most worlds it is considered the highest honor to be selected as a candidate for mating with the sons and daughters of the garden." P. 585.
3. **The violet race is a monogamous people.**
"The violet race is a monogamous people, and every evolutionary man or woman uniting with the Adamic sons and daughters pledges not to take other mates and to instruct his or her children in single-matedness. The children of each of these unions are educated and trained in the schools of the Planetary Prince and then are permitted to go forth to the race of their evolutionary parent, there to marry among the selected groups of superior mortals." P. 586.
4. **Cardinal characteristics of the violet race founded by Adam and Eve.**
"Adam and Eve were the founders of the violet race of men, the ninth human race to appear on Urantia. Adam and his offspring had blue eyes, and the violet peoples were characterized by fair complexions and light hair color—yellow, red, and brown.

"Eve did not suffer pain in childbirth; neither did the early evolutionary races. Only the mixed races produced by the union of evolutionary man with the Nodites and later with the Adamites suffered the severe pangs of childbirth." P. 850.

5. **Adam and Eve had a dual nutrition. Their children had only the mortal type of nutrition.**

   "Adam and Eve, like their brethren on Jerusem, were energized by dual nutrition, subsisting on both food and light, supplemented by certain superphysical energies unrevealed on Urantia. Their Urantia offspring did not inherit the parental endowment of energy intake and light circulation. They had a single circulation, the human type of blood sustenance. They were designedly mortal though long-lived, albeit longevity gravitated toward the human norm with each succeeding generation." P. 851.

6. **Dietetic habits of Adam and his offspring.**

   "Adam and Eve and their first generation of children did not use the flesh of animals for food. They subsisted wholly upon 'the fruits of the trees.' After the first generation all of the descendants of Adam began to partake of dairy products, but many of them continued to follow a nonflesh diet. Many of the southern tribes with whom they later united were also nonflesh eaters. Later on, most of these vegetarian tribes migrated to the east and survived as now admixed in the peoples of India." P. 851.

7. **Adam and Eve had superior special senses.**

   "Both the physical and spiritual visions of Adam and Eve were far superior to those of the present-day peoples. Their special senses were much more acute, and they were able to see the midwayers and the angelic hosts, the Melchizedeks, and the fallen Prince Caligastia, who several times came to confer with his noble successor. They retained the ability to see these celestial beings for over one hundred years after the default. These special senses were not so acutely present in their children and tended to diminish with each succeeding generation." P. 851.

8. **The early beginning of the Andite race.**

   "After becoming established in the second garden on the Euphrates, Adam elected to leave behind as much of his life plasm as possible to benefit the world after his death. Accordingly, Eve was made the head of a commission of twelve on race improvement, and before Adam died this commission had selected 1,682 of the highest type of women on Urantia, and

PART V — *Anthropology*

these women were impregnated with the Adamic life plasm. Their children all grew up to maturity except 112, so that the world, in this way, was benefited by the addition of 1,570 superior men and women. Though these candidate mothers were selected from all the surrounding tribes and represented most of the races on earth, the majority were chosen from the highest strains of the Nodites, and they constituted the early beginnings of the mighty Andite race. These children were born and reared in the tribal surroundings of their respective mothers." P. 851.

D. **Story of Adamson and Ratta—the origin of secondary midwayers.**

1. **Adamson elected to remain on earth. After the establishment of the second garden he set out to find the home of Van and Amadon.**

    "Adamson was among that group of the children of Adam and Eve who elected to remain on earth with their father and mother. Now this eldest son of Adam had often heard from Van and Amadon the story of their highland home in the north, and sometime after the establishment of the second garden he determined to go in search of this land of his youthful dreams.

    "Adamson was 120 years old at this time and had been the father of thirty-two pure-line children of the first garden. He wanted to remain with his parents and assist them in upbuilding the second garden, but he was greatly disturbed by the loss of his mate and their children, who had all elected to go to Edentia along with those other Adamic children who chose to become wards of the Most Highs.

    "Adamson would not desert his parents on Urantia, he was disinclined to flee from hardship or danger, but he found the associations of the second garden far from satisfying. He did much to forward the early activities of defense and construction but decided to leave for the north at the earliest opportunity. And though his departure was wholly pleasant, Adam and Eve were much grieved to lose their eldest son, to have him go out into a strange and hostile world, as they feared, never to return." P. 861.

2. **Adamson met and married Ratta, a pure-line descendant of the Prince's staff.**

    "A company of twenty-seven followed Adamson northward in quest of these people of his childhood fantasies. In a little over three years Adamson's party actually found the object of their adventure, and among these people he discovered a wonderful and beautiful woman, twenty years old, who claimed to be the last pure-line descendant of the Prince's staff. This woman, Ratta, said that her ancestors were all descendants of two of the fallen staff of the Prince. She was the last of her race, having no living brothers or sisters. She had about decided not to mate, had about made up her mind to die without issue, but she lost her heart to the majestic Adamson. And when she heard the story of Eden, how the predictions of Van and Amadon had really come to pass, and as she listened to the recital of the Garden default, she was encompassed with but a single thought—to marry this son and heir of Adam. And quickly the idea grew upon Adamson. In a little more than three months they were married." P. 861.

3. **Origin of secondary midwayers.**

"Adamson and Ratta had a family of sixty-seven children. They gave origin to a great line of the world's leadership, but they did something more. It should be remembered that both of these beings were really superhuman. Every fourth child born to them was of a unique order. It was often invisible. Never in the world's history had such a thing occurred. Ratta was greatly perturbed—even superstitious—but Adamson well knew of the existence of the primary midwayers, and he concluded that something similar was transpiring before his eyes. When the second strangely behaving offspring arrived, he decided to mate them, since one was male and the other female, and this is the origin of the secondary order of midwayers. Within one hundred years, before this phenomenon ceased, almost two thousand were brought into being.

"Adamson lived for 396 years. Many times he returned to visit his father and mother. Every seven years he and Ratta journeyed south to the second garden, and meanwhile the midwayers kept him informed regarding the welfare of his people. During Adamson's life they did great service in upbuilding a new and independent world center for truth and righteousness.

"Adamson and Ratta thus had at their command this corps of marvelous helpers, who labored with them throughout their long lives to assist in the propagation of advanced truth and in the spread of higher standards of spiritual, intellectual, and physical living. And the results of this effort at world betterment never did become fully eclipsed by subsequent retrogressions." P. 861-2.

4. **The culture of the Adamsonites.**

"The Adamsonites maintained a high culture for almost seven thousand years from the times of Adamson and Ratta. Later on they became admixed with the neighboring Nodites and Andonites and were also included among the 'mighty men of old.' And some of the advances of that age persisted to become a latent part of the cultural potential which later blossomed into European civilization.

"This center of civilization was situated in the region east of the southern end of the Caspian Sea, near the Kopet Dagh. A short way up in the foothills of Turkestan are the vestiges of what was onetime the Adamsonite headquarters of the violet race. In these highland sites, situated in a narrow and ancient fertile belt lying in the lower foothills of the Kopet range, there successively arose at various periods four diverse cultures respectively fostered by four different groups of Adamson's descendants. It was the second of these groups which migrated westward to Greece and the islands of the Mediterranean. The residue of Adamson's descendants migrated north and west to enter Europe with the blended stock of the last Andite wave coming out of Mesopotamia, and they were also numbered among the Andite-Aryan invaders of India." P. 862.

III. Present-day Problems Resulting from Rebellion and Default

A. **Repercussions of the Lucifer rebellion.**

1. **Problems of true and false liberty growing out of the Lucifer rebellion.**

"Of all the perplexing problems growing out of the Lucifer rebellion, none has occasioned more difficulty than the failure of immature evolutionary mortals to distinguish between true and false liberty.

"True liberty is the quest of the ages and the reward of evolutionary progress. False liberty is the subtle deception of the error of time and the evil of space. Enduring liberty is predicated on the reality of justice—intelligence, maturity, fraternity, and equity.

"Liberty is a self-destroying technique of cosmic existence when its motivation is unintelligent, unconditioned, and uncontrolled. True liberty is progressively related to reality and is ever regardful of social equity, cosmic fairness, universe fraternity, and divine obligations.

"Liberty is suicidal when divorced from material justice, intellectual fairness, social forbearance, moral duty, and spiritual values. Liberty is nonexistent apart from cosmic reality, and all personality reality is proportional to its divinity relationships.

"Unbridled self-will and unregulated self-expression equal unmitigated selfishness, the acme of ungodliness. Liberty without the associated and ever-increasing conquest of self is a figment of egoistic mortal imagination. Self-motivated liberty is a conceptual illusion, a cruel deception. License masquerading in the garments of liberty is the forerunner of abject bondage." P. 613.

2. **Three hundred fifty thousand years of evolutionary progress were lost.**

"By fifty thousand years after the collapse of the planetary administration, earthly affairs were so disorganized and retarded that the human race had gained very little over the general evolutionary status existing at the time of Caligastia's arrival three hundred and fifty thousand years previously. In certain respects progress had been made; in other directions much ground had been lost." P. 761.

3. **The rebellion deprived the mortal races of much of the benefit of the Adamic inheritance.**

"Sin on Urantia did very little to delay biologic evolution, but it did operate to deprive the mortal races of the full benefit of the Adamic inheritance. Sin enormously retards intellectual development, moral growth, social progress, and mass spiritual attainment. But it does not prevent the highest spiritual achievement by any individual who chooses to know God and sincerely do his divine will." P. 761.

B. **Eugenics—race problems.**

1. **It is neither wise nor altruistic to perpetuate the lowest of the inferior human stocks.**

"It is neither tenderness nor altruism to bestow futile sympathy upon degenerated human beings, unsalvable abnormal and inferior mortals. There exist on even the most normal of the evolutionary worlds sufficient differences between individuals and between numerous social groups to provide for the full exercise of all those noble traits of altruistic sentiment and unselfish mortal ministry without perpetuating the socially unfit and the morally degenerate strains of evolving humanity. There is abundant opportunity for the exercise of tolerance and the function of altruism in behalf of those unfortunate and needy individuals who have not irretrievably lost their moral heritage and forever destroyed their spiritual birthright." P. 592.

2. **The Adamic progeny mate only with the higher and selected racial strains.**

    "This age usually witnesses the completion of the elimination of the unfit and the still further purification of the racial strains; on normal worlds the defective bestial tendencies are very nearly eliminated from the reproducing stocks of the realm.
    "The Adamic progeny never amalgamate with the inferior strains of the evolutionary races. Neither is it the divine plan for the Planetary Adam or Eve to mate, personally, with the evolutionary peoples. This race-improvement project is the task of their progeny. But the offspring of the Material Son and Daughter are mobilized for generations before the racial-amalgamation ministry is inaugurated." P. 593.

3. **It would be folly to undertake broad-scale interracial mixtures at the present time.**

    "But while the pure-line children of a planetary Garden of Eden can bestow themselves upon the superior members of the evolutionary races and thereby upstep the biologic level of mankind, it would not prove beneficial for the higher strains of Urantia mortals to mate with the lower races; such an unwise procedure would jeopardize all civilization on your world. Having failed to achieve race harmonization by the Adamic technique, you must now work out your planetary problem of race improvement by other and largely human methods of adaptation and control." P. 586.

4. **Race blending favors appearance of new characteristics—superior, if the stocks are superior.**

    "Race blending greatly contributes to the sudden appearance of *new* characteristics, and if such hybridization is the union of superior strains, then these new characteristics will also be *superior* traits." P. 920.

5. **The pros and cons of the intermingling of present-day human races.**

    "As long as present-day races are so overloaded with inferior and degenerate strains, race intermingling on a large scale would be most detrimental, but most of the objections to such experiments rest on social and cultural prejudices rather than on biological considerations. Even among inferior stocks, hybrids often are an improvement on their ancestors. Hybridization makes for species improvement because of the role of the *dominant genes*. Racial intermixture increases the likelihood of a larger number of the desirable *dominants* being present in the hybrid." P. 920.

6. **No more new human races will appear on Urantia. Scientific supervision could greatly improve present-day human races.**

    "Mankind on Urantia must solve its problems of mortal development with the human stocks it has—no more races will evolve from prehuman sources throughout all future time. But this fact does not preclude the possibility of the attainment of vastly higher levels of human development through the intelligent fostering of the evolutionary potentials still resident in the mortal races. That which we, the Life Carriers, do toward fostering and conserving the life strains before the appearance of human will, man must do for himself after such an event and subsequent to our retirement from active participation in evolution. In a general way, man's evolutionary destiny is in his own hands, and scientific intelligence must sooner or later supersede the random functioning of uncontrolled natural selection and chance survival." P. 734.

C. **Health problems.**

1. **Urantia scientists must work to compensate for the loss through default of resistance to disease.**

    "The body cells of the Material Sons and their progeny are far more resistant to disease than are those of the evolutionary beings indigenous to the planet. The body cells of the native races are akin to the living disease-producing microscopic and ultramicroscopic organisms of the realm. These facts explain why the Urantia peoples must do so much by way of scientific effort to withstand so many physical disorders. You would be far more disease resistant if your races carried more of the Adamic life." P. 851.

Part V — *Anthropology*

Section Six
THE RACES OF URANTIA AFTER THE SECOND GARDEN

I. Racial and Cultural Distribution

"The second Eden was the cradle of civilization for almost thirty thousand years. Here in Mesopotamia the Adamic peoples held forth, sending out their progeny to the ends of the earth, and latterly, as amalgamated with the Nodite and Sangik tribes, were known as the Andites. From this region went those men and women who initiated the doings of historic times, and who have so enormously accelerated cultural progress on Urantia." P. 868.

A. Summary of racial and cultural distribution thirty-five thousand years ago.

"Adam and Eve also contributed much that was of value to the social, moral, and intellectual progress of mankind; civilization was immensely quickened by the presence of their offspring. But thirty-five thousand years ago the world at large possessed little culture. Certain centers of civilization existed here and there, but most of Urantia languished in savagery. Racial and cultural distribution was as follows:

"1. *The violet race—Adamites and Adamsonites.* The chief center of Adamite culture was in the second garden, located in the triangle of the Tigris and Euphrates rivers; this was indeed the cradle of Occidental and Indian civilizations. The secondary or northern center of the violet race was the Adamsonite headquarters, situated east of the southern shore of the Caspian Sea near the Kopet mountains. From these two centers there went forth to the surrounding lands the culture and life plasm which so immediately quickened all the races.

"2. *Pre-Sumerians and other Nodites.* There were also present in Mesopotamia, near the mouth of the rivers, remnants of the ancient culture of the days of Dalamatia. With the passing millenniums, this group became thoroughly admixed with the Adamites to the north, but they never entirely lost their Nodite traditions. Various other Nodite groups that had settled in the Levant were, in general, absorbed by the later expanding violet race.

"3. *The Andonites* maintained five or six fairly representative settlements to the north and east of the Adamson headquarters. They were also scattered throughout Turkestan, while isolated islands of them persisted throughout Eurasia, especially in mountainous regions. These aborigines still held the northlands of the Eurasian continent,

- 329 -

together with Iceland and Greenland, but they had long since been driven from the plains of Europe by the blue man and from the river valleys of farther Asia by the expanding yellow race.

"4. *The red man* occupied the Americas, having been driven out of Asia over fifty thousand years before the arrival of Adam.

"5. *The yellow race.* The Chinese peoples were well established in control of eastern Asia. Their most advanced settlements were situated to the northwest of modern China in regions bordering on Tibet.

"6. *The blue race.* The blue men were scattered all over Europe, but their better centers of culture were situated in the then fertile valleys of the Mediterranean basin and in northwestern Europe. Neanderthal absorption had greatly retarded the culture of the blue man, but he was otherwise the most aggressive, adventurous, and exploratory of all the evolutionary peoples of Eurasia.

"7. *Pre-Dravidian India.* The complex mixture of races in India—embracing every race on earth, but especially the green, orange, and black—maintained a culture slightly above that of the outlying regions.

"8. *The Sahara civilization.* The superior elements of the indigo race had their most progressive settlements in what is now the great Sahara desert. This indigo-black group carried extensive strains of the submerged orange and green races.

"9. *The Mediterranean basin.* The most highly blended race outside of India occupied what is now the Mediterranean basin. Here blue men from the north and Saharans from the south met and mingled with Nodites and Adamites from the east." P. 868-9.

II. The Adamites

A. Nature and culture.

1. **The heroism of the early Adamites constitutes an inspiring chapter of Urantia history.**
   "Adam and Eve had left behind a limited but potent progeny, and the celestial observers on Urantia waited anxiously to find out how these descendants of the erring Material Son and Daughter would acquit themselves." P. 869.
   "The heroism displayed in the leadership of the second garden

constitutes one of the amazing and inspiring epics of Urantia's history. These splendid souls never wholly lost sight of the purpose of the Adamic mission, and therefore did they valiantly fight off the influences of the surrounding and inferior tribes while they willingly sent forth their choicest sons and daughters in a steady stream as emissaries to the races of earth. Sometimes this expansion was depleting to the home culture, but always these superior peoples would rehabilitate themselves." P. 869.

2. **The civilization of the Adamites was comparatively high, but was not evolved, and therefore was doomed to deterioration.**

   "The civilization, society, and cultural status of the Adamites were far above the general level of the evolutionary races of Urantia. Only among the old settlements of Van and Amadon and the Adamsonites was there a civilization in anyway comparable. But the civilization of the second Eden was an artifical structure-*it had not been evolved*—and was therefore doomed to deteriorate until it reached a natural evolutionary level." P. 870.
   "But the Adamites were a real nation around 19,000 B.C., numbering four and a half million, and already they had poured forth millions of their progeny into the surrounding peoples." P. 870.

B. **Early expansions.**

1. **The violet race did not attempt territorial conquest, but sent forth teachers.**

   "The violet race retained the Edenic traditions of peacefulness for many millenniums, which explains their long delay in making territorial conquests. When they suffered from population pressure, instead of making war to secure more territory, they sent forth their excess inhabitants as teachers to the other races. The cultural effect of these earlier migrations was not enduring, but the absorption of the Adamite teachers, traders, and explorers was biologically invigorating to the surrounding peoples." P. 870.

2. **The expansion of the Adamites was generally north and west.**

   "Some of the Adamites early journeyed westward to the valley of the Nile; others penetrated eastward into Asia, but these were a minority. The mass movement of the later days was extensively northward and thence westward. It was, in the main, a gradual but unremitting northward push, the greater number making their way north and then circling westward around the Caspian Sea into Europe.

"About twenty-five thousand years ago many of the purer elements of the Adamites were well on their northern trek. And as they penetrated northward, they became less and less Adamic until, by the times of their occupation of Turkestan, they had become thoroughly admixed with the other races, particularly the Nodites. Very few of the pure-line violet peoples ever penetrated far into Europe or Asia." P. 870.

III. The Andites

"The Andite races were the primary blends of the pure-line violet race and the Nodites plus the evolutionary peoples. In general, Andites should be thought of as having a far greater percentage of Adamic blood than the modern races. In the main, the term Andite is used to designate those peoples whose racial inheritance was from one-eighth to one-sixth violet. Modern Urantians, even the northern white races, contain much less than this percentage of the blood of Adam." P. 871.

A. Origin and nature.
  1. **Andite peoples took origin around Mesopotamia.**
     "The earliest Andite peoples took origin in the regions adjacent to Mesopotamia more than twenty-five thousand years ago and consisted of a blend of the Adamites and Nodites. The second garden was surrounded by concentric circles of diminishing violet blood, and it was on the periphery of this racial melting pot that the Andite race was born. Later on, when the migrating Adamites and Nodites entered the then fertile regions of Turkestan, they soon blended with the superior inhabitants, and the resultant race mixture extended the Andite type northward." P. 871.
  2. **The Andites were the best all-round human stock since the violet people. They were neither Occidental nor Oriental.**
     "The Andites were the best all-round human stock to appear on Urantia since the days of the pure-line violet peoples. They embraced most of the highest types of the surviving remnants of the Adamite and Nodite races and, later, some of the best strains of the yellow, blue, and green men.
     "These early Andites were not Aryan; they were pre-Aryan. They were not white; they were pre-white. They were neither an Occidental nor an Oriental people. But it is Andite inherit

PART V — *Anthropology*

ance that gives to the polyglot mixture of the so-called white races that generalized homogeneity which has been called Caucasoid." P. 872.

3. **The Andites were skillful militarists; they were adventurous.**

   "The purer strains of the violet race had retained the Adamic tradition of peace-seeking, which explains why the earlier race movements had been more in the nature of peaceful migrations. But as the Adamites united with the Nodite stocks, who were by this time a belligerent race, their Andite descendants became, for their day and age, the most skillful and sagacious militarists ever to live on Urantia. Thenceforth the movements of the Mesopotamians grew increasingly military in character and became more akin to actual conquests.

   "These Andites were adventurous; they had roving dispositions. An increase of either Sangik or Andonite stock tended to stabilize them. But even so, their later descendants never stopped until they had circumnavigated the globe and discovered the last remote continent." P. 872.

4. **Infusion of Adamic stock quickened civilization and stimulated adventure and exploration.**

   "Infusion of the Adamic stock into the human races not only quickened the pace of civilization, but it also greatly stimulated their proclivities toward adventure and exploration to the end that most of Eurasia and northern Africa was presently occupied by the rapidly multiplying mixed descendants of the Andites." P. 904.

B. **Early Andite migrations.**

1. **The culture of the second garden declined until about 15,000 B.C. when a great renaissance took place.**

   "For twenty thousand years the culture of the second garden persisted, but it experienced a steady decline until about 15,000 B.C., when the regeneration of the Sethite priesthood and the leadership of Amosad inaugurated a brilliant era. The massive waves of civilization which later spread over Eurasia immediately followed the great renaissance of the Garden consequent upon the extensive union of the Adamites with the surrounding mixed Nodites to form the Andites." P. 872.

2. **Andites upstepped the civilizations of Turkestan, Europe, China, and India. A few reached Japan, Formosa, and the East Indies.**

"The civilization of Turkestan was constantly being revived and refreshed by the newcomers from Mesopotamia, especially by the later Andite cavalrymen. The so-called Aryan mother tongue was in process of formation in the highlands of Turkestan; it was a blend of the Andonic dialect of that region with the language of the Adamsonites and later Andites. Many modern languages are derived from this early speech of these central Asian tribes who conquered Europe, India, and the upper stretches of the Mesopotamian plains. This ancient language gave the Occidental tongues all of that similarity which is called Aryan.

"By 12,000 B.C. three quarters of the Andite stock of the world was resident in northern and eastern Europe, and when the later and final exodus from Mesopotamia took place, sixty-five per cent of these last waves of emigration entered Europe.

"The Andites not only migrated to Europe but to northern China and India, while many groups penetrated to the ends of the earth as missionaries, teachers, and traders. They contributed considerably to the northern groups of the Saharan Sangik peoples. But only a few teachers and traders ever penetrated farther south in Africa than the headwaters of the Nile. Later on, mixed Andites and Egyptians followed down both the east and west coasts of Africa well below the equator, but they did not reach Madagascar.

"These Andites were the so-called Dravidian and later Aryan conquerors of India; and their presence in central Asia greatly upstepped the ancestors of the Turanians. Many of this race journeyed to China by way of both Sinkiang and Tibet and added desirable qualities to the later Chinese stocks. From time to time small groups made their way into Japan, Formosa, the East Indies, and southern China, though very few entered southern China by the coastal route." P. 872-3.

3. **Some reached the Polynesian islands and South America and helped establish the ancestry of the Incas.**

"One hundred and thirty-two of this race, embarking in a fleet of small boats from Japan, eventually reached South America and by intermarriage with the natives of the Andes established the ancestry of the later rulers of the Incas. They crossed the Pacific by easy stages, tarrying on the many islands they found along the way. The islands of the Polynesian group were both more numerous and larger then than now, and these Andite

PART V — *Anthropology*

sailors, together with some who followed them, biologically modified the native groups in transit. Many flourishing centers of civilization grew up on these now submerged lands as a result of Andite penetration. Easter Island was long a religious and administrative center of one of these lost groups. But of the Andites who navigated the Pacific of long ago none but the one hundred and thirty-two ever reached the mainland of the Americas." P. 873.

4. **Andites contributed humor, art, adventure, music, and manufacture.**

"The migratory conquests of the Andites continued on down to their final dispersions, from 8000 to 6000 B.C. As they poured out of Mesopotamia, they continuously depleted the biologic reserves of their homelands while markedly strengthening the surrounding peoples. And to every nation to which they journeyed, they contributed humor, art, adventure, music, and manufacture. They were skillful domesticators of animals and expert agriculturists. For the time being, at least, their presence usually improved the religious beliefs and moral practices of the older races. And so the culture of Mesopotamia quietly spread out over Europe, India, China, northern Africa, and the Pacific Islands." P. 873.

C. **Later Andite migrations.**

1. **Three waves of Andites poured out of Mesopotamia between 8000 and 6000 B.C.**

"The last three waves of Andites poured out of Mesopotamia between 8000 and 6000 B.C. These three great waves of culture were forced out of Mesopotamia by the pressure of the hill tribes to the east and the harassment of the plainsmen of the west. The inhabitants of the Euphrates valley and adjacent territory went forth in their final exodus in several directions:

"Sixty-five per cent entered Europe by the Caspian Sea route to conquer and amalgamate with the newly appearing white races—the blend of the blue men and the earlier Andites.

"Ten per cent, including a large group of the Sethite priests, moved eastward through the Elamite highlands to the Iranian plateau and Turkestan. Many of their descendants were later driven into India with their Aryan brethren from the regions to the north.

"Ten per cent of the Mesopotamians turned eastward in their

northern trek, entering Sinkiang, where they blended with the Andite yellow inhabitants. The majority of the able offspring of this racial union later entered China and contributed much to the immediate improvement of the northern division of the yellow race.

"Ten per cent of these fleeing Andites made their way across Arabia and entered Egypt.

"Five per cent of the Andites, the very superior culture of the coastal district about the mouths of the Tigris and Euphrates who had kept themselves free from intermarriage with the inferior neighboring tribesmen, refused to leave their homes. This group represented the survival of many superior Nodite and Adamite strains." P. 873-4.

2. **Floods in Mesopotamia, particularly the one during the days of Noah, completed the disruption of Andite civilization, and destroyed the second garden.**

"The river dwellers were accustomed to rivers overflowing their banks at certain seasons; these periodic floods were annual events in their lives. But new perils threatened the valley of Mesopotamia as a result of progressive geologic changes to the north.

"For thousands of years after the submergence of the first Eden the mountains about the eastern coast of the Mediterranean and those to the northwest and northeast of Mesopotamia continued to rise. This elevation of the highlands was greatly accelerated about 5000 B.C., and this, together with greatly increased snowfall on the northern mountains, caused unprecedented floods each spring throughout the Euphrates valley. These spring floods grew increasingly worse so that eventually the inhabitants of the river regions were driven to the eastern highlands. For almost a thousand years scores of cities were practically deserted because of these extensive deluges.

"Almost five thousand years later, as the Hebrew priests in Babylonian captivity sought to trace the Jewish people back to Adam, they found great difficulty in piecing the story together; and it occurred to one of them to abandon the effort, to let the whole world drown in its wickedness at the time of Noah's flood, and thus to be in a better position to trace Abraham right back to one of the three surviving sons of Noah." P. 874.

"These floods completed the disruption of Andite civilization.

PART V — *Anthropology*

With the ending of this period of deluge, the second garden was no more. Only in the south and among the Sumerians did any trace of the former glory remain.

"The remnants of this, one of the oldest civilizations, are to be found in these regions of Mesopotamia and to the northeast and northwest. But still older vestiges of the days of Dalamatia exist under the waters of the Persian Gulf, and the first Eden lies submerged under the eastern end of the Mediterranean Sea." P. 875.

D. **The Sumerians—last of the Andites.**

1. **The remnant of Andites in Mesopotamia constituted the Sumerians.**

   "When the last Andite dispersion broke the biologic backbone of Mesopotamian civilization, a small minority of this superior race remained in their homeland near the mouths of the rivers. These were the Sumerians, and by 6000 B.C. they had become largely Andite in extraction, though their culture was more exclusively Nodite in character, and they clung to the ancient traditions of Dalamatia. Nonetheless, these Sumerians of the coastal regions were the last of the Andites in Mesopotamia. But the races of Mesopotamia were already thoroughly blended by this late date, as is evidenced by the skull types found in the graves of this era." P. 875.

2. **Barbarians from Turkestan and Iran overran all Mesopotamia, assimilating the remaining Andites, and developed into the mixed people who were the ancestors of the Babylonians.**

   "The peaceful grain growers of the Euphrates and Tigris valleys had long been harassed by the raids of the barbarians of Turkestan and the Iranian plateau. But now a concerted invasion of the Euphrates valley was brought about by the increasing drought of the highland pastures. And this invasion was all the more serious because these surrounding herdsmen and hunters possessed large numbers of tamed horses. It was the possession of horses which gave them a tremendous military advantage over their rich neighbors to the south. In a short time they overran all Mesopotamia, driving forth the last waves of culture which spread out over all of Europe, western Asia, and northern Africa.

   "These conquerors of Mesopotamia carried in their ranks many of the better Andite strains of the mixed northern races of

Turkestan, including some of the Adamson stock. These less advanced but more vigorous tribes from the north quickly and willingly assimilated the residue of the civilization of Mesopotamia and presently developed into those mixed peoples found in the Euphrates valley at the beginning of historic annals. They quickly revived many phases of the passing civilization of Mesopotamia, adopting the arts of the valley tribes and much of the culture of the Sumerians. They even sought to build a third tower of Babel and later adopted the term as their national name." P. 875-6.

3. **About 2500 B.C. the Sumerians were defeated and absorbed into the ranks of the Semites. The Garden culture yielded the ferments which have produced present-day civilization.**

"About 2500 B.C. the Sumerians suffered severe reverses at the hands of the northern Suites and Guites. Lagash, the Sumerian capital built on flood mounds, fell. Erech held out for thirty years after the fall of Akkad. By the time of the establishment of the rule of Hammurabi the Sumerians had become absorbed into the ranks of the northern Semites, and the Mesopotamian Andites passed from the pages of history." P. 876.

"And this is the story of the violet race after the days of Adam and of the fate of their homeland between the Tigris and Euphrates. Their ancient civilization finally fell due to the emigration of superior peoples and the immigration of their inferior neighbors. But long before the barbarian cavalrymen conquered the valley, much of the Garden culture had spread to Asia, Africa, and Europe, there to produce the ferments which have resulted in the twentieth century civilization of Urantia." P. 877.

IV. ANDITE EXPANSION IN THE ORIENT

"Asia is the homeland of the human race. It was on a southern peninsula of this continent that Andon and Fonta were born; in the highlands of what is now Afghanistan, their descendant Badonan founded a primitive center of culture that persisted for over one-half million years. Here at this eastern focus of the human race the Sangik peoples differentiated from the Andonic stock, and Asia was their first home, their first hunting ground, their first battlefield. Southwestern Asia witnessed the successive civilizations of Dalamatians, Nodites, Adamites, and Andites, and from these regions the potentials of modern civilization spread to the world." P. 878.

PART V — *Anthropology*

A. **The Andites of Turkestan.**
1. **The Andites infiltrated Turkestan on their way to eastern Asia, Europe, and India.**
   "For over twenty-five thousand years, on down to nearly 2000 B.C., the heart of Eurasia was predominantly, though diminishingly, Andite. In the lowlands of Turkestan the Andites made the westward turning around the inland lakes into Europe, while from the highlands of this region they infiltrated eastward. Eastern Turkestan (Sinkiang) and, to a lesser extent, Tibet were the ancient gateways through which these peoples of Mesopotamia penetrated the mountains to the northern lands of the yellow men. The Andite infiltration of India proceeded from the Turkestan highlands into the Punjab and from the Iranian grazing lands through Baluchistan. These earlier migrations were in no sense conquests; they were, rather, the continual drifting of the Andite tribes into western India and China." P. 878.
2. **Increasing aridity drove the Andites southward and caused them to become traders and to build cities.**
   "By 8000 B.C. the slowly increasing aridity of the highland regions of central Asia began to drive the Andites to the river bottoms and the seashores. This increasing drought not only drove them to the valleys of the Nile, Euphrates, Indus, and Yellow rivers, but it produced a new development in Andite civilization. A new class of men, the traders, began to appear in large numbers.
   "When climatic conditions made hunting unprofitable for the migrating Andites, they did not follow the evolutionary course of the older races by becoming herders. Commerce and urban life made their appearance. From Egypt through Mesopotamia and Turkestan to the rivers of China and India, the more highly civilized tribes began to assemble in cities devoted to manufacture and trade. Adonia became the central Asian commercial metropolis, being located near the present city of Ashkhabad. Commerce in stone, metal, wood, and pottery was accelerated on both land and water." P. 878-9.
3. **Even in more recent times there is evidence of Andite blood among the Asiatic peoples.**

"But even in the twentieth century after Christ there are traces of Andite blood among the Turanian and Tibetan peoples, as is witnessed by the blond types occasionally found in these regions. The early Chinese annals record the presence of the red-haired nomads to the north of the peaceful settlements of the Yellow River, and there still remain paintings which faithfully record the presence of both the blond-Andite and the brunet-Mongolian types in the Tarim basin of long ago.

"The last great manifestation of the submerged military genius of the central Asiatic Andites was in A.D. 1200, when the Mongols under Genghis Khan began the conquest of the greater portion of the Asiatic continent. And like the Andites of old, these warriors proclaimed the existence of 'one God in heaven.' The early breakup of their empire long delayed cultural intercourse between Occident and Orient and greatly handicapped the growth of the monotheistic concept in Asia." P. 879.

B. The Andites in India.

1. **India is the only locality where all the Urantia races were blended.**

    "India is the only locality where all the Urantia races were blended, the Andite invasion adding the last stock. In the highlands northwest of India the Sangik races came into existence, and without exception members of each penetrated the subcontinent of India in their early days, leaving behind them the most heterogeneous race mixture ever to exist on Urantia. Ancient India acted as a catch basin for the migrating races. The base of the peninsula was formerly somewhat narrower than now, much of the deltas of the Ganges and Indus being the work of the last fifty thousand years." P. 879.

2. **About 15,000 B.C. population pressure in Turkestan caused the Andites to move into India. The topography of India prevented inferior stocks from emigrating; the Andites, despite a desperate attempt to preserve their identity, became submerged, but the whole mass of people had been improved.**

    "About 15,000 B.C. increasing population pressure throughout Turkestan and Iran occasioned the first really extensive Andite movement toward India. For over fifteen centuries these superior peoples poured in through the highlands of Baluchistan, spreading out over the valleys of the Indus and Ganges and slowly moving southward into the Deccan. This

Part V — Anthropology

Andite pressure from the northwest drove many of the southern and eastern inferiors into Burma and southern China but not sufficiently to save the invaders from racial obliteration.

"The failure of India to achieve the hegemony of Eurasia was largely a matter of topography; population pressure from the north only crowded the majority of the people southward into the decreasing territory of the Deccan, surrounded on all sides by the sea. Had there been adjacent lands for emigration, then would the inferiors have been crowded out in all directions, and the superior stocks would have achieved a higher civilization.

"As it was, these earlier Andite conquerors made a desperate attempt to preserve their identity and stem the tide of racial engulfment by the establishment of rigid restrictions regarding intermarriage. Nonetheless, the Andites had become submerged by 10,000 B.C., but the whole mass of the people had been markedly improved by this absorption." P. 880.

3. **Andite admixture with the native stock of India produced the Dravidians, who did much to elevate the social and religious levels of the inhabitants of India.**

"The blending of the Andite conquerors of India with the native stock eventually resulted in that mixed people which has been called Dravidian. The earlier and purer Dravidians possessed a great capacity for cultural achievement, which was continuously weakened as their Andite inheritance became progressively attenuated. And this is what doomed the budding civilization of India almost twelve thousand years ago. But the infusion of even this small amount of the blood of Adam produced a marked acceleration in social development. This composite stock immediately produced the most versatile civilization then on earth." P. 881.

"The superior culture and religious leanings of the peoples of India date from the early times of Dravidian domination and are due, in part, to the fact that so many of the Sethite priesthood entered India, both in the earlier Andite and in the later Aryan invasions. The thread of monotheism running through the religious history of India thus stems from the teachings of the Adamites in the second garden." P. 881.

"But for more than seven thousand years, down to the end of the Andite migrations, the religious status of the inhabitants of

India was far above that of the world at large. During these times India bid fair to produce the leading cultural, religious, philosophic, and commercial civilization of the world. And but for the complete submergence of the Andites by the peoples of the south, this destiny would probably have been realized." P. 881.

"The Dravidians were among the earliest peoples to build cities and to engage in an extensive export and import business, both by land and sea. By 7000 B.C. camel trains were making regular trips to distant Mesopotamia; Dravidian shipping was pushing coastwise across the Arabian Sea to the Sumerian cities of the Persian Gulf and was venturing on the waters of the Bay of Bengal as far as the East Indies. An alphabet, together with the art of writing, was imported from Sumeria by these seafarers and merchants." P. 881.

4. **The second Andite penetration, the Aryan invasion, upstepped the northern part of India, but amalgamation with inferior natives, in spite of the caste system, resulted in an inferior civilization.**

"The second Andite penetration of India was the Aryan invasion during a period of almost five hundred years in the middle of the third millennium before Christ. This migration marked the terminal exodus of the Andites from their homelands in Turkestan.

"The early Aryan centers were scattered over the northern half of India, notably in the northwest. These invaders never completed the conquest of the country and subsequently met their undoing in this neglect since their lesser numbers made them vulnerable to absorption by the Dravidians of the south, who subsequently overran the entire peninsula except the Himalayan provinces." P. 882.

"On the Gangetic plain Aryan and Dravidian eventually mingled to produce a high culture, and this center was later reinforced by contributions from the northeast, coming from China." P. 882.

"When the Aryans entered India, they brought with them their concepts of Deity as they had been preserved in the lingering traditions of the religion of the second garden. But the Brahman priests were never able to withstand the pagan momentum built up by the sudden contact with the inferior religions of the Deccan after the racial obliteration of the Aryans. Thus

PART V — *Anthropology*

the vast majority of the population fell into the bondage of the enslaving superstitions of inferior religions; and so it was that India failed to produce the high civilization which had been foreshadowed in earlier times." P. 882.

C. **The Andites and the yellow races of China.**
   1. **Enough of the Andites migrated to northern centers of culture in China to stimulate their civilization.**

      "About fifteen thousand years ago the Andites, in considerable numbers, were traversing the pass of Ti Tao and spreading out over the upper valley of the Yellow River among the Chinese settlements of Kansu. Presently they penetrated eastward to Honan, where the most progressive settlements were situated. This infiltration from the west was about half Andonite and half Andite.

      "The northern centers of culture along the Yellow River had always been more progressive than the southern settlements on the Yangtze. Within a few thousand years after the arrival of even the small numbers of these superior mortals, the settlements along the Yellow River had forged ahead of the Yangtze villages and had achieved an advanced position over their brethren in the south which has ever since been maintained.

      "It was not that there were so many of the Andites, nor that their culture was so superior, but amalgamation with them produced a more versatile stock. The northern Chinese received just enough of the Andite strain to mildly stimulate their innately able minds but not enough to fire them with the restless, exploratory curiosity so characteristic of the northern white races. This more limited infusion of Andite inheritance was less disturbing to the innate stability of the Sangik type." P. 886.

   2. **The lack of stimulus of danger, and the Chinese tendencies toward agriculture, led to ancestor worship and comparative stagnation.**

      "While the red man suffered from too much warfare, it is not altogether amiss to say that the development of statehood among the Chinese was delayed by the thoroughness of their conquest of Asia. They had a great potential of racial solidarity, but it failed properly to develop because the continuous driving stimulus of the ever-present danger of external aggression was lacking.

"With the completion of the conquest of eastern Asia the ancient military state gradually disintegrated—past wars were forgotten. Of the epic struggle with the red race there persisted only the hazy tradition of an ancient contest with the archer peoples. The Chinese early turned to agricultural pursuits, which contributed further to their pacific tendencies, while a population well below the land-man ratio for agriculture still further contributed to the growing peacefulness of the country.

"Consciousness of past achievements (somewhat diminished in the present), the conservatism of an overwhelmingly agricultural people, and a well-developed family life equaled the birth of ancestor veneration, culminating in the custom of so honoring the men of the past as to border on worship. A very similar attitude prevailed among the white races in Europe for some five hundred years following the disruption of Graeco-Roman civilization.

"The belief in, and worship of, the 'One Truth' as taught by Singlangton never entirely died out; but as time passed, the search for new and higher truth became overshadowed by a growing tendency to venerate that which was already established. Slowly the genius of the yellow race became diverted from the pursuit of the unknown to the preservation of the known. And this is the reason for the stagnation of what had been the world's most rapidly progressing civilization." P. 887.

3. **Though several factors delayed the development of statehood among the Chinese, they have caused the development of family life which helped produce the stability of the Chinese.**

"Between 4000 and 500 B.C. the political reunification of the yellow race was consummated, but the cultural union of the Yangtze and Yellow river centers had already been effected. This political reunification of the later tribal groups was not without conflict, but the societal opinion of war remained low; ancestor worship, increasing dialects, and no call for military action for thousands upon thousands of years had rendered this people ultrapeaceful." P. 887.

"The great weakness of ancestor veneration is that it promotes a backward-looking philosophy. However wise it may be to glean wisdom from the past, it is folly to regard the past as the exclusive source of truth. Truth is relative and expanding; it *lives* always in the present, achieving new expression in each generation of men—even in each human life.

"The great strength in a veneration of ancestry is the value that such an attitude places upon the family. The amazing stability and persistence of Chinese culture is a consequence of the paramount position accorded the family, for civilization is directly dependent on the effective functioning of the family; and in China the family attained a social importance, even a religious significance, approached by few other peoples." P. 888.

"And so the ancient civilization of the yellow race has persisted down through the centuries. It is almost forty thousand years since the first important advances were made in Chinese culture, and though there have been many retrogressions, the civilization of the sons of Han comes the nearest of all to presenting an unbroken picture of continual progression right on down to the times of the twentieth century. The mechanical and religious developments of the white races have been of a high order, but they have never excelled the Chinese in family loyalty, group ethics, or personal morality.

"This ancient culture has contributed much to human happiness; millions of human beings have lived and died, blessed by its achievements. For centuries this great civilization has rested upon the laurels of the past, but it is even now reawakening to envision anew the transcendent goals of mortal existence, once again to take up the unremitting struggle for never-ending progress." P. 888.

V. ANDITE EXPANSION IN THE OCCIDENT

"Although the European blue man did not of himself achieve a great cultural civilization, he did supply the biologic foundation which, when its Adamized strains were blended with the later Andite invaders, produced one of the most potent stocks for the attainment of aggressive civilization ever to appear on Urantia since the times of the violet race and their Andite successors.

"The modern white peoples incorporate the surviving strains of the Adamic stock which became admixed with the Sangik races, some red and yellow but more especially the blue. There is a considerable percentage of the original Andonite stock in all the white races and still more of the early Nodite strains." P. 889.

A. The Andites along the Nile.

1. **The Adamites and Andites found Nodite centers of civilization in Egypt. A stream of Mesopotamians for 30,000 years enriched the civilization of the Nile valley, though the ingress of large numbers of black Saharans greatly deteriorated the culture.**

"Before the last Andites were driven out of the Euphrates valley, many of their brethren had entered Europe as adventurers, teachers, traders, and warriors. During the earlier days of the violet race the Mediterranean trough was protected by the Gibraltar isthmus and the Sicilian land bridge. Some of man's very early maritime commerce was established on these inland lakes, where blue men from the north and the Saharans from the south met Nodites and Adamites from the east.

"In the eastern trough of the Mediterranean the Nodites had established one of their most extensive cultures and from these centers had penetrated somewhat into southern Europe but more especially into northern Africa. The broad-headed Nodite-Andonite Syrians very early introduced pottery and agriculture in connection with their settlements on the slowly rising Nile delta. They also imported sheep, goats, cattle, and other domesticated animals and brought in greatly improved methods of metalworking, Syria then being the center of that industry.

"For more than thirty thousand years Egypt received a steady stream of Mesopotamians, who brought along their art and culture to enrich that of the Nile valley. But the ingress of large numbers of the Sahara peoples greatly deteriorated the early civilization along the Nile so that Egypt reached its lowest cultural level some fifteen thousand years ago.

"But during earlier times there was little to hinder the westward migration of the Adamites. The Sahara was an open grazing land overspread by herders and agriculturists. These Saharans never engaged in manufacture, nor were they city builders. They were an indigo-black group which carried extensive strains of the extinct green and orange races. But they received a very limited amount of the violet inheritance before the upthrust of land and the shifting water-laden winds dispersed the remnants of this prosperous and peaceful civilization." P. 889.

2. **After the terminal migration of Andites from Mesopotamia, Egypt became the headquarters of the most advanced group on earth.**

"From the times of the terminal Andite migrations, culture declined in the Euphrates valley, and the immediate center of civilization shifted to the valley of the Nile. Egypt became the successor of Mesopotamia as the headquarters of the most advanced group on earth.

"The Nile valley began to suffer from floods shortly before the Mesopotamian valleys but fared much better. This early setback was more than compensated by the continuing stream of Andite immigrants, so that the culture of Egypt, though really derived from the Euphrates region, seemed to forge ahead. But in 5000 B.C., during the flood period in Mesopotamia, there were seven distinct groups of human beings in Egypt; all of them, save one, came from Mesopotamia.

"When the last exodus from the Euphrates valley occurred, Egypt was fortunate in gaining so many of the most skillful artists and artisans. These Andite artisans found themselves quite at home in that they were thoroughly familiar with river life, its floods, irrigations, and dry seasons. They enjoyed the sheltered position of the Nile valley; they were there much less subject to hostile raids and attacks than along the Euphrates. And they added greatly to the metalworking skill of the Egyptians. Here they worked iron ores coming from Mount Sinai instead of from the Black Sea regions." P. 894.

3. **The Andites built the first stone structures in Egypt, but internal warfare laid them open to invasion by the inferior tribes from Arabia and the south.**

"The Egyptians very early assembled their municipal deities into an elaborate national system of gods. They developed an extensive theology and had an equally extensive but burdensome priesthood. Several different leaders sought to revive the remnants of the early religious teachings of the Sethites, but these endeavors were short-lived. The Andites built the first stone structures in Egypt. The first and most exquisite of the stone pyramids was erected by Imhotep, an Andite architectural genius, while serving as prime minister. Previous buildings had been constructed of brick, and while many stone structures had been erected in different parts of the world, this was the first in Egypt. But the art of building steadily declined from the days of this great architect.

"This brilliant epoch of culture was cut short by internal warfare along the Nile, and the country was soon overrun, as Mesopotamia had been, by the inferior tribes from inhospitable Arabia and by the blacks from the south. As a result, social progress steadily declined for more than five hundred years." P. 894.

B. The Adamites and the blue race.

1. **Geographic conditions coupled with sex attraction between the violet and blue races caused a migration of Adamites to Europe.**

    "Adam's blood has been shared with most of the human races, but some secured more than others. The mixed races of India and the darker peoples of Africa were not attractive to the Adamites. They would have mixed freely with the red man had he not been far removed in the Americas, and they were kindly disposed toward the yellow man, but he was likewise difficult of access in faraway Asia. Therefore, when actuated by either adventure or altruism, or when driven out of the Euphrates valley, they very naturally chose union with the blue races of Europe.

    "The blue men, then dominant in Europe, had no religious practices which were repulsive to the earlier migrating Adamites, and there was great sex attraction between the violet and the blue races. The best of the blue men deemed it a high honor to be permitted to mate with the Adamites. Every blue man entertained the ambition of becoming so skillful and artistic as to win the affection of some Adamite woman, and it was the highest aspiration of a superior blue woman to receive the attentions of an Adamite.

    "Slowly these migrating sons of Eden united with the higher types of the blue race, invigorating their cultural practices while ruthlessly exterminating the lingering strains of Neanderthal stock. This technique of race blending, combined with the elimination of inferior strains, produced a dozen or more virile and progressive groups of superior blue men, one of which you have denominated the Cro-Magnons.

    "For these and other reasons, not the least of which was more favorable paths of migration, the early waves of Mesopotamian culture made their way almost exclusively to Europe. And it

PART V — *Anthropology*

was these circumstances that determined the antecedents of modern European civilization." P. 890.

2. **The lowering of the Gibraltar isthmus and the Sicilian land bridge brought about the greatest flood in history and delayed the migration of Adamites into Europe.**

"About the time of these climatic changes in Africa, England separated from the continent, and Denmark arose from the sea, while the isthmus of Gibraltar, protecting the western basin of the Mediterranean, gave way as the result of an earthquake, quickly raising this inland lake to the level of the Atlantic Ocean. Presently the Sicilian land bridge submerged, creating one sea of the Mediterranean and connecting it with the Atlantic Ocean. This cataclysm of nature flooded scores of human settlements and occasioned the greatest loss of life by flood in all the world's history.

"This engulfment of the Mediterranean basin immediately curtailed the westward movements of the Adamites, while the great influx of Saharans led them to seek outlets for their increasing numbers to the north and east of Eden. As the descendants of Adam journeyed northward from the valleys of the Tigris and Euphrates, they encountered mountainous barriers and the then expanded Caspian Sea. And for many generations the Adamites hunted, herded, and tilled the soil around their settlements scattered throughout Turkestan. Slowly this magnificent people extended their territory into Europe. But now the Adamites enter Europe from the east and find the culture of the blue man thousands of years behind that of Asia since this region has been almost entirely out of touch with Mesopotamia." P. 890-1.

C. **The Andite invasions of Europe.**

1. **There were seven major invasions of Europe by Andites, interspersed with an invasion of Andonites.**

"While the Andites poured into Europe in a steady stream, there were seven major invasions, the last arrivals coming on horseback in three great waves. Some entered Europe by way of the islands of the Aegean and up the Danube valley, but the majority of the earlier and purer strains migrated to northwestern Europe by the northern route across the grazing lands of the Volga and the Don.

"Between the third and fourth invasions a horde of Andonites entered Europe from the north, having come from Siberia by way of the Russian rivers and the Baltic. They were immediately assimilated by the northern Andite tribes." P. 892.

2. **The Adamites were pacific, the Nodites were belligerent; the union of these stocks with the Sangiks produced the aggressive Andites.**

"The earlier expansions of the purer violet race were far more pacific than were those of their later semimilitary and conquestloving Andite descendants. The Adamites were pacific; the Nodites were belligerent. The union of these stocks, as later mingled with the Sangik races, produced the able, aggressive Andites who made actual military conquests." P. 892.

3. **The horse was an important factor in the Andite conquest of Europe.**

"But the horse was the evolutionary factor which determined the dominance of the Andites in the Occident. The horse gave the dispersing Andites the hitherto nonexistent advantage of mobility, enabling the last groups of Andite cavalrymen to progress quickly around the Caspian Sea to overrun all of Europe. All previous waves of Andites had moved so slowly that they tended to disintegrate at any great distance from Mesopotamia. But these later waves moved so rapidly that they reached Europe as coherent groups, still retaining some measure of higher culture.

"The whole inhabited world, outside of China and the Euphrates region, had made very limited cultural progress for ten thousand years when the hard-riding Andite horsemen made their appearance in the sixth and seventh millenniums before Christ. As they moved westward across the Russian plains, absorbing the best of the blue man and exterminating the worst, they became blended into one people. These were the ancestors of the so-called Nordic races, the forefathers of the Scandinavian, German, and Anglo-Saxon peoples.

"It was not long before the superior blue strains had been fully absorbed by the Andites throughout all northern Europe. Only in Lapland (and to a certain extent in Brittany) did the older Andonites retain even a semblance of identity." P. 892-3.

4. **Tribes in northern Europe were continuously upstepped by Andites, but the blue men in the south resisted them.**

"The tribes of northern Europe were being continuously reinforced and upstepped by the steady stream of migrants

PART V — *Anthropology*

from Mesopotamia through the Turkestan-south Russian regions, and when the last waves of Andite cavalry swept over Europe, there were already more men with Andite inheritance in that region than were to be found in all the rest of the world.

"For three thousand years the military headquarters of the northern Andites was in Denmark. From this central point there went forth the successive waves of conquest, which grew decreasingly Andite and increasingly white as the passing centuries witnessed the final blending of the Mesopotamian conquerors with the conquered peoples.

"While the blue man had been absorbed in the north and eventually succumbed to the white cavalry raiders who penetrated the south, the advancing tribes of the mixed white race met with stubborn and protracted resistance from the Cro-Magnons, but superior intelligence and ever-augmenting biologic reserves enabled them to wipe the older race out of existence." P. 893.

5. **The decisive struggles between the blue man and the white man took place in the valley of the Somme.**

    "The decisive struggles between the white man and the blue man were fought out in the valley of the Somme. Here, the flower of the blue race bitterly contested the southward-moving Andites, and for over five hundred years these Cro-Magnoids successfully defended their territories before succumbing to the superior military strategy of the white invaders. Thor, the victorious commander of the armies of the north in the final battle of the Somme, became the hero of the northern white tribes and later on was revered as a god by some of them." P. 893.

6. **Commerce, intermarriage, and extermination of inferiors completed conquest of the blue man by the white races.**

    "The strongholds of the blue man which persisted longest were in southern France, but the last great military resistance was overcome along the Somme. The later conquest progressed by commercial penetration, population pressure along the rivers, and by continued intermarriage with the superiors, coupled with the ruthless extermination of the inferiors.

    "When the tribal council of the Andite elders had adjudged an inferior captive to be unfit, he was, by elaborate ceremony, committed to the shaman priests, who escorted him to the river and administered the rites of initiation to the 'happy hunting grounds' —lethal submergence. In this way the white invaders of Europe exterminated all peoples encountered who were not quickly absorbed into their own ranks, and thus did the blue man come to an end-and quickly." P. 893.

7. **The legacy of the Cro-Magnoid blue man.**
"The Cro-Magnoid blue man constituted the biologic foundation for the modern European races, but they have survived only as absorbed by the later and virile conquerors of their homelands. The blue strain contributed many sturdy traits and much physical vigor to the white races of Europe, but the humor and imagination of the blended European peoples were derived from the Andites. This Andite-blue union, resulting in the northern white races, produced an immediate lapse of Andite civilization, a retardation of a transient nature. Eventually, the latent superiority of these northern barbarians manifested itself and culminated in present-day European civilization." P. 893.

D. **The Andites of the Mediterranean Isles.**

1. **A superior group of Andites settled in Crete, while descendants of Adamson migrated from Mesopotamia into Greece.**
"About 12,000 B.C. a brilliant tribe of Andites migrated to Crete. This was the only island settled so early by such a superior group, and it was almost two thousand years before the descendants of these mariners spread to the neighboring isles. This group were the narrow-headed, smaller-statured Andites who had intermarried with the Vanite division of the northern Nodites. They were all under six feet in height and had been literally driven off the mainland by their larger and inferior fellows. These emigrants to Crete were highly skilled in textiles, metals, pottery, plumbing, and the use of stone for building material. They engaged in writing and carried on as herders and agriculturists.

"Almost two thousand years after the settlement of Crete a group of the tall descendants of Adamson made their way over the northern islands to Greece, coming almost directly from their highland home north of Mesopotamia. These progenitors of the Greeks were led westward by Sato, a direct descendant of Adamson and Ratta.

"The group which finally settled in Greece consisted of three hundred and seventy-five of the selected and superior people comprising the end of the second civilization of the Adamsonites. These later sons of Adamson carried the then most valuable strains of the emerging white races. They were of a high intellectual order and physically regarded, the most beautiful of men since the days of the first Eden.

"Presently Greece and the Aegean Islands region succeeded Mesopotamia and Egypt as the Occidental center of trade, art, and culture. But as it was in Egypt, so again practically all of the art and science of the Aegean world was derived from Mesopotamia except for the culture of the Adamsonite forerunners of the Greeks. All the art and genius of these latter people is a direct legacy of the posterity of Adamson, the first son of Adam and Eve, and his extraordinary second wife, a daughter descended in an unbroken line from the pure Nodite staff of Prince Caligastia. No wonder the Greeks had mythological traditions that they were directly descended from gods and superhuman beings." P. 895.

2. **Origin of the mother cult.**

"The Aegean region passed through five distinct cultural stages, each less spiritual than the preceding, and ere long the last glorious era of art perished beneath the weight of the rapidly multiplying mediocre descendants of the Danubian slaves who had been imported by the later generations of Greeks.

"It was during this age in Crete that the *mother cult* of the descendants of Cain attained its greatest vogue. This cult glorified Eve in the worship of the 'great mother.' Images of Eve were everywhere. Thousands of public shrines were erected throughout Crete and Asia Minor. And this mother cult persisted on down to the times of Christ, becoming later incorporated in the early Christian religion under the guise of the glorification and worship of Mary the earth mother of Jesus." P. 895.

3. **In spite of deterioration due to influxes of inferior peoples, civilization in Cyprus and in northern Africa was improved by Andite movement migrations from Mesopotamia.**

"By 5000 B.C. the three purest strains of Adam's descendants were in Sumeria, northern Europe, and Greece. The whole of Mesopotamia was being slowly deteriorated by the stream of mixed and darker races which filtered in from Arabia. And the coming of these inferior peoples contributed further to the scattering abroad of the biologic and cultural residue of the

Andites. From all over the fertile crescent the more adventurous peoples poured westward to the islands. These migrants cultivated both grain and vegetables, and they brought domesticated animals with them.

"About 5000 B.C. a mighty host of progressive Mesopotamians moved out of the Euphrates valley and settled upon the island of Cyprus; this civilization was wiped out about two thousand years subsequently by the barbarian hordes from the north.

"Another great colony settled on the Mediterranean near the later site of Carthage. And from north Africa large numbers of Andites entered Spain and later mingled in Switzerland with their brethren who had earlier come to Italy from the Aegean Islands." P. 896.

4. **The Greeks were great traders and colonizers as well as teachers and artists.**

"The Greeks were not only great teachers and artists, they were also the world's greatest traders and colonizers. Before succumbing to the flood of inferiority which eventually engulfed their art and commerce, they succeeded in planting so many outposts of culture to the west that a great many of the advances in early Greek civilization persisted in the later peoples of southern Europe, and many of the mixed descendants of these Adamsonites became incorporated in the tribes of the adjacent mainlands." P. 896.

E. **The Danubian Andonites.**

The northern and southern Andites were separated by Andonites who were dispersed throughout central and southeastern Europe. The Hittites and descendants of Abraham carried some of this strain.

"The Andite peoples of the Euphrates valley migrated north to Europe to mingle with the blue men and west into the Mediterranean regions to mix with the remnants of the commingled Saharans and the southern blue men. And these two branches of the white race were, and now are, widely separated by the broad-headed mountain survivors of the earlier Andonite tribes which had long inhabited these central regions.

"These descendants of Andon were dispersed through most of the mountainous regions of central and southeastern Europe. They were often reinforced by arrivals from Asia Minor, which region they occupied in considerable strength. The ancient Hittites stemmed directly from the Andonite stock; their pale skins and broad heads were typical of that race. This strain was carried in Abraham's ancestry and contributed much to the characteristic facial appearance of his later Jewish descendants who, while having a culture and religion derived from the Andites, spoke a very different language. Their tongue was distinctly Andonite.

"The tribes that dwelt in houses erected on piles or log piers over the lakes of Italy, Switzerland, and southern Europe were the expanding fringes of the African, Aegean, and, more especially, the Danubian migrations.

"The Danubians were Andonites, farmers and herders who had entered Europe through the Balkan peninsula and were moving slowly northward by way of the Danube valley. They made pottery and tilled the land, preferring to live in the valleys. The most northerly settlement of the Danubians was at Liege in Belgium. These tribes deteriorated rapidly as they moved away from the center and source of their culture. The best pottery is the product of the earlier settlements.

"The Danubians became mother worshipers as the result of the work of the missionaries from Crete. These tribes later amalgamated with groups of Andonite sailore who came by boats from the coast of Asia Minor, and who were also mother worshipers. Much of central Europe was thus early settled by these mixed types of the broad-headed white races which practiced mother worship and the religious rite of cremating the dead, for it was the custom of the mother cultists to burn their dead in stone huts." P. 896-7.

F. **The three white races.**
    1. **The origin, nature, and distribution of the three white races.**
        "The racial blends in Europe toward the close of the Andite migrations became generalized into the three white races as follows:
        "1. *The northern white race.* This so-called Nordic race consisted primarily of the blue man plus the Andite but also contained a considerable amount of Andonite blood, together with smaller amounts of the red and yellow Sangik. The northern white race thus encompassed these four most desirable human stocks. But the largest inheritance was from the blue man. The typical early Nordic was long-headed, tall, and blond. But long ago this race became thoroughly mixed with all of the branches of the white peoples.

"The primitive culture of Europe, which was encountered by the invading Nordics, was that of the retrograding Danubians blended with the blue man. The Nordic-Danish and the Danubian-Andonite cultures met and mingled on the Rhine as is witnessed by the existence of two racial groups in Germany today.

"The Nordics continued the trade in amber from the Baltic coast, building up a great commerce with the broadheads of the Danube valley via the Brenner Pass. This extended contact with the Danubians led these northerners into mother worship, and for several thousands of years cremation of the dead was almost universal throughout Scandinavia. This explains why remains of the earlier white races, although buried all over Europe, are not to be found-only their ashes in stone and clay urns. These white men also built dwellings; they never lived in caves. And again this explains why there are so few evidences of the white man's early culture, although the preceding Cro-Magnon type is well preserved where it has been securely sealed up in caves and grottoes. As it were, one day in northern Europe there is a primitive culture of the retrogressing Danubians and the blue man and the next that of a suddenly appearing and vastly superior white man.

"2. *The central white race.* While this group includes strains of blue, yellow, and Andite, it is predominantly Andonite. These people are broad-headed, swarthy, and stocky. They are driven like a wedge between the Nordic and Mediterranean races, with the broad base resting in Asia and the apex penetrating eastern France.

"For almost twenty thousand years the Andonites had been pushed farther and farther to the north of central Asia by the Andites. By 3000 B.C. increasing aridity was driving these Andonites back into Turkestan. This Andonite push southward continued for over a thousand years and, splitting around the Caspian and Black seas, penetrated Europe by way of both the Balkans and the Ukraine. This invasion included the remaining groups of Adamson's descendants and, during the latter half of the invasion period, carried with it considerable numbers of the Iranian Andites as well as many of the descendants of the Sethite priests.

PART V —— *Anthropology*

"By 2500 B.C. the westward thrust of the Andonites reached Europe. And this overrunning of all Mesopotamia, Asia Minor, and the Danube basin by the barbarians of the hills of Turkestan constituted the most serious and lasting of all cultural setbacks up to that time. These invaders definitely Andonized the character of the central European races, which have ever since remained characteristically Alpine.

"3. *The southern white race.* This brunet Mediterranean race consisted of a blend of the Andite and the blue man, with a smaller Andonite strain than in the north. This group also absorbed a considerable amount of secondary Sangik blood through the Saharans. In later times this southern division of the white race was infused by strong Andite elements from the eastern Mediterranean.

"The Mediterranean coastlands did not, however, become permeated by the Andites until the times of the great nomadic invasions of 2500 B.C. Land traffic and trade were nearly suspended during these centuries when the nomads invaded the eastern Mediterranean districts. This interference with land travel brought about the great expansion of sea traffic and trade; Mediterranean sea-borne commerce was in full swing about forty-five hundred years ago. And this development of marine traffic resulted in the sudden expansion of the descendants of the Andites throughout the entire coastal territory of the Mediterranean basin.

"These racial mixtures laid the foundations for the southern European race, the most highly mixed of all. And since these days this race has undergone still further admixture, notably with the blue-yellow-Andite peoples of Arabia. This Mediterranean race is, in fact, so freely admixed with the surrounding peoples as to be virtually indiscernible as a separate type, but in general its members are short, long-headed, and brunet." P. 897-8.

2. **Because of subsequent blending it is a fallacy to classify the white people as Nordic, Alpine, and Mediterranean.**
"But it is a fallacy to presume to classify the white peoples as Nordic, Alpine, and Mediterranean. There has been altogether too much blending to permit such a grouping. At one time there was a fairly well-defined division of the white race into such classes, but widespread intermingling has since occurred, and it is no longer possible to identify these distinctions with any clarity. Even in 3000 B.C. the ancient social groups were no

more of one race than are the present inhabitants of North America." P. 899.

VI. The Mixed Races

A. Classification of present-day races.

1. **The human races of today are a result of the blending of the five basic human stocks.**
   "As contact is made with the dawn of historic times, all of Eurasia, northern Africa, and the Pacific Islands is overspread with the composite races of mankind. And these races of today have resulted from a blending and reblending of the five basic human stocks of Urantia." P. 904.

2. **Physical characteristics of the basic human races.**
   "Each of the Urantia races was identified by certain distinguishing physical characteristics. The Adamites and Nodites were long headed; the Andonites were broad-headed. The Sangik races were medium-headed, with the yellow and blue men tending to broadheadedness. The blue races, when mixed with the Andonite stock, were decidedly broad-headed. The secondary Sangiks were medium to long-headed." P. 904.

3. **The five basic human races.**
   "Although these skull dimensions are serviceable in deciphering racial origins, the skeleton as a whole is far more dependable. In the early development of the Urantia races there were originally five distinct types of skeletal structure:
   "1. Andonic, Urantia aborigines.
   "2. Primary Sangik, red, yellow, and blue.
   "3. Secondary Sangik, orange, green, and indigo.
   "4. Nodites, descendants of the Dalamatians.
   "5. Adamites, the violet race." P. 904.

4. **The Lapps and Eskimos are nearest to the original Andonic stock.**
   "As these five great racial groups extensively intermingled, continual mixture tended to obscure the Andonite type by Sangik hereditary dominance. The Lapps and the Eskimos are blends of Andonite and Sangik-blue races. Their skeletal structures come the nearest to preserving the aboriginal Andonic type. But the Adamites and the Nodites have become so admixed with the other races that they can be detected only as a generalized Caucasoid order." P. 904.

5. **Study of skeletal structure discloses three present-day types of mankind:**

PART V — *Anthropology*

    a. *Caucasoid.*
    b. *Mongoloid.*
    c. *Negroid.*

"In general, therefore, as the human remains of the last twenty thousand years are unearthed, it will be impossible clearly to distinguish the five original types. Study of such skeletal structures will disclose that mankind is now divided into approximately three classes:

"1. *The Caucasoid*—the Andite blend of the Nodite and Adamic stocks, further modified by primary and (some) secondary Sangik admixture and by considerable Andonic crossing. The Occidental white races, together with some Indian and Turanian peoples, are included in this group. The unifying factor in this division is the greater or lesser proportion of Andite inheritance.

"2. *The Mongoloid*—the primary Sangik type, including the original red, yellow, and blue races. The Chinese and Amerinds belong to this group. In Europe the Mongoloid type has been modified by secondary Sangik and Andonic mixture; still more by Andite infusion. The Malayan and other Indonesian peoples are included in this classification, though they contain a high percentage of secondary Sangik blood.

"3. *The Negroid*—the secondary Sangik type, which originally included the orange, green, and Indigo races. This is the type best illustrated by the Negro, and it will be found through Africa, India, and Indonesia wherever the secondary Sangik races located." P. 905.

6. There are no pure races in the world today.

"There are no pure races in the world today. The early and original evolutionary peoples of color have only two representative races persisting in the world, the yellow man and the black man; and even these two races are much admixed with the extinct colored peoples. While the so-called white race is predominantly descended from the ancient blue man, it is admixed more or less with all other races much as is the red man of the Americas." P. 919.

7. The three primary and the three secondary human races.

"Of the six colored Sangik races, three were primary and three were secondary. Though the primary races—blue, red, and yellow —were in many respects superior to the three secondary peoples, it should be remembered that these secondary races had many desirable traits which would have considerably enhanced the primary peoples if their better strains could have been absorbed." P. 919.

B. **Factors that influenced the development of civilization.**

1. **The effects of climatic and geologic changes on early migrations.**

   "It was the great climatic and geologic changes in northern Africa and western Asia that terminated the early migrations of the Adamites, barring them from Europe by the expanded Mediterranean and diverting the stream of migration north and east into Turkestan. By the time of the completion of these land elevations and associated climatic changes, about 15,000 B.C., civilization had settled down to a world-wide stalemate except for the cultural ferments and biologic reserves of the Andites still confined by mountains to the east in Asia and by the expanding forests in Europe to the west." P. 900.

2. **Climatic changes forced man to abandon hunting for herding and farming. Evolution may be slow, but it is terribly effective.**

   "Climatic evolution is now about to accomplish what all other efforts had failed to do, that is, to compel Eurasian man to abandon hunting for the more advanced callings of herding and farming. Evolution may be slow, but it is terribly effective." P. 900.

3. **The trader and explorer did more to advance historic civilization than all other influences combined.**

   "The traveling trader and the roving explorer did more to advance historic civilization than all other influences combined. Military conquests, colonization, and missionary enterprises fostered by the later religions were also factors in the spread of culture; but these were all secondary to the trading relations, which were ever accelerated by the rapidly developing arts and sciences of industry." P. 904.

PART V — *Anthropology*

SECTION SEVEN
THE DEVELOPMENT OF CIVILIZATION

"Civilization is a racial acquirement; it is not biologically inherent; hence must all children be reared in an environment of culture, while each succeeding generation of youth must receive anew its education. The superior qualities of civilization—scientific, philosophic, and religious—are not transmitted from one generation to another by direct inheritance. These cultural achievements are preserved only by the enlightened conservation of social inheritance." P. 763.

I. STEPS IN THE EVOLUTION OF CIVILIZATION

A. Socialization.

1. **Association became the price of survival.**
   "Association early became the price of survival. The lone man was helpless unless he bore a tribal mark which testified that he belonged to a group which would certainly avenge any assault made upon him. Even in the days of Cain it was fatal to go abroad alone without some mark of group association. Civilization has become man's insurance against violent death, while the premiums are paid by submission to society's numerous law demands.
   "Primitive society was thus founded on the reciprocity of necessity and on the enhanced safety of association. And human society has evolved in agelong cycles as a result of this isolation fear and by means of reluctant co-operation." P. 763.

2. **Primitive man early learned that organization and co-operation were essential to successful resolution of difficulties.**
   "Primitive human beings early learned that groups are vastly greater and stronger than the mere sum of their individual units. One hundred men united and working in unison can move a great stone; a score of well-trained guardians of the peace can restrain an angry mob. And so society was born, not of mere association of numbers, but rather as a result of the *organization* of intelligent co-operators. But co-operation is not a natural trait of man; he learns to co-operate first through fear and then later because he discovers it is most beneficial in meeting the difficulties of time and guarding against the supposed perils of eternity.
   "The peoples who thus early organized themselves into a primitive society became more successful in their attacks on nature as well as in defense against their fellows; they possessed greater survival possibilities; hence has civilization

steadily progressed on Urantia, notwithstanding its many setbacks. And it is only because of the enhancement of survival value in association that man's many blunders have thus far failed to stop or destroy human civilization." P. 763-4.

3. **Four factors which contributed to the association of human beings were food hunger, sex love, vanity, and fear.**
"The herd instinct in natural man is hardly sufficient to account for the development of such a social organization as now exists on Urantia. Though this innate gregarious propensity lies at the bottom of human society, much of man's sociability is an acquirement. Two great influences which contributed to the early association of human beings were food hunger and sex love; these instinctive urges man shares with the animal world. Two other emotions which drove human beings together and *held* them together were vanity and fear, more particularly ghost fear.

"History is but the record of man's agelong food struggle. *Primitive man only thought when he was hungry*; food saving was his first self-denial, self-discipline. With the growth of society, food hunger ceased to be the only incentive for mutual association. Numerous other sorts of hunger, the realization of various needs, all led to the closer association of mankind. But today society is top-heavy with the overgrowth of supposed human needs. Occidental civilization of the twentieth century groans wearily under the tremendous overload of luxury and the inordinate multiplication of human desires and longings. Modern society is enduring the strain of one of its most dangerous phases of far-flung interassociation and highly complicated interdependence.

"Hunger, vanity, and ghost fear were continuous in their social pressure, but sex gratification was transient and spasmodic. The sex urge alone did not impel primitive men and women to assume the heavy burdens of home maintenance. The early home was founded upon the sex restlessness of the male when deprived of frequent gratification and upon that devoted mother love of the human female, which in measure she shares with the females of all the higher animals. The presence of a helpless baby determined the early differentiation of male and female activities; the woman had to maintain a settled residence where she could cultivate the soil. And from earliest times, where woman was has always been regarded as the home.

PART V — *Anthropology*

"Woman thus early became indispensable to the evolving social scheme, not so much because of the fleeting sex passion as in consequence of *food requirement*; she was an essential partner in self-maintenance. She was a food provider, a beast of burden, and a companion who would stand great abuse without violent resentment, and in addition to all of these desirable traits, she was an everpresent means of sex gratification." P. 765.

"If vanity be enlarged to cover pride, ambition, and honor, then we may discern not only how these propensities contribute to the formation of human associations, but how they also hold men together, since such emotions are futile without an audience to parade before. Soon vanity associated with itself other emotions and impulses which required a social arena wherein they might exhibit and gratify themselves. This group of emotions gave origin to the early beginnings of all art, ceremonial, and all forms of sportive games and contests." P. 765.

"Probably the greatest single factor in the evolution of human society was the ghost dream. Although most dreams greatly perturbed the primitive mind, the ghost dream actually terrorized early men, driving these superstitious dreamers into each other's arms in willing and earnest association for mutual protection against the vague and unseen imaginary dangers of the spirit world. The ghost dream was one of the earliest appearing differences between the animal and human types of mind. Animals do not visualize survival after death." P. 766.

4. **Help from superhuman sources is necessary to keep the associations built up through hunger, love, vanity, and fear.**

"Hunger and love drove men together; vanity and ghost fear held them together. But these emotions alone, without the influence of peace-promoting revelations, are unable to endure the strain of the suspicions and irritations of human interassociations. Without help from superhuman sources the strain of society breaks down upon reaching certain limits, and these very influences of social mobilization—hunger, love, vanity, and fear—conspire to plunge mankind into war and bloodshed.

"The peace tendency of the human race is not a natural endowment; it is derived from the teachings of revealed religion, from the accumulated experience of the progressive races, but more especially from the teachings of Jesus, the Prince of Peace." P. 766.

5. **Though early man was a slave to custom or usage, custom has been the thread of continuity which held civilization together.**

"Prior to the liberating and liberalizing instruction of the Dalamatia teachers, ancient man was held a helpless victim of the ritual of the mores; the primitive savage was hedged about by an endless ceremonial. Everything he did from the time of awakening in the morning to the moment he fell asleep in his cave at night had to be done just so—in accordance with the folkways of the tribe. He was a slave to the tyranny of usage; his life contained nothing free, spontaneous, or original. There was no natural progress toward a higher mental, moral, or social existence.

"Early man was mightily gripped by custom; the savage was a veritable slave to usage; but there have arisen ever and anon those variations from type who have dared to inaugurate new ways of thinking and improved methods of living. Nevertheless, the inertia of primitive man constitutes the biologic safety brake against precipitation too suddenly into the ruinous maladjustment of a too rapidly advancing civilization.

"But these customs are not an unmitigated evil; their evolution should continue. It is nearly fatal to the continuance of civilization to undertake their wholesale modification by radical revolution. Custom has been the thread of continuity which has held civilization together. The path of human history is strewn with the remnants of discarded customs and obsolete social practices; but no civilization has endured which abandoned its mores except for the adoption of better and more fit customs.

"The survival of a society depends chiefly on the progressive evolution of its mores. The process of custom evolution grows out of the desire for experimentation; new ideas are put forward-competition ensues. A progressing civilization embraces the progressive idea and endures; time and circumstance finally select the fitter group for survival. But this does not mean that each separate and isolated change in the composition of human society has been for the better. No! indeed no! for there have been many, many retrogressions in the long forward struggle of Urantia civilization." P. 767.

6. **In the Eastern Hemisphere there were four great steps in the forward march of civilization.**

"The earliest human cultures arose along the rivers of the Eastern Hemisphere, and there were four great steps in the forward march of civilization. They were:

"1. *The collection stage.* Food coercion, hunger, led to the first form of industrial organization, the primitive food-gathering lines. Sometimes such a line of hunger march would be ten miles long as it passed over the land gleaning food. This was the primitive nomadic stage of culture and is the mode of life now followed by the African Bushmen.

"2. *The hunting stage.* The invention of weapon tools enabled man to become a hunter and thus to gain considerable freedom from food slavery. A thoughtful Andonite who had severely bruised his fist in a serious combat rediscovered the idea of using a long stick for his arm and a piece of hard flint, bound on the end with sinews, for his fist. Many tribes made independent discoveries of this sort, and these various forms of hammers represented one of the great forward steps in human civilization. Today some Australian natives have progressed little beyond this stage.

"The blue men became expert hunters and trappers; by fencing the rivers they caught fish in great numbers, drying the surplus for winter use. Many forms of ingenious snares and traps were employed in catching game, but the more primitive races did not hunt the larger animals.

"3. *The pastoral stage.* This phase of civilization was made possible by the domestication of animals. The Arabs and the natives of Africa are among the more recent pastoral peoples.

"Pastoral living afforded further relief from food slavery; man learned to live on the interest of his capital, the increase in his flocks; and this provided more leisure for culture and progress.

"Prepastoral society was one of sex co-operation, but the spread of animal husbandry reduced women to the depths of social slavery. In earlier times it was man's duty to secure the animal food, woman's business to provide the vegetable edibles. Therefore, when man entered the pastoral era of his existence, woman's dignity fell greatly. She must still toil to produce the vegetable necessities of life, whereas the man need only go to his herds to provide an abundance of animal food. Man thus became relatively independent of woman; throughout the entire pastoral age woman's status steadily declined. By the close of this era she had become scarcely more than a human animal, consigned to work and to bear human offspring, much as the animals of the herd were expected to labor and bring forth young. The men of the pastoral ages had great love for their cattle; all the more pity they could not have developed a deeper affection for their wives.

"4. *The agricultural stage.* This era was brought about by the domestication of plants, and it represents the highest type of material civilization. Both Caligastia and Adam endeavored to teach horticulture and agriculture. Adam and Eve were gardeners, not shepherds, and gardening was an advanced culture in those days. The growing of plants exerts an ennobling influence on all races of mankind.

"Agriculture more than quadrupled the land-man ratio of the world. It may be combined with the pastoral pursuits of the former cultural stage. When the three stages overlap, men hunt and women till the soil.

"There has always been friction between the herders and the tillers of the soil. The hunter and herder were militant, warlike; the agriculturist is a more peace-loving type. Association with animals suggests struggle and force; association with plants instills patience, quiet, and peace. Agriculture and industrialism are the activities of peace. But the weakness of both, as world social activities, is that they lack excitement and adventure.

"Human society has evolved from the hunting stage through that of the herders to the territorial stage of agriculture. And each stage of this progressive civilization was accompanied by less and less of nomadism; more and more man began to live at home.

"And now is industry supplementing agriculture, with consequently increased urbanization and multiplication of nonagricultural groups of citizenship classes. But an industrial era cannot hope to survive if its leaders fail to recognize that even the highest social developments must ever rest upon a sound agricultural basis." P. 768-9.

7. **The land-man ratio determined the value of human life.**
"Human society is controlled by a law which decrees that the population must vary directly in accordance with the land arts and inversely with a given standard of living. Throughout these early ages, even more than at present, the law of supply and demand as concerned men and land determined the estimated

PART V — *Anthropology*

value of both. During the times of plentiful land—unoccupied territory—the need for men was great, and therefore the value of human life was much enhanced; hence the loss of life was more horrifying. During periods of land scarcity and associated overpopulation, human life became comparatively cheapened so that war, famine, and pestilence were regarded with less concern.

"When the land yield is reduced or the population is increased, the inevitable struggle is renewed; the very worst traits of human nature are brought to the surface. The improvement of the land yield, the extension of the mechanical arts, and the reduction of population all tend to foster the development of the better side of human nature." P. 769-70.

8. **Overpopulation, though seldom a problem in the past, may become a test of the wisdom of Urantia rulers.**

"From a world standpoint, overpopulation has never been a serious problem in the past, but if war is lessened and science increasingly controls human diseases, it may become a serious problem in the near future. At such a time the great test of the wisdom of world leadership will present itself. Will Urantia rulers have the insight and courage to foster the multiplication of the average or stabilized human being instead of the extremes of the supernormal and the enormously increasing groups of the subnormal? The normal man should be fostered; he is the backbone of civilization and the source of the mutant geniuses of the race. The subnormal man should be kept under society's control; no more should be produced than are required to administer the lower levels of industry, those tasks requiring intelligence above the animal level but making such low-grade demands as to prove veritable slavery and bondage for the higher types of mankind." P. 770.

B. **Social institutions.**

1. **Man should control his institutions—not be controlled by them.**

"All human institutions minister to some social need, past or present, notwithstanding that their overdevelopment unfailingly detracts from the worthwhileness of the individual in that personality is overshadowed and initiative is diminished. Man should control his institutions rather than permit himself to be dominated by these creations of advancing civilization." P. 772.

2. **Primitive industry grew up as insurance against famine.**
   "Primitive industry slowly grew up as an insurance against the terrors of famine. Early in his existence man began to draw lessons from some of the animals that, during a harvest of plenty, store up food against the days of scarcity." P. 773.
3. **Poverty is man's natural estate. Wealth is derived from labor, knowledge, and organization.**
   "Before the dawn of early frugality and primitive industry the lot of the average tribe was one of destitution and real suffering. Early man had to compete with the whole animal world for his food. Competition-gravity ever pulls man down toward the beast level; poverty is his natural and tyrannical estate. Wealth is not a natural gift; it results from labor, knowledge, and organization." P. 773.
4. **The relation of capital to modern civilization.**
   "Though capital has tended to liberate man, it has greatly complicated his social and industrial organization. The abuse of capital by unfair capitalists does not destroy the fact that it is the basis of modern industrial society. Through capital and invention the present generation enjoys a higher degree of freedom than any that ever preceded it on earth. This is placed on record as a fact and not in justification of the many misuses of capital by thoughtless and selfish custodians." P. 777.
5. **The evolution of human government.**
   "Every human institution had a beginning, and civil government is a product of progressive evolution just as much as are marriage, industry, and religion. From the early clans and primitive tribes there gradually developed the successive orders of human government which have come and gone right on down to those forms of social and civil regulation that characterize the second third of the twentieth century." P. 788.
6. **Only very primitive and very advanced civilizations are free from those human inequalities which create social classes.**
   "The mental and physical inequality of human beings insures that social classes will appear. The only worlds without social strata are the most primitive and the most advanced. A dawning civilization has not yet begun the differentiation of social levels, while a world settled in light and life has largely effaced these divisions of mankind, which are so characteristic of all intermediate evolutionary stages." P. 792.

PART V — *Anthropology*

7. **Profit-motivated economy is doomed unless it is augmented by service motives. Exclusive self-service motives are incompatible with the teachings of Jesus.**
"Present-day profit-motivated economics is doomed unless profit motives can be augmented by service motives. Ruthless competition based on narrow-minded self-interest is ultimately destructive of even those things which it seeks to maintain. Exclusive and selfserving profit motivation is incompatible with Christian ideals-much more incompatible with the teachings of Jesus." P. 805.

8. **In economics, profit motivation is to service motivation what fear is to love in religion.**
"In economics, profit motivation is to service motivation what fear is to love in religion. But the profit motive must not be suddenly destroyed or removed; it keeps many otherwise slothful mortals hard at work. It is not necessary, however, that this social energy arouser be forever selfish in its objectives." P. 805.

9. **Profit-making can only be transcended by wisdom, brotherhood, and spiritual attainment.**
"The profit motive of economic activities is altogether base and wholly unworthy of an advanced order of society; nevertheless, it is an indispensable factor throughout the earlier phases of civilization. Profit motivation must not be taken away from men until they have firmly possessed themselves of superior types of nonprofit motives for economic striving and social serving—the transcendent urges of superlative wisdom, intriguing brotherhood, and excellency of spiritual attainment." P. 805.

C. **Fire and animals.**

1. **Fire is a civilizing influence.**
"Fire was a great civilizer, providing man with his first means of being altruistic without loss by enabling him to give live coals to a neighbor without depriving himself. The household fire, which was attended by the mother or eldest daughter, was the first educator, requiring watchfulness and dependability. The early home was not a building but the family gathered about the fire, the family hearth. When a son founded a new home, he carried a firebrand from the family hearth." P. 777.

2. **Fire, along with water and food, contributed to early human foresight.**

   "The first human foresight was directed toward the preservation of fire, water, and food. But primitive man was a natural-born gambler; he always wanted to get something for nothing, and all too often during these early times the success which accrued from patient practice was attributed to charms. Magic was slow to give way before foresight, self-denial, and industry." P. 773.

3. **The part played by animals in advancing civilization.**

   "To start with, the entire animal world was man's enemy; human beings had to learn to protect themselves from the beasts. First, man ate the animals but later learned to domesticate and make them serve him.

   "The domestication of animals came about accidentally. The savage would hunt herds much as the American Indians hunted the bison. By surrounding the herd they could keep control of the animals, thus being able to kill them as they were required for food. Later, corrals were constructed, and entire herds would be captured." P. 778.

D. **War and slavery.**

   1. **War is natural to evolving man; peace is the yardstick measuring civilization.**

      "War is the natural state and heritage of evolving man; peace is the social yardstick measuring civilization's advancement. Before the partial socialization of the advancing races man was exceedingly individualistic, extremely suspicious, and unbelievably quarrelsome. Violence is the law of nature, hostility the automatic reaction of the children of nature, while war is but these same activities carried on collectively. And wherever and whenever the fabric of civilization becomes stressed by the complications of society's advancement, there is always an immediate and ruinous reversion to these early methods of violent adjustment of the irritations of human interassociations." P. 783.

   2. **The gains and losses of war. While curing some social evils, war sometimes kills the patient.**

      "In past ages a fierce war would institute social changes and facilitate the adoption of new ideas such as would not have occurred naturally in ten thousand years. The terrible price paid for these certain war advantages was that society was temporarily thrown back into savagery; civilized reason had to abdicate. War is strong medicine, very costly and most dangerous; while often curative of certain social disorders, it sometimes kills the patient, destroys the society." P. 785.

3. **The social gains of war.**
"The constant necessity for national defense creates many new and advanced social adjustments. Society, today, enjoys the benefit of a long list of useful innovations which were at first wholly military and is even indebted to war for the dance, one of the early forms of which was a military drill.
"War has had a social value to past civilizations because it:
"1. Imposed discipline, enforced co-operation.
"2. Put a premium on fortitude and courage.
"3. Fostered and solidified nationalism.
"4. Destroyed weak and unfit peoples.
"5. Dissolved the illusion of primitive equality and selectively stratified society." P. 785.

4. **Ancient wars selected leaders. Today, science and industry must do this.**
"But even in passing, war should be honored as the school of experience which compelled a race of arrogant individualists to submit themselves to highly concentrated authority—a chief executive. Old-fashioned war did select the innately great men for leadership, but modern war no longer does this. To discover leaders society must now turn to the conquests of peace: industry, science, and social achievement." P. 786.

5. **Enslavement of war captives was a forward and merciful advance in civilization.**
"Enslavement was a forward step in the merciful treatment of war captives. The ambush of Ai, with the wholesale slaughter of men, women, and children, only the king being saved to gratify the conqueror's vanity, is a faithful picture of the barbaric slaughter practiced by even supposedly civilized peoples. The raid upon Og, the king of Bashan, was equally brutal and effective. The Hebrews 'utterly destroyed' their enemies, taking all their property as spoils. They put all cities under tribute on pain of the 'destruction of all males.' But many of the contemporary tribes, those having less tribal egotism, had long since begun to practice the adoption of superior captives." P. 779.

6. **The contribution of slavery to advancing civilization.**
"Slavery was an indispensable link in the chain of human civilization. It was the bridge over which society passed from

chaos and indolence to order and civilized activities; it compelled backward and lazy peoples to work and thus provide wealth and leisure for the social advancement of their superiors." P. 779.

E. **Communism and private ownership.**

1. **The pros and cons of primitive communism.**

   "While primitive society was virtually communal, primitive man did not adhere to the modern doctrines of communism. The communism of these early times was not a mere theory or social doctrine; it was a simple and practical automatic adjustment. Communism prevented pauperism and want; begging and prostitution were almost unknown among these ancient tribes.

   "Primitive communism did not especially level men down, nor did it exalt mediocrity, but it did put a premium on inactivity and idleness, and it did stifle industry and destroy ambition. Communism was indispensable scaffolding in the growth of primitive society, but it gave way to the evolution of a higher social order because it ran counter to four strong human proclivities." P. 780.

2. **Private ownership followed the failure of communism. And now, following slavery, comes the machine age.**

   "Private ownership brought increased liberty and enhanced stability; but private ownership of land was given social sanction only after communal control and direction had failed, and it was soon followed by a succession of slaves, serfs, and landless classes. But improved machinery is gradually setting men free from slavish toil." P. 782.

3. **The advantages of modern civilization have grown up around the private ownership of property.**

   "The right to property is not absolute; it is purely social. But all government, law, order, civil rights, social liberties, conventions, peace, and happiness, as they are enjoyed by modern peoples, have grown up around the private ownership of property." P. 782.

4. **Present social order is not divine, but if we change—we should be sure to change for the better.**

   "The present social order is not necessarily right—not divine or sacred—but mankind will do well to move slowly in making changes. That which you have is vastly better than any system known to your ancestors. Make certain that when you change the social order you change for the better. Do not be persuaded to experiment with the discarded formulas of your forefathers. Go forward, not backward! Let evolution proceed! Do not take a backward step." P. 782.

F. Human rights—justice.

1. **Nature confers no rights on man—only life.**
    "Nature confers no rights on man, only life and a world in which to live it. Nature does not even confer the right to live, as might be deduced by considering what would likely happen if an unarmed man met a hungry tiger face to face in the primitive forest. Society's prime gift to man is security." P. 793.

2. **Natural justice is a myth. Justice, as conceived by man, is a matter of progressive evolution.**
    "Natural justice is a man-made theory; it is not a reality. In nature, justice is purely theoretic, wholly a fiction. Nature provides but one kind of justice—inevitable conformity of results to causes.
    "Justice, as conceived by man, means getting one's rights and has, therefore, been a matter of progressive evolution. The concept of justice may well be constitutive in a spirit-endowed mind, but it does not spring full-fledgedly into existence on the worlds of space." P. 794.

3. **Evolution of justice.**
    "Justice was thus first meted out by the family, then by the clan, and later on by the tribe. The administration of true justice dates from the taking of revenge from private and kin groups and lodging it in the hands of the social group, the state." P. 796.
    "But as time passed, it was learned that the severity of the punishment was not so valuable a deterrent to crime as was its certainty and swiftness." P. 796.

4. **Evolution of laws and courts.**
    "It is just as difficult to draw sharp distinctions between mores and laws as to indicate exactly when, at the dawning, night is succeeded by day. Mores are laws and police regulations in the making. When long established, the undefined mores tend to crystallize into precise laws, concrete regulations, and well-defined social conventions.
    "Law is always at first negative and prohibitive; in advancing

civilizations it becomes increasingly positive and directive. Early society operated negatively, granting the individual the right to live by imposing upon all others the command, 'you shall not kill.' Every grant of rights or liberty to the individual involves curtailment of the liberties of all others, and this is effected by the taboo, primitive law. The whole idea of the taboo is inherently negative, for primitive society was wholly negative in its organization, and the early administration of justice consisted in the enforcement of the taboos. But originally these laws applied only to fellow tribesmen, as is illustrated by the later-day Hebrews, who had a different code of ethics for dealing with the gentiles." P. 796.

"Law is a codified record of long human experience, public opinion crystallized and legalized. The mores were the raw material of accumulated experience out of which later ruling minds formulated the written laws. The ancient judge had no laws. When he handed down a decision, he simply said, 'It is the custom.'" P. 797.

"Property disputes were handled in many ways, such as:

"1. By destroying the disputed property.

"2. By force—the contestants fought it out.

"3. By arbitration—a third party decided.

"4. By appeal to the elders—later to the courts." P. 797.

"The whole idea of primitive justice was not so much to be fair as to dispose of the contest and thus prevent public disorder and private violence. But primitive man did not so much resent what would now be regarded as an injustice; it was taken for granted that those who had power would use it selfishly. Nevertheless, the status of any civilization may be very accurately determined by the thoroughness and equity of its courts and by the integrity of its judges." P. 797.

5. **The state is the net gain of war and suffering. It was automatic in origin.**

"The state is a useful evolution of civilization; it represents society's net gain from the ravages and sufferings of war. Even statecraft is merely the accumulated technique for adjusting the competitive contest of force between the struggling tribes and nations.

"The modern state is the institution which survived in the long struggle for group power. Superior power eventually prevailed, and it produced a creature of fact—the state—together with the moral myth of the absolute obligation of the citizen to live and die for the state. But the state is not of divine genesis; it was not even produced by volitionally intelligent human action; it is purely an evolutionary institution and was wholly automatic in origin." P. 800.

6. **Social idealists should protect themselves against those who would exploit or destroy their civilization.**

    "The appearance of genuine brotherhood signifies that a social order has arrived in which all men delight in bearing one another's burdens; they actually desire to practice the golden rule. But such an ideal society cannot be realized when either the weak or the wicked lie in wait to take unfair and unholy advantage of those who are chiefly actuated by devotion to the service of truth, beauty, and goodness. In such a situation only one course is practical: The 'golden rulers' may establish a progressive society in which they live according to their ideals while maintaining an adequate defense against their benighted fellows who might seek either to exploit their pacific predilections or to destroy their advancing civilization." P. 804.

7. **The test of idealism—having power to resist aggression, but refusing to use such power for self-aggrandizement.**

    "Idealism can never survive on an evolving planet if the idealists in each generation permit themselves to be exterminated by the baser orders of humanity. And here is the great test of idealism: Can an advanced society maintain that military preparedness which renders it secure from all attack by its war-loving neighbors without yielding to the temptation to employ this military strength in offensive operations against other peoples for purposes of selfish gain or national aggrandizement? National survival demands preparedness, and religious idealism alone can prevent the prostitution of preparedness into aggression. Only love, brotherhood, can prevent the strong from oppressing the weak." P. 804.

G. Marriage.

"Marriage—mating—grows out of bisexuality. Marriage is man's reactional adjustment to such bisexuality, while the family life is the sum total resulting from all such evolutionary and adaptative adjustments. Marriage is enduring; it is not inherent in biologic evolution, but it is the basis of all social evolution and is therefore certain of continued existence in some form. Marriage has given mankind the home, and the home is the crowning glory of the whole long and arduous evolutionary struggle." P. 913.

1. **Marriage represents the effort of society to control the sex urge of self-perpetuation.**

    "As an institution, marriage, from its early beginnings down to modern times, pictures the social evolution of the biologic propensity for self-perpetuation. The perpetuation of the evolving human species is made certain by the presence of this racial mating impulse, an urge which is loosely called sex attraction. This great biologic urge becomes the impulse hub for all sorts of associated instincts, emotions, and usages—physical, intellectual, moral, and social." P. 914.

2. **With advancing civilization, the sex drive transcends the food urge and must be subjected to social control.**

    "With the savage, the food supply was the impelling motivation, but when civilization insures plentiful food, the sex urge many times becomes a dominant impulse and therefore ever stands in need of social regulation. In animals, instinctive periodicity checks the mating propensity, but since man is so largely a self-controlled being, sex desire is not altogether periodic; therefore does it become necessary for society to impose self-control upon the individual." P. 914.

3. **Nature insists on reproduction, but the problems of sex control must be solved by society.**

    "The story of the evolution of marriage is simply the history of sex control through the pressure of social, religious, and civil restrictions. Nature hardly recognizes individuals; it takes no cognizance of so-called morals; it is only and exclusively interested in the reproduction of the species. Nature compellingly insists on reproduction but indifferently leaves the consequential problems to be solved by society, thus creating an everpresent and major problem for evolutionary mankind. This social conflict consists in the unending war between basic instincts and evolving ethics." P. 914.

4. **Marriage is society's response to the biologic urge to reproduction.**

    "Marriage is the institutional response of the social organism to the ever-present biologic tension of man's unremitting urge to reproduction—self-propagation. Mating is universally natural, and as society evolved from the simple to the complex, there was a corresponding evolution of the mating mores, the genesis of the marital institution. Wherever social evolution has progressed to the stage at which mores are generated, marriage will be found as an evolving institution." P. 915.

5 **In primitive times marriage was the price of social standing. From age to age the purpose of marriage has been regarded differently.**

"In primitive times marriage was the price of social standing; the possession of a wife was a badge of distinction. The savage looked upon his wedding day as marking his entrance upon responsibility and manhood. In one age, marriage has been looked upon as a social duty; in another, as a religious obligation; and in still another, as a political requirement to provide citizens for the state." P. 915.

6. **Primitive marriage was an investment; it involved an exchange of property.**

"Primitive marriage was an investment, an economic speculation; it was more a matter of business than an affair of flirtation. The ancients married for the advantage and welfare of the group; wherefore their marriages were planned and arranged by the group, their parents and elders. And that the property mores were effective in stabilizing the marriage institution is borne out by the fact that marriage was more permanent among the early tribes than it is among many modern peoples.

"As civilization advanced and private property gained further recognition in the mores, stealing became the great crime. Adultery was recognized as a form of stealing, an infringement of the husband's property rights; it is not therefore specifically mentioned in the earlier codes and mores. Woman started out as the property of her father, who transferred his title to her husband, and all legalized sex relations grew out of these pre-existent property rights. The Old Testament deals with women as a form of property; the Koran teaches their inferiority. Man had the right to lend his wife to a friend or guest, and this custom still obtains among certain peoples." P. 917.

7. **Though inbreeding sometimes resulted in the upbuilding of strong tribes, the frequent bad results led primitive man to formulate taboos against in-marriage.**

"While the inbreeding of good stock sometimes resulted in the upbuilding of strong tribes, the spectacular cases of the bad results of the inbreeding of hereditary defectives more forcibly impressed the mind of man, with the result that the advancing mores increasingly formulated taboos against all marriages among near relatives." P. 918.

"Many tribes finally forbade marriages within the clan; others limited mating to certain castes. The taboo against marriage with a woman of one's own totem gave impetus to the custom of stealing women from neighboring tribes. Later on, marriages were regulated more in accordance with territorial residence than with kinship. There were many steps in the evolution of in-marriage into the modern practice of outmarriage. Even after the taboo rested upon in-marriages for the common people, chiefs and kings were permitted to marry those of close kin in order to keep the royal blood concentrated and pure. The mores have usually permitted sovereign rulers certain licenses in sex matters." P. 919.

8. **Marriage is society's regulator of sex relations and inheritance.**

"Marriage is society's mechanism designed to regulate and control those many human relations which arise out of the physical fact of bisexuality. As such an institution, marriage functions in two directions:

"1. In the regulation of personal sex relations.
"2. In the regulation of descent, inheritance, succession, and social order, this being its older and original function." P. 922.

9. **The wedding ceremony resulted from the fact that marriage was a community affair. The luck element culminated in church weddings.**

"The wedding ceremony grew out of the fact that marriage was originally a community affair, not just the culmination of a decision of two individuals. Mating was of group concern as well as a personal function." P. 924.

"The luck element, that in spite of all premarital tests certain marriages turned out bad, led primitive man to seek insurance protection against marriage failure; led him to go in quest of priests and magic. And this movement culminated directly in modern church weddings. But for a long time marriage was generally recognized as consisting in the decisions of the contracting parents—later of the pair—while for the last five hundred years church and state have assumed jurisdiction and now presume to make pronouncements of marriage." P. 925.

PART V — *Anthropology*

10. **Marriage progressed from the promiscuity of the herd to group marriages and then to polygamy.**

    "The next step in mating evolution was the *group marriage*. This communal phase of marriage had to intervene in the unfolding of family life because the marriage mores were not yet strong enough to make pair associations permanent. The brother and sister marriages belonged to this group; five brothers of one family would marry five sisters of another. All over the world the looser forms of communal marriage gradually evolved into various types of group marriage. And these group associations were largely regulated by the totem mores. Family life slowly and surely developed because sex and marriage regulation favored the survival of the tribe itself by insuring the survival of larger numbers of children.

    "Group marriages gradually gave way before the emerging practices of polygamy—polygyny and polyandry—among the more advanced tribes. But polyandry was never general, being usually limited to queens and rich women; furthermore, it was customarily a family affair, one wife for several brothers. Caste and economic restrictions sometimes made it necessary for several men to content themselves with one wife. Even then, the woman would marry only one, the others being loosely tolerated as 'uncles' of the joint progeny." P. 925-6.

11. **Monogamy is the ideal of sex life, but it demands self-control.**

    "Monogamy always has been, now is, and forever will be the idealistic goal of human sex evolution. This ideal of true pair marriage entails self-denial, and therefore does it so often fail just because one or both of the contracting parties are deficient in that acme of all human virtues, rugged self-control." P. 927.

12. **Monogamy is the yardstick which measures the advance of social civilization. It fosters the best in marriage for both parents and children.**

    "Monogamy is the yardstick which measures the advance of social civilization as distinguished from purely biologic evolution. Monogamy is not necessarily biologic or natural, but it is indispensable to the immediate maintenance and further development of social civilization. It contributes to a delicacy of sentiment, a refinement of moral character, and a spiritual growth which are utterly impossible in polygamy. A woman never can become an ideal mother when she is all the while compelled to engage in rivalry for her husband's affections.

"Pair marriage favors and fosters that intimate understanding and effective co-operation which is best for parental happiness, child welfare, and social efficiency. Marriage, which began in crude coercion, is gradually evolving into a magnificent institution of self-culture, self-control, self-expression, and self-perpetuation." P. 927-8.

13. **Marriage is man's most exalted institution, but it should not be considered a sacrament. Marriage is not consummated by divine action.**

"Marriage which culminates in the home is indeed man's most exalted institution, but it is essentially human; it should never have been called a sacrament. The Sethite priests made marriage a religious ritual; but for thousands of years after Eden, mating continued as a purely social and civil institution.

"The likening of human associations to divine associations is most unfortunate. The union of husband and wife in the marriage-home relationship is a material function of the mortals of the evolutionary worlds. True, indeed, much spiritual progress may accrue consequent upon the sincere human efforts of husband and wife to progress, but this does not mean that marriage is necessarily sacred. Spiritual progress is attendant upon sincere application to other avenues of human endeavor." P. 929.

"It is also unfortunate that certain groups of mortals have conceived of marriage as being consummated by divine action. Such beliefs lead directly to the concept of the indissolubility of the marital state regardless of the circumstances or wishes of the contracting parties. But the very fact of marriage dissolution itself indicates that Deity is not a conjoining party to such unions. If God has once joined any two things or persons together, they will remain thus joined until such a time as the divine will decrees their separation. But, regarding marriage, which is a human institution, who shall presume to sit in judgment, to say which marriages are unions that might be approved by the universe supervisors in contrast with those which are purely human in nature and origin?" P. 929.

14. **Marriage was the result of the attachment of primitive woman to her offspring and of food hunger of primitive man.**

"Marriage was not founded on sex relations; they were incidental thereto. Marriage was not needed by primitive man, who indulged his sex appetite freely without encumbering himself with the responsibilities of wife, children, and home.

"Woman, because of physical and emotional attachment to her offspring, is dependent on co-operation with the male, and this urges her into the sheltering protection of marriage. But no direct biologic urge led man into marriage—much less held him in. It was not love that made marriage attractive to man, but food hunger which first attracted savage man to woman and the primitive shelter shared by her children." P. 931.

15. The mother-child association was the nucleus from which marriage and the home sprang.

"While the mother-child association is neither marriage nor home, it was the nucleus from which both sprang. The great advance in the evolution of mating came when these temporary partnerships lasted long enough to rear the resultant offspring, for that was homemaking." P. 932.

16. Chances of survival were improved by the male-female partnership.

"Regardless of the antagonisms of these early pairs, notwithstanding the looseness of the association, the chances for survival were greatly improved by these male-female partnerships. A man and a woman, co-operating, even aside from family and offspring, are vastly superior in most ways to either two men or two women. This pairing of the sexes enhanced survival and was the very beginning of human society. The sex division of labor also made for comfort and increased happiness." P. 932.

17. The change from the mother-family to the father-family was a radical readjustment that led to improved social improvement.

"With the passing of the hunter mores, when herding gave man control of the chief food supply, the mother-family came to a speedy end. It failed simply because it could not successfully compete with the newer father-family. Power lodged with the male relatives of the mother could not compete with power concentrated in the husband-father. Woman was not equal to the combined tasks of childbearing and of exercising continuous authority and increasing domestic power. The oncoming of wife stealing and later wife purchase hastened the passing of the mother-family.

"The stupendous change from the mother-family to the father-family is one of the most radical and complete right-about-face adjustments ever executed by the human race. This change led at once to greater social expression and increased family adventure." P. 933.

18. **Woman's status reflected the type of society and the degree of development of civilization. As man changed from hunter to herdsman, her status changed, but was improved when man became agriculturist.**

"It may be that the instinct of motherhood led woman into marriage, but it was man's superior strength, together with the influence of the mores, that virtually compelled her to remain in wedlock. Pastoral living tended to create a new system of mores, the patriarchal type of family life; and the basis of family unity under the herder and early agricultural mores was the unquestioned and arbitary authority of the father. All society, whether national or familial, passed through the stage of the autocratic authority of a patriarchal order." P. 933.

"But man was no more to blame for his low opinion of woman during past ages than was woman herself. She failed to get social recognition during primitive times because she did not function in an emergency; she was not a spectacular or crisis hero. Maternity was a distinct disability in the existence struggle; mother love handicapped women in the tribal defense." P. 934.

"Among the more advanced races, women are not so large or so strong as men. Woman, being the weaker, therefore became the more tactful; she early learned to trade upon her sex charms. She became more alert and conservative than man, though slightly less profound. Man was woman's superior on the battlefield and in the hunt; but at home woman has usually outgeneraled even the most primitive of men.

"The herdsman looked to his flocks for sustenance, but throughout these pastoral ages woman must still provide the vegetable food. Primitive man shunned the soil; it was altogether too peaceful, too unadventuresome. There was also an old superstition that women could raise better plants; they were mothers. In many backward tribes today, the men cook the meat, the women the vegetables, and when the primitive tribes of Australia are on the march, the women never attack game, while a man would not stoop to dig a root." P. 934.

"Woman's first liberation came when man consented to till the soil, consented to do what had theretofore been regarded as woman's work. It was a great step forward when male captives were no longer killed but were enslaved as agriculturists. This

PART V — *Anthropology*

brought about the liberation of woman so that she could devote more time to homemaking and child culture.

"The provision of milk for the young led to earlier weaning of babies, hence to the bearing of more children by the mothers thus relieved of their sometimes temporary barrenness, while the use of cow's milk and goat's milk greatly reduced infant mortality. Before the herding stage of society, mothers used to nurse their babies until they were four and five years old.

"Decreasing primitive warfare greatly lessened the disparity between the division of labor based on sex. But women still had to do the real work while men did picket duty. No camp or village could be left unguarded day or night, but even this task was alleviated by the domestication of the dog. In general, the coming of agriculture has enhanced woman's prestige and social standing; at least this was true up to the time man himself turned agriculturist. And as soon as man addressed himself to the tilling of the soil, there immediately ensued great improvement in methods of agriculture, extending on down through successive generations. In hunting and war man had learned the value of organization, and he introduced these techniques into industry and later, when taking over much of woman's work, greatly improved on her loose methods of labor." P. 934.

"Generally speaking, during any age woman's status is a fair criterion of the evolutionary progress of marriage as a social institution, while the progress of marriage itself is a reasonably accurate gauge registering the advances of human civilization.

"Woman's status has always been a social paradox; she has always been a shrewd manager of men; she has always capitalized man's stronger sex urge for her own interests and to her own advancement. By trading subtly upon her sex charms, she has often been able to exercise dominant power over man, even when held by him in abject slavery." P. 935.

"Childbearing was once generally looked upon as rendering a woman dangerous and unclean. And many tribal mores decreed that a mother must undergo extensive purification ceremonies subsequent to the birth of a child. Except among those groups where the husband participated in the lying-in, the expectant mother was shunned, left alone. The ancients even avoided having a child born in the house. Finally, the old women were permitted to attend the mother during labor, and this practice gave origin to the profession of midwifery. During labor, scores of foolish things were said and done in an effort to facilitate delivery. It was the custom to sprinkle the newborn with holy water to prevent ghost interference." P. 935.

"A great advance was made when a man was denied the right to kill his wife at will. Likewise, it was a forward step when a woman could own the wedding gifts. Later, she gained the legal right to own, control, and even dispose of property, but she was long deprived of the right to hold office in either church or state. Woman has always been treated more or less as property, right up to and in the twentieth century after Christ. She has not yet gained world-wide freedom from seclusion under man's control. Even among advanced peoples, man's attempt to protect woman has always been a tacit assertion of superiority.

"But primitive women did not pity themselves as their more recently liberated sisters are wont to do. They were, after all, fairly happy and contented; they did not dare to envision a better or different mode of existence." P. 936.

19. **The improvement of woman's status was an unplanned episode of social evolution. Science, not religion, really emancipated woman.**

"The modern idea of sex equality is beautiful and worthy of an expanding civilization, but it is not found in nature. When might is right, man lords it over woman; when more justice, peace, and fairness prevail, she gradually emerges from slavery and obscurity. Woman's social position has generally varied inversely with the degree of militarism in any nation or age.

"But man did not consciously nor intentionally seize woman's rights and then gradually and grudgingly give them back to her; all this was an unconscious and unplanned episode of social evolution. When the time really came for woman to enjoy added rights, she got them, and all quite regardless of man's conscious attitude. Slowly but surely the mores change so as to provide for those social adjustments which are a part of the persistent evolution of civilization. The advancing mores slowly provided increasingly better treatment for females; those tribes which persisted in cruelty to them did not survive." P. 936-7.

"Science, not religion, really emancipated woman; it was the modern factory which largely set her free from the confines of the home. Man's physical abilities became no longer a vital essential in the new maintenance mechanism; science so changed the conditions of living that man power was no longer so superior to woman power.

"These changes have tended toward woman's liberation from domestic slavery and have brought about such a modification of her status that she now enjoys a degree of personal liberty and sex determination that practically equals man's. Once a woman's value consisted in her food-producing ability, but invention and wealth have enabled her to create a new world in which to function—spheres of grace and charm. Thus has industry won its unconscious and unintended fight for woman's social and economic emancipation. And again has evolution succeeded in doing what even revelation failed to accomplish." P. 937.

"In the ideals of pair marriage, woman has finally won recognition, dignity, independence, equality, and education; but will she prove worthy of all this new and unprecedented accomplishment? Will modern woman respond to this great achievement of social liberation with idleness, indifference, barrenness, and infidelity? Today, in the twentieth century, woman is undergoing the crucial test of her long world existence!" P. 937.

20. **The partnership of man and woman.**

"The reproductive urge unfailingly brings men and women together for self-perpetuation but, alone, does not insure their remaining together in mutual co-operation—the founding of a home.

"Every successful human institution embraces antagonisms of personal interest which have been adjusted to practical working harmony, and homemaking is no exception. Marriage, the basis of home building, is the highest manifestation of that antagonistic cooperation which so often characterizes the contacts of nature and society. The conflict is inevitable. Mating is inherent; it is natural. But marriage is not biologic; it is sociologic. Passion insures that man and woman will come together, but the weaker parental instinct and the social mores hold them together." P. 938.

"The differences of nature, reaction, viewpoint, and thinking between men and women, far from occasioning concern, should be regarded as highly beneficial to mankind, both individually and collectively. Many orders of universe creatures are created in dual phases of personality manifestation. Among mortals, Material Sons, and midsoniters, this difference is described as male and female; among seraphim, cherubim, and Morontia Companions, it has been denominated positive or aggressive and negative or retiring. Such dual associations greatly multiply versatility and overcome inherent limitations, even as do certain triune associations in the Paradise-Havona system." P. 938.

"Men and women need each other in their morontial and spiritual as well as in their mortal careers. The differences in viewpoint between male and female persist even beyond the first life and throughout the local and superuniverse ascensions. And even in Havona, the pilgrims who were once men and women will still be aiding each other in the Paradise ascent. Never, even in the Corps of the Finality, will the creature metamorphose so far as to obliterate the personality trends that humans call male and female; always will these two basic variations of humankind continue to intrigue, stimulate, encourage, and assist each other; always will they be mutually dependent on co-operation in the solution of perplexing universe problems and in the overcoming of manifold cosmic difficulties." P. 939.

21. **The great threat against marriage is the rising tide of selfgratification.**

"The great threat against family life is the menacing rising tide of self-gratification, the modern pleasure mania. The prime incentive to marriage used to be economic; sex attraction was secondary. Marriage, founded on self-maintenance, led to self-perpetuation and concomitantly provided one of the most desirable forms of self-gratification. It is the only institution of human society which embraces all three of the great incentives for living." P. 942.

22. **The pleasure mania threatens all of our social institutions especially the home.**

"Originally, property was the basic institution of self-maintenance, while marriage functioned as the unique institution of self-perpetuation. Although food satisfaction, play, and humor, along with periodic sex indulgence, were means of self-gratification, it remains a fact that the evolving mores have failed to build any distinct institution of self-gratification. And it is due to this failure to evolve specialized techniques of pleasurable enjoyment that all human institutions are so completely shot through with this pleasure pursuit. Property accumulation is becoming an instrument for augmenting all forms of self-gratification, while marriage is often viewed only as a means of pleasure. And this overindulgence, this widely spread pleasure mania, now constitutes the greatest threat that has ever been leveled at the social evolutionary institution of family life, the home." P. 942.

23. **The chief pleasures should be found in play, humor, and food—not in sex gratification.**
"The violet race introduced a new and only imperfectly realized characteristic into the experience of humankind—the play instinct coupled with the sense of humor. It was there in measure in the Sangiks and Andonites, but the Adamic strain elevated this primitive propensity into the *potential of pleasure*, a new and glorified form of self-gratification. The basic type of self-gratification, aside from appeasing hunger, is sex gratification, and this form of sensual pleasure was enormously heightened by the blending of the Sangiks and the Andites." P. 942.

H. **Religion and fear.**
1. **Fear and ignorance in relation to worship.**
"At one time or another mortal man has worshiped everything on the face of the earth, including himself. He has also worshiped about everything imaginable in the sky and beneath the surface of the earth. Primitive man feared all manifestations of power; he worshipped every natural phenomenon he could not comprehend. The observation of powerful natural forces, such as storms, floods, earthquakes, landslides, volcanoes, fire, heat, and cold, greatly impressed the expanding mind of man. The inexplicable things of life are still termed 'acts of God' and 'mysterious dispensations of Providence.'" P. 944.

2. **Fear and uncertainty contributed to making man a gambler.**
"Early man lived in uncertainty and in constant fear of chance-bad luck. Life was an exciting game of chance; existence was a gamble. It is no wonder that partially civilized people still believe in chance and evince lingering predispositions to gambling. Primitive man alternated between two potent interests: the passion of getting something for nothing and the fear of getting nothing for something. And this gamble of existence was the main interest and the supreme fascination of the early savage mind." P. 950.

3. **The mystery of natural death fostered religion among primitive men.**
   "Death was the supreme shock to evolving man, the most perplexing combination of chance and mystery. Not the sanctity of life but the shock of death inspired fear and thus effectively fostered religion. Among savage peoples death was ordinarily due to violence, so that nonviolent death became increasingly mysterious. Death as a natural and expected end of life was not clear to the consciousness of primitive people, and it has required age upon age for man to realize its inevitability." P. 952.

4. **Early man accepted life as a fact, death as a visitation of some sort.**
   "Early man accepted life as a fact, while he regarded death as a visitation of some sort. All races have their legends of men who did not die, vestigial traditions of the early attitude toward death. Already in the human mind there existed the nebulous concept of a hazy and unorganized spirit world, a domain whence came all that is inexplicable in human life, and death was added to this long list of unexplained phenomena." P. 952

5. **Death and disease were believed to be due to spirit influences.**
   "All human disease and natural death was at first believed to be due to spirit influence. Even at the present time some civilized races regard disease as having been produced by 'the enemy' and depend upon religious ceremonies to effect healing. Later and more complex systems of theology still ascribe death to the action of the spirit world, all of which has led to such doctrines as original sin and the fall of man." P. 952.

6. **Death-survival concepts.**
   "Early man entertained no ideas of hell or future punishment. The savage looked upon the future life as just like this one, minus all ill luck. Later on, a separate destiny for good ghosts and bad ghosts—heaven and hell—was conceived. But since many primitive races believed that man entered the next life just as he left this one, they did not relish the idea of becoming old and decrepit. The aged much preferred to be killed before becoming too infirm.

   "Almost every group had a different idea regarding the destiny of the ghost soul. The Greeks believed that weak men must

Part V — *Anthropology*

have weak souls; so they invented Hades as a fit place for the reception of such anemic souls; these unrobust specimens were also supposed to have shorter shadows. The early Andites thought their ghosts returned to the ancestral homelands. The Chinese and Egyptians once believed that soul and body remained together. Among the Egyptians this led to careful tomb construction and efforts at body preservation. Even modern peoples seek to arrest the decay of the dead. The Hebrews conceived that a phantom replica of the individual went down to Sheol; it could not return to the land of the living. They did make that important advance in the doctrine of the evolution of the soul." P. 953.

7. **Early man's belief in ghosts and spirits led to superstition and this constituted man's only religion until the times of revelation.**

 "Very early in the history of mankind the realities of the imaginary world of ghosts and spirits became universally believed, and this newly imagined spirit world became a power in primitive society. The mental and moral life of all mankind was modified for all time by the appearance of this new factor in human thinking and acting.

 "Into this major premise of illusion and ignorance, mortal fear has packed all of the subsequent superstition and religion of primitive peoples. This was man's only religion up to the times of revelation, and today many of the world's races have only this crude religion of evolution." P. 955.

8. **To the savage, religion was the payment of premiums on insurance against bad luck.**

 "The savage felt the need of insurance, and he therefore willingly paid his burdensome premiums of fear, superstition, dread, and priest gifts toward his policy of magic insurance against ill luck. Primitive religion was simply the payment of premiums on insurance against the perils of the forests; civilized man pays material premiums against the accidents of industry and the exigencies of modern modes of living." P. 956.

II. CULTS AND PRIESTS.

1. **The origin, nature, and mission of cults.**

 "The cult type of social organization persisted because it provided a symbolism for the preservation and stimulation of moral sentiments and religious loyalties. The cult grew out of the traditions of 'old families' and was perpetuated as an established institution; all families have a cult of some sort. Every inspiring ideal grasps for some perpetuating symbolism—seeks some technique for cultural manifestation which will insure survival and augment realization—and the cult achieves this end by fostering and gratifying emotion." P. 965.

2. **The good and the evil associated with cults.**
"From the dawn of civilization every appealing movement in social culture or religious advancement has developed a ritual, a symbolic ceremonial. The more this ritual has been an unconscious growth, the stronger it has gripped its devotees. The cult preserved sentiment and satisfied emotion, but it has always been the greatest obstacle to social reconstruction and spiritual progress." P. 965.

3. **Though cults retarded social progress, they provided mutual support—something to belong to.**
"Notwithstanding that the cult has always retarded social progress, it is regrettable that so many modern believers in moral standards and spiritual ideals have no adequate symbolism—no cult of mutual support—nothing to *belong* to. But a religious cult cannot be manufactured; it must grow. And those of no two groups will be identical unless their rituals are arbitrarily standardized by authority." P. 965.

4. **The effective Christian cult has lost many of its fundamental ideas.**
"The early Christian cult was the most effective, appealing, and enduring of any ritual ever conceived or devised, but much of its value has been destroyed in a scientific age by the destruction of so many of its original underlying tenets. The Christian cult has been devitalized by the loss of many fundamental ideas." P. 965.

5. **In olden times man attempted to do by magic what in modern times he achieves by science.**
"Civilized man attacks the problems of a real environment through his science; savage man attempted to solve the real problems of an illusory ghost environment by magic. Magic was the technique of manipulating the conjectured spirit environment whose machinations endlessly explained the inexplicable; it was the art of obtaining voluntary spirit cooperation and of coercing involuntary spirit aid through the use of fetishes or other and more powerful spirits." P. 970.

Part V — *Anthropology*

6. **Magic evolves into science.**
   "Magic was the branch off the evolutionary religious tree which eventually bore the fruit of a scientific age. Belief in astrology led to the development of astronomy; belief in a philosopher's stone led to the mastery of metals, while belief in magic numbers founded the science of mathematics." P. 972.

7. **The technique of ritual was all important—hence the evolution of ritual specialists—priests.**
   "The essence of the ritual is the perfection of its performance; among savages it must be practiced with exact precision. It is only when the ritual has been correctly carried out that the ceremony possesses compelling power over the spirits. If the ritual is faulty, it only arouses the anger and resentment of the gods. Therefore, since man's slowly evolving mind conceived that the *technique of ritual* was the decisive factor in its efficacy, it was inevitable that the early shamans should sooner or later evolve into a priesthood trained to direct the meticulous practice of the ritual. And so for tens of thousands of years endless rituals have hampered society and cursed civilization, have been an intolerable burden to every act of life, every racial undertaking." P. 992.

8. **Rituals sanctify custom, perpetuate myths, and dignify religious ceremonials.**
   "Ritual is the technique of sanctifying custom; ritual creates and perpetuates myths as well as contributing to the preservation of social and religious customs. Again, ritual itself has been fathered by myths. Rituals are often at first social, later becoming economic and finally acquiring the sanctity and dignity of religious ceremonial. Ritual may be personal or group in practice-or both—as illustrated by prayer, dancing, and drama." P. 992.

9. **While priests have delayed science and hindered spiritual progress, they have helped stabilize civilization and enhance culture.**
   "The priesthoods have done much to delay scientific development and to hinder spiritual progress, but they have contributed to the stabilization of civilization and to the enhancement of certain kinds of culture. But many modern priests have ceased to function as directors of the ritual of the worship of God, having turned their attention to theology—the attempt to define God.

"It is not denied that the priests have been a millstone about the neck of the races, but the true religious leaders have been invaluable in pointing the way to higher and better realities." P. 993.

III. THE MAINTENANCE OF CIVILIZATION

A. **The civilization which is now evolving on Urantia grew out of, and is predicated on, the following factors:**

1. "*Natural circumstances.* The nature and extent of a material civilization is in large measure determined by the natural resources available. Climate, weather, and numerous physical conditions are factors in the evolution of culture." P. 906.
2. "*Capital goods.* Culture is never developed under conditions of poverty; leisure is essential to the progress of civilization. Individual character of moral and spiritual value may be acquired in the absence of material wealth, but a cultural civilization is only derived from those conditions of material prosperity which foster leisure combined with ambition." P. 907.
3. "*Scientific knowledge.* The material aspects of civilization must always await the accumulation of scientific data. It was a long time after the discovery of the bow and arrow and the utilization of animals for power purposes before man learned how to harness wind and water, to be followed by the employment of steam and electricity. But slowly the tools of civilization improved. Weaving, pottery, the domestication of animals, and metalworking were followed by an age of writing and printing. "Knowledge is power. Invention always precedes the acceleration of cultural development on a world-wide scale. Science and invention benefited most of all from the printing press, and the interaction of all these cultural and inventive activities has enormously accelerated the rate of cultural advancement." P. 907.
4. "*Human resources.* Man power is indispensable to the spread of civilization. All things equal, a numerous people will dominate the civilization of a smaller race. Hence failure to increase in numbers up to a certain point prevents the full realization of national destiny, but there comes a point in population increase where further growth is suicidal. Multiplication of numbers beyond the optimum of the normal man-land ratio means either a lowering of the standards of living or an immediate expansion of territorial boundaries by peaceful penetration or by military conquest, forcible occupation.

"You are sometimes shocked at the ravages of war, but you should recognize the necessity for producing large numbers of mortals so as to afford ample opportunity for social and moral development; with such planetary fertility there soon occurs the serious problem of overpopulation. Most of the inhabited worlds are small. Urantia is average, perhaps a trifle undersized. The optimum stabilization of national population enhances culture and prevents war. And it is a wise nation which knows when to cease growing." P. 907-8.

5. "*Effectiveness of material resources*. Much depends on the wisdom displayed in the utilization of natural resources, scientific knowledge, capital goods, and human potentials. The chief factor in early civilization was the *force* exerted by wise social masters; primitive man had civilization literally thrust upon him by his superior contemporaries. Well-organized and superior minorities have largely ruled this world.

"Might does not make right, but might does make what is and what has been in history. Only recently has Urantia reached that point where society is willing to debate the ethics of might and right." P. 908.

6. "*Effectiveness of language*. The spread of civilization must wait upon language. Live and growing languages insure the expansion of civilized thinking and planning. During the early ages important advances were made in language. Today, there is great need for further linguistic development to facilitate the expression of evolving thought." P. 908.

7. "*Effectiveness of mechanical devices*. The progress of civilization is directly related to the development and possession of tools, machines, and channels of distribution. Improved tools, ingenious and efficient machines, determine the survival of contending groups in the arena of advancing civilization." P. 909.

8. "*Character of torchbearers*. Social inheritance enables man to stand on the shoulders of all who have preceded him, and who have contributed aught to the sum of culture and knowledge. In this work of passing on the cultural torch to the next generation, the home will ever be the basic institution. The play and social life comes next, with the school last but equally indispensable in a complex and highly organized society." P. 909.

9. "*The racial ideals.* The ideals of one generation carve out the channels of destiny for immediate posterity. The *quality* of the social torchbearers will determine whether civilization goes forward or backward. The homes, churches, and schools of one generation predetermine the character trend of the succeeding generation. The moral and spiritual momentum of a race or a nation largely determines the cultural velocity of that civilization." P. 909.

10. "*Co-ordination of specialists.* Civilization has been enormously advanced by the early division of labor and by its later corollary of specialization. Civilization is now dependent on the effective co-ordination of specialists. As society expands, some method of drawing together the various specialists must be found." P. 910.

11. "*Place-finding devices.* The next age of social development will be embodied in a better and more effective co-operation and coordination of ever-increasing and expanding specialization. And as labor more and more diversifies, some technique for directing individuals to suitable employment must be devised. Machinery is not the only cause for unemployment among the civilized peoples of Urantia. Economic complexity and the steady increase of industrial and professional specialism add to the problems of labor placement." P. 910.

12. "*The willingness to co-operate.* One of the great hindrances to the progress of human society is the conflict between the interests and welfare of the larger, more socialized human groups and of the smaller, contrary-minded asocial associations of mankind, not to mention antisocially-minded single individuals." P. 910. "The maintenance of world-wide civilization is dependent on human beings learning how to live together in peace and fraternity. Without effective co-ordination, industrial civilization is jeopardized by the dangers of ultraspecialization: monotony, narrowness, and the tendency to breed distrust and jealousy." P. 911.

13. "*Effective and wise leadership.* In civilization much, very much, depends on an enthusiastic and effective load-pulling spirit. Ten men are of little more value than one in lifting a great load unless they lift together—all at the same moment. And such

PART V — *Anthropology*

teamwork—social co-operation—is dependent on leadership. The cultural civilizations of the past and the present have been based upon the intelligent co-operation of the citizenry with wise and progressive leaders; and until man evolves to higher levels, civilization will continue to be dependent on wise and vigorous leadership." P. 911.

14. "*Social changes.* Society is not a divine institution; it is a phenomenon of progressive evolution; and advancing civilization is always delayed when its leaders are slow in making those changes in the social organization which are essential to keeping pace with the scientific developments of the age. For all that, things must not be despised just because they are old, neither should an idea be unconditionally embraced just because it is novel and new." P. 911.

15. "*The prevention of transitional breakdown.* Society is the offspring of age upon age of trial and error; it is what survived the selective adjustments and readjustments in the successive stages of mankind's agelong rise from animal to human levels of planetary status. The great danger to any civilization—at any one moment-is the threat of breakdown during the time of transition from the established methods of the past to those new and better, but untried, procedures of the future." P. 911.

B. Education.

1. **The purpose of education; the function of education in an ideal state.**

   "The enduring state is founded on culture, dominated by ideals, and motivated by service. The purpose of education should be acquirement of skill, pursuit of wisdom, realization of selfhood, and attainment of spiritual values.

   "In the ideal state, education continues throughout life, and philosophy sometime becomes the chief pursuit of its citizens. The citizens of such a commonwealth pursue wisdom as an enhancement of insight into the significance of human relations, the meanings of reality, the nobility of values, the goals of living, and the glories of cosmic destiny." P. 806.

2. **Education is the business of living. It ascends to the seven insights of wisdom and God-consciousness.**

   "Education is the business of living; it must continue throughout a lifetime so that mankind may gradually experience the ascending levels of mortal wisdom, which are:

"1. The knowledge of things.
"2. The realization of meanings.
"3. The appreciation of values.
"4. The nobility of work—duty.
"5. The motivation of goals—morality.
"6. The love of service—character.
"7. Cosmic insight—spiritual discernment.

"And then, by means of these achievements, many will ascend to the mortal ultimate of mind attainment, God-consciousness." P. 806.

PART V — *Anthropology*

SECTION EIGHT
THE CULMINATION OF HUMAN EVOLUTION

I. RELIGION IN HUMAN EXPERIENCE

A. Man's spiritual estate.

1. **Religion ranges from the lowest to the highest in human nature-it is the inspiration of human evolution.**
"Religion, as a human experience, ranges from the primitive fear slavery of the evolving savage up to the sublime and magnificent faith liberty of those civilized mortals who are superbly conscious of sonship with the eternal God.
"Religion is the ancestor of the advanced ethics and morals of progressive social evolution. But religion, as such, is not merely a moral movement, albeit the outward and social manifestations of religion are mightily influenced by the ethical and moral momentum of human society. Always is religion the inspiration of man's evolving nature, but it is not the secret of that evolution." P. 1104.

2. **The mechanistic despair of a bewildered soul can be dispelled by one stretch of faith.**
"To the unbelieving materialist, man is simply an evolutionary accident. His hopes of survival are strung on a figment of mortal imagination; his fears, loves, longings, and beliefs are but the reaction of the incidental juxtaposition of certain lifeless atoms of matter. No display of energy nor expression of trust can carry him beyond the grave. The devotional labors and inspirational genius of the best of men are doomed to be extinguished by death, the long and lonely night of eternal oblivion and soul extinction. Nameless despair is man's only reward for living and toiling under the temporal sun of mortal existence. Each day of life slowly and surely tightens the grasp of a pitiless doom which a hostile and relentless universe of matter has decreed shall be the crowning insult to everything in human desire which is beautiful, noble, lofty, and good.
"But such is not man's end and eternal destiny; such a vision is but the cry of despair uttered by some wandering soul who has become lost in spiritual darkness, and who bravely struggles on in the face of the mechanistic sophistries of a material philosophy, blinded by the confusion and distortion of a complex learning. And all this doom of darkness and all this destiny of despair are forever dispelled by one brave stretch of faith on the part of the most humble and unlearned of God's children on earth." P. 1118.

3. **Philosophy is the mediator between science and religion.**
   "The union of the scientific attitude and the religious insight by the mediation of experiential philosophy is part of man's long Paradise-ascension experience. The approximations of mathematics and the certainties of insight will always require the harmonizing function of mind logic on all levels of experience short of the maximum attainment of the Supreme." P. 1138.

4. **Without truth insight, logic can never reconcile science and religion.**
   "But logic can never succeed in harmonizing the findings of science and the insights of religion unless both the scientific and the religious aspects of a personality are truth dominated, sincerely desirous of following the truth wherever it may lead regardless of the conclusions which it may reach." P. 1138.

5. **The interworking of logic, reason, and religious faith in human experience.**
   "Logic is the technique of philosophy, its method of expression. Within the domain of true science, reason is always amenable to genuine logic; within the domain of true religion, faith is always logical from the basis of an inner viewpoint, even though such faith may appear to be quite unfounded from the inlooking viewpoint of the scientific approach. From outward, looking within, the universe may appear to be material; from within, looking out, the same universe appears to be wholly spiritual. Reason grows out of material awareness, faith out of spiritual awareness, but through the mediation of a philosophy strengthened by revelation, logic may confirm both the inward and the outward view, thereby effecting the stabilization of both science and religion. Thus, through common contact with the logic of philosophy, may both science and religion become increasingly tolerant of each other, less and less skeptical." P. 1138.

6. **Both science and religion need more self-criticism.**
   "What both developing science and religion need is more searching and fearless self-criticism a greater awareness of incompleteness in evolutionary status. The teachers of both science and religion are often altogether too self-confident and dogmatic. Science and religion can only be self-critical of their *facts*. The moment departure is made from the stage of facts, reason abdicates or else rapidly degenerates into a consort of false logic." P. 1138.

PART V — *Anthropology*

7. **Revelation assists philosophy in co-ordinating science and religion.**
    "The science of the material world enables man to control, and to some extent dominate, his physical environment. The religion of the spiritual experience is the source of the fraternity impulse which enables men to live together in the complexities of the civilization of a scientic age. Metaphysics, but more certainly revelation, affords a common meeting ground for the discoveries of both science and religion and makes possible the human attempt logically to correlate these separate but interdependent domains of thought into a well-balanced philosophy of scientific stability and religious certainty." P. 1139.

8. **Both science and religion are founded on assumptions.**
    "In the mortal state, nothing can be absolutely proved; both science and religion are predicated on assumptions. On the morontia level, the postulates of both science and religion are capable of partial proof by mota logic. On the spiritual level of maximum status, the need for finite proof gradually vanishes before the actual experience of and with reality; but even then there is much beyond the finite that remains unproved." P. 1139.

9. **The basic assumptions of science and religion.**
    "All divisions of human thought are predicated on certain assumptions which are accepted, though unproved, by the constitutive reality sensitivity of the mind endowment of man. Science starts out on its vaunted career of reasoning by *assuming* the reality of three things: matter, motion, and life. Religion starts out with the assumption of the validity of three things: mind, spirit, and the universe—the Supreme Being." P. 1139.

10. **Vastness of the problem of the unification of the material and the spiritual.**
    "Science becomes the thought domain of mathematics, of the energy and material of time in space. Religion assumes to deal not only with finite and temporal spirit but also with the spirit of eternity and supremacy. Only through a long experience in mota can these two extremes of universe perception be made to yield analogous interpretations of origins, functions, relations, realities, and destinies. The maximum harmonization

of the energy-spirit divergence is in the encircuitment of the Seven Master Spirits; the first unification thereof, in the Deity of the Supreme; the finality unity thereof, in the infinity of the First Source and Center, the I AM." P. 1139.

11. **The nature, mission, and limitations of revelation.**
"Revelation is evolutionary but always progressive. Down through the ages of a world's history, the revelations of religion are ever-expanding and successively more enlightening. It is the mission of revelation to sort and censor the successive religions of evolution. But if revelation is to exalt and upstep the religions of evolution, then must such divine visitations portray teachings which are not too far removed from the thought and reactions of the age in which they are presented. Thus must and does revelation always keep in touch with evolution. Always must the religion of revelation be limited by man's capacity of receptivity." P. 1007.

B. **The acme of religious living.**

1. **A portrait of the personality of Jesus.**
"Jesus was an unusually cheerful person, but he was not a blind and unreasoning optimist. His constant word of exhortation was, 'Be of good cheer.' He could maintain this confident attitude because of his unswerving trust in God and his unshakable confidence in man. He was always touchingly considerate of all men because he loved them and believed in them. Still he was always true to his convictions and magnificently firm in his devotion to the doing of his Father's will.

"The Master was always generous. He never grew weary of saying, 'It is more blessed to give than to receive.' Said he, 'Freely you have received, freely give.' And yet, with all of his unbounded generosity, he was never wasteful or extravagant. He taught that you must believe to receive salvation. 'For every one who seeks shall receive.'

"He was candid, but always kind. Said he, 'If it were not so, I would have told you.' He was frank, but always friendly. He was outspoken in his love for the sinner and in his hatred for sin. But throughout all this amazing frankness he was unerringly *fair*.

"Jesus was consistently cheerful, notwithstanding he sometimes drank deeply of the cup of human sorrow. He fearlessly faced the realities of existence, yet was he filled with enthusiasm for the gospel of the kingdom. But he controlled his enthusiasm; it never controlled him. He was unreservedly dedicated to 'the Father's business.' This divine enthusiasm led his unspiritual brethren to think he was beside himself, but the onlooking universe appraised him as the model of sanity and the pattern of supreme mortal devotion to the high standards of spiritual living. And his controlled enthusiasm was contagious; his associates were constrained to share his divine optimism.

"This man of Galilee was not a man of sorrows; he was a soul of gladness. Always was he saying, 'Rejoice and be exceedingly glad.' But when duty required, he was willing to walk courageously through the 'valley of the shadow of death.' He was gladsome but at the same time humble.

"His courage was equaled only by his patience. When pressed to act prematurely, he would only reply, 'My hour has not yet come.' He was never in a hurry; his composure was sublime. But he was often indignant at evil, intolerant of sin. He was often mightily moved to resist that which was inimical to the welfare of his children on earth. But his indignation against sin never led to anger at the sinner.

"His courage was magnificent, but he was never foolhardy. His watchword was, 'Fear not.' His bravery was lofty and his courage often heroic. But his courage was linked with discretion and controlled by reason. It was courage born of faith, not the recklessness of blind presumption. He was truly brave but never audacious.

"The Master was a pattern of reverence. The prayer of even his youth began, 'Our Father who is in heaven, hallowed by your name.' He was even respectful of the faulty worship of his fellows. But this did not deter him from making attacks on religious traditions or assaulting errors of human belief. He was reverential of true holiness, and yet he could justly appeal to his fellows, saying, 'Who among you convicts me of sin?'

"Jesus was great because he was good, and yet he fraternized with the little children. He was gentle and unassuming in his personal life, and yet he was the perfected man of a universe. His associates called him Master unbidden.

"Jesus was the perfectly unified human personality. And today, as in Galilee, he continues to unify mortal experience and to coordinate human endeavors. He unifies life, ennobles character, and simplifies experience. He enters the human mind to elevate, transform, and transfigure it. It is literally true: 'If any man has Christ Jesus within him, he is a new creature; old things are passing away; behold, all things are becoming new.'" P. 1102-3.

II. HUMAN DESTINY

A. Evolutionary ascension.

1. **The evolutionary destiny of human beings.**
"The evolutionary planets are the spheres of human origin, the initial worlds of the ascending mortal career. Urantia is your starting point; here you and your divine Thought Adjuster are joined in temporary union. You have been endowed with a perfect guide; therefore, if you will sincerely run the race of time and gain the final goal of faith, the reward of the ages shall be yours; you will be eternally united with your indwelling Adjuster. Then will begin your real life, the ascending life, to which your present mortal state is but the vestibule. Then will begin your exalted and progressive mission as finaliters in the eternity which stretches out before you. And throughout all of these successive ages and stages of evolutionary growth, there is one part of you that remains absolutely unaltered, and that is personality —permanence in the presence of change." P. 1225.

2. **The ministry of angels.**
"The Most Highs rule in the kingdoms of men through many celestial forces and agencies but chiefly through the ministry of seraphim.

"At noon today the roll call of planetary angels, guardians, and others on Urantia was 501,234,619 pairs of seraphim. There were assigned to my command two hundred seraphic hosts—597,196,800 pairs of seraphim, or 1,194,393,600 individual angels. The registry, however, shows 1,002,469,238 individuals; it follows therefore that 191,924,362 angels were absent from this world on transport, messenger, and death duty. (On Urantia there are about the same number of cherubim as seraphim, and they are similarly organized.)

"Seraphim and their associated cherubim have much to do with the details of the superhuman government of a planet, especially of worlds which have been isolated by rebellion. The angels, ably assisted by the midwayers, function on Urantia as the actual supermaterial ministers who execute the mandates of the resident governor general and all his associates and subordinates. Seraphim as a class are occupied with many assignments other than those of personal and group guardianship." P. 1250.

3. **The nature, mission, and composition of the reserve corps of destiny.**

"The reserve corps of destiny consists of living men and women who have been admitted to the special service of the superhuman administration of world affairs. This corps is made up of the men and women of each generation who are chosen by the spirit directors of the realm to assist in the conduct of the ministry of mercy and wisdom to the children of time on the evolutionary worlds. It is the general practice in the conduct of the affairs of the ascension plans to begin this liaison utilization of mortal will creatures immediately they are competent and trustworthy to assume such responsibilities. Accordingly, as soon as men and women appear on the stage of temporal action with sufficient mental capacity, adequate moral status, and requisite spirituality, they are quickly assigned to the appropriate celestial group of planetary personalities as human liaisons, mortal assistants.

"When human beings are chosen as protectors of planetary destiny, when they become pivotal individuals in the plans which the world administrators are prosecuting, at that time the planetary chief of seraphim confirms their temporal attachment to the seraphic corps and appoints personal destiny guardians to serve with these mortal reservists. All reservists have self-conscious Adjusters, and most of them function in the higher cosmic circles of intellectual achievement and spiritual attainment.

"Mortals of the realm are chosen for service in the reserve corps of destiny on the inhabited worlds because of:

"1. Special capacity for being secretly rehearsed for numerous possible emergency missions in the conduct of various activities of world affairs.

"2. Wholehearted dedication to some special social, economic, political, spiritual, or other cause, coupled with willingness to serve without human recognition and rewards.

"3. The possession of a Thought Adjuster of extraordinary versatility and probable pre-Urantia experience in coping with planetary difficulties and contending with impending world emergency situations." P. 1257.

Science In *The Urantia Book*

4. **Nature and mission of Thought Adjusters.**

   "The Adjusters are the actuality of the Father's love incarnate in the souls of men; they are the veritable promise of man's eternal career imprisoned within the mortal mind; they are the essence of man's perfected finaliter personality, which he can foretaste in time as he progressively masters the divine technique of achieving the living of the Father's will, step by step, through the ascension of universe upon universe until he actually attains the divine presence of his Paradise Father. "God, having commanded man to be perfect, even as he is perfect, has descended as the Adjuster to become man's experiential partner in the achievement of the supernal destiny which has been thus ordained. The fragment of God which indwells the mind of man is the absolute and unqualified assurance that man can find the Universal Father in association with this divine Adjuster, which came forth from God to find man and sonship him even in the days of the flesh." P. 1176.

B. **The triumph of faith.**

   1. **Man liberated by religion becomes conscious of the fact that the divine hosts of the universes are on his side.**

   "When you experience such a transformation of faith, you are no longer a slavish part of the mathematical cosmos but rather a liberated volitional son of the Universal Father. No longer is such a liberated son fighting alone against the inexorable doom of the termination of temporal existence; no longer does he combat all nature, with the odds hopelessly against him; no longer is he staggered by the paralyzing fear that, perchance, he has put his trust in a hopeless phantasm or pinned his faith to a fanciful error.

   "Now, rather, are the sons of God enlisted together in fighting the battle of reality's triumph over the partial shadows of existence. At last all creatures become conscious of the fact that God and all the divine hosts of a well-nigh limitless universe are on their side in the supernal struggle to attain eternity of life and divinity of status. Such faith-liberated sons have certainly enlisted in the struggles of time on the side of the supreme forces and divine personalities of eternity; even the stars in their courses are now doing battle for them; at last they gaze upon the universe from within, from God's view point, and all is transformed from the uncertainties of material isolation to the sureties of eternal spiritual progression. Even time itself becomes but the shadow of eternity cast by Paradise realities upon the moving panoply of space." P. 1117.

CONCLUSION

"True it is, you mortals are of earthly, animal origin; your frame is indeed dust. But if you actually will, if you really desire, surely the heritage of the ages is yours, and you shall someday serve throughout the universes in your true characters—children of the Supreme God of experience and divine sons of the Paradise Father of all personalities." P. 1240.

NOTES

NOTES

NOTES